ADULT READING

ii

ADULT READING

The Fifty-fifth Yearbook of the
National Society for the Study of Education

PART II

Prepared by the Yearbook Committee: DAVID H. CLIFT *(Chairman)*, LESTER E.
ASHEIM, EDGAR DALE, CYRIL O. HOULE, *and* GRACE T. STEVENSON

Edited by
NELSON B. HENRY

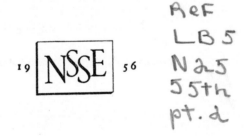

Distributed by THE UNIVERSITY OF CHICAGO PRESS • CHICAGO, ILLINOIS

The responsibilities of the Board of Directors of the National Society for the Study of Education in the case of Yearbooks prepared by the Society's committees are (1) to select the subjects to be investigated, (2) to appoint committees calculated in their personnel to insure consideration of all significant points of view, (3) to provide appropriate subsidies for necessary expenses, (4) to publish and distribute the committees' reports, and (5) to arrange for their discussion at the annual meetings.

The responsibility of the Yearbook Editor is to prepare the submitted manuscripts for publication in accordance with the principles and regulations approved by the Board of Directors.

Neither the Board of Directors, nor the Yearbook Editor, nor the Society is responsible for the conclusions reached or the opinions expressed by the Society's yearbook committees.

Published 1956 by

THE NATIONAL SOCIETY FOR THE STUDY OF EDUCATION

5835 Kimbark Avenue, Chicago 37, Illinois

First printing, 10,000 Copies

Printed in the United States of America

The Society's Committee on Adult Reading

LESTER E. ASHEIM

Dean, Graduate Library School, University of Chicago
Chicago, Illinois

DAVID H. CLIFT

(Chairman)
Executive Secretary, American Library Association
Chicago, Illinois

EDGAR DALE

Professor of Education, Ohio State University
Columbus, Ohio

CYRIL O. HOULE

Professor of Education, University of Chicago
Chicago, Illinois

GRACE T. STEVENSON

Associate Executive Secretary, American Library Association
Chicago, Illinois

Associated Contributors

JEANNE S. CHALL

Assistant Professor of Education, City College of the City of New York
New York, New York

WILLIAM S. GRAY

Emeritus Professor of Education, University of Chicago
Chicago, Illinois

ARTHUR T. HAMLIN

Executive Secretary, Association of College and Reference Libraries
Chicago, Illinois

v

ASSOCIATED CONTRIBUTORS

DAN LACY

Managing Director, American Book Publishers Council
New York, New York

WILBUR SCHRAMM

Dean, Division of Communications, University of Illinois
Urbana, Illinois

PAUL A. WITTY

Professor of Education, Northwestern University
Evanston, Illinois

Editor's Preface

Several of the earlier yearbooks of the National Society have dealt with important aspects of theory and practice in the teaching of reading. Those dealing with such general functions of formal education as minimum essentials in school subjects, economy of time, and new materials of instruction have recognized reading as a dominant activity in the pursuit of knowledge in all subject fields. These, together with the volume on silent reading (Twentieth Yearbook, Part II), provided the setting for the advent of the National Committee on Reading, appointed by the United States Commissioner of Education in January, 1923. The report of this committee was published as Part I of the Twenty-fourth Yearbook of this Society. Part I of our Thirty-sixth Yearbook, designed to describe the developments in reading instruction and to interpret the outcomes of a decade of research and experience under the stimulus of the National Committee's report, was published in 1937 as a second report on the teaching of reading.

In 1945, the Board of Directors organized a new committee on reading with the view of defining the current status of reading instruction in the American schools and of preparing such a publication as the needs of the times might suggest. In April, 1946, Professsor Gray, chairman of the committee, reported that it was the consensus of the committee that the various lines of development in reading could not be adequately treated in a single yearbook. In addition to the revision of the Thirty-sixth Yearbook, the committee urged the early publication of a volume on reading instruction at the secondary-school and college levels. The further suggestion was made that the Board of Directors give consideration to the possible publication of supplementary reports on adult reading and parent education. Although the plan of supplementing the series of yearbooks by issuing special reports at appropriate times was not adopted, interest in the proposal regarding adult reading was revived in 1952 in connection with the discussion of the inquiry of officers of the Adult Education Association regarding the possible interest of the National Society in publishing a yearbook in the area of adult education. At the meeting of the Board in February, 1954, the committee for the yearbook on adult reading was selected and an appropriation authorized for the expenses involved in the preparation of this volume.

In this enterprise, as in connection with many other professional services, the National Society has enjoyed the cordial co-operation of talented representatives of related professional groups. Their contributions to this volume and their generous support of our endeavor are as invaluable from the point of view of the purposes of this Society as is their devotion to the aims of their chosen professions. It is a pleasure to record here this expression of the appreciation of the officers and members of the National Society for their good will and neighborly interest.

NELSON B. HENRY

Table of Contents

Introduction

DAVID H. CLIFT

In a world in which the adult is hard put to cope with the ideas that strive for and require his attention, reading remains the single most important form of communication available to him and the most effective tool for his continuing education. There are, of course, other forms of communication. Beginning with 1900, various communication media have come along to stand beside the book, either as competitor or ally, but the book holds the leading position it has occupied for hundreds of years. There's good reason to feel, as President Dodds of Princeton University observed at the National Book Committee's 1955 Conference on American Books Abroad, that "books will remain the best visual aids to education."

Our concerns in this yearbook are with the adult reader and the several agencies that have an interest in and a responsibility for adult reading. In this picture, the largely unknown element is the adult reader. Something is known of why he reads what he reads when he does read. But our knowledge is made up of many fragments, all of which when pieced together do not produce a clear picture of the adult reader. We get, instead, an image that stands out imperfectly with only some of the features clear and distinct.

Those concerned with adult reading have accepted the responsibility, laid upon them by society, to help the individual in his efforts to improve himself through reading according to his own desires and his own motivations. These include the schools which prepare for adulthood and where the individual begins to learn how to read and where habits and desires may be inculcated that will lead to a lifetime reliance upon reading. The home is important, because, best of all, books and reading can here be made a socially acceptable and desirable part of everyday living. In this company, too, are the makers of books, including authors with the skills of communication and the publishers who bring books into physical existence. Included, also, are the persons who devote their skills to making books more readable. There is the teacher of adults with his deep concern over the effect of reading. There is the library and the bookstore, each so vital to the distribution and availability of reading materials. Not one of these agencies is limited to a single concern in adult reading; the concerns of each are the concern of all.

All who have a part in the reading of adults seek to understand the adult reader better, for his needs, his requirements, his desires, his capabilities, and his limitations all affect the extent and depth of voluntary reading.

The amount of reading materials published each year, the educational level of the people, and the notable absence of illiteracy in this country indicate that we should be a nation of readers. This is far from the case, although everyone who can read does read something. The known facts on individual reading, library use, and bookstore sales contribute strongly to the uncomfortable feeling that we are very nearly a nation of nonreaders. Many demands and many deterrents come between the adult and his desire or need to read. He has many other things to do. He has duties and tasks and responsibilities for which the rewards are more obvious and more tangible. Many activities compete for the time which might go into reading. His ability to read with understanding and with pleasure is often limited either by his own shortcomings or by the poor writing which he undertakes to read. He might want and need to read a book but find himself frustrated by a lack of guidance as to which book to read or by the unavailability of books in general. The factor of availability can be a formidable road block, for availability means more than the presence of books and other reading materials in the home, the library, or the bookstore. The effort required by the reader, involving his skill and his time, contribute heavily to the degree of availability.

Reading is one of the good things in life. It is good in itself and, like a good wine, needs no bush. Reading is a factor of great importance in the individual's development. Persons who read do so for many different reasons, as different as men are different one from another. We read for the rich enjoyment that comes from sharing the experiences of a penetrating mind or following the magic of a master storyteller. We read as one of the tasks of daily living. We read, particularly in these confused times, to understand the trials that beset mankind and to help keep even our sense of balance in a changing world. We read, consciously, to advance ourselves either in our social spheres or in our fields of endeavor. We read because we seek to understand many viewpoints and to evaluate many situations in order that we may bring an intelligent interest to our community life and to our daily work. We read to escape the world of reality just as we must read to live in that world. We read because we like to, and we read because we must.

And yet an appalling number of Americans do not do any reading that is socially valuable. This fact stands out clearly from a score of studies on reading. A fairly accurate estimate can be made of the large portion of our population that must be classed as nonreaders. The better education of these nonreaders, their development into more rounded individuals, their good-citizenship potential, their enjoyment of life will not necessarily be assured if all become good readers in the best sense of the word. However, the odds rest in that direction. It is, therefore, distinctly in the public interest to improve the quality and quantity of reading as one of the instruments of social and individual progress.

The purpose of this yearbook is to explore the many aspects of adult reading including those that contribute to and those that retard its development. We shall, in the pages that follow, attempt a review and an analysis of what is known about the adult reader and of the efforts aiming at improvement in adult reading which are either under way or strongly indicated. The yearbook will look at the adult reader to see what he reads, how well he reads, and why he reads. We shall examine audio-visual materials as allied and reinforcing media. From the adult reader, as we can picture him, we will turn to the efforts being made to improve his reading. These will include the programs of the general libraries and the functions of college libraries, the use of print in adult educational agencies, the work of schools and colleges in adult reading, the development of readable materials, and the physical availability of reading materials.

The Committee hopes that this yearbook will be helpful to the many individuals and groups that are concerned with adult reading. We hope that the teacher will find these studies helpful to him in his preparation of the student for adult life. We hope there will be aid here for the teacher of adult classes in increasing participation and depth of learning in both formal and informal adult education. Librarians will, we hope, find something within these pages that will broaden their understanding of the readers who come to the library and the ones who stay away. We hope that the concerns and findings recorded here will be of help and interest to the publisher and bookseller, for in their hands rests a considerable opportunity and a considerable challenge. We hope, too, that the several areas in which studies and investigations are needed will be noted so that further efforts may be undertaken to fill in some of the gaps in our knowledge of the adult reader.

Finally, we can hope that, if these pages bring some clarification to the problems of adult reading and lead to further efforts at improvement, the result will mean a somewhat happier lot for the adult reader.

CHAPTER I

What Do Adults Read?

LESTER ASHEIM

Available Reading Materials

To assist us in our exploration of the role of voluntary adult reading in the United States, certain kinds of information would be useful. How much reading is actually being done in this country today? Who are the readers? What kinds of things do they read? The answers to such questions can help us define what would constitute an "improvement" in adult reading and give direction to any programs we may devise for enlarging the role of reading and increasing its importance in the education of adults.

At first glance one might find the picture of reading in America an encouraging one. One indicator which is frequently used to gauge the amount of reading done is found in the figures for newspaper and magazine circulation and for book publication—and these figures are impressive. In 1954, according to the annual summary in the *Publishers' Weekly*,[1] there were 11,901 new books and new editions of old titles published in the United States, a figure which, although slightly less than the 12,050 titles published during the preceding year, is nevertheless more than the number published in any of the pre-TV years from 1946 to 1950. Magazines make a similarly strong showing with 7,648 periodicals published in 1955, representing a total circulation in the neighborhood of 175,000,000.[2] In 1955, also, 1,765 English-language daily newspapers were being

---

1. "American Book Publication—1954," *Publishers' Weekly*, CLXVII (January 22, 1955), 335.

2. *N. W. Ayer & Son's Directory: Newspapers and Periodicals, 1955*, p. 8. Philadelphia: N. W. Ayer & Son's, Inc., 1955.

published in the United States with a combined circulation of close to 55,000,000.[3]

Another indicator would be the state of literacy in the United States. These figures, too, are encouraging. In 1952 only 2.5 per cent of the civilian population 14 years of age and over were illiterate by census standards.[4]

Finally the attention paid to education is an indicator, and again the indicator is a favorable one. Seventy-three per cent of the total population of the United States between the ages of 5 and 20 are enrolled in school, and one-third of the population 25 years of age or over has a high-school education or better (20 per cent have completed four years of high school; 7 per cent have had from one to three years of college work; and 6 per cent have four or more years of college education.) [5] With college enrolment on the upswing since World War II, one can predict for the years to come a continuing increase in the proportion of adults over 25 years of age who will have had at least some college education. Surely this represents a lot of available reading material and a lot of potential readers. But what do the figures mean?

There are many ways of looking at them. For one thing, we know that the fact that one is able to read does not necessarily mean that he will do so. Thus, literacy is prerequisite to reading but does not guarantee it. The high literacy rate in the United States tells us merely that reading *could* be done by a large majority of our citizens. We know also that, because a person is exposed to classrooms and has spent a lot of time in school buildings, he is not necessarily "educated" in the richest sense of the word. Thus, compulsory education, like the high literacy level to which it leads, merely provides a potential audience, not necessarily an actual one. Finally, we know that books on the shelves of libraries, bookstores, and even home collections are not necessarily books read. Total publication figures or total sales figures, therefore, tell us only what is available for reading but not whether readers use it.

3. *Editor and Publisher International Yearbook, 1955*, p. 20. New York: Editor & Publisher, 1955.

4. United States Bureau of the Census, *Statistical Abstract of the United States, 1954*. Washington: Government Printing Office, 1954.

5. *Ibid.*, pp. 115, 121.

Thus, although the book industry in the United States issues enough titles to provide three books for every adult in our population, not every book published is purchased, nor is every book read which is purchased. Even if everyone did read as many as three books a year—and we know they do not—we should hardly be a nation of voracious book-readers. But it is to be feared that even so modest a showing is a goal to strive for rather than an accomplished achievement.

It should be recognized, however, that book reading is not the only reading in which the average man or woman indulges. We tend to forget how natural a part of our daily lives reading has become and that our society is organized on the assumption of widespread literacy. Nearly everyone in the United States depends upon his ability to read to see him through most of his waking day. Each of us reads—and sometimes even acts upon—such verbal information as "No Admittance," "This Way Out," "No Parking," "Sale Ends Friday," "Bus Stop," or "Today's Television Programs." As a matter of fact, it is reading on this level which has the most immediate measurable effect upon us. Our conduct is definitely altered by our reading a traffic sign ("Right Turn on Green Arrow Only"), while it would be difficult to show that our reading of *Moby Dick* had any effect at all. Yet it is the reading of the Moby Dick type of content with which we are really concerned when we worry about the reading of adults. And when we say that Americans—by and large—are not readers, we mean that they are not sustained readers of serious content; not that they do not indulge in the simple act of deriving meaning from written symbols.

For we do say that Americans, by and large, are not serious readers, and we say this on the basis of a fairly solid core of studies of reading which provide verifiable data on the reading of adults. We do not yet know all we want to know about adult reading, but from existing studies, the findings of which are sufficiently consistent with each other to establish their over-all reliability, we can draw up—in general terms—a fairly accurate picture of how much reading is done and by whom. That picture is far less encouraging than the indirect picture which publication figures painted.

How Many Readers?

The first finding, which appears in study after study, is that not much more than one-fourth of the adult population reads even as little as one book a month. In cross-section polls of the population the question is frequently asked, "Are you reading a book now?" or "Have you read a book within the past month?" The percentage of persons who answer "No" to such questions consistently hovers around the same figure, as shown in the following tabulation:

Study A (1950)................79 per cent
Study B (1949)................79 per cent
Study C (1948)................74 per cent
Study D (1948)................70 per cent

Other studies ask different questions and cannot be exactly compared with this table, but the over-all pattern is overwhelmingly the same: "Active" readers seldom make up more than 25 to 30 per cent of any group that reflects, with reasonable accuracy, a cross section of the total population. If we bear in mind the prestige which reading is presumed to carry in the United States, we should certainly guess that the tendency of the respondent would be to claim book-reading wherever possible rather than to suppress the report of reading. We must, therefore, assume that these reports represent the upper limit of book-reading among the respondents.

But book-reading is only one aspect of reading, even if we rule out the casual—almost inadvertent—reading of signs, markers, instructions, and notices with which we have elected not to be concerned in this chapter. When we leave the realm of the book, reports are a little more encouraging. The studies show that between 60 and 70 per cent of the adult population read one or more *magazines* regularly; and between 85 and 90 per cent read a *newspaper* more or less regularly. Thus, the majority of the population do have ready access to printed sources of ideas, information, knowledge, and recreation and utilize them to some extent. But even the newspaper—the most widely used medium of print—does not reach all its potential audience. The question immediately arises: Who are the users of print and who are not? How do the two groups differ? What are the characteristics which tend to make a person a reader?

Here again we have data from studies which help supply some answers. The answers are not as detailed nor as refined as we might wish them to be, but they reveal some interesting information which is essential to those concerned with promoting and extending the use of reading by adults. Whether the study is made in an exclusive residential community, an industrial neighborhood, or a slum; whether it centers upon highly educated people, the "average" man, or the underprivileged; whether it is based on existing records maintained by book agencies, on questionnaires to interested parties, or on personal interviews over a broad sampling of the population, the same general results appear.

Generally speaking, the studies have shown that a far greater proportion of the young adults (between 21 and 29 years of age) than of people over 50 years of age will be in the reader group. A larger proportion of the professional people and skilled workers than of wage-earners or unskilled will be represented. A higher percentage of persons in the upper than in the lower income groups will be readers. And most important of all: We know that *the readers are the ones with the most education*. Education is the major correlate of reading, no matter how you approach it. It is clear that in each of the other groupings mentioned above—age, occupation, and economic status—education is a hidden factor. And within each group the difference between those who read much and those who read little is education.

What Do They Read?

Knowing something about the amount of reading of different kinds and about the characteristics of readers is useful, but our concern is more specifically with reading which is socially valuable, not just with reading *per se*. It is generally recognized that the content of the printed media vary so widely that we cannot universally equate the undifferentiated reading act with socially desirable conduct. It is clear that some kinds of reading have greater social and artistic value than others, and there is reason to believe that some reading might even be harmful, although we have little evidence to prove this. At any rate, there is a lot of reading which, if not harmful, does not represent the most fruitful use of the time spent. Thus, it is important for us to know not only *that* people read but also *what* they read.

The "what," as we have noted, has been established pretty well for broad categories of reading material. We know that almost everyone does some newspaper reading; about two-thirds of the adult population read one or more magazines with some regularity; and that books—reaching about a quarter of the adult population— are read less than any other medium of print. But very little research has yet been done which probes deeply enough to tell us what this means in terms of actual content. Certain broad assumptions have been made: Books represent the more serious and important content, and magazines the less serious; newspapers, although they deal with matter essential for the informed citizen, represent the least thoughtful, the least detailed, and the least analytical presentation of information. These generalizations have a partial validity. It is probably true that a more solid contribution to complete understanding of a complex concept can be obtained from a book-length analysis than from the limited attention which can be paid in a newspaper column or a short magazine article. But it is also true that neither books, magazines, nor newspapers represent homogeneous categories; each represents a range of content from profound to shallow, serious to frivolous, lasting to ephemeral. If it is true that book-readers, by and large, tend to be better informed than newspaper readers, it is partially because book-readers are also newspaper and magazines readers as well (as our studies also show.)[6] The generalization really is less related to book-reading as an isolated phenomenon than it is to the more obvious fact that people who actively use many sources of information are likely to be better informed than those who limit the number of sources they consult.

But even this generalization has flaws in it—the same flaws that marred the generalization that books are more serious than magazines. That flaw is that we are, in a sense, judging a book by its cover or—to state it more accurately—judging content by format. Until we know what kinds of things are read in the newspapers,

6. This fact helps to explain the apparent discrepancy between the great number of publications and the high figures for circulation and the small number of actual readers. A few people are counted again and again in such figures, while many people are not included among the readers at all. George Gallup reports, for example, that three-fourths of all pocket-size books are bought by approximately 10 per cent of the population and that there are 72 million persons who have never bought a single copy in their lives. The buyers— who buy many different titles of the small books—are quite probably also subscribers to several magazines and among the major purchasers of hardbound books.

magazines, and books, we should be extremely cautious about our assumptions concerning the comparative importance of the several media to the development of the individual reader. A mystery novel, just because it is bound in hard covers, is not more profound than a serious discussion of contemporary social conditions in a scholarly journal; nor is a romantic short story in a magazine more important than a newspaper column by Walter Lippmann. Specific content, not the shape, size, or frequency of publication, is the key. And content is not sufficiently well described by the mere identification of the medium. Is the newspaper read for its editorials or its comic pages? Does the reader of *Life* direct his attention to "The History of Western Culture" or to the pin-up pictures? Is the subscriber to the *New Yorker* necessarily reached by the edition devoted to John Hersey's *Hiroshima* or is he a devotee of the cartoons? It seems quite clear that we can say only this of the reader of the *New York Times*, or the subscriber to the *Atlantic Monthly*, or the owner of a library card in the Detroit Public Library: He has the opportunity to read materials of importance if he takes advantage of it. But there is always the "if."

Another popular, but dubious, generalization is frequently voiced: Nonfiction tends to be more "important" than fiction. Here again such a generalization is only occasionally true; *The Power of Positive Thinking* is not a more serious work than *The Brothers Karamazov*. Yet librarians and publishers seem to be gratified whenever they can point to an increase in the reading of nonfiction, and many educators consider this to be a desirable goal to promote.[7] Much has been made recently of the growing interest in nonfiction; of the increasing proportion of nonfiction articles in the popular magazines. These trends have been taken as an indicator of a growing seriousness and intelligence on the part of the reading public. But if closer analysis of these shifts from fiction to nonfiction should reveal that people are reading less Melville and Tolstoy and more books on how to play Scrabble and Canasta, we should have to revise our assumption that the trend from fiction to nonfiction is a trend toward more serious reading.

7. See, for example, Ray H. Simpson and Kenneth L. Camp, "Diagnosing Community Reading," *School Review*, LXI (February, 1953), 98-100.

Unfortunately few of the studies have made a refined enough analysis of specific reading to tell us these things precisely. We have studies by medium, with some analysis of parts of a particular newspaper or magazine read; studies by such a gross breakdown as fiction/nonfiction; and a few studies of nonfiction by the Dewey classifications of subject matter, and of fiction by very broad categories of quality level. The findings reveal something like the following:

1) *Newspaper reading.* As in all reading situations, the more "serious" articles in the newspapers (editorials, public affairs news, etc.) are read much more frequently by the better-educated. Newspaper readers on the lower end of the educational curve tend to use the newspaper for entertainment, sensational news, and pictorial material; those at the top of the education curve tend to use it less for entertainment, more for information on public affairs.[8] A continuing ten-year study of newspaper reading habits conducted by George Gallup [9] revealed that while both men and women read the general news stories (96 per cent of the women, 97 per cent of the men reported one or more news stories read), there are very great differences in subject interest. Twice as many men as women reported reading the editorials; four times as many men as women had read the stocks and bonds information; ten times as many men as women had read the lead sport story. On the other hand, five times as many women as men had read the fiction feature; four times as many women as men had read the advertisement of the leading department store; and about thirty times as many women as men had read such features as recipes, styles, love advice, beauty advice, health, etiquette, and child-care features. Younger people tend to read the comics and sensational news, although reading of comics tends to decrease from the middle-teens on. Reading of public affairs and editorials increases with age, with education, and with higher economic status (characteristics which are, of course, related to each other).

8. Wilbur Schramm and David M. White, "Age, Education, and Economic Status as Factors in Newspaper Reading," *Mass Communications*, p. 404. Edited by Wilbur Schramm. Urbana, Illinois: University of Illinois, 1949.

9. George Gallup, "I Asked 100,000 People What They Read in Newspapers," *Advertising and Selling*, XXXI (January, 1938), 41-43.

But another factor must be taken into account—the amount of space and attention given to articles in the press. There is a definite correlation between the amount of space and the amount of reader familiarity with the subject matter. This leads to a certain circularity in the field of all the media of print; the reader pays attention to that which is most emphasized, but the producers of the media tend to give the most space to those kinds of content in which the readers have demonstrated the most interest. We shall find this phenomenon again in magazine and book publishing, and it raises an interesting question concerning "real" versus "created" reader interest—and how they can be measured.

2) *Magazine reading.* Magazine reading reveals similar differences which seem to be correlated with sex, education, and economic status. Women read the advertisements more than men do and tend to prefer fiction to a greater extent than do men. They like romantic love stories, although this is truer of the young than of the older women. Men like articles and stories about adventure, intrigue, war, sports, and those with historical and foreign locales. As in the newspapers, the political articles appeal to men more than women; fashions and homemaking, to women more than men. And as in all cases of reading, a very real difference in the kinds of magazines read can be correlated with differences in amount of education. These differences are obvious enough. No studies are needed to show which of the magazines, *True Romance, American Magazine, Reporter,* and *Partisan Review,* are likely to be most popular, respectively, with those who have had only a grade-school education, a high-school education, or a college education.

3) *Book-reading.* Book-reading, despite its much more limited and selective audience, reveals similar trends. Women read more fiction than men; men read more books on business and public affairs. Generally speaking, women do more "recreational" reading than men; men more work-related reading than women. In terms of total amount of reading, women read more, but men read more "seriously"—for study, for reference, for vocational advancement. In fiction, women read more best-selling novels; men more standard and classic titles. And again, education is the major correlate: Women read more than men if education is held constant, but the more-educated women read the most among the women, and the

better-educated men read more than the less-well-educated women.

A statistical summary and categorization of best sellers from 1912 to 1950 [10] reveals certain subject-matter areas which seem constantly to appeal to book-readers. Of the 345 books on the best-seller lists during the 36-year period mentioned, 22 per cent (76 titles) were biography and autobiography. The next most popular categories of nonfiction were social problems and self-help; together, these three groups comprise fully 46 per cent of all the nonfiction best-sellers on the list.

Fiction, which represents a variety as great as nonfiction, is still dealt with as a homogeneous category in most studies. Yet, in the best-seller lists have appeared the works of writers whose critical acclaim is high (Willa Cather, Ernest Hemingway, William Faulkner) and writers whose novels cannot, by any relaxation of critical standards, be considered anything more than time-filling trifles. The subject matter ranges from historical novels to novels about contemporary social problems; from philosophical novels to novels of "pure" entertainment; from novels of character to novels of incident. While recurrent themes and appeals could undoubtedly be traced in this seemingly unpatterned mass, no solid studies have yet appeared which have attempted to do this.

The Study of Reading Interests

More detailed studies of subject interest in reading have been made. One of the pioneer studies in this field was *What People Want To Read About*,[11] in which the authors attempted to isolate the factors which make for common reading interests. Their concern was with *group* interests, not with individual interest, and their approach was to make a check list of subjects to which groups alike in respect to one or more factors could react. The high reliability which marked the results seemed to argue that they had indeed isolated group factors related to reading interests—and subsequent studies and observation since the Waples and Tyler book have supported their findings.

10. Garry R. Austin, "Nonfiction Best Sellers: Types and Trends," *Journal of Social Psychology*, XXXVIII (August, 1953), 141-43.

11. Douglas Waples and Ralph Tyler, *What People Want To Read About*. Chicago: American Library Association and the University of Chicago Press, 1931.

In order of their relative importance, Waples and Tyler found that the factors which make for differences in reading interest are: sex, amount of schooling, occupation, environment, age, and time spent in reading. The more factors that groups have in common, the more closely their reading interests will agree. In other words, groups are interested in themselves, in people like themselves, and in problems and situations with which they can identify. The interests revealed above in magazine, newspaper, and book reflect this: Women read about other women, about homemaking and child-rearing, about fashion and—when they are young and still involved in emotional problems—romantic love. Men read about business, political affairs, sports, and how to get along in the army. This does not so much reflect a higher seriousness on the part of men readers as it does the greater immediacy to men of these problems.

Editors and others who are concerned with finding out what people want to read about have reached similar conclusions from observation. Their approach to these problems is empirical rather than theoretical. "We have attempted at various times to get the readers to give us their opinions on the items read—tell how they like them. But we find the public not very analytical. We believe that the 'box-office' appeal of any item, as manifested by the number of readers it attracts tells more than a dozen pages of comments," says the director of research for the Crowell-Collier Publishing Company.[12] While the scholar may look with distrust at the use of "box-office" reports as a measuring device, it must be acknowledged that the practical businessman and the theoretical student have uncovered identical results. Paralleling Waples and Tyler, although probably arriving at his conclusions independently, John Siddall, a former editor of *American Magazine*, has found that "the most interesting thing in the world to a man is himself, and the next most interesting thing is another human being in his image and likeness."

"Box-office appeal," circulation figures, number of sales—these have traditionally been taken as convincing indicators of where

12. Raymond A. Robinson, "Fact and Fiction in Magazine Reading," *Writer*, LXVI (June, 1953), 180.

majority interests lie in the content of newspapers, magazines, and books. Yet the studies which followed the Waples and Tyler research uncovered the interesting and rather disturbing fact that interest is less important as a factor in determining what a person will read than is accessibility.[13] In other words, unless the reader is very strongly motivated, he is likely to read what is there, whether he is particularly interested or not. And this is where the disconcerting circularity mentioned above (p. 13) comes into play. People tend to choose for reading what is ready to hand. The producers of printed media tend to publish more and more of the kinds of things that have been chosen by readers in the past. Which means that an apparent demand could be created for something which the producers themselves have made available, rather than what readers would freely select if they had unrestricted choice. It becomes difficult to establish which of the two influences is greater in creating the best-seller—the real interest of the reading audience or the saturation of the market by the astute producer.

These are important factors for us to isolate if we are ever going to learn why people read what they do and how they could learn to read better. But our investigations are considerably hampered if we can neither ask the readers themselves nor judge from an overview of the actual reading done.

It does not necessarily follow that we cannot utilize such methods. There is no reason for us arbitrarily to assume, for example, that the producers of the printed media must be wrong in their judgments about the interests of readers. While they may be able occasionally to drum up a false interest in a particular book or magazine, we know that they can not fool all the people all the time; some of their favorite promotional schemes fall dead on the market, and many a "sleeper" rises to popularity almost in spite of the publisher and the bookseller. Favorite authors sometimes carry an audience with them on many of their lesser efforts, it is true, but many a best-selling author ends up on the remainder tables with particular works which did not "catch on." Apparently the audi-

13. Douglas Waples, "The Relation of Subject Interests to Actual Reading," *Library Quarterly*, II (January, 1932), 42-70; Leon Carnovsky, "A Study of the Relationship between Reading Interest and Actual Reading," *Library Quarterly*, IV (January, 1934), 76-110.

ence does have something to say about what it will like and what it will not.

Nor are we being accurate when we assume that interest is only a subject-matter thing. To say that people read what other people are reading, rather than what they themselves are interested in, is to overlook an important element in what is interesting, i.e., "what other people are reading." Interest may well be whetted by the comments of others, the opportunity to talk over a reading with those who have read the same thing. Thus, a best-seller is interesting for the very reason that it *is* a best-seller, and publishers' promotions can whip up some of this interest. But the reader is not as hapless a victim as some critics would like to have us think.

The truth of the matter is that every reader does not read what every other reader does. The best-seller lists themselves cover a wide-enough range of interest and quality to suggest that several different audiences are responsible for the titles on the top of the list—not one homogeneous mass of readers of best-sellers. There are very real individual differences which even the group approach of Waples and Tyler revealed, and it is here that we begin to approach some sense of the several appeals, the several motivations, the several hoped-for effects which lure people to reading. The refinements in categories for which we called earlier in the chapter are now beginning to be introduced into reading studies, in the form of more intensive analyses of the reading of specific groups, rather than extensive studies of the total reading audience.

One of the first of these applied the Waples and Tyler method and was conducted by Waples himself.[14] Extending the technique of his general study to a specific group, Waples tried to compare the stated interest of public school teachers with the reading that they actually do. The study was limited to avowed interest and actual reading in subjects which had been rated by a jury of social economists as of social importance. Underlying the study was the assumption that teachers *should* show an interest in such subjects and, because of their education, the nature of their profession, and the availability of materials, could reasonably be expected to read

14. Douglas Waples and A. M. W. Birkeland, "Reading Interests of Teachers," in B. W. Frazier *et al.*, *Special Survey Studies*, pp. 233-46. Washington: Government Printing Office, 1935.

more widely and more intelligently in this field than the average man.

To a certain extent it was true that the actual reading that public school teachers did was a little "better" than average—a reflection of the materials available in the school library and the nature of class assignments. But the total pattern of the reading of the teachers is characterized by the same interests as those of the population at large. As studies of the general audience have shown, the women read about 10 per cent more in general than do the men, but the men—among the teachers as among the general population—read more on social subjects and show more interest in them. In the field of social subjects, teachers of both sexes were found to prefer conventional subject matter, sensational treatment, and provincial attitudes. That they read a little bit more of it than the average man is not particularly encouraging.

Waples did not pursue the social significance of this phenomenon, although its implications are clearly stated in his report. When social scientists and educators begin to seek for the causes for the low status of serious reading in our society, for the limited audience for the serious book, and for the failure of those who could most profit by reading to take advantage of a readily accessible tool, they must eventually come to a consideration of the determining role of the teacher. If the teachers themselves do not read, or read only a limited amount, or read without discrimination and taste, the coming generation of potential readers is considerably handicapped in the development of its own lifetime reading habits. The teacher's is not the sole responsibility by any means, but he shares a considerable part of that responsibility with parents and others. And if we push far enough, we must face the fact that the failure of the parents is also often ultimately the failure of *their* teachers.

When the students of reading turn their attention to higher academic levels, they find some equally disconcerting facts. Holt attempted to discover who reads the "best" histories by analyzing the sale records for a group of historical studies which had been adjudged as the best of the last thirty years by a jury of over one hundred scholars.[15] He found that the total sales for eight of the

15. W. Stull Holt, "Who Reads the Best Histories?" *Mississippi Valley Historical Review*, XL (March, 1954), 613-19.

books for which he could find more or less exact figures were less than four thousand copies. On the basis of the number of college and university libraries and the number of professors of American history in the United States, he was forced to conclude that the total number sold (of Hick's *The Populist Revolt,* for example) was not enough to supply each college and university library, to say nothing of the professors of American history. Considering the fact that the larger universities buy multiple copies and that a significant number of the books have been sold to the general public and to public libraries, Mr. Holt concludes that "most of our scholarly history, including the best, is not by specialists for specialists, but is by specialists for a small fraction of the specialists." [16]

Here again the intensive study of a highly specialized group serves merely to confirm what more general studies have already found. Not only is reading the occupation of a small segment of the population but serious and continued reading is limited to a smaller segment within that one. This is most clearly shown in the figures we have for library use. About 25 per cent of the adult population of a library community is registered with the public library, but actually only about 18 per cent use the library at least once a year, and only about 10 per cent use it as often as once a month. This concentration of library use is typical of reading activity generally; it is probably safe to say—borrowing figures from library studies—that about three-fourths of the books that are read are read by less than 5 per cent of the adult population.

A more limited study of a more limited group at a high level of subject specialization was made among members of the American Psychological Association, who were asked to check articles, reviews, and notes which they had read in the *Psychological Bulletin.* It was found that "the reader-audience of specific items ranged from 9 per cent to 58 per cent . . . of the eleven literature surveys appearing on the check list, seven were read by one-third or more of the respondents . . . and most book reviews were read by one-third or more of the A.P.A., and some by as many as half. . . ." [17] The

16. *Ibid.,* p. 619.

17. Wayne Dennis and Edward Girden, "Do Psychologists Read? The Case of the *Psychological Bulletin," American Psychologist,* VIII (May, 1953), 199.

writers of the article found these data gratifying and concluded that "psychologists not only write, but also read." But if we take into consideration what is being measured here, the results are not particularly encouraging to those who believe in the importance and promotion of reading. The membership of the A.P.A. is made up of the type of people who are most likely to read the most—men on a high educational level, with high economic and social status, whose special subject interest is great, and who are dealing with readily available material. This combination of factors is the most favorable for reading, yet, if only about a third of the group reads a piece of material, it is considered to be a comparatively widely-read article. If this is the most favorable reading situation, we must expect even less reading in a cross section of the general public.

Another special group whose reading has been investigated is that of businessmen, with special emphasis on executives. Here again, one would expect that those who successfully rise to the top would be those who utilize the materials of print to keep them informed, to broaden their outlook, to help them in making business decisions. By and large, however, the executive differs little from the ordinary run of Americans; he follows the best-seller lists if he reads at all for recreation; he reads most in those areas of his special interest which promise an immediate, tangible reward, and he reads hardly at all in the area of profound and abstract thought. A high percentage of his reading is in mysteries (recreation) and in management books (practical). Books dealing with theories of economics, in contrast with books on the techniques of management, hold little appeal.

These generalizations are based on a survey conducted by *Fortune* magazine and the Research Institute of America, which included a sampling through questionnaires of executive groups in several corporations, a poll by the R.I.A. of its fifteen thousand company subscribers, and more than one hundred personal interviews.[18] The poll turned up the fact that only 4.6 per cent of the respondents were willing to say that they never read any books; another 5.4 per cent declined to say whether they read anything

---

18. Duncan Norton-Taylor, "Why Don't Businessmen Read Books?" *Fortune,* XLIX (May, 1954), 115-17 ff.

or nothing. But "on the basis of spot sampling in several corporations and its interviews, *Fortune* would guess that not more than
20 per cent of executives might read as many as a dozen books a
year dealing with general subjects." [19] The rest of their reading is
of the highly "practical" type which they see as essential to their
success. An attempt to start a kind of book-of-the-month club for
executives which would feature books having a "lasting value" was
completely unsuccessful; refurbished to offer "how-to" books for
young executives, it was a great success. *Fortune* concludes: "The
executive's explanation for not reading books is that he hasn't time
for them. But what his comments unwittingly suggest is that the
reading he doesn't get around to is merely the reading he doesn't
think is necessary to his success." [20]

In the top ranks of labor, these underlying principles are even
more clearly illustrated. A short survey of the books which labor
leaders have read or recommend for young people of today to
read to inform themselves on the aims and principles of the labor
movement reveals that few of the labor leaders can mention specific
titles when called upon to do so.[21] Among these men there is also
a kind of defensiveness about the failure to read. On the one hand,
apologies are offered: In their youth they had little leisure, limited
schooling, were actively engaged in the activities of men, etc. On
the other hand, their biographies and autobiographies contain many
passages indicating that they loved to read, would read everything
they could get their hands on, etc. Pinned down, the biographers
are hard put to it to mention specific titles. The biographies abound
in such phrases as: "He must surely have read . . . ," or "Although
no lists survive, it is safe to say . . . ," or "He is said to have read. . . ."
In the end, the major conclusion is that "most of the leaders in the
needle trades in New York City and in the large metropolitan areas
trace their early beliefs to participation in various radical movements
rather than to direct reading or study." [22]

19. *Ibid.*, p. 117.

20. *Ibid.*, p. 154.

21. Mark Starr, "American Labor and the Book," *Saturday Review*, XXXVII
(September 4, 1954), 10-11 ff.

22. *Ibid.*, p. 11.

It would be useful to have more studies of specific groups, and even more useful to have some really intensive case studies of individual readers (or nonreaders). But from the studies which now exist, covering many different kinds of persons in many different kinds of situations, there seems to be an over-all pattern which cannot be lightly brushed aside. That pattern reveals that there are very few adults in the United States today who do much reading of a purely voluntary sort. Reading—and in this it is probably very little different from most of our activities—is undertaken when some immediate reward can be foreseen. Thus reading, book-buying, and borrowing of books from libraries show a significant drop at the school-leaving point. Those who drop out of school at the end of high school virtually stop all reading activity outside of newspapers and magazines. Those who continue through college continue to read while in college but reduce the amount of their reading drastically when college ends. Those who continue in the academic world continue to read—but in this atmosphere reading is part of the job as much as it is voluntary recreation. It cannot be denied that much of the reading of these groups is pursued for a specific and tangible end and not for its own sake.

Among businessmen and others outside the academic field, reading is almost completely business-related. Seventy-five per cent of a sample of business executives took one or more *trade* publications as compared to 2 per cent who subscribed to *Harper's*.[23] More than one-half of the young managers enrolled at the well-known advanced management course at Harvard read virtually no books except textbooks and business treatises.[24] Business reading tastes are highly correlated with work interests according to the latest intensive studies. And what is true of businessmen is true of almost all groups, as Waples and Tyler were able to report in their pioneering study twenty-five years ago. People read what they feel they must; and reading, despite the high level of literacy in the United States, is not a "must" activity for very many of them.

23. Edward C. Bursk and Donald T. Clark, "Reading Habits of Business Executives," *Harvard Business Review*, XXVII (May, 1949), 330-45.

24. Norton-Taylor, *op. cit.*, p. 154.

The Status of Reading

It is interesting to analyze the reports, and the apologies, of those whose failure to read is revealed in these studies. Throughout, one finds the same emphasis, either directly stated or implicit: One doesn't have time to do "unnecessary" things—and reading is apparently one of these unnecessary activities to the average man. When a piece of information can be found only in a book, when a reading will lead to a specific proficiency for which an immediate reward is forthcoming, when social or business success can be shown to be dependent upon what books make available, people will read. Delayed rewards have little appeal. In an abstract and friendly discussion of principles, for example, few businessmen would deny that to be a successful businessman one probably should understand the world in which the business operates. But faced with the realities of choice, understanding the world must wait while one learns, instead, which button to push on a specific machine.

This is neatly summarized in Schramm's "fraction of selection" (chap. iii, pp. 64), where the value of the fraction can be increased either by increasing the expectation of reward or decreasing the effort required. Let us look at the implications of the relationship between these two factors for the reading of adults.

We have spoken of the reluctance of the average man to engage in activities for which the foreseeable reward is delayed, and we have shown how he seeks, as immediate rewards from his reading, tangible effects in his business or social world. In other words, the average reader does not find an immediate reward in reading itself; it is not sufficiently pleasurable to warrant the expenditure of time and money which he more readily gives to moving pictures and television. This is revealed in an analysis of the distribution of recreational expenditures compiled from Department of Commerce data.[25]

Activity	Per Cent of Total Recreational Expenditure
Radio, TV, records, musical instruments	19.8
Spectator amusements (movies, sports events, etc.)	13.5
Magazines, newspapers	12.5

25. "The Leisured Masses," *Business Week*, September 12, 1953, p. 143.

Activity	Per Cent of Total Recreational Expenditure
Nondurable toys	11.0
Flowers, seeds	7.1
Sporting goods	6.7
Books, maps	5.4
Participation amusements	3.8
Gambling	3.6
All other	16.6

Much time and money is spent in leisure-time activities. The trend, while not yet great enough to displace spectator amusements and the mass media from the head of the list, is more and more toward those in which people participate as individuals or in small groups. The "active arts have flourished mightily," for example, with a boom in art supplies, musical instruments, do-it-yourself materials, etc. But there are "a couple of major artistic fields that have lagged well behind the general advance. The theater—whose share of the recreation dollar has plummeted since 1929—is one. Reading is the other." [26]

One very clear reason for the comparatively poor showing which books make in contrast with the other competitors for leisure time lies in the denominator in our fraction of selection: the effort required. It is not that the reader could not get pleasure, enlightenment, enjoyment, or refreshment from his reading as great as that available on the screens to which he now devotes so much of his time. It is that, to get a similar reward from reading, he has to work harder for it. For reading is *a highly developed skill;* it is not the mere passive acceptance of the efforts of others. It is no accident that amount of reading correlates so highly with education; one must be educated to be able to read at all; and one must have had considerable practice in reading to be able to read well. To be able to read with pleasure and with ease requires continual practice, continual exercise, continual improvement in the skill. Higher education automatically supplies some of this, and thus the college graduate is more likely to turn to a book for pleasure than is a high-

26. "Where Leisure Time—and Money—Goes," *Business Week*, September 19, 1953, p. 150.

school graduate. These are not reflections of intelligence but of stages in the development of an acquired proficiency. But the average man is still—even in the middle of the twentieth century, and even in the United States—not a college graduate (see p. 6). He lacks, usually through no fault of his own, the ability to read sufficiently well to give serious reading a very high value in the fraction of selection.

To compensate for this lack, some of those interested in the promotion of reading advocate simplifying reading materials to fit the average level of reading proficiency. Recent trends in the development of readability formulas, in condensation and abridgement, in simplification and popularization are a reflection of the growing recognition that serious reading requires a level of skill which the average man does not possess.

Another attack upon the "effort required" is made by those who are trying to make reading materials more readily available. The effort required just to get hold of the materials to read is great. We have seen (pp. 15-16) that accessibility is as important—maybe more important—than subject interest in dictating what a person will choose to read. Therefore, to promote serious reading, we must make it as available as the moving picture theater, the television set, the magazine at the corner newsstand. Otherwise, the reader does not really have an equal choice. We have increased the effort required, lowered the value of the fraction, and set up a barrier against widespread reading.

Here the phenomenon of the paper-bound book becomes a matter of interest. The paper binding has applied to the book the same distribution treatment accorded the popular magazine. It is handily on the counters of cigar store and newsstand, its price is comparable to that of the magazine, the variety of its content compares favorably with that formerly represented by the racks of magazines in the corner drugstore. To a certain extent we have seen that such availability does indeed affect the use of the book. According to the "Census of Manufactures," about 14.3 million dollars worth of paper-bound books were sold in 1947; in 1952 the estimated sales were around $47,000,000.[27] Estimates for 1953 set production of

27. *Publishers Weekly*, CLXVII (January 22, 1955), 323.

paper-back books at 292 million copies—some 100 million copies ahead of the hard-cover production for that year.[28]

But availability can only go so far in promoting reading before it comes up against the other aspect of effort—reading difficulty. When the paper-bound boom was at its height, there were those who predicted a new age of popular education. It was the hope of the more enthusiastic publishers and educators that, with the best in books within reach of the smallest pocketbook, no further barriers would exist between the serious book and the audience which had never before had access to it. For a while it actually seemed as if this new age had dawned. But it is becoming apparent that, in reality, no great new audience has been tapped by the soft-cover book. The light romantic stories, the mysteries, and the westerns found—not a new audience—but the audience which formerly read material on this same level of difficulty and challenge in the pulp magazines. It was these, not the "good" books, which represented the major part of the total sales of paper-bounds, replacing the pulps, finding the same audience, and creating here no really new audience at all.

The "serious" book apparently found its audience in much the same way—among the students and the better-educated who always were the readers of such content. While the publishers tried to convince themselves that new audiences were being reached, the distributors and book-sellers were much more realistic. They placed their titles in those outlets which were patronized by the "natural" audience for different types of content. The drugstore, newsstands, and cigar stores are seldom the places where one finds the serious content even though he does find the soft-cover book. The books which represent the delayed reward or the reward of aesthetic pleasure are available, even in paper covers, almost exclusively in the college and university bookstores and those which deliberately cater to the "carriage trade."

More than that, the very interesting phenomenon which is presently occurring in the paper-bound industry seems to lend support to these hypotheses. The cheap (in both senses of the term), popu-

28. Kurt Enoch, "The Paper-bound Book: Twentieth-Century Publishing Phenomenon," *Library Quarterly*, XXIV (July, 1954), 213.

lar (in its pejorative sense) book is no longer the big news in the paper-bound field. The lasting item in the field turns out to be the serious book of more permanent value which, although less expensive than its hard-cover edition, cannot be considered a truly inexpensive item. Such series as Anchor, Vintage, Image, Meridian, Harvest, and the Viking Portables in paper-back editions are priced at a little less than a dollar for some titles and over a dollar for many others. Such titles and such prices are no longer aiming at the mass market; they are being sold to that limited audience—the better-educated, higher-income group—which has always been the buyers of books whether in hard or soft covers. In reality, they represent the kind of publishing which has long been with us in such series as *Modern Library* and *Everyman's Library*, carrying titles of similar quality and charging prices comparable to the *Modern Library* and *Everyman* prices of a couple of decades ago. That they are now paper-bound, rather than hard-bound, for 95 cents and $1.25 is less a reflection of a new approach to publishing than it is of rising production costs.

It would appear, then, that the audience for the book is self-limiting. So long as the reading skill is not highly developed in the majority of our population, it is foolish to imagine a majority audience reading widely and seriously. As higher education becomes more and more the possession of the average man, an increase in serious reading may be expected, but not in a one-to-one relationship. For even when a man can read and has reading materials readily available, he does not necessarily read if the rewards of reading are not apparent to him. Some of these rewards are intangible; their appeal is greater to some people than to others; and the matter of individual differences will always make readers of some people and nonreaders of others even when they possess the basic skill.

Some of the rewards are—for want of a better term—social; they relate to the role which the individual wishes to play in his society and in relation to his peers. And here we are face to face with a much more difficult obstacle to widespread reading than any of the variables which have been studied and reported in this chapter. For the status of reading in our society cannot be ignored —and that status is a strange one. If not carried to excess, we think reading is a good thing—for somebody else. The "bookish" person is not necessarily one which the average man would wish to emulate; there is something remote, "anti-social," "impractical" about such a person in the stereotype which is now widely held. It is revealing that one of the executives interviewed in the study by *Fortune* and the Research Institute of America said, "Reading is not part of the concept of what a businessman is supposed to be or to be doing. The concept is of a man pressed by tangible problems that require tangible solutions. The businessman is a man of action. Reading doesn't fit into this concept." [29]

So long as "action" seems more desirable in our society than thought, it is going to be difficult to promote reading as a socially desirable activity. So long as rewards from any time-consuming activity must be tangible and immediate, it is going to be difficult to convince more than a few in our society that reading has a justifiable claim upon their time. So long as reading is difficult to do, it is going to suffer in competition with less difficult activities. These are formidable barriers to breach, but there is one weapon which suggests itself in every one of these instances. That weapon is education, and while it is not—in the most literal sense of the words—fool-proof, it is the most promising one we have.

29. Norton-Taylor, *op. cit.*, p. 117.

CHAPTER II

How Well Do Adults Read?

WILLIAM S. GRAY

The fact was pointed out in the preceding chapter that what adults read and the extent of their reading are influenced by their ability to read. It is equally true that the values derived—pleasure, information, thought stimulation, the solution of personal and group problems—are determined in large measure by their reading efficiency. It follows that the question of how well adults read assumes large importance in any critical analysis of adult reading problems.

As we approach this question, two issues arise. The first is concerned with the role of reading in current life and the nature of the reading attitudes and skills needed. The second relates to the level of competence in reading among adults and involves such questions as: What per cent of the adult population is unable to read? What per cent is functionally literate, that is, able to engage effectively in the reading activities normally expected of literate adults? To what extent are they able to interpret mature types of material in general, technical, and literary fields? How effectively are they able to achieve the various purposes for which they read? Obviously, we cannot provide rational answers to some of the questions pertaining to the adequacy of reading ability among adults until we consider, at least briefly, the nature of the attitudes and skills which affect the level of competence an individual may attain in reading.

The Dynamic Role of Adult Reading

As we review the role of reading in American life, three facts stand out clearly. The first is that reading has always played a significant role in the lives of people in this country.[1] Even in colonial

---

1. Nila B. Smith, *American Reading Instruction*. Newark, New Jersey: Silver, Burdett & Co., 1934.

days, great importance attached to reading as an aid in providing spiritual guidance. The second fact is that the dominant purposes for reading have varied from time to time in harmony with the changing needs, ideals, and aspirations of our people. During the revolutionary period, for example, the materials read acquainted people with the causes that impelled separation from the mother country and promoted loyalty to the new nation; during the early part of the nineteenth century, they provided needed information about the expanding frontier and the duties of good citizens; during the latter part of the century, they provided a growing acquaintance with our social and literary heritage; and during the first quarter of this century, the strictly utilitarian values of reading ranked high.

By 1925 the opportunities and demands for reading were many and varied. Personal inquiries carried on among hundreds of adults showed that they read to meet various practical needs of daily living, to know and understand current happenings, to secure immediate personal satisfaction or pleasure, to further avocational interests, to acquire added professional or vocational efficiency, to meet personal-social needs such as to maintain social prestige by being well informed, to acquire a growing understanding of social problems, to discharge their duties as citizens more intelligently, to promote self-development, to extend their cultural background, to acquire a growing acquaintance with our literary heritage, and to satisfy religious and spiritual needs.

The period since 1925 has been one of the most critical periods in our history. Within a relatively brief period of time, adults have faced a series of challenging economic, social, and political problems that have called for wide reading, clear thinking, and radical adjustments. The understandings needed have related to such matters as the soundness of our economic structure, the basic principles underlying our democratic form of government, the essential differences between various national ideologies, the causes and elimination of intergroup conflicts, the principles for which we fought during World War II, and the conditions that must be met to insure permanent peace. Because of the very character of the times, the demands made on readers have increased at an unprecedented rate.

In an effort to acquire needed information, young people and adults have read more widely and in greater numbers than ever before. As shown by numerous published reports, reading has continued to serve each of the vital purposes listed above. In addition, chief attention has focused in turn on each of the successive problems which our nation has faced. Individuals have read widely and intensively to secure a clearer understanding of the issues involved and to search for possible solutions. In the course of time they found it necessary to engage also in many other types of reading, the chief value of which was to provide release from or to escape tension. Some sought to overcome their confusion and perplexities through wide reading in the fields of psychology, psychiatry, and other approaches to personality problems. Others turned to the "Great Books" and to the literature of "power" and "imagination." Such reading, it has been claimed, does far more than entertain, soothe, or inform. It gives direction to the thought-life of the reader, prepares him to see current problems in a broader perspective, and contributes to a full, rich, and satisfying personal life.

Paralleling these developments, other agencies of mass communication have come into wide use. It was thought at first that they might largely replace the need for reading. Intensive studies such as those made by Dale [2] and Lazarsfeld [3] supply clear evidence that "there is no substitute for reading" in meeting many personal and social needs. Of special importance is its value in the deliberate study of the serious problems which we face today. Its distinctive value lies in two facts. Printed materials provide the most illuminating and varied records of human experience now available. Furthermore, they can be examined and restudied time and again at the reader's convenience and at his own pace, thus enabling him to acquire clearer understandings, to develop rational attitudes, and to reach sound conclusions.

As a result of a broad inquiry to identify the distinctive functions that reading should serve in an age of motion pictures, radio, and television, Preston [4] identified the following: "To provide a

2. Edgar Dale, "Is There a Substitute for Reading?" *Newsletter* (Bureau of Educational Research, Ohio State University), X (April, 1945).

3. Paul F. Lazarsfeld, *Radio and the Printed Page*. New York: Duell, Sloan & Pearce, 1940.

4. Ralph C. Preston, "The Changed Role of Reading," in *Reading in an Age of Mass Communication*, pp. 7-13. Edited by William S. Gray. New York: Appleton-Century-Crofts, Inc., 1949.

semblance of balance in the content of vicarious experience" and "to augment the individual's self-respect" through a discriminating choice of reading materials; to provide "a needed check on the authenticity of the content" of other mass media, due both to distorted presentations and their fleeting character; "to foster substantial human values" in contrast to the strictly materialistic motives that receive so much emphasis today through other mass media; to secure a more penetrating grasp of specific problems through re-reading, analysis, and intermittent reflection; and to promote mental and spiritual health through participation at times in private as contrasted with group experience and in silent as contrasted with noisy ones.

Developing a Broader Concept of Reading

The foregoing discussion has described all too briefly the expanding role of reading in adult life. The facts presented, however, raise pointedly the question: How well should adults be able to read to meet effectively the needs of current life? It will be helpful in attempting to answer this question to follow briefly the growth which has occurred in the concept of reading[5] during recent decades and to identify its essential aspects.

Early in the current century, reading was often defined as the act of recognizing and pronouncing words. Anything else that occurred during the act of reading was called supra-reading. As long as reading was thus conceived, attention in teaching focused on the development of accuracy and independence in word recognition and in promoting fluent habits of oral reading. Unfortunately, only minor emphasis was given to the content or meaning of what was read. During this period very low standards of literacy were adopted and applied.

Between 1910 and 1925 a much broader concept of reading began to evolve. This was due largely to two developments: first, the rapid increase in reading among adults with large emphasis on its utilitarian values; and, second, the discovery of the greater economy and efficiency of silent reading. As a result, the view was adopted

---

5. William S. Gray, "The Nature and Development of Reading," *Reading in the High School and College*, chap. iii. Forty-seventh Yearbook of the National Society for the Study of Education, Part II. Chicago: Distributed by University of Chicago Press, 1948.

that reading consists not only of the accurate recognition of words but also of the fluent grasp of meaning.

At first major emphasis was given to the literal meaning of a passage, that is, to what it says. As effort was made to promote growth in comprehension, it was found that other types of meanings were involved, such as implied meanings, those that are intended by the author but not stated; related meanings, all that the reader knows or can find out that make clear the author's intended message; and derived meanings, the conclusions or generalizations that can be deduced from the facts presented. Thus, there emerged a broader understanding of the steps involved in securing a clear grasp of meaning in reading. At the same time the need developed for increased speed in reading, both to meet the expanding uses for reading and to take fuller advantage of the opportunities to acquire pleasure, insight, and inspiration through reading.

During the late twenties and thirties, it became evident that, in order to grow in understanding of the perplexing personal and social problems faced, it is not enough merely to recognize words quickly and accurately and to secure a clear grasp of their meaning. In addition, the readers must reflect on the significance of the ideas apprehended, discover relationships among them, and clarify their thinking concerning the issues involved. Furthermore, they must react thoughtfully to what is read, rejecting that which is inaccurate, biased, and unsound and responding favorably to "the true, the beautiful, and the good."

During the forties the fact was emphasized that if reading is to make its largest contribution to personal development the reader must combine the ideas read with previous experience. Only in this way can he correct or expand his present understanding through reading, acquire more rational attitudes, and develop improved ways of thinking and behaving. Reading without integration may be likened to the dropping of a stone into a vat of liquid. Nothing happens other than a slight rise in the level of the liquid. Reading that involves integration may be compared to the pouring of a few drops of bluing into a vat of clear liquid. The bluing instantly begins to spread and soon changes both the appearance and composition of the liquid.

In harmony with the foregoing statements, reading is conceived today as a complex activitiy of four dimensions: the perception of words, a clear grasp of meaning, thoughtful reaction, and integration. All four steps are essential in varying combinations if adults are to secure through reading an adequate understanding of the conflicting issues that current life presents, to choose wisely between alternatives, to find valid solutions to the challenging personal and social problems faced, and to develop richer and more stable personalities. The belief prevails that, if adult reading is effective in the future in achieving these ends, American life will be notably improved.

It would be very desirable if we could turn at this point to the results of nation-wide studies that show how well adults read in the broad sense that has just been outlined. Unfortunately, no comprehensive appraisal of this type has ever been made. However, much information is available that provides a basis for estimating the extent of literacy and the various levels of reading ability attained by adults. In addition, numerous objective studies of adult reading have been reported, based on segments of our population. They have been carried on both among the armed forces and among civilians. In the sections that follow, the more significant data now available will be examined for the purpose of identifying possible generalizations concerning how well adults read.

Measuring the Reading Ability of Adults

ESTIMATES BASED ON UNITED STATES CENSUS REPORTS

For the major part of a century the federal government has been vitally concerned with the size of the adult reading public and its ability to read. Prior to 1940 interest centered largely on the per cent of illiteracy among adults. The records secured were based on responses to the question: Can you read or write, or both? It was assumed that all who were classified as literate by the census enumerators had made at least a beginning in learning to read.

Through the use of the procedures just described, the extent of literacy in this country was found to be as follows: 80 per cent in 1870; 83.3 per cent in 1880; 86.7 per cent in 1890; 89.3 per cent in 1900; 92.3 per cent in 1910; 94 per cent in 1920, and 95.7 per cent in 1930. In 1952 it was estimated that the corresponding per cent was 97.5. These findings were very gratifying from two points of view. They implied that steady progress had been made during the last century in developing a literate nation. They also suggested that within a relatively short time practically all adults would be able to read, as measured by the standards used. Further evidence of progress was found in the fact that the percentage of illiteracy was distinctly less among the younger as contrasted with the older adults questioned at any given census period.

Gratifying as these findings may be, they are far from satisfactory for several reasons. The literacy standards used were so low that the data secured had little value. Stated differently, they assumed little more than ability to recognize a limited number of simple words and bore little relationship to the high level of competence in reading that current life demands. The methods used in securing the data were such that pointed questions arose concerning their reliability in estimating ability to read. Furthermore, the data secured gave no indication of the level at which given adults could read. This proved to be a serious limitation because no conclusions could be drawn concerning the reading needs of adults or their ability to engage in the various types of reading essential to individual welfare or social progress.

For the reasons enumerated, the Census Bureau discontinued in 1940 the use of traditional literacy tests. It adopted instead the plan of securing a record of the number of years of schooling completed. This was done on the assumption that such a record would provide a truer measure of literacy than the traditional tests. Furthermore, some evidence had accumulated that a reasonably close correlation existed between the amount of education and the average reading ability of classified groups. It was believed, therefore, that the information secured would have value in estimating the levels of literacy attained by adults.

The records secured during the 1940 and the 1950 censuses are summarized in Table 1. They show the per cent of adults, 25 years of age or older, who completed certain specified school grades during their last year in school. The entries in the table supply a far broader view of the cultural level and probable reading ability of adults than the literacy records previously secured. Those in the right-hand column show that, in 1940, the median number of school grades completed by adults was 8.6. It was, therefore, assumed that the average reading ability of all adults could be represented by a grade score of 8.6 This is equivalent to the average score in reading made by pupils who are in the sixth month of their eighth year in school. The median for 1950 shows that the cultural status and presumably the reading ability of adults had improved by distinctly more than a half-grade during the intervening decade.

TABLE 1

PERCENTAGE DISTRIBUTION OF PERSONS TWENTY-FIVE YEARS OLD OR OLDER, CLASSIFIED BY NUMBER OF YEARS OF SCHOOL COMPLETED *

CENSUS YEAR	PER CENT OF TOTAL POPULATION ACCORDING TO YEARS OF SCHOOL COMPLETED							MEDIAN YEARS OF SCHOOL COMPLETED
	Elementary School			High School		College		
	Less than 5 years	5 to 7 Years	8 Years	1 to 3 Years	4 Years	1 to 3 Years	4 Years	
1940.........	13.5	18.3	27.8	14.9	14.1	5.4	4.6	8.6
1950.........	10.8	15.9	20.2	16.9	20.2	7.2	6.0	9.3

* Based on data in Table 135, *Statistical Abstract of the United States, 1954*, p. 121. Washington: Bureau of Census, Department of Commerce. (Not included in this table are 1.4 per cent of the adults in 1940 and 2.8 per cent in 1950.)

Further study of the entries in the table show that the adults interviewed varied widely in the extent of their education. In 1940 at least 13.5 per cent of the adult population had received less than five years of schooling and presumably had acquired only limited reading ability. In 1950 the corresponding per cent was 10.8. At the opposite extreme, 10 per cent of the adults in 1940 and 13.2 per cent in 1950 had acquired the cultural advantages that attach to one or more years of college education. They were also presumably equipped to read with a relatively high degree of penetration and discrimination. Additional evidence of progress [6] is found in the fact that the younger adults involved in the 1950 census ranked distinctly higher in amount of schooling than the older adults. Such findings are very encouraging.

As the foregoing census records were studied, questions arose concerning the minimum amount of schooling that could be accepted as an index of literacy. Following wide discussion of this problem, the concept of "functional literacy" evolved. It was defined as ability to engage in all those reading activities essential to the welfare of all citizens in a culture. Further study led to the tentative conclusion that the minimum ability in reading needed by adults was the equivalent of that possessed on the average by pupils

6. *Statistical Abstract of the United States, 1954*, p. 121. Washington: Bureau of the Census, Department of Commerce, 1955.

who had completed the fourth grade. Accordingly, "persons completing fewer than five years of schooling were called functionally illiterate." [7]

This definition has been used widely during recent years in estimating the extent of functional illiteracy. In 1953, for example, Caliver reported that approximately ten million, or 11 per cent of the adults in this country, had less than a fifth-grade education and were, by definition, functionally illiterate. The percentage of illiteracy which he reported on this basis for the respective states is shown in Table 2.

The discussion thus far has reviewed briefly the estimates made

TABLE 2

PERCENTAGE OF ADULTS TWENTY-FIVE YEARS AND ABOVE IN EACH STATE
WHO COMPLETED LESS THAN FIVE YEARS OF SCHOOLING *

State	Per Cent	State	Per Cent
Continental U.S.	11.0	Missouri	8.4
Iowa	3.9	North Dakota	8.8
Oregon	4.3	Connecticut	8.9
Utah	4.3	New Jersey	9.2
Idaho	4.5	Pennsylvania	9.4
Washington	4.7	New York	9.5
Nebraska	4.9	Delaware	9.7
Kansas	5.0	Rhode Island	9.7
Vermont	5.5	Maryland	10.9
Wyoming	5.7	Oklahoma	10.9
Minnesota	5.8	West Virginia	13.7
South Dakota	5.8	Florida	13.8
Montana	6.3	Arizona	14.2
New Hampshire	6.3	Texas	15.8
Indiana	6.6	Kentucky	16.8
Maine	6.7	Virginia	17.5
California	6.8	New Mexico	18.0
District of Columbia	6.8	Tennessee	18.3
Nevada	6.8	Arkansas	19.8
Ohio	6.9	North Carolina	21.1
Colorado	7.1	Alabama	22.6
Wisconsin	7.2	Georgia	24.2
Michigan	7.5	Mississippi	25.2
Illinois	7.8	South Carolina	27.4
Massachusetts	7.9	Louisiana	28.7

* Adapted from Ambrose Caliver, *Literacy Education: National Statistics and Other Related Data*, Table 2. United States Office of Education, Circular No. 376, 1953. Washington: Government Printing Office, 1953.

7. "Illiteracy in the United States, October, 1947," *Current Population Reports: Population Characteristics*. Washington: Department of Commerce, Bureau of the Census, September 22, 1948.

by the federal government of the cultural level of adults in terms of last school grade attended. Assuming, first, that there is a fairly close correspondence between number of years of schooling and the average reading ability of adults, the following tentative conclusions appear to be valid. The average reading ability of the current generation of adults is about equal to the average ability of pupils in the early part of the ninth grade. Furthermore, the range in reading ability extends from complete illiteracy to a superior level of interpretation and discrimination. Assuming, second, that adults who have not completed the fourth grade are functionally illiterate, approximely 11 per cent of our adult population is illiterate. Furthermore, the per cent of illiteracy varies for the various states from 3.9 to 28.7. It follows that the task faced by the different states in developing a literate citizenry varies widely.

As an aid in checking the validity of the foregoing conclusions, attention will be directed next to the results of objective studies of the reading ability of adults.

READING SCORES OBTAINED BY OBJECTIVE TESTS

Although objective studies of reading achievement have been made widely among children during the last four decades, this is is not true in the case of adults. Unfortunately the limited number of studies reported relate to only very small segments of our civilian population or to specialized groups, such as men in the armed forces. Furthermore, many of the civilian studies which are most valuable in checking on the foregoing conclusions and in suggesting fruitful generalizations were made about two decades ago.

Reading Ability of Men in the Armed Forces. Without doubt more objective tests of reading have been given to members of the armed forces than to any other adult group. The results have been used widely in determining the basic qualifications of young men for service and the nature and type of activities in which inductees can engage to best advantage. Unfortunately, most of the data reported pertain to those of limited reading ability.

In 1917-18, during the draft, 1,522,256 [8] men were given tests.

8. *Five Questions on American Education Week*, pp. 1280-81. Research Bulletin of the National Education Association, Vol. I, No. 4. Washington: National Education Association, 1923.

The results showed that 24.9 per cent of those tested "were unable to read and understand newspapers and to write letters" in English. As a result of tests given to inductees during World War II, it was estimated that from 12 to 15 per cent of the adults in this country were functionally illiterate. These findings attracted wide attention [9] because the percentages given were notably higher than the census estimates of illiteracy. The data also showed that a surprisingly large number of individuals who had gone to school were unable as adults to read. Further study revealed the fact that various factors contributed to their inability to read, such as limited learning capacity, ill-health, poor vision and hearing, emotional disturbances, lack of motivation, limited amount of schooling, and irregularity in attendance.

During recent years, the army has followed the plan of administering the *Armed Forces Qualification Test* to all men who entered the service. Those who were accepted have been given the *Army Classification Battery*. Those who appeared to be deficient in reading and arithmetic were given the *California Achievement Test, Intermediate Level.* During the period from January to June, 1955, the induction centers in the thirteen states of the Fifth Army Area processed 20,684 inductees.[10] This area embraces the North Central States which, according to Table 2, rank relatively high in functional literacy.

The data secured show that, of the number processed, 7.5 per cent had reading abilities below the fifth-grade level and 18.2 per cent ranked between the fifth and eighth grades in reading. These percentages do not include the approximately 3,000 who fell below the minimum army requirements. That the 1955 group may have been above average, or that the situation may be improving, is shown by the fact that, in 1952, approximately 18.5 per cent of the inductees processed at the Fort Custer Reception Center were unable to read at the fourth-grade level. Whereas no data were reported for the states which rank highest in illiteracy according

9. Eli Ginzberg and Douglas W. Bray, *The Uneducated.* New York: Columbia University Press, 1952.

10. The information and data relative to the Fifth Army Area have been supplied through the courtesy of the Commanding General, Fifth Army, Major General P. D. Ginder, U.S.A., Chicago, Illinois.

to Table 2, it may be assumed that the percentages unable to read at the fourth-grade level would be very high.

It is now customary for the army to provide training in reading for those who rank below the level of functional literacy. Of large significance is the fact that 75 per cent of the trainees attain functional literacy during 96 hours of academic training. Others require additional training. Noncommissioned officers who rank below the eighth grade in reading ability are also given training in reading. An average of 250 hours of instruction enables 75 per cent of these officers to learn to read well enough to attain eighth-grade reading ability.

The additional fact was pointed out by Major General Ginder that the raising of the educational level of the noncommissioned officers is of great importance today. With the rapid technological advances of the armed forces, it is vital that all officers operate at a high literacy level. Once they have attained the eighth-grade level they can qualify for the armed services schools with the possibility of further advancement. On the basis of both evidence and experience, it has been found that many men who read only at the eighth-grade level "are not able to reach their potential level." Such findings doubtless apply also to advancement in many fields of civilian service. They indicate that many otherwise capable men are not able to live up to their fullest potentialities in activities in an age when the use of print is essential.

The importance of increased speed and comprehension on the part of officers has been recognized by various branches of the armed services. As a result, testing and reading-improvement programs have been developed in all of them. In 1948, for example, the Air University of the Maxwell Air Force Base reported the results of reading tests given to ninety National Guard and Reserve Officers.[11] The findings showed that the group read at an average of 291 words per minute, the range being from about 170 to 470. To use another example, tests were given to a volunteer group of officers and nonofficers at one of the army headquarters. The average speed score was 303 words per minute and the range was from

11. *The Air University Reading Improvement Program*, pp. 21-24. Montgomery, Alabama: Air University, Maxwell Air Force Base, June, 1948.

204 to 485. The percentile distribution of comprehension scores was from 1 to 99. As a result of the training now given, which makes large use of reading-rate controllers and other types of speed exercises, far greater increases have been secured in speed of reading than in comprehension. The training given has proved valuable in enabling the officers to do more quickly the large amount of paper work which their positions require.

The foregoing findings are very revealing. The men in the armed forces represent practically all levels of reading ability found among adults in our population. Unfortunately, thousands are lost to the services due to limited capacity, in general, and to inability to read. From 5 to almost 30 per cent of the men accepted from different parts of the country require specific training to attain functional literacy. This is deemed essential for even reasonably effective service. Extensive training programs in reading are also provided beyond the fourth-grade level to enable otherwise capable men to render intelligent service as noncommissioned officers and to prepare for advancement. The experiments with reading programs among men who have had a high-school or college education shows that gratifying increases in reading ability are possible. These findings indicate the great responsibility which schools, colleges, and adult agencies face if they are to prepare men and women to use reading as effectively as possible as an aid to personal development, national service, and social progress.

Reading Ability of Civilian Groups. Interest in how well civilians read has increased very rapidly during recent years. It stems from a keenly felt need among adults throughout the nation to be able to read with greater ease and understanding. It finds expression also in the effort of industrial, commercial, and professional organizations to provide their members with the training needed to meet more effectively the reading demands made upon them. Equally important is the wide interest of teachers and research workers in the field of education to identify the causes of poor reading and the most effective types of guidance in securing improvements.

For the reasons indicated, reading tests have been given to many specialized groups and to various small segments of our population. In many cases standardized tests prepared for use in schools and colleges have been given. In other cases special tests, including content based on the interests of adults, have been prepared and used. Unfortunately, the various tests used measure different aspects of reading and the results cannot be readily compared. Furthermore, most of the studies reported have been concerned with adults who encounter serious difficulty in reading and are in need of corrective training. Unfortunately, also, the results of tests given to employees by large industrial and commercial organizations have not been published. As a result we are sorely handicapped in our effort to present a comprehensive picture of how well civilians in general read. Through reference to the results of a few carefully selected studies, an effort will be made to reach certain valid conclusions.

One of the most illuminating studies now available was designed to find out in detail how well adults read. For this purpose, Buswell [12] selected 982 adults with great care. In respect to occupation, they were classified as follows: professional, 102; office and sales, 504; skilled labor, 104; unskilled labor, 245; unclassified, 27. They were somewhat equally distributed over the age range from 25 to 45. Few subjects more than 45 years of age were used due to the onset of farsightedness. Their classification in terms of last school grade attended was as follows: Grade VI or below, 143; VII-VIII, 253; IX-X, 213; XI-XII, 209; XIII or above, 164. Of the total number tested, 48 were Negroes. Scores made on the Otis Self-Administering Tests of Mental Ability, Form A, were quite normally distributed. As indicated by these facts, the group was fairly representative of the adult population in general, particularly in urban communities.

The tests used were prepared specifically for use in this study. They aimed to measure ability to engage in a number of adult reading activities, such as finding the price of given items from a price list; finding from a series of advertisements the name of the theater where a specific movie could be seen; answering questions based on paragraphs read; selecting from a series of words the one which means the same as a given word. In order to make certain comparisons, the tests were given to eighty junior and senior high school pupils. Eye-movement records while reading were also

12. Guy T. Buswell, *How Adults Read.* Supplementary Educational Monographs, No. 45. Chicago: University of Chicago, 1937.

secured from 38 of the adults, the 80 junior and senior high school pupils, and 26 elementary-school pupils.

The results of the tests given to 897 adults are summarized in Table 3. The entries in the table confirm the findings reported earlier to the effect that reading achievements among adults increase in general with the number of years of schooling. They also supply

TABLE 3

SCORES MADE ON READING TESTS BY 897 ADULTS GROUPED ACCORDING TO
LAST SCHOOL GRADE ATTENDED *

| TEST SCORES | NUMBER OF ADULTS GROUPED BY LAST SCHOOL GRADE ATTENDED | | | | | TOTAL SUBJECTS |
	VI or Below	VI-VIII	IX-X	XI-XII	XIII or Above	
76-93.............	0	4	6	9	23	42
57-75.............	2	38	74	92	101	307
38-56.............	25	96	88	91	29	329
19-37.............	53	58	31	7	4	153
0-18.............	44	16	5	1	0	66
Total subjects.....	124	212	204	200	157	897
Median score.....	25.0	43.8	51.8	56.7	65.1	50.8

* *Statistical Abstract of the United States, op. cit., p. 33.*

clear evidence that adults with given amounts of schooling differ widely in ability to read. This corresponds with the results of reading tests among children. It is due largely to innate differences among individuals and to variations in environmental factors that influence progress in reading.

The relationship between amount of schooling and reading ability was studied further through a comparison of amount of schooling of the 100 adults ranking highest in the test and the 100 adults ranking lowest. These groups were sharply separated by a span of 40 points. The data showed that 79 per cent of the 100 best readers had gone beyond the tenth grade before leaving school, whereas 96 per cent of the 100 poorest readers had not gone as far as the ninth grade.

A study was made next to find out the influence of amount of schooling and ability to read on the reading interests and habits of the adults tested. It was found that newspapers were read regularly by 77.5 per cent of those with six years of schooling or less and by 92 to 95 per cent of all other grade groups. Magazines were reported as read regularly by 21.1 per cent of those with six or less years of schooling; by 34.3 per cent of those with nine or ten years of schooling; and by 69.1 per cent of those with 13 or more years of schooling. Books were reported as read by 9.2, 35.2, and 62.3 per cent, respectively, of these three groups. As evidenced by all the data secured, amount of schooling exerts a vital influence on both the average reading achievement of adults and the amount and kind of reading done.

Finally, Buswell was concerned to know if adults made any progress in reading after they left school. He, therefore, classified the adults tested in terms of both last school grade attended and number of years out of school. In the latter case he classified the adults under three headings: 14 years or less out of school, 15 to 19 years, and 20 or more years. The data thus arranged showed that up to 20 years out of school the reading scores increased. Beyond that period the trend was uncertain. He found also that those who left school in Grades VI, VII, and VIII ranked higher than those who left school in later grades. This was explained by the statement that "greater gains are possible at a low level of ability than at a high level."

The foregoing findings are supported in general by those of other investigators. Lorge and Blau,[13] for example, gave the Thorn-dike-McCall Reading Test to 867 eighth-grade pupils in 1921-22. The tests were repeated again in 1932 and 1941. The number of volunteers for these two tests were 163 and 133, respectively. Unfortunately the average scores compared were not for the same individuals in all cases, and a number of those tested had received some school training after leaving the eighth grade. Nevertheless, the investigators concluded that "adults who are subject to the usual tasks and activities of post-adolescent life do on the average improve in their comprehension." The data further indicated that the period of greatest improvement was during the first ten years beyond leaving the eighth grade.

Lorge and Blau supported their findings by reference to those of Norris [14] who gave the New Stanford Reading Test to 851 un-

13. Irving Lorge and Raphael Blau, "Reading Comprehension of Adults," *Teachers College Record*, XLIII (December, 1941), 189-98.

14. K. E. Norris, *The Three R's and the Adult Worker*, pp. 127-28. Montreal, Canada: McGill University, 1940.

employed adults in Canada and classified those tested in terms of the last school grade attended. The average scores made for those thus classified increased from Grades VI to IX, inclusive, but decreased for those in Grades X and XI. These average scores were then compared with the scores made by pupils completing the respective grades at the time the study was made. On this basis, there appeared to be a "quite general improvement in reading" among adults who left school on completing Grades VI to IX, inclusive, and a slight loss among those who left school in Grades X and XI.

Reference is here made to a study of adults in a rural community because of the additional light it throws on our problem.[15] It included as its basic group all of the adults of a rural community of 200 who were willing to participate. Seventy-five who took the tests lived in a small village in western Illinois, and 76 lived on adjacent farms. The median age of the village group was 44.9; of the rural group, 43.5. The mean school grade last attended was the eighth in both cases. In general ability, occupational interests, and economic status the group, as a whole, was quite typical of midwest rural America. Both the Standardized Oral Reading Test and the Monroe Silent Reading Test were given to all who cooperated.

When the scores on the oral and silent reading tests were compared, it was found that both the villagers and the farmers scored at least one and one-half grades higher on the former. On the basis of eight years of experience as a pupil in the village school of this community, the writer would attribute this difference to vigorous emphasis on oral reading and meager attention to thoughtful interpretation. The statement should be added that such evidence supports the contention that the nature of the reading competence of any generation of adults is determined to a large extent by the kind and amount of the instruction given when they were in school.

The scores made on the Monroe Silent Reading Test varied from a grade score of 2.9 or less to 16.9 or above. They indicated that, whereas some of the adults were unable to read even the simplest material with any degree of understanding, others could read ma-

---

15. William S. Gray and Bernice Leary. *What Makes a Book Readable*, pp. 86-90. Chicago: University of Chicago Press, 1935.

terials as difficult as those commonly read by college seniors. Furthermore, those who discontinued school at any given grade level varied widely in reading ability. As was true in the case of Buswell's findings, there was a fair degree of correlation between the last school grade attended and the average reading ability of the respective groups.

Further analysis of the data showed two distinct variations from the trend just described. On the one hand, those who did not remain in school beyond the fifth grade usually made scores as adults below that level. This may have been due in part to the fact that some of those who dropped out of school early did so because they had found it difficult to learn to read and had made little or no progress. Others who dropped out of school before reaching the sixth grade had acquired only limited reading ability even though they had made normal progress. As a result, they could read adult material only with great difficulty. They, therefore, read very little and, in the course of time, a part if not all of the ability they had acquired in school was lost through disuse.

On the other hand, the pupils who remained in school for six years or more tended to read as adults above the level of the last school grade attended. This was explained by the fact that they were able, on leaving school, to read simple material with reasonable ease. They used reading to a considerable extent, at first, in meeting the practical needs of daily life and, later, in extending their range of experience, in securing pleasure during leisure hours, and in solving personal and social problems. As a result of the motivated reading in which they engaged, growth in reading efficiency occurred.

The facts presented thus far justify a series of very useful conclusions: First, adults vary in general reading ability from complete inability to read to the highest levels of efficiency that have been measured; second, there is a fair degree of relationship in the case of groups, between last school grade attended and average reading ability; and, third, individuals vary from this trend in several respects. Of large significance is the fact that those who leave school before the fifth grade tend, as adults, to read below the expected grade level; on the other hand, those who continue in school beyond the fifth grade tend, in general, to read above the level of the last school grade attended. Moreover, the greatest gains are made by those who drop out of school in the upper grades and junior high school and during the first ten to twenty years out of school rather than later. Further research is needed to confirm or modify these conclusions.

A Projected View of Adult Reading Ability

As the foregoing findings were identified, a plan evolved for developing a more detailed and illuminating description of adult reading ability than appears in previous sections of this chapter. It included, as a first step, the securing of accurate records of the reading ability of children when the present generation of adults were in school. By interpreting such records in the light of the tentative conclusions stated above, it would be possible, it was believed, to secure a reasonably accurate picture of the extent and distribution of the reading ability of the current generation of adults.

Accordingly, a search was made for reading scores secured from pupils a decade or more ago through the use of a valid test of reading ability. An effort was made, also, to secure the records of pupils from as many grades as possible under reasonably comparable conditions. After reviewing all of the test records that could be found, the data summarized in Table 4 were selected for use.

The entries in the table represent the reading scores made by 14,007 pupils in Grades IV to XII, inclusive, on the elementary and advanced forms of the Iowa Silent Reading Test. The records for Grades IV to VIII, inclusive, were secured in the autumn of 1944 from pupils in as many as 61 schools. Those for Grades IX to XII, inclusive, were secured a year later from pupils in as many as 95 schools. The tests were administered under the general direction of the Educational Records Bureau, which endeavors to secure test records from many schools under fairly comparable conditions. Unfortunately, the data presented are subject to certain limitations. For example, the pupils tested were from private as contrasted with public schools. Furthermore, pupils below the fourth grade and college and university students are not represented, due to the fact that comparable scores could not be secured. The influence of these limitations will be considered more fully later.

TABLE 4

Scores Made on the Iowa Silent Reading Test:

Elementary Form Given in the Fall, 1944, to Pupils in Grades IV to VIII;[1]
Advanced Form Given in the Fall, 1945, to Pupils in Grades IX to XII[2]

Raw Score	Grade Score	IV	V	VI	VII	VIII	IX	X	XI	XII	Grade Score	Raw Score
									1	2		216
									5	9		214
									11	25		212
							1	3	9	15		210
								8	32	61		208
							1	7	19	32		206
								10	12	16		204
							5	19	60	86		202
							8	32	77	106		200
							8	33	85	113		198
							23	50	101	100		196
							14	27	56	69)		194
							26	62	122	154)		192
							33	68	139	124)		190
196					1	1	36	89	145)	117)		188
194							67	118	165)	131)_		186
192						3	89	152	192)	161)		184
190						8	43	53)	75)	56)		182
188					8	21	128	189)	246)_	175)		180
186	16.3		2	4	13	30	83	99)	101)	97)		178
184	15.5			1	9	36	99)	122)	133)	103	13.0	176
182	14.1			8	18	58	120)	201)_	146)	105	12.4	174
180	13.1			7	26	50	136)	145)	139)	77 *	11.8	172
178	12.3		2	5	24	52	73)	110)	87)	52	11.3	170
176	11.6		1	9	25	72)	222)	256)	201 *	125	10.9	168
174	11.0		1	13	41	49)	68)_	77)*	66	41	10.4	166
172	10.5		2	7	43	63)	189)	147)	126	78	10.0	164
170	10.0	1	4	20	42)	83)_	114)	101	70	40	9.6	162
168	9.6		6	24	54)	70)	122)*	117	72	25	9.2	160
166	9.2		4	24	53)	67)	131)	91	47	25	8.8	158
164	8.8		9	26)	62)_	58)*	113)	92	54	34	8.5	156
162	8.5	3	10	31)	67)	71)	115	74	49	20	8.2	154
160	8.2	2	10	32)	49)	63	100	50	25	17	7.9	152
158	7.9	4	11	40)	58)	39	98	58	26	9	7.6	150
156	7.6	7	22	38)_	50)*	37	67	38	12	7	7.3	148
154	7.3	5	23	26)	35	29	45	29	10	2	7.0	146
152	7.1	8	23)	34)	32	18	57	22	12	6	6.8	144
150	6.8	6	22)	33)	30	19	43	13	5	4	6.5	142
148	6.5	4	21)	26)*	25	17	33	11	5	1	6.2	140
146	6.3	7	21)	23	16	10	10	3	2	1	6.0	138
144	6.1	14	19)_	19	27	10	8	5	1	2	5.8	136
142	5.8	14	32)	27	15	6	32	10	6	2	5.5	134
140	5.6	18)	35)*	21	12	10	9	1	1		5.3	132
138	5.4	19)	23)	7	11	5	8	1			5.1	130
136	5.2	23)	27)	7	7	2	8				4.9	128
134	5.0	10	21	6	9	1		2			4.7	126
132	4.8	13)*	8	5	2	1		1			4.5	124
130	4.6	16)	20	4	5	2	1				4.3	122
128	4.4	15)	16	7	3	3	1					120
126	4.2	20	16	6								
124	4.0	15	11	1								
122	3.8	14	6	1								
120	3.6	18	13	1								
118	3.4	19	4	3								
116	3.2	6	6		1							
114	3.0	10	4	1								
112	2.8	5	1									
110	2.6	3		1								
108	2.4			1								
106	2.2											
104	2.0											
102		1										
100		1										
Total		301	456	551	872	1064	2581	2804	2948	2426		

− Medians for the groups tested
* National norms

TABLE 4—Continued

Raw Score	Grade Score	Frequency of Scores by Grades									Grade Score	Raw Score
		IV	V	VI	VII	VIII	IX	X	XI	XII		
Q3		142.	153.	165.	172.	178.	176.	183.	190.	195.		
Md		133.	143.	157.	164.	170.	166.	173.	181.	185.		
Q1		124.	135.	146.	155.	162.	156.	164.	170.	175.		
Range		100	112	108	116	128	119	125	129	132		
		171	187	187	196	196	210	212	217	216		
Schools		26	36	43	55	61	95	86	87	81		

1. Adapted from Table 15, 1944, *Fall Testing Program in Independent Schools and Supplementary Studies*, p. 21. Educational Records Bureau, Bulletin No. 42, January, 1945.

2. Adapted from Table 12, 1945, *Fall Testing Program in Independent Schools and Supplementary Studies*, p. 20. Educational Records Bureau, Bulletin No. 44, January, 1946.

In interpreting the entries in the table, the following facts should be kept clearly in mind. Both the raw scores and the grade scores shown in the two left-hand columns apply to the entries for pupils in Grades IV to VIII on the elementary form of the Iowa Silent Reading Test. Those in the two right-hand columns apply to the entries for pupils in Grades IX to XII on the advanced form of that test. The two columns of grade scores have been so placed that grade scores of 9.2 on the two forms of the test come at the same horizontal level. Higher and lower grade scores come at about the same levels for the primary and advanced forms of the test, excepting near the extreme ends of the scale. The slight differences that occur, however, are not great enough to invalidate comparisons for our present purpose.

As we survey the table as a whole, three facts stand out impressively. The first is that the median reading scores for the pupils tested advance regularly from the fourth-grade level to the twelfth. This shows that the pupils who were in school a decade or more ago attained successively higher median scores from the fourth to the twelfth grades. Data from other sources show that this was true also of the pupils in the primary grades and of college students. The rate of increase at the college level was not quite as rapid as at the high-school level.

The second fact is that the range in reading ability at each grade level is tremendous. As shown by the entries in the table, fourth-grade pupils a decade ago varied over a range of more than six grades, and ninth-grade pupils over a range of fourteen grades. It follows that pupils who left school at the end of any given grade a decade ago varied widely in reading ability. The third fact is that the medians (represented by short horizontal bars) for the pupils tested above the fifth grade are about a grade higher than the national norms (represented by stars). It follows that the reading ability of all pupils who were in school in 1944 and 1945 would be more accurately represented if the distributions of scores were lowered by a grade or more for all grades above the fifth.

As shown by the results of tests given at various times since 1925, the general level and distribution of reading ability has not changed significantly. It follows that, with the exceptions referred to above, the entries in Table 4 present a reasonably accurate picture of the present generation of adults at the time they left school. We are concerned next with the probable changes which have occurred in their reading ability since leaving school.

Attention is directed, first, to those who completed less than five years of schooling. As shown in Table 1, they included 10.8 per cent of the adults in 1950. The scores made on various reading tests in the primary grades during the last quarter of a century show that pupils advance steadily, on the average, throughout these grades at about the same rate as is shown for the middle grades in Table 4. Furthermore, the distribution of scores increases rapidly from grade to grade, many pupils in the second and third grades far surpassing the norm for the fourth grade.

In harmony with the findings reported earlier, a large majority of the adults who discontinued school during the first four grades and who did not attain the fifth-grade norm now read no better, and in all probability less well, than when they left school. When to these are added those pupils in the higher grades who failed to attain the fifth-grade norm in reading and also those who never attended school, it is apparent that the number of functionally illiterate adults in this country approximates 15 per cent of the population over twenty-five years of age. The entries in the table supply striking evidence also that the last school grade attended is not a satisfactory measure of functional literacy for those of limited schooling. Actual measures of reading ability are needed in reaching conclusions concerning the literacy level of individuals.

The status of those who discontinued school in Grades V and VI is superior to those who left school in the primary grades. They included about 11 per cent of the adult population in 1950. Whereas those who left school in the fifth grade probably made no gain, or may even have lost in reading ability, those in the sixth grade doubtless made some improvement in general. As indicated earlier, the greatest gains are made, as a rule, by adults who left school at Grade VII, VIII, or IX. This group included about 30 per cent of the adult population in 1950. It is fair to assume, therefore, that the median reading ability of adults today may be considerably in advance of 9.2, which was the median last school grade attended for that date. Those who left school during the senior high school or college years have, in all probability, made some improvement in general but not as much as those who left school in Grade VII, VIII, or IX.

Although the foregoing analysis is not satisfactory in many respects, it provides the most detailed view of adult reading ability today that could be secured from available evidence. The two most impressive facts revealed are, first, the steady increase in the median reading ability of adults from one educational level to the next and, second, the great diversity in reading ability among those of similar amounts of schooling. It is apparent that at least half of our adult population is able to read at the ninth-grade level or above. This enables them to read with ease and understanding the more popular types of newspapers, magazines, and books.

As shown by numerous readability studies, much of the serious reading material published today ranks above the ninth grade in difficulty. Before adults of average reading ability can read widely and interpret such materials critically, they must acquire increased reading efficiency. This is true also if they are to have ready access to much of our literary heritage.

Evidence that thousands of adults who rank above the average in reading ability feel the need of continued guidance in reading is found in several facts. During the last few years they have participated in surprisingly large numbers in various types of reading activities, such as group study of the "Great Books," course work relating to popular themes offered by universities, or guided practice in reading provided by public and private agencies. Of special note is the insistent demand for training which aims to improve speed of reading. For example, thousands of business and professional men find that they read too slowly to meet the reading demands made upon them. Through the training provided, many have been able to increase their speed of reading from 50 to 200 per cent, or more, with no decrease in comprehension.

Somewhat less than half of our adult population still read below the ninth-grade level. Of this number, approximately a third are functionally illiterate, that is, unable to read at the fifth-grade level. Many of the remainder cannot read easily and with understanding much of the popular materials provided for adults today. Neither are they able to use reading effectively in the study of personal and social problems.

These adults form one of the neglected or forgotten groups in our population. Before they can take advantage of the wealth of pleasurable and enriching materials now available and assume more fully their responsibilities as informed citizens, they need to acquire greater competence in reading. This need defines one of the very challenging educational problems at the adult level faced by our nation today. The effort of volunteer organizations to meet this need is wholly inadequate. Steps should be taken at once to provide throughout the nation, at public expense, the training needed by millions of adults of limited reading ability.

The Characteristics of Superior Readers

Before concluding this discussion of how well adults read, it seems advisable to examine in some detail the characteristics of superior readers. The facts revealed should not only provide added understanding of the nature and extent of their reading attitudes and skills; they should also aid in establishing goals in efforts to improve reading among both children and adults.

As a part of an intensive study of maturity in reading,[16] Gray and Rogers carried on interviews with three groups of adults. The

16. William S. Gray and Bernice Rogers, *Maturity in Reading: Its Nature and Appraisal*. Chicago: University of Chicago Press, 1956.

first included individuals representing various occupations and educational levels who were selected wherever co-operation could be secured. The second included residents of a midwestern city selected in terms of amount of schooling in proportion to the total number of adults in the city who had completed an elementary, a high-school, or a college education. A third group included twenty-one reputedly well-read, superior readers in a metropolitan area.

The study as a whole sought information concerning five basic aspects of efficient reading, namely, "interest in reading," "purposes for reading," "the recognition and construing of meaning," "reaction to and use of the ideas read," and "kinds of material read." Each of these basic items was analyzed into a series of elements which were called "criteria of maturity." The outline that follows includes the criteria relating to competence in reading:

I. The recognition and construing of meaning
   a) Grasping the literal or sense meaning of a passage
   b) Recognizing meanings implied but not stated
   c) Recalling related meanings that enrich one's understanding of a passage
   d) Reaching valid conclusions or making generalizations not stated by the author

II. Evaluative reactions to the materials read
   a) Adopting an attitude of inquiry concerning such items as the accuracy, value, and quality of what is read
   b) Suspending decisions and using rational standards of judgment in making evaluative responses

III. Use and application of the ideas acquired
   a) Recognizing that what is read may have personal or social value
   b) Insightfulness, breadth, and penetration in using or applying the ideas acquired

Each adult who participated in the study was asked to read two short selections relating to topics of wide current interest. After reading each article, the interviewer and the adult discussed at length its meaning and implications. Questions were raised wherever necessary to determine how well the adults had read in terms of each of the criteria listed above. A record was made of their responses as the interview progressed. As an aid in determining the effectiveness of the reading, an "instrument of appraisal" was developed which consisted of a scale of values for each criterion of maturity. It extended from Level 1, which represented "an extremely low level" of performance, to Level 5, which represented "superior" performance. Each level was defined and illustrated in terms of the actual performance of readers, varying from the poorest to the most capable. The instrument was then applied to each participant in an effort to determine his efficiency as a reader.

Attention is directed first to the findings for the reputedly superior readers. They represented many areas of business, professions, and cultural interests. Whereas most of them were college or university graduates, a few of them had never gone to college. Of the twenty-one cases interviewed, eleven attained Level 5 in all aspects of the recognition and construing of meaning and of thoughtful reaction to and use of the ideas apprehended. Six did not rise above Level 3 in these aspects of reading, and the remainder were intermediate between these two groups. All were classified at Level 5, however, in one or more of the basic aspects of reading.

Stated in descriptive terms, the superior reader is characterized by a clear and "accurate grasp of meaning, the use of a rich and vivid background of related meanings, facility in deducing insightful and penetrating generalizations, constant and active curiosity about the accuracy, value, and prejudicial nature of the material read, and full and insightful use of the ideas acquired." Whereas all of these qualities contribute to a high level of competence in reading, only a small proportion of all the adults interviewed functioned normally at a superior level in each of the characteristics mentioned.

The foregoing statements assume added significance in the light of the following common characteristics of the distinctly superior readers as revealed by this study.

1. In every case, "reading was an inseparable part of day-to-day living."
2. Each displayed "a vital interest in people, places, and problems outside his or her daily sphere of life." There was invariably "some compelling area of interest, a radix or focal point which extended far beyond the individual's survival needs."
3. Each recognized clearly the value of reading as an aid to individual growth. The reading which was done, however limited in scope, was "so interpreted and applied as to contribute to many aspects of the personal and social development of the individual."

4. In interpreting what was read, each assumed an objective, impartial attitude toward the subject or issue under discussion and sought diligently to differentiate between that which was biased, false, and unsound and that which could be rationally defended.
5. Each expressed in word or action some interest in the search for the good life and a better society.
6. Each had had the advantage of some degree of cultural stimulation at home and stimulating contacts with good literature at some point in his formative years.
7. Rarely did an adult evidence a high degree of maturity in reading in general without being able to interpret with discrimination and penetration and to react thoughtfully to and apply the ideas acquired through reading. In their own areas of specialization these adults gave evidence of outstanding capacity in these respects.

As an integral part of this study, the responses of the adults who were selected in terms of amount of schooling were also studied through the use of "the instrument of appraisal." The aim was to find out how elementary-, high-school, and college graduates distributed themselves on such a scale. The striking fact revealed was the relatively low rankings assigned to them. With but few exceptions they varied from Level 1 to Level 3.

In harmony with expectation, the college graduates ranked highest. In general they read at about the mid-point in the total range from gross immaturity to superior ability to understand and interpret what they read. Their relatively low rank can be explained in part in terms of selective factors that operated in choosing them as subjects. Each of them held a responsible position of one type or another in a large department store. Apparently college graduates who find employment in such organizations either have not acquired compelling motives for contemplative reading before accepting their positions or are not stimulated to engage in such reading while thus employed. Evidence secured from other groups shows that many college graduates approximate the high levels in reading ability attained by superior readers.

Both the elementary- and the high-school graduates read at about Level 2 both in "recognizing and construing meaning" and in "reacting to and applying what is read." The latter group ranked slightly above the former. Furthermore, only slight differences between the two groups were indicated for "interest in reading," "purpose for reading" and "kinds of material read." Further studies are needed to determine the extent to which these findings are representative of high-school graduates in general. In partial explanation of the distinct lag in the reading interests and abilities of high-school graduates, two facts may be cited: the failure of many high schools in the past to provide carefully organized developmental and corrective reading programs; and the notable decrease in reading interest as revealed by studies among high-school students. Consequently those who leave school during high-school years do so at a time when interest in reading is at a low ebb.

These findings justify the conclusion that elementary schools, high schools, and colleges face a challenging responsibility in stimulating strong motives for reading and in promoting growth in reading in harmony with the increasing maturity of pupils. As revealed by the interviews held during the study, many of the superior readers did not acquire until adulthood the interests that led to wide reading. It follows that adult-education agencies face today both the opportunity and the responsibility of providing in every way possible the stimulus and guidance needed to insure broader reading interests and to promote continuous growth both in and through reading.

CHAPTER III

Why Adults Read

WILBUR SCHRAMM

Purpose of the Chapter

Why do adults read? Because it is one of the most powerful resources they have at hand. Reading is one of the first high skills they learn as children. It is an activity in which they have nearly lifelong practice and are consistently rewarded for success. Through reading they get much of their information about what is happening over the horizon; many of the opinions and facts that let them take part in the process of arriving at social consensus; a large part of the knowledge, mental skills, and role patterns that socialize and educate them to take their part in society. From reading they derive a large proportion of their entertainment and aesthetic pleasure. Although they use reading for the most specific instrumental purposes (such as learning how to repair the vacuum cleaner, or where to buy the cheapest groceries), they use it also, perhaps, unwittingly, for the most general and pervasive of purposes: throughout life their picture of reality builds up, so slowly they hardly realize it is building, largely from bits of fact and opinion cast up and saved out of the great ocean of print that constantly flows around them. And as the skill becomes familiar and practiced, the mere act of reading gives them pleasure and contributes to their sense of well-being and security.

It is our task in this paper to take this large picture apart. We shall consider this lifelong behavior of man as a series of decisions to read or not to read a given piece of writing at a given time in a given situation. We shall suggest some general models as to why these decisions take place, but we must also record great variations in the models and great individual differences among readers.

Let us at the very beginning admit the inadequacy of our knowledge and understanding of this process which seems so clear and potent in the large, but often so complex and baffling in detail. It is one of those frequent situations in human science which are exasperating to lay observers. For when we ask, why do adults read, the common-sense answer is, because they want to. And this is doubtless true, but it is no answer at all from our point of view because it does not consider what kinds of "wants" these are, what gives rise to them, and how many of them are conscious. Another common answer is that adults read because they *need* to, which is as true and about as satisfactory as the first answer. More technically, we might say that adults read because they are *motivated* to read. But we need to know also *what* motivates them and under what conditions, for the act of deciding whether or not to read obviously includes some assessment of the availability of communication, of competing possibilities, of personal abilities, and of social restrictions and encouragements. Perhaps the easiest answer is simply to say that we do not know in any detail why adults read; and that is altogether too true, because our knowledge in this area is fragmentary, often conjectural, and altogether less firm than our knowledge of *what* and *how* people read.

Probably the best place to begin, therefore, is with some discussion of *why* adults read, as related to *what* and *how* they read.

How—What—and Why

It is obvious that some measurements of *what* people read (through readership surveys) and of *how* people read (through tests of reading rate, eye cameras, and similar devices) are a great deal easier and more objective than the study of *why* they read, which must largely be inferred on the basis of *what* and *how*. It is also clear that these three are intimately related. Very little that we can say about why people read makes much sense except in terms of *what* and *how* they read. Therefore, the reader of this paper is advised to examine the evidence in chapters i and ii of this volume. Whereas it would be inappropriate to review that evidence here, still it is necessary to make some additional statements about *what* individuals read, and *how* they read, before talking about *why*.

In the first place, it is evident that there are great individual differences among readers in their skills, tastes, and perceptions and in the availability to them of reading opportunities. Consider the case of Professor A. of Columbia University who reads the *New York Times* at his breakfast table, spends most of his day in a book-lined office a few hundred feet from a great library, and comes home in the evening to a home where current magazines and new books are beside his easy chair. Contrast this with the case of Mr. B., a sheepherder in Montana, who rides the range by day and sleeps under a tarpaulin on the ground at night. Obviously, the first of these men will read as easily and naturally as he breathes; reading is a part of his everyday life, a familiar, valued, and well-mastered behavior. To the second of these men, on the other hand, reading may be something unfamiliar, extraordinary behavior, valued but seldom attainable, or foreign and suspect. To be sure, we have chosen nearly polar opposites, but to some extent the availability of reading material must necessarily affect all reading behavior.

Between these two individuals, there will be considerable skill differences. Professor A. will probably read along at 400 to 500 words a minute. He will be able to bring to his reading both a sharp critical ability and a rich sounding board for allusions. Foreign-language quotations will not deter him, and he will be at home in the mathematical symbols or other scholarly codes in which his colleagues communicate. Mr. B., on the other hand, will probably read at a rate of 100 to 200 words a minute. His usable vocabulary may be one-third to one-half as large as that of Professor A. He will not be a critical reader except of subject matter which deals with horses or sheep or range land or other items close to his experience. He will probably be frightened away from technical or highly literary language. His sounding board will be considerably more restricted than that of Professor A., and if a writer expects to stir reverberations in Mr. B. he must aim his allusions at a much smaller world of experience. Here again, of course, we are dealing with individuals whose experience is poles apart, and yet similar though usually smaller differences are demonstrated to some degree in every community reading survey, every broad test of vocabulary and reading rate, and every questionnaire or interview on reading interests.

It would not be surprising if such surveys and tests as we have just been talking about would reveal noteworthy differences in reading tastes between Professor A. and Mr. B. Professor A. is fond of the *New Yorker;* Mr. B. would find it too exotic a diet. Mr. B. is probably interested in the trade journals of sheepherding; Professor A., in the scholarly journals of his field. Professor A. values criticism, satire, suggestive, allusive, indirect writing; Mr. B. likes writing done with a broader brush, more straightforward, down to earth. Professor A. likes to read himself to sleep with science fiction or an Agatha Christie mystery; Mr. B., too, likes to relax and read adventure or love stories, but this reading—occupying, as it does, a much larger part of his total reading time—means rather more to him than it does to his New York opposite. To Mr. B., it is an important way of getting vicarious experience and contact, supplementing his limited experience with this window into an outside world. These taste differences are not at all extraordinary, in view of the evidence we have at hand. It is a revealing experience to review the early pages of Waples and Tyler [1] in which those authors record their examination of previous work on reading patterns and tastes and their despair at ever finding trends and generalizations among the welter of individual patterns.

Even these differences are hardly as impressive as the differences that must exist in the way Professor A. and Mr. B. perceive what they read. We can perceive only in terms of what we know. We search for meaning in everything we meet. We select and structure and fill out new experience until it "fits" with old experience. Obviously, there are vast areas of Mr. B.'s experience which are not duplicated in Professor A.'s, and vice versa. Even in areas where each of them has had experience, there may be only superficial likenesses. For example, "night" to Professor A. will probably mean the city night, shiny with neon and street lights, a time for concerts and lectures and parties and leisurely reading and television, house slippers or dress clothes. To Mr. B. it will mean the clear hushed night of the high plains, with the stars sharp and the Milky Way

1. Douglas Waples and Ralph W. Tyler, *What People Want To Read About.* Chicago: American Library Association and the University of Chicago Press, 1931.

stretching across the midnight blue of the heavens, the sheep grazing quietly, and the feel of the hard ground under the tarpaulin. To understand the full magnitude of these perceptual differences, we don't have to ask, as do Krech and Crutchfield [2] in their insightful treatment of perception, how a savage who had never before seen an airplane would perceive an airplane which landed beside his village. We can test ourselves by remembering how we perceived our parents when we were very young and again when we were older and married and parents ourselves; or how we perceived a foreign country when we first read about it and again after we had lived in it six months; or how we perceived a classic on first meeting it in school, and again upon rereading it twenty years later.

It is, therefore, important to recognize that perceptual differences may result in readers getting quite different experiences from the same material. It is dangerous to project from the material read to the motivations and gratifications of a reader. What may be pure escape for an adult, may be, for a teen-ager, an opportunity to learn some of the role patterns expected of him. For a well-adjusted child a crime story may be a harmless release of aggressions; for a mal-adjusted child, the same crime story may be an opportunity to learn the trick of burglarizing a store or outwitting the police. What may be for one reader a delightful excursion into humor, may be for another a deeply shocking experience because some of his firmly held values are challenged. Take a homely and common example: Consider how a minister, a physician, an insurance agent, an auto-mobile mechanic, the wife of one of the accident victims, an automobile salesman, and a beginning driver would perceive a newspaper picture of a serious auto accident. In effect, two individuals reading the same page may actually be reading different materials, so different are their perceptions of the material.

Consider what these differences mean in practice. Mr. B. may classify as "long-hair," and avoid, a piece of reading material which Professor A. may pick up with eagerness and excitement. A story which comfortably fits Mr. B.'s reading skill and metaphorical experience may be discarded impatiently by Professor A. A piece of

2. David Krech and Richard S. Crutchfield, *Theory and Problems of Social Psychology*. New York: McGraw-Hill Book Co., Inc., 1948.

writing about nature which is profoundly moving and illuminating to Mr. B. may mean little or nothing to Professor A. because he has an inadequate perception of it. To be sure these are not the only reasons why Mr. B. reads what he does and why Professor A. reads something else, but these qualities are important in the total situation which surrounds the instant of decision as to whether a given selection will or will not be read.

Let us say something about this so-called "instant of decision." Reading presents itself to our attention in the form of materials organized around index cues. These cues represent our way of scanning environment. We are constantly being presented with stimuli, countless stimuli, far more than we could possibly attend to. As we scan our surrounding environment we tend to organize these offered stimuli into cues, some of which have the quality of representing and predicting others. These are the index cues. When we hear an auto horn behind us, when we see a light appearing to come from a blind curve in the road, when we feel an irregularity in the pulse of our automobile engine, we are receiving cues which demand and usually receive our attention because of what they represent. The people who prepare the messages of mass communication try to organize their materials so that such cues will have a high probability of coming to our attention. They put tables of contents in books, headlines in newspapers and magazines, cue words in newscasts. Making these index cues is one of the heaviest responsibilities of the editor or the broadcaster. For one thing, he must accurately represent the meaning of the material; if he does not, the interpretation of the whole item may be affected. A series of experiments at the University of Illinois [3] has shown that different headlines on the same story can make a reader believe that a certain person on trial for a crime is or is not guilty. Different captions on a news picture can result in wholly different interpretations of the tone of the picture—from happy to sad, victorious to defeated, evil to good. But accuracy of content is not the only responsibility of the mass communicator in making his cues. He must also estimate the probable importance of the item to his audience and give the cue a size or intensity which is neither too great nor too little. If he

3. Under the direction of Percy H. Tannenbaum and Jean Kerrick,

often guesses wrong, he loses the confidence of his audience. It has been shown that the cue "Flash!" or "Bulletin!" in a newscast will soon lose its attention-getting power if the item heralded is one that does not justify such an extraordinary cue. An announcer who consistently screams his commercials, or a paper that consistently spreads large headlines and red ink over its front page, soon will get no more attention (probably less attention) for their lead items than a calm announcer or a more restrained paper for theirs. In addition, the screamers will lose the advantage of being able to emphasize an extraordinary message when they have one.

The instant of decision is, therefore, the time when our previously learned expectations and our current motivations are related to these index cues and we accept or reject. There is some feedback process operative here which we do not as yet entirely understand. We need not go into that here. But it is clear that our learned and stored experience with cues, our estimates of difficulty and probable reward, the motivations and values which lead us at any given moment to be more concerned with some topics than others—it is clear that these enter into the total situation in which we select or reject a cue and give or withhold our attention.

At least four important variables, then, are active at the instant of decision. These are:

Content to be read →	Index cues → Decision	Personality ← characteristics	Active ← environment
which may be perceptually different for different readers, although objectively identical to printers and proofreaders.	which may or may not accurately represent the content and which differ widely in availability over time and among individuals.	of the reader at a given time —chiefly the relevant skills, motivations, and values, and, of course, intelligence.	including competition for an individual's attention, factors which make for a comfortable or uncomfortable reading situation, and values and mores attached to reading by his society and valued groups.

If all these variables could be described for a given individual at a given moment, we could doubtless predict his reading behavior at a very high level of confidence. But it is unrealistic to think of describing in detail the "total situation" or the "total field." Our problem is to find some practical model by which to structure the field so that we can think about it and analyze information from it.

A General Model of Reading Choice

An approximation to such a model is what I have elsewhere [4] called the "fraction of selection"—that is,

$$\frac{\text{Expectation of reward}}{\text{Effort required}}$$

Obviously if we increase the upper term (make the reading seem more worth while) or decrease the lower term (make it easier to do) then the fraction grows larger: the likelihood of selection becomes greater. When Dickens was at the height of his reputation and was publishing his novels in serial form, the expectation of reward was great enough to cause Americans to rush down to the docks in New York and meet the ships from England in hope of finding out as soon as possible what happened in the new Dickens installment. Likewise, because so little effort is required, many of us sit at home and look at old movies on TV rather than going to the theater to see new ones. But the longer the trip to the docks, the less likely it was to be made—other things being equal. For example, fewer people must have come from Albany than from upper Manhattan. And in the case of TV *vs.* movies, the more attractive the new movie, the more likely we are to break away from TV—*ceteris paribus*—and make the trip to the theater.

This formulation has a deceptive simplicity. It is necessary to interpret these terms carefully. *Expectation of reward* is merely a broader way of saying *motivation*. *Effort required* is a broader way of talking about *availability*. Let us examine *availability* first.

---

4. *The Nature and Process of Mass Communication.* Edited by Wilbur Schramm. Urbana, Illinois: University of Illinois Press, 1954.

Wilbur Schramm, "Procedures and Effects of Mass Communication," *Mass Media and Education,* chap. vi. Fifty-third Yearbook of the National Society for the Study of Education, Part II. Chicago: Distributed by the University of Chicago Press, 1954.

AVAILABILITY

To make any sense of this problem, we must conceive availability in terms much broader than books on the shelf or magazines in the stand.[5] We must think of it at least in terms of the *skill* a given act of reading is likely to require, the *time* it is likely to require, the *space* which is interposed between reader and reading, and the *economic* difficulties involved.

Let us mention some of the *skill* considerations. How does the individual's reading skill measure up against the apparent magnitude of the reading task he sees before him? (Many a reader has been frightened away by the sheer bulk of a book.) How does his vocabulary measure against the vocabulary level of the material to be read? (It is probably true that only 10 per cent of Americans can easily read college-level books.) How does his ability to conceptualize and abstract measure up against the amount and level of abstraction in the reading material? (This quality more than any other seems to distinguish between the better and the less well-educated readers.) What is the relation of his auditory to his visual skills? (This relationship would help to determine whether he turns to print or to broadcasting.)

Think of some of the *time* considerations: How much leisure time has the individual, and what patterns has he worked out for its use? (E.g., on a leisurely ocean cruise, anyone finds it easy to turn to reading; but on land an inveterate golfer, given three hours of daylight leisure, is more likely to spend them on the links than with a magazine.) What competition from other mass communications does reading have? (On vacation in a mountain cabin, with no radio and with the nearest movies fifty miles away, one gives reading a virtual monopoly on mass-communication time; but in the city with four television and ten radio channels, and half a dozen movies within a few blocks, the media competition is intense.) What is the relation of reading to work and to working time? (For example, a teacher might have considerable time and reason to read during the work day.) What is the competitive appeal, in relation

---

5. George K. Zipf, in *Human Behavior and the Principle of Least Effort* (Cambridge, Massachusetts: Addison-Wesley, 1949), sets an example for treating the concept of "effort" with a great deal of generality.

to available time, of short cuts (e.g., news summaries for newspapers, digests for magazines)?

The principal *space* consideration is, what has the individual at hand compared to what he has to go after? Home reading is easier than going to the library. Listening to a news broadcast is easier than going out after a newspaper. Reading a magazine one takes is easier than getting a magazine at the newsstand or library. The scarcity of bookstores in this country has undoubtedly restricted the circulation of hard-bound books, and the ubiquity of racks for paper-bound books is undoubtedly a factor in the large sales of those titles.

Economic considerations may be illustrated in a number of ways. One of them is the price of paper-bound *vs.* hard-bound books. Digests are cheaper than a group of magazines. Very large expenditures (e.g., a television set) tend to crowd out some of the other forms of mass communication in the family budget. On the other hand, there is some positive appeal in high-priced communication items. Belonging to the subscribers of a high-priced magazine carries prestige value; and when one pays $1.25 for a copy of a magazine, he is likely to read it. So, likewise, when he pays several hundred dollars for a television set, he is likely not only to use it but to expect high-quality entertainment out of it.

All these kinds of availability will vary not only by individuals but also by age, sex, education, economic status, social roles (e.g., occupation, class, family and community position), location (e.g., urban or rural, south, east, or west), and surrounding events (e.g., war, crisis, vocational needs). For example, a teen-ager is going to find it relatively less effort than will his father to go to the library for a book. A college graduate will find it easier than will a grade-school graduate to read the *Yale Review*. A wealthy family is likely to have more at hand to read, and to read more, than a poor family. A rural family ordinarily has less competition than city families from movies, finds it harder to get daily newspapers, and usually has less leisure time. And we might continue in this fashion to construct a three-sided matrix out of the classes of reading content, the four kinds of effort mentioned above, and the categories of age, sex, education, etc., until we could make some general predictions, for example, about what degree and kinds of effort—other things being equal—reading a given kind of material would require of a 25-year-old unmarried female, junior-college educated, living in the rural South, teaching school, and receiving a low, moderate income, in wartime.

But compiling such a matrix is not a task for this paper. Let us here say merely that an individual is likely to read: (*a*) what he can read without unduly taxing his skills (but also what is not so far below his skill as to bore him); (*b*) what he can easily fit into his available time; (c) what he can easily bring to hand; and (*d*) what he feels he can afford without undue strain.

Strong motivation, of course, may so change the situation that an individual will choose the less easily available material even at the cost of a much greater effort. Therefore we must look at the problem of motivation.

MOTIVATION

A motive is a directed drive. Motivation is the kind of inner patterning that directs us toward certain behavior because we expect it to reduce inner tension or uneasiness. It is, therefore, the kind of patterning that directs us toward most of our behavior. There is little undirected behavior in the human adult. You can see an example of undirected behavior in the flopping of a chicken after its head is cut off. A baby in its first hours of life appears to indulge in a large proportion of undirected behavior. Panic brings a moment of indirection. But chiefly the behavior of adults is motivated and purposeful. The drive signals the need; motivation takes aim on a particular goal.

Now, what are the motivations that lead to reading?

It might be well to look at some of the evidence on that point before making generalizations. Our evidence on reading motivation comes from at least five kinds of data. The largest body of fact deals with reading habits and patterns, from which motives can be "inferred." There is a small but interesting collection of evidence on what people "miss" when the opportunity to read is taken from them. Another small but interesting bit of evidence is the attempt to derive factors or clusters of preferences within reading patterns. Still another scanty but promising source is in the attempts to relate personality measurements to reading choices. Finally, we have a considerable number of cases and depth interviews which have attempted to get people to introspect on the reasons why they read and why they prefer one kind of reading to another. Let us look briefly at each of these bodies of evidence.

Reading Habits and Patterns. The most extensive work on reader interests has been done at the University of Chicago, the published materials representing a combination of sociology, education, and library-school interests. In other chapters of this yearbook, as well as in this one, frequent mention will be made of some of the Chicago reports: Gray and Munroe, *The Reading Interests and Habits of Adults;* Waples and Tyler, *What People Want To Read About;* and Waples, Berelson, and Bradshaw, *What Reading Does to People.* From other institutions and agencies have come upwards of two hundred studies of newspaper readership, as, for example: The Advertising Research Foundation's *Continuing Study of Newspaper Reading* (including several surveys a year and frequent summaries); Chilton R. Bush's *Five-Year Summary of 25 Western Hometown Daily Newspaper Readership Studies* (Stanford University Press, 1950); and a few studies like that of Schramm and White in which newspaper-reading was analyzed in terms of age, sex, education, and economic status. Magazine reading has also been studied extensively for the mass audience. And there have been studies on the relation of book-reading to newspaper and magazine reading, and to the use of other mass communications, which are summarized in Berelson's report for the Library Inquiry, *The Library's Public* (Columbia University Press, 1949), and in Lazarsfeld and Kendall, *Radio Listening in America* (Prentice-Hall, 1948).

Because this material is considered elsewhere in this volume, it will not be treated in detail here. In general, the usable result of all this study is to establish certain personal factors which correlate with patterns of content choice. Thus, Waples and Tyler, studying 107 groups, found that certain factors seemed much more likely than others to correlate with differences in reading interest. They say:

In order of relative importance the factors are sex, amount of schooling, type of occupation, environment, age, and time spent per week in reading. The more of these factors which are common to any two or more groups, the more closely the reading interest of the groups will agree. Any groups alike in respect to sex, schooling, and occupation are found to have very similar interests in the field of non-fiction.[6]

The greatest differences they found in reading interest correlated with sex differences. They say:

It is evident that sex has a predominant effect upon reading interest. Between no two groups we have studied that differ in sex has there been found a correlation in reading interest higher than .62. When sex and other factors vary, the coefficients are all much lower. When sex is the same and the other factors are all constant, the coefficients are all much higher."[7]

These differences are expressed notably in a greater feminine interest in personality and low feminine interest in politics and business matters. "Taken as a whole, the topics in which groups of women express more than average interest suggest a universal feminine desire to escape boredom by a fuller understanding of themselves and their associates, by good health, by reading about foreign countries, and, of course, by successful marriage."[8] The nearest they could come to a common denominator of reading interest, and to a suggestion of basic motivation, is that *"people like to read about themselves.* The more closely a subject relates to what is familiar to the given reader, the more interesting it is. The common denominator of reading interest, in the field of non-fiction at least, is *self*."[9]

Taking Schramm and White as an example of the research on newspaper reading, the conclusion is that "amount of news reading increases very rapidly with age, with education, and with economic status," and that this is true for both men and women, although education seems to make a greater difference in women's reading, economic status a greater difference in men's.[10] Teen-agers, persons

6. Waples and Tyler, *op. cit.*, 189.

7. *Ibid.*, p. 128.

8. *Ibid.*, p. 75.

9. *Ibid.*, p. xxiii.

10. Wilbur Schramm and David M. White, "Age, Education, Economic Status: Factors in Newspaper Reading," *Journalism Quarterly*, XXVI (1949), 259.

who have had only grade-school education, and persons in the lower economic groups are "more likely to read crime and disaster news than any other broad class of news." Reading of crime news decreases with more education. Reading of public affairs news and editorials increases with education, age, and economic status. Higher economic status makes for a considerable increase in women's reading of society news. Reading of sports news is at its height in the 20's, thereafter tapers off. Reading of comics is at its height in the teens and decreases after the age of 15. It decreases also with more education. The general pattern that comes out of this kind of study, then, is for a gradually increasing use of the newspaper, with more education and age, as a medium of serious information rather than entertainment.

These same patterns appear to go through other studies of reading habits and interests. In magazines, books, or newspapers, there seems to be a difference between men's and women's reading, and the difference appears to relate to the different roles the two sexes play in society. There is likewise a difference in reading according to education: The higher the education, the less likely entertainment material is to be chosen in preference to nonentertainment. Magazine and newspaper reading increases with age; book-reading does not—which apparently reflects the greater relative effort required to use libraries after the school years. Reading material which comes close to an individual's experience seems to have a special interest for him. Examples are articles about an individual's occupation, or his illness, or his city. Waples and Tyler say, "Whenever a topic which is not familiar to the point of boredom, touches upon vocational interest, it invariably tops the list." [11]

What Readers Miss. Berelson's study on "What 'Missing the Newspaper' Means" [12] is an especially intriguing approach to the study of motivations for reading. During a two-week period when deliverymen for New York newspapermen were on strike, Berelson or his representatives conducted 60 interviews stratified by rental

11. Waples and Tyler, *op. cit.,* p. 85.

12. Bernard Berelson, "What 'Missing the Newspaper' Means" in *Communications Research, 1948-49.* Edited by Paul Lazarsfeld and Frank Stanton. New York: Harper & Bros., 1949.

areas in Manhattan. He attempted to find out, not *whether* people missed their newspaper, but *what it was* they missed. Indeed, as the interviews probed deeper, they turned up evidence of an important difference between the general protestations of interest in the newspaper's "serious" purpose and the specific motivations and practices of the readers. That is, it was the accepted and automatic thing to say that the newspaper "keeps me informed about the world," but only about one-third of the individuals who said that had any idea what they wanted more information about. On the basis of further probing, Berelson constructed a typology of uses of the newspaper, of which "information about and interpretation of public affairs" was only one category and not necessarily the dominant one. Others were "as a tool of daily living" (e.g., radio programs, stock quotations, obituaries), "respite" (e.g., comics, human interest, which "take your mind off other things"), "social prestige" (meaning not that the newspaper is good in itself, but that it is good *for* something—in this case, for making one appear informed before his colleagues), and "social contact" (vicarious participation in private lives of famous people; some of the respondents indicated that they missed the paper because, so to speak, "some of their friends" resided in its pages). In addition to these conscious motivations, Berelson came to the conclusion that at least two other elements were powerful motivations toward reading and missing the newspaper. For one thing, he concluded, the act of reading itself appears to be highly valued in our society, and therefore provides certain basic satisfaction without primary regard for the content of the reading matter. This is really not surprising when we consider how we reward children for success in reading, and how we connect reading in later life with approved symbols like "education," "the well-read man," "the informed man," etc. Finally, Berelson found a good deal of evidence for the "ritualistic and near-compulsive" character of newspaper reading. This apparently grows out of the fact that we usually read our newspaper at a particular period of the day and often as a secondary activity (e.g., at breakfast or while riding to work). Therefore, depriving us of this habitual time-filler is especially noticeable.

Factors in Reading Habits. At least one attempt has been made to study reading interests by means of factor analysis. Nafziger,

MacLean, and Engstrom [13] applied this method to two readership surveys of Minnesota papers. Although they used only ten categories of content, they found three general factors or clusters to account for most of the variation in readership. These were: (*a*) easy-to-read entertainment material (pictures, comics for the smaller paper; pictures, comics, and sports for the city paper); (*b*) general and public affairs news; and (*c*) news about people and society, arts and hobbies. In the big-city paper, factors (*b*) and (*c*) were so highly intercorrelated that they were in reality a single factor. This means that the average reader's pattern for newspaper reading (excluding advertising) can be described in terms of how much he is interested in two or three kinds of material (entertainment, public affairs news, human-interest news). If we know his relative interest in these three categories we can pretty well predict what he will read in any given newspaper. We can also assume that each of these categories tends to represent a clustering or an averaging of motivations beneath the surface of reading behavior. We can guess at the nature of these motivations (for example, the entertainment cluster must represent a group of motivations toward respite and vicarious excitement, the public affairs cluster must represent a group of motivations toward serious scanning of the horizon, using the newspaper as a tool of daily living, and perhaps the social prestige of being well informed). But let us remember that we can *only* guess. Furthermore, as we have pointed out, two people may read the same material with quite different motivations.

Work was recently completed on a much larger factor analysis of reader interest in news. This work has been done by Schramm at Illinois and Stanford universities, using electronic digital computers so as to be able to handle a matrix approximately 100 x 100. Preliminary results show six types of readers: the general public-affairs reader; the reader who carefully avoids all threatening or anxiety-producing news; the feature reader; the reader of ego-involving news; the "local" reader; and the sensation (crime, accident, disaster, etc.) reader.

13. Ralph O. Nafziger, Malcolm MacLean, Jr., and Warren Engstrom, "Useful Tools for Interpreting Readership Data," *Journalism Quarterly*, XXVIII (1951), 441.

Relation of Reading Choices to Personality Measurements. From a number of scattered sources and experiments, we know something of the relation of attitudes and other personality measurements to reading habits. We know, for example:

1. Individuals tend to read material in which their existing attitudes and opinions are reinforced. This has been demonstrated notably in the way people use the mass media during election campaigns.[14] This suggests that the need of a sense of security may be a strong motivation for reading.
2. Given a choice of newspaper, individuals who rate high on the F-scale of authoritarianism tend to prefer the paper which more often sponsors authoritarian policies.
3. It has been demonstrated experimentally that an individual's personal values are related, in at least some degree, to his reading choices. Individuals whose personal values were measured by the Allport-Vernon scale significantly skewed their choices of newspaper reading toward items which mirrored at least two of the six values on the scale.
4. Raising the level of a reader's anxiety will apparently make some change in his reading patterns.

Case Histories and Depth Interviews. A large number of such detailed studies have been made.[15] This would seem to be the most satisfactory—indeed almost the only satisfactory—way of exploring an individual's motives for reading, were it not for the difficulty of introspecting in a field like this, the complex nature of motivations, and the fact that only the most superficial layers of motivation are readily revealed to the interviewer. To get below this surface level requires considerable skill and analytical power on the part of the interviewer. What usually comes out of such interviews, therefore, is the easily verbalizable motivation and often the motivation which an individual thinks he *ought* to have. For example, Berelson was invariably told by his interviewees that they missed the newspaper for its coverage of public affairs, and it took a lot of probing to get below that answer to the more basic reasons. Here is a summary report of the purposes of silent reading which came out of confer-

14. See, for example, Bernard Berelson, Paul F. Lazarsfeld, and William McPhee, *Voting*. Chicago: University of Chicago Press, 1954.

15. For a partial list, see Waples and Tyler, *op. cit.*

ences conducted by Parsons and Gray with more than nine hundred
adults:

To keep informed concerning current events; to secure specific information of value in making plans; to learn more about events or problems of special interest; to secure the opinion of others concerning civic,
social, and industrial problems; to keep in touch with business or professional developments; to secure suggestions concerning efficient methods of doing work; to determine the important items in correspondence,
messages, instructions; to follow directions; to advance in one's field of
work; to broaden one's range of information; to keep the mind stimulated with important things to think about; to develop a broad outlook
on life; to secure pleasure and recreation during leisure hours; to
satisfy curiosity.[16]

On about the same level is the list of motives for recreational
reading arrived at by Montgomery after interviewing 410 persons.
Following is a partial list of uses which he found were made of
recreatory reading.[17]

MOTIVE	FREQUENCY OF MENTION
For diversion	203
Because one likes author	174
For recommendation of book	156
For interesting title	151
For physical rest	145
To relieve common, everyday experiences	139
To visualize	132
To get away from real life	131
For pleasure	115
For description	100

Somewhat more revealing is the kind of information reported by
Gray and Munroe on the influences which enter into the forming of
reading habits. This is a summary:

The studies which have been reported suggest a variety of experiences that influence reading habits. In many cases the reading habit was
stimulated early by parents, friends, or relatives who had literary tastes
and who enjoyed reading. Not infrequently, the influence of the parent
was greatly increased, if there was a strong emotional bond between
parent and child. The mere presence of books in the home or an

16. William S. Gray and Ruth Munroe, *The Reading Interests and Habits
of Adults*, p. 53. New York: Macmillan Co., 1929.

17. As reported by Gray and Munroe, *ibid.*, p. 62.

attractive library in the community has often proved a sufficiently strong influence to initiate independent reading habits. The influence of teachers has been reported many times; also the fact that school work was often closely related to library reading. The skill of teachers and librarians in placing interesting books in a child's hands at the right time has been commented on by some adults. Encouragement given by a father to his son to engage in mechanical activities led one boy to become keenly interested in reading along scientific lines. The fact that her father discussed poetry with a girl one evening each week after she was thirteen and her mother read and discussed poetry with her regularly were referred to as valuable influences. Such examples suggest various steps which may be taken by parents, teachers and librarians to stimulate the development of desirable reading interests.

In many of the cases studied, the experiences of the reader and the influences reported were of an entirely different order from those mentioned above. For example, one child was physically handicapped. As a result he withdrew more or less from the social group and found satisfaction in reading. In a second case a long period of idleness because of illness with every encouragement to read stimulated interest which became more or less permanent. A boy who was unable to compete successfully with a younger brother in games found reading a pleasurable retreat from an embarrassing situation. A slight social maladjustment in one case and a long illness emphasized the tendency to find stimulation and satisfaction in reading. A child who was reared in a strict home and denied most of the social pleasures of her friends found refuge in daydreaming and books. The narrow atmosphere of the same home oppressed the young lady after graduation from college and she again sought relief in wide reading.

A third group of influences relate more particularly to those which modified the habits of readers after reaching maturity. In one case superior intelligence and conscious effort toward self-improvement led to wide reading. In a second case, the habit of doing everything thoroughly and well led to the organization of a well-planned reading program. Several adults reported they were associated with friends and professional workers of literary tastes which made wide reading necessary and also stimulated interest in independent reading. One adult was profoundly impressed with his own greatness and power and read widely as a means of realizing ambitions. Another adult engaged in wide reading of mystery stories which provided mild vicarious excitement in an otherwise serene existence. Several adults were engaged in occupations, such as library work, which made wide reading necessary. In some cases the reading habit was stimulated by the fact that the keen pleasure was derived by reading "perfect writing about beautiful happenings."[18]

18. *Ibid.*, pp. 269-71.

Even more interesting is the kind of psychological analysis which is represented by Wolfe and Fiske.[19] On the basis of a number of interviews, these authors decided that for a normal child the reading of comics is simply a means of ego-strengthening. "In the early or funny-animal stage, he expands his ego-experience through projection. Later, in the adventure stage, he inflates his ego by identification with an invincible hero. Finally, he stands on his own feet, and employs 'true' comics as a tool for the real adventure which is life itself. He may turn back to his earlier comic favorites, but he now reads them only as a means of relaxation." For the maladjusted child, however, "the comics satisfy, just as efficiently, an equally intense emotional need, but here the need is not so readily outgrown." The child, searching for a more perfect father-figure, finds such a figure in "Superman" and the other authority and power figures of the comics. The child becomes a comic fan. He goes to the comics, in one sense, as to a religion; in another, as to a drug. The religion (or the habit) of comics is not easily given up.

From Wolfe and Fiske analyzing the reasons why children read comics, to Gray and Munroe analyzing the influences that enter into reading habits, to Berelson inquiring why people miss newspapers, to the surveyors finding out what people actually read is a long road through highly varied country. The evidence from these studies is not easy to put together. There is no single place where all of it has been put together. However, if the reader of this paper is looking for a wise and balanced treatment of many of these types of evidence, he would do well to look at Waples, Berelson, and Bradshaw,[20] and particularly to the chapter entitled "The Readers' Predispositions." This book was published in 1940 and lacks some of the new studies but still stands up very well.

Systematizing the Evidence on Motivation. Most writers in this field, looking at the evidence at hand, have set down a list of anywhere from six to fifty apparent "motives" or "reasons" for reading. Waples, Berelson, and Bradshaw go farther in proposing a two-fold

19. Katherine Wolfe and Marjorie Fiske, "Why Children Read Comics," in *Communications Research, 1948-49.* Edited by Paul F. Lazarsfeld and Frank Stanton. New York: Harper & Bros., 1949.

20. Douglas Waples, Bernard Berelson, and Franklyn R. Bradshaw, *What Reading Does to People.* Chicago: University of Chicago Press, 1940.

classification of reading motives that would include all the lesser ones. They say: "Motives may be classified as intrapersonal and interpersonal. Intrapersonal motives impel the reader to publications likely to stimulate his feelings about himself. Interpersonal motives impel the reader toward publications involving his relationship with others." But they couple this classification with a warning: "Of course, the satisfaction of either one type of motive often tends to satisfy the other. For example, desires for prestige which explain reading the Bible for intrapersonal satisfactions may also improve the reader's status with others, because of their respect for people who read the Bible." [21]

This model has an intuitive validity because it approximates a total field—the individual plus his social environment. But, on the other hand and perhaps for that very reason, the model is not very easy to use in explaining or understanding behavior. As the authors say, motives tend to be mixed. It is hard to distinguish between motivations which clearly "stimulate feelings about one's self" and those which "involve relationships with others." In fact, it could be argued that very few of an adult's "feelings about himself" fail to involve "relationships with others." Thus, even reading for respite or escape constitutes an escape from surrounding reality and a judgment on one's relations with others. Reading for self-improvement is usually aimed toward an ultimate social goal. Reading up on current politics may serve both to enhance one's status in a group and also to raise one's feeling of prestige. Reading the current best-seller is seldom either exclusively for self-stimulation or for social prestige. Therefore, the usefulness of this model will be somewhat tempered by the fact that it appears not to make clear distinctions in practice.

The Waples-Berelson-Bradshaw classification might be thought of as a sociological model. Several years ago, the present writer suggested another model which was grounded in psychological learning theory,[22] and which might be described thus:

21. *Ibid.*, p. 92.

22. For the kind of learning theory underlying this model, see O. H. Mowrer, *Learning Theory and Personality Dynamics*. New York: Ronald Press, 1950.

1. The socialization of a young human involves a combination of problem-solving and associative [or conditioning] learning.

   For example, the child learns, by trial and error, how to reduce certain drives and tensions [such as hunger and loneliness], and he also learns to respond in equivalent ways to associated stimuli [such as the mother and the word "mother"].

2. But as the process of socialization goes on, the child learns [by a kind of emotional conditioning] some of the drives and tensions he *ought* to have in order to play the social roles that will be expected of him.

   For example, he learns that he ought to feel sorry when he tips over his glass of milk; that he ought to like to pet the dog; a little later, that he ought to like to read comic books.

3. Then he learns further problem-solving so as to reduce these *learned* drives and tensions.

   That is, he learns to apologize for tipping over his glass of milk, to pet the dog when the creature comes close to him, to read comic books.

4. As socializing goes on, the individual learns certain problem-solving behavior which actually and deliberately induces further tensions and drives, on the supposed theory that a certain amount of continuing tension is necessary for the survival of the human animal.

   For example, he learns to go to the dentist, have regular medical check-ups, take exercises, read alarming news.

5. The question is then raised whether the difference between the kind of problem-solving behavior in (4) and that in (3) and (1) does not offer a useful distinction between kinds of reading?

   For example, the reading of comics is ordinarily a different order of behavior from the reading of editorials. A mother reads the news about a polio epidemic, regardless of how the news disturbs her, so that she can be ready to defend her children against the disease. This kind of reading is clearly a different order of behavior from the way she reads the human-interest news. But two individuals may display quite different motivations in reading the same material. For example, consider the way a coach reads the story of his next opponent's most recent game as compared to the way one of the opponent's fans reads that same story. In other words, we have a distinction here between reading in which immediate drive reduction ("immediate reward") is sought and reading in which temporary uneasiness, even increased tension, is tolerated because it will supposedly lead to later social rewards in prestige, status, or survival.

Obviously, many of the same reservations which were made to the previous model can also be made to this one. Motives are usually mixed. It is hard to tell from the outside, or even from introspection, exactly what combination of drive-reduction and drive-stimulation is accomplished by any act of reading. It is obviously impossible to test the theory in terms of *what* is read, because, as the example of the coach illustrates, individuals may read the same material with quite different motivations and apparently with different effects on their level of tension. Nevertheless, this model has considerable validity when it is examined in light of what we know about the process of socializing human beings.

It would seem on the surface as though both these models might be attempts to get at the same felt distinction. Intuitively, it is apparent to us that reading the comics usually satisfies a different order of need from the one we satisfy by reading the editorials; that reading about a sexy actress in Hollywood is a different order of behavior from reading an article on the problems of keeping children from becoming delinquents; that watching wrestling on TV is a different order of behavior from watching experts analyze the President's budget message. It is also intuitively apparent that one group of these behaviors (comic reading, Hollywood gossip reading, watching the wrestling matches) requires less in the way of socialization than does the other group. And it seems reasonable that if we were to regard the structure of reading motivations as a continuum stretching from one of these poles to the other, we ought to be able to place any number of identified motivations somewhere on this continuum. That is what we are going to try to do in the following section.

A TYPOLOGY OF READING MOTIVATIONS

Suppose that we were to start from one extreme of motivation which we might call "immediate reward" (although we call it that reluctantly and only in the absence of a better term, inasmuch as "immediate reward" and "delayed reward" may be misleading)—suppose that we were to start at that end of the continuum and move toward the other end, then we might arrange a list of reading motives in some such order as this:

1. *Compulsive ritualistic reading*—reading so well learned and habitual that the original motivation is completely submerged if not forgotten. This is, for example, the habit of reading the paper at breakfast, or the afternoon paper late in the day, so that when the paper does not come, one feels as though something is missing, life is somehow disorganized—and all this quite apart from any specific content of the paper.

2. *Reading for respite*—reading as a tool for relaxing, escaping from burdensome realities, submerging problems, refreshing one's self in a world of fantasy where no mistakes are counted and no hurts are lasting. This is typified by the harried executive reading himself to sleep with a mystery novel; the research physicist, weary from trying to solve a real-life laboratory problem, relaxing with science fiction, etc.

3. *Reading for a sense of personal security*—reading for identification with characters who win admiration and success, either in fiction or in news. By sharing vicariously in these successes, the reader shores up his own deflated ego.

4. *Reading for a sense of social security in a changing world*—reading for reinforcement of one's attitudes and values. Perhaps one has become aware of challenges to his viewpoints and persuasion away from them. He goes to the media for reassurance. And, as we know, he tends to select reading which will mirror and strengthen his own viewpoints.

5. *Reading for vicarious experience*—reading as the magic carpet to take one into homes and adventures where one would never otherwise go. Thus many readers flew the Atlantic with Lindbergh, climbed Everest with Tensing and Hilary, wandered around the theaters of battle with Ernie Pyle.

6. *Reading for social contact*—reading which replaces direct with mediated contact, and especially which provides vicarious contact with interesting personalities. This is the kind of reading that permits one to think of Hollywood as one's own neighborhood, to argue mentally with Marilyn Monroe over divorcing Joe Dimaggio, to feel on first-name terms with Ike and Mamie. An important variety of this is the way a child reads to find out the roles that will be expected of him as he grows older, or a country girl reads to find out what city life is like.

7. *Reading for aesthetic experience*—on one level this has elements of escape (2), and on another it partakes of vicarious experience (5), but at its height this kind of reading results in meeting an interesting mind and being shown a penetrating view of life.

8. *Reading as a value in society*—the prestige value that society puts upon reading: the concept that reading anything is better than reading nothing, that it is good to be considered intellectually

curious or well-read, to take good magazines or have good books lying around, to have read the news regardless of its importance on any particular day.

9. *Reading as a tool of daily living*—reading to find out about the radio program, the sale prices, the stock quotations, the weather, the marriages, divorces, and deaths so that one will be able to express the proper sentiments.

10. *Reading as a tool of self-improvement*—to learn how to do it, how to get a better job, how to bring up a family, how to get along with one's wife, etc.

11. *Reading as a device for scanning the horizon*—this is news-reading intended to point out dangers and opportunities, results and outlooks, strengths and weaknesses in society, and forecasts.

12. *Reading for interpretation*—reading as an aid to understanding of and consensus on public issues: what the news means, what automation is likely to mean, what to think about foreign policy, how to evaluate current criticisms of the schools, etc.

This catalogue, as we have said, is arranged roughly in order from the most immediate to the most delayed reward, as we have used those terms. You may well quarrel with the order. And let us say again that these motivations will seldom occur separately. We may read for interpretation but combine with this a wish to have our own opinions reinforced. We may read for respite and for the excitement of identifying with glamorous characters or great adventures but also for the prestige of being thought well-read. It is safe to say that a grouping of motives, usually with one motive dominating the combination, lies behind almost every act of reading. But you will probably find it helpful to think of reading motivations, whether pure or mixed, in terms of their position on some continuum such as this.

Reading as Opposed to Other Channels

The catalogue of motivations which we have just constructed applies to other communication channels as well as to reading. We must, therefore, ask what are the factors that lead a person to choose to reduce his drives by reading rather than by listening or viewing.[23]

23. For an interesting treatment of media differences, see Joseph Klapper, "The Comparative Effects of the Various Media" in *The Nature and Process of Mass Communication*. Edited by Wilbur Schramm. Urbana, Illinois: University of Illinois, 1954.

There are undoubtedly some individuals whose visual skills are relatively greater than their auditory ones, or vice versa, or whose skill with print may be relatively less (or more) than their skill with pictures. Supposing that sensory equipment is normal, such persons must have acquired these differential skills mostly by learning them, and therefore earlier motivation must have lead to learning one set of skills better than the other. Perhaps there was more opportunity to practice one than the other, or one was valued and rewarded more than the other in the primary group.

Differences in availability often occur among the media. When the current is off, you aren't going to look at television. When the paper is late, you are going to enjoy some other kind of communication (if any) until it comes. When you are up late at night, you are more likely to read than to listen to the radio, which might waken the sleeping family.

But these are individual differences or situational accidents. We are more interested in the broad differences between media which help us to predict more generally whether a person will choose one or the other.

The most apparent difference among the media is that reading, more than any other channel, permits the receiver to *control the speed,* the *repetition,* and the *emphasis.* Once he has selected a channel, the television or radio listener is at the mercy of the TV or radio communicator so far as speed, repetition, and emphasis go. Once he has chosen a theater, he is at the mercy of the movie producer and exhibitor. But in reading he can go as fast or slow as he wishes, repeat as often as necessary, concentrate on one paragraph or one idea, if he so desires, at no cost to others. Therefore, reading has some advantage for the person who is trying to study or to make up his mind. Furthermore, very fast or very slow readers can more easily find reading material to fit their skills than they can find such material in radio, TV, or films.

Reading may be thought of as a *more active* kind of participation. Listening and viewing are more passive. In reading, as we have already pointed out, the reader is in charge. In the other media, the producers are in charge; the audience can only open the channel and let content flow. A person reading a newspaper selects what he wants to read; a person listening to a newscast finds the content preselected and preindexed for him. Some people doubtless have the personalities to prefer the more active experience; others, the more passive. At some times, anyone may prefer the more active— for example, when he knows exactly what he wants from the media and is in a hurry for it. At other times, anyone may prefer the passive—for example, when he is weary and in quest of relaxation.

There are some *space* advantages on one side or the other. You can read in bed, do the housework while listening to the radio, go out to movies (which you may or may not desire to do), stay home for the other media (which you may or may not decide to do). Books are less likely to be available at home, but if one goes out to the library one can find books on almost any subject. That is not true of radio, TV, and movies, which offer a much more limited choice, at home or elsewhere.

There are also *time* advantages. Radio brings quicker reports from the horizon. TV brings quicker and more life-like portrayals of special events. On the other hand, newspapers carry more news. And on the whole the printed media are more flexible. They are not divided into five- and fifteen-minute segments. They can afford to give a topic the coverage it deserves. And they last. They can be referred to again and again, if necessary. Nothing is more striking about mass communications than the evanescence, the impermanence, of radio and television programs.

There are also some *status* considerations. These are not the same in all cultures or in all times. Reading is broadly valued, but during the early years of television there has been special prestige in owning (or rather lack of prestige in not owning) a television set. There is prestige to be gained by having read the current best-seller or the revelation in the local newspaper, or having viewed the currently popular TV program. For individuals of one age, there is prestige in reading comics; for individuals of a later age, reading comics may be something to be rather ashamed of.

And there are also *economic* considerations. In general, print requires more frequent expenditures than radio or TV, but the expenditures associated with radio and TV are larger. Movies require frequent expenditures, but not so large as book cost or magazine subscriptions. Obviously, the state of one's individual economy, and behind that the national economy, will have something to do with the size and frequency of communication purchases. On the other hand, the size and immediacy of purchases will also have an effect on use. You tend to look immediately at the paper you buy at the newsstand. When you lay out several hundred dollars for a television set, you tend to give it a lot of use the first few days.

It is interesting to look at some of these broad generalizations against a set of cross-media preferences obtained in interviewing 200 middle western adults, who were asked the question which appears at the head of Table 1. The answers are arranged in average rank order of choice.

TABLE 1
MEDIA PREFERENCES EXPRESSED BY 200 MIDDLE WESTERN ADULTS

Query: Suppose that for a whole month you were unable to get any newspapers or any magazines, hear any radio, view any television, or go to any movies—in other words, all mass communication were taken away from you. Which of the media do you think you would miss most for each of the following services: (For example, if for "local news" you think you would miss movies the most, follow the row over from "local news" and put a check under *movies.* Put only one check in each row.)

SERVICE	NEWSPAPER	RADIO	TV	MAGAZINES	MOVIES
Local news	1	2	3	4	5
Washington news	1	1	3	3	5
Foreign news	2	1	3	3	5
Interpretation of the news	2	2	3	1	5
Opinions you value on the news	3	1	3	2	5
Information about "how to do it"	2	3	4	1	5
Information about science	2	3	3	1	5
Information about business and economics	2	3	4	1	5
Information about health	2	3	4	1	5
Useful information in general	2	3	4	1	5
Entertainment in general	5	4	1	2	3
Laughs	5	2	1	4	2
Sports	1	3	1	4	5
Advertisements you look at when you have decided to buy a certain thing, but not where or what kind to buy	1	4	3	2	—
Advertisements you look at when you want ideas for Christmas shopping or some similar purpose	2	4	2	1	—
Advertisements you look at to see what the new products are like	3	4	2	1	—

The Total Act of Decision

We have been taking the process apart. We have been fractionating it, explaining it as best we can from the limited evidence we have, in the hope of understanding it better when we put it back together. But always with this atomistic treatment there is the danger that the pieces will never be put back together.

That is what we must avoid. The act of decision is a totality. These separate motives, conditions, and factors do not exist separately. They cluster. They blend. The act of deciding whether to read or not to read is a balancing of availabilities and motivations, in terms of a particular environment, and as against competing possibilities—a very broad canvas which we should have the greatest difficulty analyzing in detail for ourselves at any instant of decision. Most of the readers will be concerned with broad patterns of reading choice, related to media or to personalities. Therefore, let us return to the broad canvas as we come near the end of this paper.

In the early pages we talked about Professor A. and Mr. B. Now let us talk briefly about Miss C. and Mr. D. in terms of what the "fraction of selection" means to them in various points of their lives.

Consider C. and D. at the age of six. This is a critical time in their reading careers. They are learning to sound out, "Come. See. See the tree," or whatever equally exciting reading matter appears in their first books. In this country, at least, such reading opportunities are almost universally available, and in school there will be sufficient motivation to get them over the first hump. But what then? What opportunities for reading will they find at home? Will there be a ladder of books difficult enough to challenge them, but not too difficult to discourage them from the next step? And what value is put on reading by the people they respect and admire? Is reading a valued behavior at home? Do the parents and older brothers and sisters read, and if so, what, and for what purposes? Do the peer groups like to read, or do they look down on the reading child as "queer"? In other words, at this time the pattern of motivations and availabilities is most flexible, and the school can only do a part of the work toward determining how skills will develop and how that pattern will organize itself for the years to come.

Now consider Miss C. and Mr. D. at age fifteen. They have boundless energy and lots of time. They are not home-bound. A walk to the library or to the newsstand, which might be a chore for their parents, is a pleasure to them. They are seeking out social experience; therefore, going to the movies or library has an added attraction. Their minds are perhaps more open, their appetites for experience more voracious than they will ever be again. Furthermore, their school work requires them to do a certain amount of reading and to learn where reading may be found. Therefore, if reading material is relatively easily available and if a value pattern has developed around the act of reading, they are likely to read a great deal. In school, of course, they read because they are motivated by the desire for self-improvement and by the prestige of grades, praise, and preferment. They read a great deal to find out about the roles they will have to play when they are older—lovers, husband, wife, soldier, college student, homemaker, business or professional man. They read a great deal for respite and for identification with glamorous personalities, and they are open and flexible to new aesthetic experiences. But mixed with this reading is the desire for social contact—the wish to meet other people and other places and lives through reading. From their school work and the adult conversations they overhear, they are beginning to become interested in public questions, and so they read occasionally to get an interpretation of the draft and the likelihood of war, or the differences between the political parties. At this time, of course, there are some kinds of reading which they do because of their roles as adolescents; D. reads sports and comics, C. reads love stories and film-stars' biographies. There is an element of ritual and compulsion about this reading. But chiefly as we look at the reading patterns of C. and D. at 15, we are impressed by the important part reading is playing in socializing them and in giving them a sense of security and by the remarkable combination of time, energy, and availability they have.

This is probably the most critical period in the reading history of Miss C. and Mr. D. They are better reading "prospects" than they will ever be again. Their skills and interests have increased very rapidly ever since the age of six. Perhaps never again will they have the same appetite for new experience and freedom to pursue it. In a few years responsibilities will close in on them, and their reading patterns will harden. Therefore, they are at a turning point. As Gray and Munroe say, they can choose either of two paths: "The one is for young people under the right kind of home and school influence to continue desirable reading habits; the other is for young people both in and out of school to discontinue reading because of prominence of other interests and activities. The period from twelve to sixteen is recognized both in this country and abroad as a critical period in the development of desirable reading interests that persist." [24] In other words, this is the time when C. and D. are setting a pattern for themselves as to how much motivation they are willing to pit against the greater effort that will be required of them in the future. They are setting a pattern for how much they are going to seek "delayed-reward" reading in the years when it will become increasingly important for them to do so.

Consider C. and D. at 35. Miss C. is now Mrs. E. The third child is on the way. She is largely home-bound. During the day she is quite busy with housework but lonely in the house so she lets the radio play while she works. In the early evening, she hears one of the children read his lesson: "Come. See. See the tree." When the children are tucked away in bed, she wearily turns to respite reading or probably to mass circulation, "common denominator" publications. They own few books. She looks over the newspaper to see what, if anything, has happened to her friends, and what the grocers have on sale this weekend. It is a real effort for Mrs. E. to do much reading and especially to do much serious, "delayed-reward" reading. Her economic situation will make some difference, and so will the valuation her husband puts on reading. Two other factors, though, may be even more important: the pattern she established in her teens, and the peer group she comes to belong to and value. Do her clubs talk about public affairs or sew? Do her friends discuss art or cooking, politics or gossip?

Mr. D. at 35 has less time and energy than at 15, more responsibility. He is work-bound by day, home-bound in the evening. He has more money, but worries more about it. It is a greater effort for him to go to movies or use libraries. Both his book-reading and his movie-going have fallen off. TV, newspaper, and magazines are more easily available. Some of his reading is now quite ritualistic—the evening paper, for example. He grouses and grumbles if the paper is late. He reads himself to sleep with a "whodunit." That

24. Gray and Munroe, *op. cit.*, p. 272.

ritual seems to relax him; and he notices that business tires and tenses him more than it used to. He reads occasionally for specific purposes: to learn how to finish the basement room in knotty pine, or how to understand his growing children. He pays less attention to socialization now, for he has learned his role. But he is more serious, both about his vocation and about politics. How much he uses reading for that purpose will again depend to a great extent on the pattern he established in his teens. Did he learn to value reading as an instrument, so that he would go to the effort of getting the reading material he needs? Did he learn to read about public affairs, and think about conflicting viewpoints, and make up his mind; or does he talk over public questions with his barber and vote what the majority of his role group vote?

This is another critical time for C. and D., though not nearly so critical as the age period from twelve to sixteen. This is the time when they are balancing out motivations against effort for the last half of life. This is the time when the decision is foreshadowed whether reading will be a major or a minor tool for the rest of life, whether it will continue to contribute to their growth in wisdom or understanding, and whether it will contribute to the serenity of old age.

This is the large picture. Throughout most of this paper we have necessarily been concerned with the countless *little* pictures, the factors and details and interrelationships. For the readers of this paper, we can only hope that understanding more of the ingredients will help them to put the larger picture together as they teach or advise Miss C. and Mr. D., or when they analyze their own behavior as Mr. D. or Mrs. E.

CHAPTER IV

Reading and Related Media

EDGAR DALE

Introduction

Why discuss audio-visual materials in a yearbook on adult reading? The answer is simple. The teacher of adults is interested in all the ways by which people get a rich experiential background for knowledge. He is especially interested in discovering how reading and other experiences can be most effectively interrelated and made mutually re-enforcing. Since reading is one of the most effective tools of the adult learner, it is pertinent to inquire whether the introduction of audio-visual materials might discourage the use of reading as a tool of learning and perhaps even lower the learner's esteem of reading. Are reading and audio-visual materials in competition? If not, how can one most effectively integrate the processes of varied media for use in communicating ideas?

The problem is made especially complex by the newness of the audio-visual media, with only a brief period of time available for experimentation. The reading of books has been the basic approach to education for hundreds of years, but since 1900 we have had to assimilate a new mass medium every twenty years. First came the motion picture; in 1920 radio arrived; and about 1940 television came on the scene. Indeed, television is so new that it was not included in the title of the 1946 report of the Hutchins Commission on Freedom of the Press, "A General Report on Mass Communication: Newpapers, Radio, Motion Pictures, Magazines, and Books."

Reading may be defined as the process of getting meaning from print by putting meaning into the print. Reading taste and ability are always tethered to past experience. But reading, itself, is one way of increasing this capital fund of cultural experience. Reading must, therefore, be thought of as involving more than *saying* the words, more than seeing the sentences and paragraphs. Good reading is the way a person brings his whole life to bear on the new ideas which he finds on the printed page. It is reading the lines, reading between the lines, and reading beyond the lines.

The lines read are those of an author who in turn has brought his whole life to bear on what he has written. Or as Dorothy Canfield Fisher put it:

> Every novel and story and poem and essay—every book, in fact, of first-rate quality—brings to bear upon the reader the total impact of the author's conception of human life, and the effect of this impact remains with the reader long after he has forgotten plot and character.[1]

Even though reading is hundreds of years older than our modern audio-visual media, we must remember that it, too, was a late-comer on the historical scene. Frances Henne has reported:

> In the old Stone Age communication included pictures of horses, bison, mammoths, and other animals drawn on cave walls; these were probably records of hunting seasons or a type of invocation. Carvings and pictures scratched on bone, stone, and bark served a similar purpose. The earliest phases in the development of writing, particularly the pictographic, hieroglyphic, and ideographic forms, utilized the drawn picture. The history of the development of the book contains many examples of the effectiveness of pictures as means of conveying messages. Such examples occur in ancient Egyptian rolls, the illuminated manuscript, moralized Bibles with picture columns, image prints, block books, and early printed books.[2]

Not only is reading a relatively new device for communicating ideas but we must remember that it has also had its early critics. We know, of course, that the Greeks learned chiefly by oral communication and that they discussed what they learned as they learned it. Greek adults were educated through the spoken word. Public recitation of the *Odyssey* and *Iliad* was not merely a custom but an occupation carried on by professionals. Hall explains that the literature of early times in Greece consisted essentially of the spoken

---

1. *Good Reading*, p. 200. A Mentor Book. Edited by the Committee on College Reading. New York: New American Library of World Literature, Inc., 1954 (revised).

2. Frances Henne, "Whence the Comic Strip: Its Development and Content" in *Adapting Reading Programs to Wartime Needs*, p. 156. Supplementary Educational Monographs, No. 57. Chicago: University of Chicago Press, 1943.

word for the reason that it was composed for recitation.[3] Herodotus read his *History* aloud in Athens (and received a prize in money because it was so well liked by his listeners). Toynbee reminds us:

> Where "write" and "writer" or "read" and "reader" occur in the English translation, the English reader must not forget that "recite" and "composer" or "hear" and "hearer" are generally the equivalents in Greek. . . . From Herodotus' day to Simocatta's [the seventh century] a public recital to a select audience by the author himself was the ordinary method of publication.[4]

A rigorous defense of speaking and listening and a criticism of reading as an adult-education device is found in Plato's *Seventh Letter* where he makes the point that the best method of communication is from individual teacher to individual pupil who live and talk together. He notes that, when the teacher commits his message to a fixed form of written words, there is loss in precision or effectiveness or both.

The teacher of adult classes needs, therefore, to think clearly about the role of reading, what it can and cannot do. D. W. Brogan says:

> It is possible . . . that we put reading too high as a test of culture. The Anglo-Saxon culture we grew up with has been pre-eminently a literary culture. Literature has had no rival in prestige like music in Germany and Italy, like painting in France. But music (in France and England as well as in America) is, I think, partly replacing literature, poetry, the drama, the novel as the cultural resource of the minority on whom the burden of maintaining high standards falls. If we think too much in terms of what people read, what plays they see, we may be missing the most important cultural developments of our times.[5]

Acquiring Reading Skills

We hope that this introduction has served to make the point that reading is only one way, though an excellent one, to master symbolically condensed experiences. But since it is not the only way,

---

3. T. W. Hall, *A Companion to Classical Texts*, p. 25. New York: Clarendon Press, 1913.

4. Arnold J. Toynbee, *Greek Historical Thought from Homer to the Age of Heraclitus*, p. 25. New York: E. P. Dutton & Co., 1924.

5. D. W. Brogan, "The Taste of the Common Man," *Saturday Review*, XXXVI (February 28, 1953), 49.

to make reading the sole method of adult education is failing to make use of some good resources. Furthermore, reading itself is improved and enhanced by the rich and varied meanings gained through such media as motion pictures, radio, and television. Reading, to be productive, needs constant fertilization from ideas expressed in other ways.

We shall next look at some of these media and note their strengths and weaknesses as communication devices. Before we do this, however, two points need to be cleared up. First, some persons read badly because they have not mastered the *skills* of reading. Buswell discovered that some graduate students in his reading clinic at the University of Chicago had a rich background of experience but read slowly and inefficiently in their field. There was something wrong with their perceptual habits or with their attitude toward reading. In one such group of 62 persons the average rate of reading was 197 words per minute. What they needed was remedial guidance in improving their *skill* as readers. Their experience background was adequate, they could comprehend what they read but they were inefficient, as far as time-spent-per-idea-gained was concerned.[6]

It becomes evident that one way to improve adult reading is to help readers master new experience, build new concepts, gain new terminology. Some of this may be achieved through using audiovisual media. That an improved background can result in improved reading is suggested by the fairly high correlation between linguistic abilities in different sensory modes of perception. It is obvious, too, that increasing one's vocabulary through viewing, listening, or conversing would help an adult read more effectively. In short, the more familiar he is with the ideas on a particular page, the faster and more effectively he can read. And this familiarity can be increased by the use of audio-visual materials.

The Role of Sensory Responses

A second point that needs to be cleared up relates to learning through different senses. Stroud points out:

6. G. T. Buswell, "The Improvement of Rate and Comprehension in Reading" in *Adapting Reading Programs to Wartime Needs.* Supplementary Educational Monographs, No. 57. Chicago: University of Chicago Press, 1943.

In the absence of valid experimental data to the contrary, it is suggested that there is no good reason to suppose there should be any very important systematic differences in the relative effectiveness of different sensory modes of presentation, except perhaps those dictated by habits of work. Learning appears to be accomplished by the making of responses. One form of sensory excitation should be as satisfactory for purposes of eliciting the putatively requisite responses as another. Academic learning is, or should be, featured by understanding and meaningful organization. The central processes loom large in learning.

These considerations, in addition to the equivocal character of the experimental results, make it unlikely that there are in general any fundamental differences in the results of different sensory modes of presentation. However, differences in interest value and differences in development of mechanical means of presenting material, for example, the perfection of the motion picture, may make one method more available than another.[7]

Furthermore, Stroud notes that the value of visual materials probably does not lie in the superiority of the visual sense but rather in the superiority of mechanical means of presentation over a verbal presentation of the content of many learning situations. That is, "the problem may well be more one of physics than of psychology." [8]

There is a commonly stated opinion that, "One picture is worth a thousand words." As an aphorism which is sometimes true it may have some value. However, an equally good case can be made for the expression, "One word is worth a thousand pictures." The one word or expression may succinctly abstract and summarize the rich meaning of hundreds of concrete experiences. Furthermore, those who assume that "One picture is worth a thousand words" simply disregard the fact that the expression itself is presented *verbally* not *pictorially*. If the statement is generally true, then the aphorism might well be illustrated by a picture instead of by recourse to words.

In adult-education classes, the teacher needs to realize that generalizations are developed out of concrete experience. Mental life consists of progressive abstraction from concrete or semiconcrete or

7. James B. Stroud, *Psychology in Education*, pp. 445-46. New York: Longmans, Green & Co., Inc., 1946.

8. *Ibid.*, p. 449.

relatively abstract experience. Less and less stands for more and more. William James is quoted as saying, "You cannot see any farther into a generalization than your knowledge of its details extends." In short, a generalization can never be more meaningful than the myriad concrete experiences out of which it grew. If we generalize on meager concrete experience, the generalization may be inaccurate. On the other hand, a mere accumulation of concrete experiences without hypothesis, without either patterning or generalization, is likely to be educationally fruitless. We don't get an education by the planless piling up of experiences, even vivid ones. It is the interaction of these experiences through thinking that makes them educational.

We conclude, therefore, that reading is not a fundamentally different process from viewing or listening. All have important verbal components; all are dependent upon language abilities. They can be made mutually re-enforcing. Hoban and Van Ormer [9] discovered, for example, that a combination of visual and auditory presentation usually is better than the poorer of the two used separately and sometimes better than either. Gibson[10] has reported that verbal descriptions of visual shapes were a help in learning the identification of aircraft.

The Still Picture

Let us look now at some of the characteristics of still pictures. These include photographs, illustrations, filmstrips, and slides. Considering first the photograph, we see that it is an excellent substitute for reality. When presented in color and in three-dimensions, it may not be easy for the viewer to see the difference between the real object and the substitute. But even photographs are abstractions and require initial help in reading. A photographer presented an Ankara shoe-shine boy with a likeness of himself. The boy did not recognize at first that he was seeing his own photograph. He

9. C. F. Hoban and E. B. Van Ormer, "Instructional Film Research, 1918-1950." Technical Report No. SDC 269-7-19, Instructional Film Research Program. Port Washington, L. I., New York: Special Devices Center, 1950.

10. *Motion Picture Testing and Research.* Army Air Forces Aviation Psychology Program Research Reports, No. 7. Edited by J. J. Gibson. Washington: Government Printing Office, 1947.

didn't "see" that a two-dimensional tiny black-and-white piece of paper could stand for him.

In the illustration just cited, the boy knew the reality for which the photograph stood. There are times, however, when we do not know the reality, and thus certain cues in the picture mean little to us. We always read our past experience into photographs just as we do with abstract symbols on the printed page. If we lack the requisite experience, we miss the meaning of the picture. That is, no background, no meaning.

The photograph and other still pictures have the advantage of being examined at one's leisure. Unlike radio, television, and the film, the pace for viewing or listening is not set by an outside source. The picture can be carefully studied if one wishes. It is especially useful in presenting concepts, the meaning of which does not require motion to portray, e.g., a landscape rather than how the blood circulates.

The still picture can be skilfully juxtaposed with reading material in a book, newspaper, or pamphlet. It can be clipped, mounted, and filed for study purposes. Continuity can be arranged for in a series of photographs, as in a strip, or through a filmstrip itself. With such materials, projection in a darkened room provides for more careful study of an enlarged view.

When we use pictures which are not photographic likenesses, additional difficulties arise in interpreting or "reading" the picture. Caricatures and stylized pictures may be hard to understand. A map is a highly condensed version of the objects and the space for which it stands. A map model may be more easily interpreted. Lines of longitude and latitude have no "real" existence, they are man-made abstractions. Adults have difficulty in reading maps, as every tourist knows.

Similar difficulties are faced in the "reading" of charts and graphs. We represent the population in 1950 as a bar occupying a certain amount of space. The reader must see it as an abstracted version of the real population at that time. Many adults need guidance in reading such graphic materials. There is also a need for writers who have skill in presenting statistical material in truly graphic form.

One of the typical weaknesses in the illustrations of books is the failure of the written text to re-enforce the picture and vice versa. The photographs selected for use in books are often an afterthought. The text is written first, and the photographs squeezed in later. One of our greatest needs is a resource file of photographs on all the subjects which adults need to be informed about. The United States Department of Agriculture has such a file. We need many others in all fields of adult education.

We also need to give more attention to guidance in the reading of pictures, whether photographs or cartoons. This is a gradual learning process, as is the moving from a literal interpretation of a statement to a metaphorical or figurative one. This is the phase of reading which requires one to infer what the author meant. It is an advanced reading skill which is paralleled in "advanced" viewing skills. An interesting report of effective guidance in learning experiences of this type is provided by a high-school teacher who started her students analyzing cartoons as a prelude to teaching "hidden meanings" in prose and poetry. The nature of the motivation in this method is indicated by the following examples.

A picture of a full dinner plate soaring into the sky, up above the heads of an awed family group, suggests that food prices are inordinately high. If it appears at a time when the front pages of the paper are full of tales of flying saucers, however, it indicates which problem the cartoonist finds more vital. A picture in the *New Yorker* of an Army barracks with the usual pin-up girls above the cots reveals the astonishment on the inspecting sergeant's face when he comes to a cot with a framed water color above it. It also gives a clue to the character of the young private lying unconcernedly beneath the painting. In another picture an amiable-looking convict points to a flower bed outside the penitentiary gates they are entering and remarks to his guard, "Say, them peonies turned out O.K., didn't they?"

In each picture, of course, the reader adds something left out. One may be sure the students will enthusiastically find many pictures of this sort.[11]

The Motion Picture

Here are some of the characteristics of the motion picture: It is attention-compelling not only through the attraction of motion

---

11. Rosemary S. Donahue, "A Problem in Developmental Reading," *English Journal*, XLII (March, 1953), 142-47.

itself but also because extraneous distractions tend to be closed off as one concentrates on the lighted screen in a darkened room.

The motion picture, like the still picture and television, can present an easily recognized counterpart of reality. It also highlights and heightens reality. It is probably inaccurate to say that it is more real than reality but it is often more emphatic and impressive than reality. The reality of the typical film is easily understood. By skilful combination of the picture and the words of the commentary, it can convey rich meaning even to the illiterate whether child or adult.

The feature motion picture not only secures a high degree of attention but may also arouse strong emotion. The evidence is clear that the motion picture can influence attitudes. Studies of Thurstone and Peterson have shown that a single film may measurably influence an attitude and that a series of films, each of which singly is too weak to produce a change in attitude, may cumulatively do so. It is likely that the emotional impact of the film can be greater than the impact of reading alone.

The film can span great distances. It can juxtapose two events broadly separated in time and space, enabling us to generalize by comparing and contrasting. Thus, we may see first a child's game in the United States, next the same game as played in Africa, with the consequent conclusion of striking similarity. Julien Bryan used this device in "Picture in Your Mind" to show that certain styles of hair-dress of American women were like those of African women. The motion-picture film enables the eye of the viewer to travel over the entire world to visualize such terms as *veldt, savanna, rain forest, desert nomad, pampas, steppes, monsoon.*

History reconstructed through the motion-picture film gains realism denied to print. The film can provide a unique record of the events that have occurred in the last fifty years. It furnishes a visual record of recent history. By means of a film such as *The Plow That Broke the Plains* we can bring present understanding to a past event such as the dust bowl storms in the early 1930's. The film can provide a record of phenomena too rare, difficult, or expensive to secure by other means—an eclipse, a rare operation, an interview with a noted scientist, or a presidential inauguration.

The eye of the motion-picture camera can see what the normal eye cannot. Thus, we can see the microscopic and the telescopic. We can zoom quickly into a room of a house, see an action such as a ballet from points of view denied the spectator in the theater.

The motion picture can both compress and expand normal time. By time-lapse photography one can see the real event in compressed time, a unique experience not available in reading or any other medium. We can expand time by use of slow-motion photography. Thus the plant which normally might take a month to grow can run its life cycle in a few minutes of film.

Through animated drawings, "life" can be given to abstract ideas. Such drawings can show the inner workings of a gasoline engine, the action of molecules, what makes a plane fly, the wind systems of the world. These may also be combined with graph and chart techniques which enable us to see animated figures whose actions express ideas clearly enough to be understood by the audience.

We have noted that the film conveys information and influences attitudes. It also is useful in teaching skills. The evidence is clear that many "how-to-do-it" skills can be learned from a motion picture. One merely imitates the excellent model which he sees as many times as needed. Reading materials prepared to accompany the film may facilitate learning.

Reading has some significant advantages over attendance at a movie. It is often easier to stay home and read than to go out to a movie. Motion-picture attendance at the theater is more of an undertaking, involves much more preparation and planning than reading a book. It costs more. A book is easily sampled, a film is not. Motion-picture attendance tends to be done as a group activity. One does not do it alone, as is usually true of reading.

Also, reading can cater to specialized tastes in a manner that film and television programs are often prohibited from doing by the high cost of production. The mass market for films and television is large, and this often means a lower common denominator of appeal. However, the art theaters are increasingly appealing to minority tastes.

Teaching Films

Reports on the production of films expressly for educational use indicate that over four thousand 16-mm. (narrow width) films have been produced by companies such as Encyclopedia Britannica, Young America Films, Coronet, and by the United States government. The films cost around $50 for an 11-minute film and rent for about two dollars. Every state has one or more film libraries from which these films can be rented. Many public libraries make films as easily available as books. Courses of study will list the films useful in reaching the objectives sought.

Educational films have been made expressly for adult training. Notable examples are the army and navy films and the several hundred vocational-training films made by the United States Office of Education during World War II. Many manufacturing and business groups make films for the training of their employees.

Hundreds of films are available for adult education. They may deal with mental health, the care of children, economics, foreign affairs, geography, or religion. Such films are frequently presented as a part of the program of discussion groups in a library, a parent-teacher association, or a church. Many of these films can be used in adult-education classes and geared into a program of reading. We like to read about what we have already experienced, in part, at first-hand. A film can serve well as an introductory experience to reading.

The following statement was taken from a piece of promotional literature for the Edison projection machine. It was written in 1898. It makes sense today, as it did then.

What is the future of the film? Ask, rather, from what conceivable phase of the future it can be debarred. In the promotion of business interests, in the advancement of science, in the revelation of unguessed worlds, in its educational and recreative powers. . . . It is the earnest of the coming age, when the great potentialities of life shall no longer be in the keeping of cloister and college . . . but shall overflow to the nethermost portions of the earth at the command of the humblest heir of the divine intelligence.

Television

To discuss television as one of several ways of transmitting or mediating ideas, we must first know its unique features and those which it shares with radio, movies, print, photographs, and other media.

How good a communication device is television? Will it gradually replace reading used for entertainment? For getting information? Television has all the advantages of film which it frequently uses, some advantages in immediacy and some disadvantages in screen size.

Television makes use of a camera which transmits and projects its picture onto a screen which may be thousands of miles away. The camera may be "witnessing" a live event or it may be "seeing" a play, a film, photograph, chart, or poster. What the camera sees is then transmitted to the viewing screen. Barring present-day physical limitations, which will probably be overcome, television can take your eye and ear to any place in the world and show what is happening there right now. Like radio, it has the impact of immediacy.

Moreover, television is both eye and ear witness. It can see and hear things as they happen. It gives us an experience of sight and sound either in color or in black and white. Sometimes television gives us more and sometimes less than we would have seen or heard as witnesses to the real event. The mobile camera may go physically where we could not go and show us a scene from many points of view. Through the use of telescopic lenses it can also get closer to the event than could the ordinary observer. The camera eye can look where we could not look, see the far away or the microscopic with equal ease.

Television is concrete, immediate, real, easily understood. It is intimate and personal. It can convey ideas and information to those unable to read. It can provide common experience to persons quite different in age, education, or maturity. It is a great equalizer of educational opportunity.

Television, more easily than print, can quickly engage the attention of millions of people, e.g., the 30 to 40 million viewers of *I Love Lucy* or the 60 or 70 million who see the "spectaculars," such as *Peter Pan*. It can occupy their time without occupying their minds. It is a comforting distraction from the fatigues and anxieties of everyday existence. Television provides an interesting, exciting change of attention, a comfortable experience obtained at low cost in one's own home.

Television, unlike the theatrical film, is viewed alone or in a small group. It is often a family experience with the consequent possibilities for group pleasure and of varying opinions of what should be viewed *now* on the single family set. However, on this point Siepmann says, "There are those . . . who question whether a family grouped in silence around a television receiver is in any true sense favorably affected in terms of family relations." [12]

Television as a medium of communication resembles the motion picture but has certain disadvantages, as well as advantages, relative to it. It can project a motion picture but must do so with a reduced screen size. Thus the sweep of *Cinerama* or *Cinemascope* is not for television. However, television does not require a darkened room— one of the handicaps in the showing of films. And no technical skill is needed to operate a television set. What will happen in a motion picture is already on the film. When a live event is being televised, the result is unpredictable. Anything can happen, as with live radio.

Television is limited to a small number of channels because of a physical limitation in wave lengths available for television. Thus, the opportunity for competition in a city or area is lessened, and the chance for monopoly of ideas is increased. Radio, on the other hand, can be tuned in from thousands of miles away. The effective distance of television is often little more than fifty miles. In many cities you must tune in the one available channel or turn off your set.

Television sets are not yet very portable so we must go where the set is. Although portability will probably come, we are not likely to have millions of television sets in autos as we now have radios. Moreover, television requires more concentration than radio. It is much less often a background experience for other things you are doing. You must stay fairly close to your set. Radio can be either background or foreground. A 16-mm. motion-picture projector can be transported but lacks the ease of handling which radio possesses. You must see the latest theatrical motion pictures in a fixed location; you must go outside the home to participate in them. Television has partially changed this and, if and when subscription television becomes a reality, will change it more.

A book or a magazine article or a news report in the newspaper can be easily reread. There is no simple way to re-view a television

12. C. A. Siepmann, *Radio, Television, and Society*, p. 342. New York: Oxford University Press, 1950.

program. Nor is there any simple way for an individual to get a record of the program to check its accuracy. Perhaps the development of television on tape may change this somewhat. Television can, of course, be repeated by the use of a kinescope, a 16-mm. (narrow-width) film made during the program, or by using the same film that may have been used on the television program. But this does not help the individual viewer very much.

Television and radio not only move at a specific pace—the same for everybody—but they are on a rigid time schedule. The medium sets the pace for absorption. We cannot stop to think or we miss what follows. With recordings or readings we can set up our own listening or reading schedule. We can use newspapers, books, or magazines when we are ready for them, but we are bound to observe the time schedules of broadcasters.

Television is chiefly a one-way communication device, like drama, film, radio, and reading. But this does not mean that there can be no interaction between viewer and the television speaker or panel. The speaker can "read" the mind of the viewer, anticipate and answer his unspoken questions. On programs such as that of the "Town Meeting" in Columbus, Ohio, which has been running for many years, questions are telephoned in. Even if there isn't time to answer all questions, the interests of the viewers can be gauged by their questions and can be taken into account in the preparation of later programs.

Radio

What are the advantages of radio as a medium of mass communication? Live radio, like live television, has immediacy. You can listen in on the event itself as it happens or as it happened if it is a speech or a similar event. One is a participant at an event, the outcome of which is uncertain. The reading materials used for adult education may be somewhat out-of-date, but radio is up-to-date.

Radio has the qualities of realism—the realism of sound. Thus, when one hears the reproduction of sounds of insects there is no intermediate experience needed to understand them. If words were used, we would try to duplicate the sound by the word. Yet when we read the sounds made by a dog, such as "arf, arf," or "woof,

woof," or the sounds of birds, or the sound of a cat, we see the difficulty even of doing this simple thing accurately. We can get authenticity with radio through the voices and sounds and ideas presented to us by the broadcasters.

Radio can surmount time and space. We can hear Nehru as he gives a speech to Congress or by a recording as he gave it five years ago. We can tune in the opening session of the United Nations and its tenth-anniversary celebration. We can get the emotional impact of listening in on history.

Radio, like motion pictures, can compress time, annihilate distance. For example, a good deal of the life of Jefferson has been compressed into a series of dramatizations titled "The Jeffersonian Heritage." Here we have an able teacher and scholar, Dumas Malone, co-operating with able dramatists to make Jefferson live again.

Radio is inexpensive, a fact which is not altogether unimportant when considered in light of the cost of equally satisfying experiences offering similar cultural and recreational benefits.

Radio is easily available. It is at hand in one's automobile, at the beach, in one's bedroom, kitchen, or living room. One can listen in the dark.

What advantage does listening have over reading? Many people say listening is easier, that it requires less attention than reading. But here we are probably thinking only of one kind of marginal listening, incidental to some other activity going on at the same time. Active listening to get the full meaning of what is said requires as careful attention as reading. But again, as with films, illiterates can understand radio without being able to read.

Through listening we can understand emotion and subtlety of meaning not always possible through reading materials or other learning materials. Indeed, all of us know what is meant by a sympathetic voice, a kindly voice, a harsh voice, a critical voice, a pleasant voice.

Listening, of course, is the counterpart of speaking. Communication is a listening-speaking process. In discussion groups we have a circular movement from speaker to listener and back again. We interact, carry on a transaction of ideas. We can ask questions; we can answer them. In a radio or recording, as with all mass media, we cannot ordinarily get this feedback, the point with which Plato was concerned as noted above.

Is there a unique role of radio and television as a supplement to the newspapers, magazines, and books in communicating information about current problems? Or, does broadcasting (radio and television) serve an intellectual function that reading does not? Frank Stanton, President of the Columbia Broadcasting System, speaking to the Convention of Sigma Delta Chi in November, 1954, at Columbus, Ohio, posed the question, "What about the operations of the intellect in our media?" He comments on some of the differences:

. . . The best newspaper pundits, the men who think hard and write lucidly and demand of their audiences that they pause and take real thought—these men can and do, on the printed page, command the attention of their readers for twenty minutes at a time. But the very greatest pundit-columnist, reading his column aloud to a microphone, with or without benefit of camera, would be switched off by the hundreds of thousands before he had talked a minute. He has written to be *read*, not to be listened to. Not enough of our pundits have given enough thought to the subtle differences between what the reading eye and the listening ear will accept, even when both are connected to the same brain. And perhaps we of broadcasting are at fault for not having studied enough, and coached enough, to translate the best of political-intellectual newspaper columns into broadcast terms. . . .

But, what about the *speech*, as a matter of record? Here I think the terms are reversed. Only the biggest metropolitan newspapers give full transcripts of important speeches; the rest content themselves with excerpts. And a verbatim transcript, the day after, can look dull, whereas radio and television have the inestimable advantage of being instantaneous with the real event. That's the magic of live broadcasting. If the speaker is to be cheered or booed or shot at; if he is to say something tremendous or put his foot into a terrible mess, the audience is there waiting for it to happen. . . .

As with the speech, so with the *panel*, so with the *discussion*, under the eyes and ears of the camera and microphone. The debates, the round tables, the critical and sometimes very rough quizzing of public figures for the benefit of a nation-wide audience of citizens, are to me among the most significant of improvements on the town hall meetings, the Lincoln-Douglas debates of an earlier America, wonderfully extended, brought up to date, and made available to all.

Characteristics of the Different Media

Let us now summarize the relative advantages and disadvantages of reading as contrasted with other media.

Motion pictures, radio and television, and reading all suffer from lack of feedback, opportunities for interaction. They are truly mass media. Occasionally with radio or television there is an opportunity for an author to meet a critic or a reader. We need, therefore, in adult education to develop ways in which the consumer can talk over his ideas with others—ideas gained from the various media. This is easiest with reading where plays and books can be read aloud and discussed. With radio, motion pictures, and television, however, language is spoken to be heard not written to be read. Still pictures usually are described verbally or are an integral part of a verbal presentation. It is, therefore, inaccurate to think of motion pictures, television, and still pictures as only visual. In reality they are more often verbal-visual.

The intellectual processes used to understand audio-visual materials are not essentially different from those required to understand reading. Yet reading requires a skill in interpreting sounds that are often known when heard. After the fourth or fifth grade in reading ability is reached, the correlations between reading and listening are fairly high. The excellent listener tends to be an excellent reader, and this is especially true for complicated material.[13]

Radio, motion pictures, television, and still pictures do not require reading ability to be understood if they are presented on a simple level. This is not because they use the senses of sight and hearing but because they usually present materials which closely approximate the life experience of the viewer or listener. They can, in short, be made simpler than reading which uses a more complicated shorthand, more abstract symbols.

However, specific radio, television, and motion-picture programs or photographs could be as difficult as any reading material. It all depends on the complexity or the abstractness of the messages sent.

13. For a more adequate and qualified statement of the relationships between reading and listening, see Robert S. Goyer, "Oral Communication: Studies in Listening," *Audio-Visual Communication Review,* II (Fall, 1954), 263-76.

For example, a diplomat might find *Foreign Affairs* easy reading but be quite unable to "read" an X-ray photograph.

Reading is the most versatile, the most transferable, of the various modes of communication. It is handy to use, requires little or no equipment. However, the symbols read must be "suffused with suggestiveness," as Whitehead asserts, if they are to come alive and be meaningful. This vigor, this concreteness, is a product of firsthand experience and can be accentuated and extended by the semiconcrete experiences of typical programs presented by radio, motion pictures, and television.

The foregoing remarks which show the value of audio-visual materials in making reading more meaningful should not lead us to conclude that the audio-visual materials are, therefore, always subsidiary aids or supplements of some kind, desirable but not essential. On the contrary, audio-visual materials have unique values of their own as noted previously.

All media of communication require and enhance language ability. Therefore, improvement in one's language through audio-visual materials is immediately available for use in reading or in writing. Moreover, we must assume that reading can improve one's listening and viewing just as much as listening and viewing can improve reading. One who listens carefully to a broadcast on the Soviet Union can later read more intelligently about various phases of Russia's agriculture and industry. Reading, writing, speaking, and listening are all correlated and interacting skills. Improve one, and you are likely to get some transfer to another.

It is sometimes argued that experience with the mass media is too easy, that one learns easily and quickly from them, that no discipline is necessary as with rigorous reading. Here, the writer would point out that, in the field of communication, we aim for clarity and relevance, not for ease or difficulty. We want the message to be no harder than it needs to be and, indeed, no easier than it needs to be. When a message is harder than it needs to be, it frustrates but does not challenge. When a message is easier than it needs to be, more material is used than is necessary and the motivation of intellectual challenge may be lost.

Furthermore, there are so many things for adults to learn, and life today is so complicated that any increased efficiency in getting ideas is to be desired. This means that we sometimes speed up reading, and sometimes we slow it down. It may mean that we substitute an audio-visual experience for reading. The aim is to secure the largest number of excellent ideas in the shortest time.

Sometimes we face the curious notion that, if an experience is enjoyable, it is not really educational. Indeed, one teacher did not want to play recordings of Shakespeare's plays because it would be too easy for the students to learn that way. The notion still exists that, if it tastes bad, it's good for you. We must remember, too, that adult groups are not captive audiences. If they don't like what they get, they don't come back.

Is it accurate to characterize reading as an active process and viewing television or films as passive? Preston, speaking of motion pictures, films, and television says: "Their content is vividly presented, supplying visual and auditory cues in a way that enables the recipient to assimilate the ideas while in a relatively passive state." [14]

Reading for entertainment can also be done "in a relatively passive state." Much popular reading material is little more than an agreeable emotional message, it soothes and comforts the troubled. It does not require active thinking. It is a sedative, not a stimulant.

Whether reading, radio, film, or television are passive or active, sedatives or stimulants, depends on their content and the purposes of the user. A recording of T. S. Eliot reading his poem, "The Waste Land," requires careful listening just as the printed copy demands careful reading. Speech may be easier for some to understand than writing, but speech as such does not induce either passivity or activity. It is what is said that matters.

Reading *Hamlet* is no more active a process than listening to it on a recording. It is probably true, however, that the materials available for adult reading certainly cover a wider range of experiences, are more complicated at the upper levels, and require more careful study than do extant materials in films, radio, or television. It is true, too, that reading a play is harder for many persons than listening to it.

14. Ralph C. Preston, "The Changed Role of Reading," in *Reading in an Age of Mass Communication*, p. 5. Edited by William S. Gray. New York: Appleton-Century-Crofts, 1949.

What evidence is there that television will undermine the ability to read and the taste for reading? This problem is engaging the serious attention of teachers, parents, and publishers. Is reading in danger of losing its hold on the adult public?

Interestingly enough the same question appeared with the introduction of pictures, then with radio. Here are some conclusions of Paul F. Lazarsfeld on this point:

People who listen to news commentators on the radio are also more likely to read news magazines and, in smaller towns, to subscribe to the Sunday edition of metropolitan newspapers.

People who read the more serious type of magazine are also more likely to listen to the more serious type of radio program.

Women who listen a great deal to the radio during the day also listen more during the evening.

Women who are interested in the "true-fiction" type of magazine are also more interested in daytime serials and prefer the romantic type of movies.

People who never go to the movies at all are also likely to listen less to the radio.

If a book has been turned into a movie the people who have read the book are more likely to see the movie and vice versa.[15]

Daniel D. Mich, in a speech before the Magazine Editors and Educators Conference in Washington, D.C., on May 11, 1955, noted the following findings of a recent study of audiences of nine major magazines; namely, *Collier's, Life, Look,* and the *Saturday Evening Post* in the general weekly field, and *Better Homes and Gardens, Good Housekeeping, Ladies' Home Journal, McCall's,* and *Woman's Home Companion:*

The study, made over a period of four months, showed that on an average-issue basis the nine magazines reached a total audience of 58,700,000 *different* people 10 years of age and older. Of these 58,700,000 readers, the study showed that 40,050,000 live in television homes as against 18,650,000 in nontelevision homes. A total of 35,250,000 read more than one of the nine magazines and 5,000,000 read at least four of the nine magazines. In all cases the survey showed that magazine reading in television homes is *more prevalent than in nontelevision homes.* For instance, 23,450,000 read one or another of the nine magazines; and of these 15,800,000 live in television homes, as against 7,650,000 in nontelevision homes. Of the 200,000 people who read all nine of the maga-

15. Paul F. Lazarsfeld, "Communication Research" in *Current Trends in Social Psychology,* pp. 233-48. Pittsburgh: University of Pittsburgh Press, 1949.

zines, 150,000 live in television homes—three times the number who live
in nontelevision homes. This ought to take care of the myth that television is destroying magazine reading—at least at any age level above
ten. And, I should point out again, this study dealt with only nine magazines. There are some 7,000-odd more being published, and the total
circulation of American magazines approaches the 200 million mark.[16]

A study of open-country families in Lancaster and Lebanon
counties in Pennsylvania showed that, for most television owners,
television had little effect on newspaper reading and attendance at
meetings, but many did reduce the time devoted to radio listening
because of television.[17]

Integrating Reading and Other Media

It is likely that television will take away radio listeners and readers who wish light entertainment. It will compete with adult comics;
with the pulp magazines; with sex crime and sensationalism in the
press; and with sexy, sadistic, paper-back books. There is no reason
to believe that serious reading will suffer from competition with
television. Indeed, whatever loss there may be is likely to be com-
pensated for by new audiences which serious television programming can develop for serious reading. If serious ideas are presented
captivatingly in films, radio, or television, they will make serious
reading more attractive.

Sometimes this joining of forces will be carefully planned. There
will be film, radio, and TV programs which are integrated with
reading. The programs of the Fund for Adult Education are an
example. (See chap. vii, pp. 174-75.) These programs typically include ten sessions and make use of varied media. Several series include as part of the program a 30-minute recording, e.g., "Ways
of Mankind" and "The Jeffersonian Heritage." Others make use of
films such as the series, "Great Men, Great Issues," and "World
Affairs Are Your Affairs." Essays are prepared to go with the
integrated unit. The "American Heritage" program of the American
Library Association combines the showing of films with the reading
of books.

16. Daniel D. Mich, quoted from report of speech given.

17. *Extension Television in Lancaster and Lebanon Counties, Pennsylvania.*
United States Department of Agriculture, Extension Service Circular 496,
April, 1955. Washington: Government Printing Office, 1955.

Sometimes the integrating of media will be less directly planned but just as real. We may expect that persons who seek serious ideas in one medium will be attracted to serious ideas in other media. It seems reasonable to conclude, therefore, that, if there is serious program content in radio, films, and television, it will influence consumers to read serious materials.

Is it possible that television, films, comics, and radio are reducing children's reading so that they are not maturing in their reading skills? Are their reading abilities and tastes geared chiefly to an easy, entertainment approach to reading? The answer seems to lie in providing reading materials which will engage their attention and provide for growth in reading. Obviously, there is need here for careful planning between parents, publishers, and librarians.

We need to plan our linking of reading with films and television programs. *Scholastic Magazine,* for example, through its Teen-Age Book Club, sold over 50,000 copies of a special paper-back edition of *The Red Badge of Courage,* an interesting tie-in of a film and a book. The Book Club sold more than 50,000 copies of *Shane* after the film appeared, and, in three months after *Magnificent Obsession* appeared, it had sold more than 40,000 copies.

Warner Brothers released a 20-minute short-subject featuring book jackets. Included were *East of Eden, Giant, Moby Dick, The Silver Chalice, Battle Cry, King Richard and the Crusaders* (from Scott's *Talisman*), and *The Spirit of St. Louis.* Librarians often publicize books such as these when the film versions are being shown in their city.

Librarians are also concerning themselves with materials other than books and pamphlets. A modern library will have available flat pictures and exhibits, recordings, and, more recently, 16-mm. films. The American Library Association, through a grant of $175,000 from the Carnegie Corporation, has made a two-year study of how existing libraries were serving American communities and the relationship of the library to new technical developments in communication.

The Cleveland Public Library, for example, has seen television not as a competitor but as a possible co-operator. The staff is alert in recognizing ways in which reading interest can be promoted by television viewing. Information regarding outstanding future television programs is prominently displayed both in the main lobby and outside in the display windows. They publicized Ed Sullivan's program which carried an excerpt of a new film version of *Moby Dick*. A television interview with Robert Frost and Carl Sandburg resulted in scores of requests for the works of these American poets.

After a television broadcast on Andrew Jackson's life, the library was swamped with requests for Jackson's biography and novels such as *The President's Lady* or *The Gorgeous Hussy*.

An alert library, then, is sensitive to and anticipates television programs likely to stimulate reading. It is ready and able to give specific help on titles which may further a reading interest aroused by the broadcast.

Libraries, as noted in chapter v, are extending their services to adults through films, recordings, and other audio-visual materials. Bernard Berelson reports on the use the public say they would make of these services:

Nearly half the public think that they would attend showings of motion pictures in the library; about one-fifth think they would borrow recordings or films or join study groups; and only one-twentieth think they would make use of meeting rooms in the library. This scale of preference indicates the public's reaction to the major current suggestions of new (nonbook) services to be offered by the public library.

Of the residents of a Michigan county, 18 per cent said they would borrow records from the public library, 14 per cent sheet music, 9 per cent pictures, and 8 per cent films.

But who are the people who would use (or more strictly, who say they would use) these services? Some librarians argue for such extension of services as a means of drawing new people into the library's clientele and thus extending the library's impact upon its community. Would such services attract new clients to the library, or would they be used mainly by the present clientele? On the whole the projected services would be used relatively more by those who at present use the library . . . than by others. Thus, the new services would not so much attract new people to the public library as provide fuller and more satisfactory services to the people who already use the library. Being more culturally alert in general, they would be more likely to extend their use to cover the new as well as the traditional services of the public library. Briefly, the new activities would provide a supplementary service for the library's present clientele.[18]

18. Bernard Berelson, *The Library's Public*, pp. 80-81. New York: Columbia University Press, 1949.

Critical Evaluation

In this chapter we have emphasized the interrelationships of reading with audio-visual materials. We have shown the unique aspects of each medium, how they are psychologically related, ways in which each could re-enforce the other.

A final point should be made about these media. All need to have a common critical judgment applied to them. The teacher of adult classes who is either preparing or selecting materials needs to ask questions such as the following:

First, will they attract attention? Will they be liked? Since adults come voluntarily to our classes, we need attractive and enticing materials. The adult must quickly see the link between what he is reading, seeing, or hearing and his own life interests. Sometimes the attractiveness of materials is increased when various materials are combined. Variety is the spice of education.

Teachers of captive students are likely to forget the importance of attractiveness and liking. As Henry James put it in "The Art of Fiction": "Nothing, of course, will ever take the place of the good old fashion of 'liking' a work of art or not liking it: the most improved criticism will not abolish that primitive, that ultimate test." He adds later: "I am quite at a loss to imagine anything (at any rate in this matter of fiction) that people *ought* to like or to dislike." [19]

Second, can the materials used be understood? A readability formula will help here. But this is only a first step. The reading material may need drawings which illustrate complicated points in the text. The charts and graphs may need simplifying. A film preceding the discussion or reading material may give concrete substance to what follows.

Third, will the teaching materials be believed? Here we face the problem of accuracy and objectivity in the materials we select or prepare. We must also, as noted above, teach adults to judge the credibility of materials, to be critical-minded not sponge-minded. Skilful reading, viewing, and listening means that one must question half-truths, recognize unsound inferences, detect bias.

19. Henry James, "The Art of Fiction" in *America's Literature*, p. 751. Edited by James D. Hart and Clarence Gohdes. New York: Dryden Press, 1955.

It is clear that adults need standards for judging the popular arts. If we do not know what we want and get what we want, we shall end up by wanting what we get. Critics can be especially helpful here, but in this country we have inadequate book, film, and television criticism. John Crosby is our only national critic of radio and television. We have only a handful of serious motion-picture critics. The able critic can tell us what he likes and why. We do not need to accept his taste, but it should help us clarify our own.

Teachers in classrooms are likely to forget that most of the reading of individuals, their viewing of films and television, and their listening to radio is when they are on their own. Children and adults come to "class" with tastes ready-made. Their tastes will reflect the tastes of their homes, the tastes of the mass media with which they are in contact. If adult education fulfils its promise, the school can then help improve tastes brought from the home and not spend its time remedying them.

The tastes of both children and adults can be improved by presenting important ideas in all the media—print, television, radio, and motion pictures. The real competition, therefore, is not between reading and broadcasting or films. It is rather a competition between entertainment and education as presented in all media. The teacher of adults must, therefore, search for ways in which all mass media can be used co-operatively for educational purposes.

CHAPTER V

The Role of the Public Library in Adult Reading[1]

GRACE T. STEVENSON

Early Motivation

The free public library is not unique to the United States, but it is here that it had its earliest beginnings and its greatest development. In 1852 the first annual report of the Boston Public Library had this to say:

It has been rightly judged that . . . under political, social, and religious institutions like ours . . . it is of paramount importance that the means of general information should be so diffused that the largest number of persons should be induced to read and understand questions going down to the very foundations of the social order, which are constantly presenting themselves, and which we, as a people, are constantly required to decide, either ignorantly or wisely.[2]

The great industrial expansion of the nineteenth century and the growth of popular education resulted in a demand for more books available to all, and the public library became the institution for the continuing education of all men. Public libraries had their early beginnings in the parish libraries of Maryland and North

---

1. The author is indebted to the following librarians for help in the preparation of this chapter: Dorothy Bendix, Detroit Public Library; Florence Craig, Cuyahoga County Public Library (Cleveland); Essae M. Culver, Louisiana State Library; Jerome Cushman, Salina (Kansas) Public Library; Leona Durkes, New York Public Library; Sigrid Edge, Simmons College School of Library Service; Edith Foster, West Georgia Regional Library (Carrollton); Ida Goshkin, Akron Public Library; Richard Hart, Enoch Pratt Free Library (Baltimore); Muriel Javelin, Boston Public Library; Fern Long, Cleveland Public Library; Margaret Monroe, Rutgers University School of Library Service; Miriam Putnam, Memorial Hall Library (Andover, Massachusetts); Eleanor Smith, Brooklyn Public Library; Mildred Stibitz, Dayton Public Library; Gertrude Thurow, LaCrosse (Wisconsin) Public Library; Ruth Warncke, Director, Library-Community Project, American Library Association Headquarters.

2. Boston Public Library, *Annual Report of the Trustees, 1852,* p. 15.

Carolina in the late seventeenth century. Later came the town libraries of New England. Early libraries were usually subscription or association libraries; mercantile or mechanics libraries founded by business houses or associations of working men to provide reading for employees. Some of these still exist. The really progressive free library became possible when Massachusetts, leading the way for other states, gave legal sanction to the expenditure of public funds for the establishment and maintenance of public libraries.

[Since that time] the public library in the United States is taken for granted. Predominantly local in character, both in support and management, it is deeply rooted in our national heritage. The community's library stands for much that is cherished in our tradition of equal educational opportunity and freedom of thought and communication. It takes its place along with the courthouse, the school, the church, and the town hall as an integral part of the American scene.[3]

Influence of the American Library Association

The founding of the American Library Association in 1876 was a milestone in the development of library service. The Association's purpose has always been to increase the use and usefulness of books. It has been responsible for developing methods and establishing standards that have made American library administration foremost in the world. These administrative philosophies and techniques have only one purpose—to make reading desirable. The simplification of classification and cataloguing, the open shelf, departmentalization, branch libraries, bookmobiles, readers' advisers, and the more recent discussion programs, book talks, and film and recordings programs are all designed to stimulate the desire for reading in all kinds of people and to make books easily available.

The A.L.A. has been responsible for several projects of some consequence which are directly related to the stimulation and improvement of reading. In 1925 it launched the "Reading with a Purpose" series. These were carefully chosen, well-annotated subject lists with an introductory essay by an expert in the field. The lists covered sixty-seven subjects when publication was discontinued in 1933, at which time approximately 850,000 copies had been sold.

3. Robert D. Leigh, *The Public Library in the United States*, p. vii. New York: Columbia University Press, 1950.

An A.L.A. committee has also spent considerable time in discovering and listing readable books. In 1926 A.L.A. and the American Association of Adult Education, with the help of a Carnegie grant, undertook a study which resulted in the book, *The Reading Interests and Habits of Adults*,[4] and the later publication, *"What People Want to Read About*.[5] In 1935 A.L.A. joined forces with A.A.A.E. in establishing at Teachers College, Columbia University, an advisory bureau on readability to experiment in writing, editing, and analyzing readable material with a view to aiding interested writers and publishers.

Procedures of the Local Public Library

The American Library Association has provided leadership and professional guidance at the national level, but it has been through the work done by hundreds of local libraries "that the largest number of persons [have been] induced to read." The local public library is an autonomous institution, governed locally, and while this sometimes results in weaknesses of financing, administration, and personnel, it also permits the unhampered development of imagination, originality, and the ingenuity required to make bricks without straw.

The role which the local library plays in adult reading is conditioned by the philosophy underlying its entire service. Its conception of the total role the library should play in the community does much to establish what the library does in reader guidance. A library which sees its role as that of "stimulator" will view its responsibilities differently from one which sees its responsibilty as ending with serving the highly motivated library-user with articulate needs which can be rather easily met. This stimulation can take place at all levels and in all types of libraries. It may affect the child to whom the wonders of the printed page have just been revealed; the mature adult broadening his cultural appreciation or intensify-

4. W. S. Gray and Ruth Munroe, *The Reading Interests and Habits of Adults.* New York: Macmillan Co., 1929.

5. Douglas Waples and Ralph W. Tyler, *What People Want To Read About.* Chicago: American Library Association and the University of Chicago Press, 1931.

ing his knowledge; or the student, who, mental curiosity thoroughly aroused, is launched on a lifetime of intellectual growth through reading.

Basic to the achievement of this role is that heart of all library service—the book collection. Most libraries now make use of a variety of information media; maps, pictures, slides, films, tapes, and recordings, but books are the basis of the materials collections. Book selection is one of the areas given the greatest emphasis in training for librarianship, and the practicing librarian regards it as his most important job. The collection must meet two kinds of needs of the community, those which are expressed, and those which are basic and universal whether expressed or not. The books which meet expressed needs are borrowed and read whether or not the library provides any encouragement. The librarian must also spend money for those books which meet a basic universal need, but in which his patrons may have expressed little interest. If he does not buy them, he has killed at its source the library's part in the possible development of the skilled and discriminating reader.

The library's book collection should foster in the individual knowledge, understanding, critical appreciation, and awareness of the world in which he lives. It must take into consideration the wide variation in reading levels and reading interests and must be based on the needs of the entire community, as well as those of the individuals and groups which make up the community. In the case of controversial questions, books presenting a variety and balance of opinion should be sought. Budget, space, and the quality of available productions make it necessary that there shall be selected a limited number of titles from the mass of books published each year. This poses the library's perennial problem—the necessity for curtailing the quantity purchase of books in demand in order to have more of those the public seemingly finds unacceptable. The decision must be based on the library's goal. If the library accepts its role as an institution deeply concerned with the education of adults, a clear basis for decision becomes apparent. A primary goal in book selection is to build a collection suited to the character of the community which it serves, including only those books which have a positive reason for being included. The maintenance of a book collection is as important as its acquisition. If a collection is to be a live and useful resource in the community, out-of-date material must be promptly discarded.

The responsibility for book selection is generally shared by a number of members of the library staff and sometimes members of the library's board of trustees also. Many of the larger libraries receive a wide selection of the publishers' output on approval for examination by the staff. In the Brooklyn Public Library, for instance, the book-ordering department maintains standing orders for all publications of many major publishing houses and checks constantly and carefully all available publishers' lists. These "on approval" volumes are reviewed by staff members as they are received and, from the wide assortment recommended, branch librarians and chiefs of subject divisions select the books to be purchased for their agencies. Librarians usually encourage their readers to make individual requests and recommendations for purchase.

It is not enough for a library to acquire a good book collection. That collection must be so organized that it is readily available and attractive to the reader, bringing to his attention the new or the unusual, encouraging him to browse. This is effected first by assigning classification numbers which bring together on the shelves the books on any given subject. There are a number of classification systems, but the one commonly used in public libraries of the United States is the Dewey Decimal, devised by Melvil Dewey, a pioneer American librarian. This system, which has been revised and kept up to date, groups books in a logical subject order and meets demands for information; but it is not so closely related to the educational needs of the public, which range in areas of broad living relationships. The parent, looking for books on child care, may also be interested in home decoration, gardening, or household budgeting. In recent years some libraries have initiated a "Reader Interest Classification" in order to bring together books as a technique in reading guidance.[6] Bringing books together in smaller subject departments and giving the reader access to the open shelf were innovations pioneered by American librarians as recently as fifty to seventy-five years ago. The open shelf was a radical change

6. Detroit Public Library, "The Reader Interest Classification," 1952 (mimeographed).

in its day and is still comparatively rare in European libraries. The simplicity and utility of these physical arrangements, plus a public catalogue constructed with the same end in view, can materially affect the reader's use of the book collection.

Librarians have developed many other ways of stimulating reading. The commonest of these is the book display. These range all the way from a few dust jackets pinned to a bulletin board or a special shelf labelled "New Books" to elaborate displays of books and other materials (often valuable materials which have been loaned) in specially constructed cases. A number of larger libraries employ personnel who devote their time to displays and employ all the latest devices.

The Free Library of Philadelphia has extensive display cases in its large foyer where the exhibition of unusual books, pictures, manuscripts, and other materials not only enhances the library's appearance but draws the reader's attention to items that may lead him to further reading. The New York Public Library is famous for its displays of materials from notable collections such as the Schomburg Collection on the Negro and a recent display on baseball memorabilia. But well-planned and meaningful displays are possible in the small library, also. The new peg boards and various types of display letters make possible attractive displays everywhere to catch the reader's attention. Memorial Hall Library, Andover, Massachusetts, reports a considerable circulation of older books from a shelf simply marked "You Always Meant To Read Them." The librarian in Salina, Kansas, maintains displays on four large peg boards, changing two of them every week. He gets display ideas from weekly magazines, government documents, the newspapers and other sources, even including the Pogo comic strip.

Displays introduce the reader to materials, add color and an air of informality, and can tie the library in with other community activities. Displays arranged in other parts of the community may have the additional advantage of being seen by people not familiar with the library. Displays of related books at the scene of other community activities serve the dual purpose of calling attention to books on the subject at the time when people are interested and of complementing the work of the groups involved.

The old attitude that it was the business of the library to deal only with that part of the community which came to it voluntarily has altered in the last generation. In 1929 Bostwick wrote:

The modern public library believes that it should find a reader for every book on its shelves and provide a book for every reader in its community, and that it should in all cases bring book and reader together. This emphasis on the reader as well as on the book—this recognition of persons as well as things, as part of the material to be dealt with by the library—may be described as a process of socialization.[7]

The modern librarian uses every means at his disposal to bring book and reader together. Next to the display, book lists are the commonest means used. These cover all subject fields and may vary from one sheet badly mimeographed to handsome two- and three-color brochures on fine paper with well-designed lay-out and type.

Some large libraries issue regular publications calling attention to their new books with a brief synopsis. Some of these well-known lists are general in nature, such as Chicago Public Library's "Book Bulletin," Cincinnati Public Library's "Guide Post," and Cleveland Public Library's "Open Shelf." Other libraries are noted for their specialized lists. Newark Public Library, which has an outstanding business department, publishes "Business Literature," and among the publications of the New York Public Library is their "New Technical Books." These are all professionally printed lists, but an effective list for a particular purpose can be done with the mimeograph machine, for example, the five small folders prepared by the Richard B. Harrison Library in Raleigh, North Carolina, for a series of discussions in the library on "Building a Better Home Town."

Most libraries prepare lists for special occasions or for specific subject fields of particular interest to their communities at that time. The Mississippi Economic Council, promoting a state-wide community development program, issued a comprehensive community guide for the use of community leaders. The Mississippi Library Commission, working with the Economic Council, using the same format and subject divisions, issued a carefully selected list of books, pamphlets, films, and slides. The Public Libraries Divi-

7. Arthur E. Bostwick, *The American Public Library*, pp. 1-2. Chicago: American Library Assn., 1929.

sion of A.L.A. prepares annually a list of notable books published during the preceding year, which thousands of readers watch for. A more personal approach to the individual is achieved by many libraries which keep a file of their readers' interests, and when a book is purchased that the librarian thinks will be of interest to a particular reader he is notified that it is available.

One of the most effective ways to interest people in books is by word of mouth. This is done in many ways: by counseling with the individual reader, by talks about books to groups and organizations either in or out of the library, by the use of radio and television. A real test of one of the qualities of a good librarian is the ability to communicate to the possible reader the value, the interest, and the magic quality of a book. To do it successfully is one of the profession's most satisfying experiences. The survey, "Adult Education Activities in Public Libraries," [8] brought out that 67 per cent of the public libraries provided book talks and 20 per cent conducted radio programs which are directly or indirectly concerned with books. This represents a good deal of time spent in making people book-conscious and is done by libraries of all sizes. Many librarians in smaller towns have established very friendly relations with their local radio stations and newspapers, both of which give fairly freely of time and space for books and for library activities. Many libraries have weekly newspaper book-columns or radio book-talk broadcasts which have gone on for years. The St. Mary's County (Maryland) Memorial Library presents over a local radio station a weekly live program of reviews and comments on books and current magazine articles, along with information on local events of cultural and civic interest, and also prepares a weekly book review for the local newspaper. This is just one instance of a practice common to hundreds of libraries all over the country. The Louisville Free Public Library has two FM radio stations which are on the air a good many hours daily.[9] Through a leased-wire network, it broadcasts educational and musical programs into forty city-wide outlets.

8. Helen Lyman Smith, "Adult Education Activities in Public Libraries," p. 17. Chicago: American Library Assn., 1954.

9. William Manchester, "Louisville Cashes in on Culture," *Harper's Magazine*, CCXI (August, 1955), 77-83.

Librarians are learning that with the coming of television, as with the increased use of other audio-visual media, the reading of books has increased, and they are also experimenting with television as a direct stimulant to reading.[10] This is not widespread. There are still many areas where there is no television, and even those libraries to which public service time is available do not always have a staff trained for this work, nor are they able to give to it the considerable amount of time and effort necessary.

Library television programs are all aimed at encouraging the viewer to make more and better use of his library. It may be a direct book program, such as that offered by the Seattle Public Library where each week four different people from the community discuss a current book of interest, a program so successful that it has been given a choice Sunday afternoon time on a commercial station. The University of Illinois Library and Library School in co-operation with the University's Television–Motion Picture Unit presented a thirteen-week series showing the resources of the libraries in the state.[11] The Cleveland Public Library presented a series called "Views and Reviews" which developed subjects and events within the framework of books and the library's collections.[12] Boston Public Library brought the cameras right into the library and televised their book services in operation. The Detroit Public Library, one of the institutions that played a major part in making the Detroit educational television station a reality, in co-operation with suburban libraries, was telecasting five and one-half hours weekly over that station in 1955.

Even the smaller libraries, in those cities and towns where there is a television station, make use of it to call attention to books and reading. In Alexandria, Louisiana, the Rapides Parish Library sponsors a program on which prominent local people discuss a current book, often a controversial one, before the TV cameras. Some

10. "Television—How Public Libraries Use It," *PLD Reporter* (American Library Assn.), February, 1955.

11. C. Walter Stone, "Libraries on TV at Urbana and Albuquerque," *Library Journal*, LXXIX (April 1, 1954), 592-97.

12. L. Quincy Mumford, "Libraries in Educational Television," *A.L.A. Bulletin*, XLIX (February, 1953), 59 ff.

libraries bring their services to the attention of televiewers by co-operating with other local institutions, such as the local art museum, in the presentation of their programs.

There is no assessing accurately how much influence all these activities have in persuading people to read. Sometimes the mention of a book through one of these avenues will cause a run on a title—sometimes not. But how often people may look for the book without finding it on the shelf, how often they get it elsewhere, is impossible to discover. These are all publicity and public relations devices—educational to be sure—directed at the general reader to help him see his public library as an interesting, informal, friendly place where books to suit his special interests may be had free of charge.

Individual Reader Guidance

Given the best book stock available, convenient arrangement, superb displays, and ample publicity, the library is still playing only a passive role in the development of adult reading if it does not have a dynamic program of reader guidance. This program involves primarily a person-to-person, librarian-to-reader relationship, which in the final analysis is the library's most potent contribution to reader development. Any librarian, and many satisfied borrowers, will tell you that every library has an active, continuing program of reader guidance, and this is true. But libraries have only scratched the surface of their potentialities in this important area of service.

Personalized help for readers was given impetus during the 1920's by the creation of the position of readers' adviser in a number of American libraries. This seemed the answer to a long-felt and much-discussed problem, that of the adult whose need for materials and information could not be met by the limited assistance provided at busy service desks. The ideal of the readers' adviser was an informed and sympathetic approach to the individual's needs in the areas of education, information, and recreation, with the emphasis upon education. The group of library-users most urgently in need of service of this kind were those on the middle and lower levels of education and privilege. In many libraries this type of service was often a continuing aid to the reader seeking self-development.

Readers applying to the readers' adviser were interviewed and their educational background, interests, and reading needs ascertained. Individual reading lists were then prepared for them and the books held in proper sequence. Records were kept of each person's reading, and the frequent interviews made it possible to alter and adapt the readings according to the reader's progress and desires.

The librarian, in his relationship with the reader, can carry the process of education beyond the stage of book use. He can help in the development of critical reading and independent thinking. When rapport has been established and the reader's interests and needs are understood, the librarian can suggest materials of gradually increasing complexity. He can suggest related materials for enrichment and extension of understanding. He can introduce to the reader materials with varying points of view of equal validity. He can share his knowledge of the process of locating materials to intensify or extend knowledge of a subject.

The West Georgia Regional Library (Carrollton, Georgia) sponsors in the senior high schools a student library association as an effective means of acquainting young adults with a wide range of reading associated with class assignments. This association has not only broadened the reading interests of the students but has also accustomed their parents and their parents' friends to seek reader guidance.

In a small library all the professional staff take part in reader guidance. To do it successfully requires personality and intelligence and the ability to be at home with both ideas and people. The same traits are required of those giving reader guidance in the large libraries, but here greater resources provide many aids. The Enoch Pratt Free Library in Baltimore has a central office headed by an experienced adult co-ordinator. It is the function of this co-ordinator, working through the subject departments and the branches, to maintain the quality of reader guidance. This is achieved through a program of in-service training, through consultation with supervisors and staff members, with production of needed tools (including a variety of informal reading guides), and through maintaining a balance of emphasis in the various subject fields. These are examples of the two extremes of reader guidance, but they are both directed to the same end, making the nonreader, or the random reader, into a purposeful reader.

Individual guidance is the most expensive service an institution can undertake. As the availability of this service gradually became known, many readers with more specific needs than general self-development turned to the readers' adviser. Problems concerning vocations, social welfare, and physical and mental health began to multiply, overtaxing the time and energy of the one or two people assigned to the work. It became increasingly necessary to refer readers to the subject departments. With the dispersal of this function among several members of a staff, there was a considerable variation in degree of competence, personal attitude, and time available. The library remains one of the dwindling number of public institutions whose primary services are directed at the individual. The ideal relation between the readers' adviser and the individual can be compared to the difference between classroom teaching and tutorial instruction. If even a pretty good appproximation of this is to be maintained, librarians need more training for it, both formally and through in-service methods. Libraries need larger staffs in order to free professional people from routine jobs. The probability of the average, too-busy librarian having the human relationship skills, the knowledge of materials, and the time to give many individuals adequate guidance is small. In actuality, partial guidance is given to many, and extensive guidance to a few. It is given only to those who seek it, and often, in a busy library, only to those who seek it with a reasonable degree of persistency.

Guidance for Community Groups

One way to reach more people with encouragement and guidance in reading is to carry the guidance function to already organized groups. A librarian approaches such a group with the assurance that they have a common interest, of varying intensity, in a single subject area. The nature of a group gives him opportunity to use additional materials such as films, recordings, maps, and so forth, to their best advantage. Library services to groups have developed in two ways: taking library services to community groups (clubs, organizations, business, industry), and bringing people to the library in groups. All group work done by the library has as its central objective the more effective use of books—more reading, more critical reading.

There is a close relationship between advisory activities within the library and the development of a broad program of service to institutions, organizations, and informal groups throughout the community. In many libraries the genesis of service to groups has been the provision of information and guidance to group representatives who are themselves habitual users of the library. If there is a point at which a library may be said to have embarked upon a program of group service, it is that point at which the library staff formulates plans for surveying those community activities in which library participation will be fruitful and for making contact with local organizations through their representatives.

Such an effort has as its first requirement an over-all knowledge of the community on the part of the librarian. In a large or medium-sized city, the fields of interest to be considered include labor and management; family welfare; groups oriented by age level, such as older men and women or young adults; men's and women's clubs; organizations, institutions, and informal groups concerned with public affairs, education, science, or the arts. Most of these are duplicated at the rural or semirural level, where we can also add the farm groups. It is obvious that no library can meet all of these needs and that a choice must be made as to where the library's limited resources can best be directed. Areas most commonly served in a library-group co-operation are: parent education and family welfare; juvenile delinquency; community planning and development; world affairs; fine arts; film- and book-discussion groups.

The assistance given to these groups can be as varied and as numerous as the groups themselves and as the libraries which serve them. The library's services are directed toward co-operating with the group in planning a program that is pertinent, meaningful, sound in content, and interestingly presented. Many libraries present an annual program-planners institute, giving many community organizations the basic fundamentals of good programming, including information on local resources, materials, and techniques. The Battle Creek (Michigan) Public Library was one of the first to develop this service which is now offered by many libraries in the country. The Detroit Public Library cosponsors an institute annually which draws several hundred people. In such institutes, emphasis is always put on more and better use of materials, books, pamphlets, periodicals, and all other media. The institutes are usually demonstrations, using several techniques of presentation, lecture, discussion, panel, films, with descriptions of the techniques and suggestions of situations in which they would be suitable. Program planners' institutes are as valuable in small-town and rural libraries as they are in the big city. Successful institutes have been held in areas as diverse from the Detroit pattern as the Cuyahoga County (Ohio) Public Library and the public library of Artesia, New Mexico (population 10,000). The follow-up on this activity is planning the separate programs with the disparate groups. The survey, "Adult-Education Activities in Libraries" indicated that more than 65 per cent of the libraries give advice in program-planning and 58 per cent participate in planning.[13]

The Akron (Oho) Public Library is a good example of how a program-planning service is handled. The program chairman is encouraged to come in with a committee to consult the librarian who is located in a central spot in the library. The librarian discusses with the committee the kind of group they are planning for, their specific interests, what kind of programs have been most successful, and those least successful. On the basis of this information, suggestions are made regarding possible subjects, methods of presentation, available speakers, films, or books and pamphlets that will help the group in building a program. Pamphlets on program-planning and subject guides are available for the committee to examine. After making these suggestions, the librarian leaves the committee to decide upon their own program. The primary purpose is not to plan programs for the committee but to help the committee analyze previous programs, point out ways of making programs meaningful to the group, and encourage them to plan more stimulating and thought-provoking programs.

Because the library serves so many and such varied community groups, it has the advantage of an overview and a perspective not available to all agencies. This sometimes enables it to see unmet community needs which others have not perceived, or at least needs

13. Helen Lyman Smith, *op. cit.*, p. 17.

which are not being filled. If these fall within the scope of the library's competency, the librarian may ask some other institution in a related field in the community to join with the library in presenting a program or series of programs on the subject. Libraries have done this most often and most successfully in the fields of family relations and child care, juvenile delinquency and mental health. There are many individuals and groups to whom these are pressing problems, and, if the library will provide program skills, materials, and possibly physical facilities, other appropriate local institutions will lend their considerable professional skills.

The Cincinnati Public Library has for several years worked closely with psychologists, psychiatrists, and local organizations such as parent-teacher associations and the Mental Hygiene Society in building a collection of films and other materials in the field of child development and mental health. Films being considered for purchase are screened by these people, and their advice is a factor in purchase. These materials are used for programs in the library, for programs of other institutions and organizations in the community, and for programs cosponsored by the library and these other groups. The Medford (Massachusetts) Public Library in 1954 cosponsored a series of lecture-discussions on world affairs with the Fletcher School of Law and Diplomacy which attracts faculty and students from all over the world.

If the library should decide to present its own program in any field, it is again likely to make use of community talent. There is hardly a community that does not have some resource in its people; distinguished citizens, competent professional and business people, writers, artists, social workers, all of whom are frequently pleased and proud to be asked to be on a program for the library. When the Jackson (Tennessee) Free Library was planning the Civic Affairs Forum,[14] for which it received a grant of funds from A.L.A., members of the staff worked with an advisory committee made up of the library trustees, the mayor and two city commissioners, executive secretary of the Chamber of Commerce, newspaper editor,

14. Gretchen Conduitte and S. F. Smith. "Civic Affairs Forum, Jackson Free Library." Nashville: Tennessee State Library and Archives, 1955 (mimeographed).

manager of the radio station, county judge, county agricultural agent, president of the League of Women Voters, a Farm Bureau leader, and city and county school superintendents. Senator Kefauver opened the series with a discussion of "Industrial Trends in the South." The Boston Public Library, in co-operation with the National Conference of Christians and Jews, presented a ten-week training institute in practical human relations for leaders of community organizations. Two staff members from the Institute of Human Relations of Boston University worked constantly with the librarian on this program from its inception.

About 40 per cent of the libraries present programs of their own, and they are always built around books and other library materials.[15] Many of these programs not only have considerable variety and ingenuity but they also show perception of community need and have more than a little influence in that community.

In 1953 the Enoch Pratt Free Library in Baltimore presented a series of programs on "Crime and the Citizen." The city had been the scene of an investigation by a special committee of the United States Senate; the incidence of crime had increased, and the citizens were both aroused and alarmed. Experts on several aspects of criminality and justice were asked to take part in the programs which hundreds of people attended. Special lists of printed materials and films were prepared, and though duplicate materials in quantity were ordered they were not sufficient to meet the demand which continued for several months after the programs were over.[16] This is an example of how a library, aware of a community need, fulfils its function by supplying information both through resource people and through books and other materials to enable informed citizens to better solve their problems.

Working with organized groups or library-sponsored groups, within or without the library, is demanding of time and effort. The advantages from an educational point of view are great. Numbers of people who would not seek an educational experience are reached in a situation in which they are somewhat receptive. The nature

15. Helen Lyman Smith, *op. cit.*, p. 17.

16. Marion E. Hawes, "Crime and the Citizen," *ALA Bulletin*, April 1954, p. 221-25.

of the experience encourages some to seek further information by reading, others are encouraged to read, listen, or discuss with more comprehension and discernment.

Library-sponsored Groups

During the past ten years libraries have sponsored an increasing number of book- and film-discussion groups. The majority of Great Books groups meet in libraries, as do World Politics, World Affairs, and many of the groups using the Experimental Discussion Programs of the Fund for Adult Education. Since September, 1951, the American Library Association, with funds provided by the Fund for Adult Education, has sponsored the American Heritage Project discussion groups in 438 libraries.[17] These are groups of fifteen to twenty-five people, with voluntary lay leaders, which meet in public libraries throughout the country to discuss political, social, and economic problems of contemporary American life. Discussions are based on readings from books and pamphlets, or on suitable films. The leaders are trained by the national staff of the Project, but the subjects for discussion and the materials to be used are determined locally.

Discussion groups require the greatest participation of people in the use of books. Here the quality of understanding which each participant brings to the discussion is brought sharply to his own attention. If he has read carelessly or without critical appraisal of the material, the opinions and interpretations of other group members will set him to assessing his own reading skills. Reading two or three selections on one topic helps to develop both critical comparison and skill in the analysis of a writer's prejudices and predispositions and stimulates wider reading on the subject. The wise selection of a book-discussion program to meet the interests and capacities of the local group means that an important and intensive reading-improvement program is under way.

The Improvement of Reading Skills

Libraries have not confined their efforts to developing critical

17. A.L.A. American Heritage Project, *Annual Report, 1953-54.* Chicago: American Library Assn., 1954.

readers. A small number, about 7 per cent, give fundamental reading instruction. About the same number give remedial reading instruction through clinics and classes, by the use of various modern devices for improving reading speed and comprehension.[18]

In the Trenton (New Jersey) Free Public Library a member of the staff aids readers interested in improving their reading skills in the selection of materials to use in connection with tachistoscopes. In the summer of 1955 the Brooklyn Public Library received a grant from the Carnegie Corporation to determine whether or not the public library is the logical place to develop reading-improvement programs for the general public. For three years they will carry on a clinic with the co-operation of the Community Services Division of Brooklyn College. The College will supply the psychologists and reading clinicians, and a librarian will guide the patron's increasing level of reading. During the last two years of the experiment the operation will be entirely a library activity, during which time they hope to demonstrate that the average person can be assisted by the use of mechanical devices if such use is tied with a personal service from the library staff. Brooklyn College will be responsible for the research and evaluation studies of the complete five-year program.

The Cuyahoga County (Ohio) Public Library has endeavored to increase reading skill and to improve critical and cultural understanding through reading aloud. This has been done with members of informal discussion groups and with the Central School of Practical Nursing in Cleveland. A part of the curriculum at this school is the care of the convalescent. In connection with this a librarian gives instruction to improve reading aloud to patients.

The Adult-Education Movement

The Library-Community Project initiated by the American Library Association in September, 1955, with funds from the Fund for Adult Education, is an expression of the philosophy that it is the function of the modern public library to assume a responsibility for the continuing education of our citizens; that its role is to provide for a well-rounded collection of materials through good organi-

18. Helen Lyman Smith, *op. cit.*, p. 17.

zation, administration, and physical facilities, and for reader guidance, group activities, and other services suited to the particular situation. The project has made subgrants to the extension agencies of state libraries in Kansas, Maryland, Michigan, and Tennessee. Working with one pilot library in each state, the project will attempt to demonstrate what can be accomplished to make more readers and better readers through a sound adult-education program, well integrated into the total library administration and tailored to that community.

How is the librarian trained for all of this? The professional librarian today must have a college education and must have completed the professional curriculum offered by a library school. With a few exceptions, this professional curriculum leads to a Master's degree. Library schools are trying to meet the need for personnel for this work partly through their recruiting program, attempting to attract well-rounded, outgoing personalities, interested in people as well as books. The present Master of Science programs are attracting more mature students, often with subject specialties which make them valuable in this field.

In the professional curriculum program less time is given to teaching techniques. There is more concern with the "why" and with ways to meet the needs of various types of readers. Greater stress is laid on the service aspect of librarianship, particularly the educational purpose of the public library and its close relationship to the adult-education movement. There is emphasis on the fact that the library's role in the dissemination of ideas requires skill not only in selecting and supplying materials on all levels but also in stimulating active use of them. These trends can be observed particularly in the courses on communication, publishing, public relations, literature, the library as a social institution, and services to adult readers.

In November, 1954, the A.L.A. Office for Adult Education, with the help of a grant from the National Committee on Study Grants of the Fund for Adult Education, arranged a conference on the "Training Needs of Librarians Doing Adult Education Work." [19]

19. Lester Asheim, *Training Needs of Librarians Doing Adult Education Work*. Report of Allerton Park Conference, November 14-16, 1954. Chicago: American Library Assn., 1955.

The conference, attended by about thirty-five administrators of libraries, library schools, and university adult-education departments, was devoted to a consideration of methods of promoting the establishment of more extensive training in attitudes, methods, and skills of adult education by exploring the establishment of sound training situations for academic study, field work, and in-service training. Better training in these attitudes and techniques should result in purposefully planned activities to better stimulate and serve the readers' interests. The director of the Simmons College School of Library Science notes the recent trends in education for librarianship thus:

> The disappearance of the specialized program in favor of the general program follows naturally from the increasing tendency in library education to minimize the techniques and skills in favor of a more philosophical and theoretical approach to librarianship and the disciplines to which it is basically related, and upon which it depends.[20]

A few of the larger libraries have in-service training programs which include service to adult readers. In most libraries book selection is a joint endeavor shared by many members of the staff and is in itself a training program. The Brooklyn Public Library has formally instituted a rounded in-service training program which, since employees so trained sometimes accept positions elsewhere, the chief librarian feels "has been able to assist in the development of the profession generally by giving these people a sounder training than they could obtain under most of the better-known methods." [21]

Various units of A.L.A., such as the Adult Education Board and Adult Education Section of the Public Libraries Division, have held institutes and worshops in this field at times, as have state and regional associations. These are usually in connection with national or local conferences. A few such institutes have been presented by library schools, such as the one given by the Graduate Library School at Rutgers University in June, 1955, and the Department of Library Science, University of Michigan, in August, 1955. Some

20. Kenneth R. Shaffer, "Personnel and the Library School," *Library Trends*, III (July, 1954), 13-21.

21. Francis R. St. John, "Selection, Orientation, and Development of the Professional Staff," *Library Trends*, III (July, 1954), 32-38.

state library extension agencies hold workshops and training institutes where a portion of time is devoted to service to adult readers. The Wisconsin Free Library Commission held a two-week workshop on "Informal Education through Libraries" in August, 1954, which considered the role of the library in adult education in the community and the organization, materials, staff, and techniques necessary to fulfil that role.

The American Library Association Office for Adult Education began in September, 1955, a consultant service in adult education for the libraries of the country. This service will be used chiefly to assist state and regional library associations and state extension agencies to plan state-wide workshops in adult education.

Underlying all library efforts to stimulate and improve reading is the belief that two things are important to good citizenship and the good life: one is that adults must be able to read well enough to continually keep themselves informed in the technological and social sciences so important in today's world; the other is that the enjoyment of reading is not only one of life's enduring pleasures but is in itself a powerful motivation to do increasingly difficult reading. Mechanical facility is only one spur toward the making of a good reader; the other is the love of reading. The potentialities for the development of readers through the library are unlimited since it is uniquely fitted to keep the channels of communication open between individual and group; to serve as a center for lifelong education; to serve as a center of carefully chosen materials, book and nonbook, old and new, controversial and experimental. A library can in a real sense be a unifying community force, coordinating community resources and helping to focalize community problems.

But it is in its relationship with the individual reader that the public library makes its greatest contribution to American life. It opens the door of knowledge, of opportunity, of understanding, of beauty to all people regardless of age, race, creed, or economic condition. One of our best known and best loved bits of folklore is the picture of the young Abraham Lincoln, almost without formal schooling, educating himself by means of borrowed books read by firelight. The pages of history, even down to the present, are filled with notable men who were self-educated. A few years ago one of them expressed his gratitude in these words, "When I stand up in meeting to make a few remarks on the Free Public Library of America, the spirit that moves me is that of an old grad who makes psalms to his alma mater. From this institution I received my literary education, and for much of this I still attend the library." [22]

22. James Stevens, *Door of Opportunity*, p. 1. Seattle: Dogwood Press, 1949.

CHAPTER VI

The Role of the College Library in Adult Reading

ARTHUR T. HAMLIN

College and university libraries are just beginning to meet their important obligation to develop adult readers on campus and in the surrounding community. The neglect of this responsibility had relatively less significance two generations ago when only 4 per cent of the college-age population received any higher education. Now more than a third of the 18-21 age group attend college, and the figure may rise to 50 per cent in the next fifteen years.[1] While reading habits are first formed in the home and the school, the college has an opportunity to awaken worth-while interests and to accustom its young adults to the feeding of these interests through the regular and independent use of books.

Students, Faculties, Librarians, and Their Books

It must be emphasized that the college or university library is the book-center of the institution, and its achievements are as much the responsibility of the teaching faculty as of the library staff. While the librarian is responsible for administration, and the library staff is in charge of operation, their efforts are only half successful unless buttressed by regular, purposeful, faculty-student contact among the books. This contact with faculty inevitably produces in the student a stimulation of interest and provides the guidance in selection and help in the use of material so important for his reading development. The library can never justify its claim to operation as "the laboratory of the mind" until it becomes the daily meeting place of student, faculty, and librarian on a basis of common intellectual purpose.

1. Ronald B. Thompson and Thomas Crane, *The Impending Tidal Wave of Students.* Report of the Committee on Special Projects, American Association of Collegiate Registrars and Admissions Officers, October, 1954 (pamphlet).

There are a few examples of college libraries which have small library staffs and yet operate successfully because the faculty members use the library daily and are extremely conscientious in guiding students in their use of the bookstacks and reference tools. Haverford College, for example, has an enviable collection of nearly two hundred thousand volumes. The budget for library staff is modest, and the faculty takes a personal interest in the building of book collections and their use. The important Quaker collection owes much to the personal interest of Rufus Jones, Douglas Steere, and others of the teaching staff. Classes are small at Haverford, and many of the courses are so conducted that the student must choose his books and dig up his own information. There is no reference department; therefore, the chief guidance in the use of the collections must come from the faculty. The library is the faculty workshop as well as the daily student workshop. In such a situation the role of library staff can, with some justification, be limited largely to the more routine operations of ordering, classifying, binding, shelving, keeping loan records, and similar tasks. A Haverford alumnus asserted recently, doubtless with considerable exaggeration, "the faculty *is* the library staff."

Occasionally librarians must undertake to develop and guide student reading interests, without much help from the teaching staff, within the four walls of the library building. Many professors are hard pressed by heavy teaching schedules and outside interests. Use of the library, if any, is made principally through messenger service and assistants. A professor at a large university was questioned recently as to why he visited the library so little. "Oh," he replied, "I don't need to go there any more. I have an assistant to take care of all of that."

Fortunately, most institutions have a liberal number of professors who put in half their work day among the bookstacks. Some are intent on their own immediate needs, but others have a word and smile for every student and are never too busy to be interrupted. A few are adept at winning young friends, probing for interests, and awakening their enthusiasms. They cajole, mock, sympathize and stir young minds, suggest reading at one moment and advise on personal problems the next. The writer's own undergraduate reading was influenced most by an English professor with whom the only contact was an occasional campus chat and many short encounters in the library. Nearly all institutions have some such, and fortunate the college which has many. The library staff which must develop students into adult readers without such faculty co-operation faces a most difficult task.

The development of students into adult readers can be materially assisted by the very planning of courses of instruction. Some teachers work principally with textbooks and a few required readings. Others are willing to allow students wide range and individual selection of study material. The student who faces and masters the problems of selecting his study material inevitably becomes interested in and competent to choose materials on topics of personal interest. Most institutions have some courses or reading programs which require a student to choose his own material (with any necessary help), but relatively few colleges emphasize this training in the curriculum.

Historical Background

To understand the present attitude of the American college library in regard to student reading, it is necessary to know something of its historical development. The college library played no appreciable role in student reading before the Civil War. In 1850 the typical collection numbered a few thousand volumes housed in one room and available to students for only several hours a week. Various restrictions throttled the book interests of those students sufficiently interested and alert to appear at the proper time. At Amherst, students had to apply to the librarian to consult any books, even those that lay before them on a table. A fee was charged for each volume withdrawn. At Yale only Juniors and Seniors could use the library at all. Another college reported: "Books are sometimes lent out to be read; but the practice is discountenanced at present on account of former abuse of the privilege." [2] Collections were strong in theology and the classics and contained little or no current literature.

The college student of this period was instructed in a very

2. W. N. Chattin Carlton, "College Libraries in Mid-nineteenth Century," *Library Journal*, XXXII (November, 1907), 479-86.

literal sense by the faculty, and his tools were a few textbooks. Only the very unusual minds had sufficient direction and sense of need to make such good use of the college library as did Ralph Waldo Emerson. The nineteenth-century substitute for the undergraduate library was the collection of books maintained by literary societies. In those days of small student bodies the faculty undoubtedly gave reading guidance to interested students. But there was little common meeting among books.

The late-nineteenth-century revolution in higher education brought about some recognition of responsibility for the reading needs and interests of all students; but, as a class, college libraries did not keep pace with the rapid development of public libraries.[3] By 1900 the college library was open for student use eight hours or more daily, the collections were reasonably strong in modern literature, and many bookstacks were open to all comers. Attention was given to the volumes required for courses and for reference. Those students who came to the library were relatively free to use its catalogues and collections. The library was often indifferent to student use. Few, if any, special services were provided, and regulations were numerous and unpleasant. Undergraduate reading interests were tolerated but not encouraged. The librarian concentrated his purchasing policies and service program on the needs of the faculty. An occasional voice spoke out on the importance of developing student reading taste and habits, but relatively little real progress was made until after the first World War.

A significant change in college libraries occurred a generation ago when a series of studies probed into many aspects of library service to the student body. It was then recognized that the college library had a definite responsibility to develop general reading interests in students as well as to supply them with the material for instruction. Furthermore, many colleges assumed some responsibility to continue book service to students after graduation. This positive role in the educational process required drastic change in library operation.[4]

3. See W. N. Chattin Carlton, "College Libraries and College Librarians: Views and Comments," *Library Journal*, XXXI (November, 1906), 751-57.

4. Louis R. Wilson, "The Emergence of the College Library," *ALA Bulletin*, XXV (September, 1931), 439-45.

The development of the modern college library as a reading and study center was given great impetus by a series of grants from the Carnegie Corporation. During the period from 1928 to 1943, approximately $2,350,000 was expended on the college libraries of the United States and Canada through a centralized program.[5] This sum does not include considerable sums allotted directly to institutions in answer to special, individual requests. Not only did the Carnegie and other foundation grants help to put a great number of libraries on their feet, so to speak, but this philanthropy stimulated study of the place and function of the college library and gave it wide publicity as a positive educational force. A Carnegie grant financed Harvie Branscomb's *Teaching with Books* (American Library Association, 1940), which is one of the most valuable and widely known studies of the college library.

Library Functions Today

For the last twenty-five years educators have been in general agreement regarding the functions of the college library. It should assist classroom instruction by providing the necessary study and reference material. It should provide the means for the teaching staff to keep up with developments in their fields and, as funds permit, collect source materials necessary for original research. Above and beyond these important functions it is recognized that the library should "encourage students to use books independently as a means to the acquisition of knowledge, not only during the college years but after, and to co-operate with the faculty in developing student interests in general reading." It should likewise "participate in any program of post-collegiate education for alumni . . ." and "co-operate with other libraries in strengthening library resources. . . ."[6] These functions relating to student reading are receiving more and more emphasis as the educational world realizes the critical importance of developing college students into habitual

---

5. William Warner Bishop, *Carnegie Corporation and College Libraries, 1928-1938:* New York: Carnegie Corporation, 1938; and Thomas R. Barcus, *Carnegie Corporation and College Libraries, 1938-1943.* New York: Carnegie Corporation, 1943.

6. Guy R. Lyle, *The Administration of the College Library,* pp. 24-25. New York: H. W. Wilson Co., 1949 (second edition).

and discerning readers with interests much broader than the horizons of their course work. A reading alumni body is the best proof of a good education. The test of the educational process is not the accumulation of data but the awakening and fostering of worthwhile interests. In all this the college library must and does play a central role through its own program and as a meeting place for student and faculty.

The community at large, as well as students and faculty, use the college library. Nearly all college and university libraries welcome any serious reader who comes to their doors. Many libraries will loan books for home use at no charge. A growing number of colleges are giving some publicity to this service. Since relatively few people have need to use the college collection, this service seldom becomes a heavy burden on the institution, and in many cases the returns in gifts of money and books have offset any costs involved. Free library use has come to be recognized as one of the most valuable and inexpensive public services which a college can offer.

The role of the librarian in collegiate education was well stated by Henry M. Wriston:

The librarian, as teacher, stimulates the student to work for himself. He is largely independent of the machinery of courses, credits, hours, and points. . . . His teaching consists not only in making accessible what professors prescribe, but in encouraging the student to go far beyond any prescription save his own ambitious curiosity.

We commonly differentiate intellectual work from recreational reading. For certain purposes and within certain limitations, this distinction has validity. In a larger and more genuine sense, however, recreational reading is often the most truly educational, even the most really intellectual, element in experience with and through books. It may well furnish an intellectual project within which the student establishes his own goals and determines his own significant values. It is the place where his tastes, aptitudes, and skills find freest play. . . . A shrewd and wise person, who knows the student and has the gift for offering stimulating suggestions, makes as direct and profound an impact upon his development as any professor, of whatever degree of distinction.[7]

William Warner Bishop made this same point subjectively when he wrote, "I am convinced that two or three books which I read

7. Henry M. Wriston, "The College Librarian and the Teaching Staff," *ALA Bulletin*, XXIX (April, 1935), 178.

quite casually in college did more to shape my development than the sum of instruction which I received." [8]

The Book Collection

Central to the library's program in developing adult readers is the nature of the book collection. This is a responsibility shared in equal measure by teaching faculty and library staff. Each department of the college normally receives a portion of the library-book budget for purchases in its area. The librarian controls funds for reference books and for certain special needs and often does some book selection in subjects covered by the faculty. In addition, the resourceful librarian sets the tone for selection by the faculty and is alert for opportunities to buy whole collections such as the Michael Sadlier collection of Victorian literature recently acquired by the University of California at Los Angeles.

In the decade following the first World War the Harvard College Library made tremendous progress in building collections largely through the initiative of its director, Archibald Cary Coolidge. Recently, similar leadership has brought a number of unusually fine collections to the universities of Kentucy, Kansas, and Yale and to Trinity College (Hartford). In other instances a member of the faculty has been primarily responsible for progress in this area. Colby College Library owes much of its pre-eminence in some subjects to the enthusiasm and zeal of Professor Carl J. Weber. College libraries with the most modest budgets wax and sometimes wane, so far as the book collection is concerned, in proportion to the vision and resourcefulness of the librarian and his faculty colleagues.

The tree which has been scarred by drought, fire, or severe cold reveals the record of these experiences in its growth rings when it is felled, perhaps centuries later. The rings also reveal periods of greatest growth. In similar fashion, larger libraries often are the unwitting recorders of strength and weakness in various departments of the faculty through the ebb and flow of the book collections in various subjects.

Libraries in predominantly undergraduate institutions vary in size from practically nothing to the 505,000 volumes at Oberlin and

8. Bishop, *op. cit.* p. 43.

the 730,000 volumes at Dartmouth. Many of the older private colleges such as Williams, Mount Holyoke, Vassar, Bowdoin, Hamilton, Bryn Mawr, and Smith have libraries in excess of 200,000 volumes. Generally speaking, these collections are periodically examined for out-dated material and, therefore, represent the current needs of the institutions.

Obviously, such large collections are needed only for the faculty. Undergraduate book needs can be completely supplied with much smaller numbers. In an important study of undergraduate reading, Harvie Branscomb discusses a study of the library needs in five colleges. An examination of the circulation records indicated "that instead of 345,000 volumes, a collection of 25,000 volumes *correctly selected* would have served undergraduate needs for the year of all five colleges, reference material excepted, and 10,000 volumes would have taken care of any one of the colleges. Of the total number of volumes available, only 6.5 per cent were used during the year." [9]

It must be emphasized that no college can maintain a high level of teaching with a collection of books selected only for undergraduate needs. The Dartmouth library justifies its high cost by its contribution to the development of the faculty. In short, the college should provide as extensive a collection for its faculty as funds allow.

Harvard University offers a striking illustration of the difference between faculty and undergraduate library requirements. Although its library is generally acknowledged to be the finest of any university in the world, the Harvard undergraduate had, until recently, relatively poor library facilities. The director of libraries stated in 1947:

A student at Amherst, Williams, Dartmouth, Bowdoin, Oberlin, or or one of the better women's colleges has at his or her disposal a much larger and better collection of books than has the Harvard undergraduate. . . . This central collection (in Widener, the principal part of the University's collection) is so large that it cannot be opened to the undergraduate except under very special circumstances, and as a result there is no large general collection freely accessible to the undergraduate at Harvard—a collection which will include a large share of volumes

9. Harvie Branscomb, *Teaching with Books*, p. 170. Chicago: American Library Association, 1940. The study referred to was made by Harry L. Johnson as an unpublished Master's thesis at the University of Iowa, 1938.

that the student will need in any of his work or in the general reading which is desirable for him to do when in college.[10]

The new Lamont Library now provides the Harvard undergraduate with the finest library facilities. This collection is to be limited to a maximum size of 100,000 volumes, a figure considered more than ample for any undergraduate reading and study needs. When that figure is reached Harvard will continue to buy books in liberal quantity for undergraduate use, but for each volume added an obsolete volume will be withdrawn. It is generally recognized that a figure lower than 100,000 could have been used for optimum, but the lower the figure the greater must be the judgment exercised in the addition and withdrawal process.

There are no universal rules or standard lists to determine what books a college library should provide for its students. Institutions vary widely in objectives, statements of purpose, course offerings, and student interests. These and similar factors determine what books should be available. The recently published catalogue of the Lamont Library [11] is widely used by other institutions as a guide to book selection. Obviously this list does not provide for the religious interests of Boston College (Catholic) or Lake Forest (Presbyterian). It is too heavy in music for institutions which offer few music courses and undoubtedly too light in some subjects for certain other colleges.

Likewise, there is divergence of opinion on the type of books suitable for undergraduates. West Liberty (West Virginia) State College provides a considerable quantity of classics in paper-bound editions because it is believed their students are accustomed to the use of books in this form and will read a classic in paper-bound format which they would not read in the less familiar and formidable hard covers. Several years ago, the University of Delaware library provided little or no literature in paper-bound editions because the librarian believed students should become more familiar with and appreciative of the better printing and artistry of hard-cover books.

10. Keyes D. Metcalf, "The Undergraduate and the Harvard Library, 1937-47," *Harvard Library Bulletin*, I (Autumn, 1947), 288-305.

11. Philip J. McNiff, *Catalog of the Lamont Library*. Cambridge, Massachusetts: Harvard University Press, 1953.

At least one professor of English [12] in a leading university considers that what his students read is not of great importance. Let it be Mickey Spillane and Kathleen Winsor, so long as they are book readers. Taste and discrimination will come. Because of this theory, the University of California (Los Angeles) library undoubtedly contains many titles which would never be accepted on a neighboring campus where light literature finds less favor.

It is clear that standardization in the selection of books for undergraduates is impractical so long as colleges do not become standardized in purpose, teaching program, student background, faculty specialization, and other factors. Such standardization hardly seems suitable for a democratic nation.

Administrative Policies

Faculty and library staff take equal responsibility for the tone of the book collection, but in other matters affecting the reading of the college community their roles are relatively separate and distinct. The librarian as administrator can provide an atmosphere so attractive and congenial that few can resist the temptation to browse. Or he can emphasize rules, multiply fines, create barriers to the books and supervise behavior to the point that only the desperate seeker after knowledge will dare to enter. As the college library has slowly recognized that use of books is more important than their preservation, it has done a great deal to create surroundings congenial to reading and study.

Nearly all educators agree that physical comfort is important in reading. The pursuit of knowledge will never compete in popular appeal with Big Ten football to the point that hard benches, cold, and crowding are matters of small consequence. College libraries have broken away from their traditional furnishings only during the last decade. Most new libraries are equipped with some easy chairs such as would be found in private homes. Surprisingly enough, it costs less to seat a student in a gay, foam rubber easy chair than on hard oak or maple at a reading-room table. Reading-room tables today are smaller, and chair spacing is more generous. Numerous

12. Leon Howard, *Los Angeles Times*, October 11, 1953 [quoted in *College and Research Libraries*, XVI (October, 1955), 397-98].

individual study-tables are provided and carrells are scattered liberally throughout bookstack areas. Air conditioning is installed in many of the new buildings.

Librarians have given special attention to illumination. They have brought lighting experts to their conferences and made many studies of improvements desirable in new buildings and in relighting old quarters. The newer buildings are equipped with a minimum of 30 foot-candles of evenly distributed light in work areas, and some buildings provide 80 or more foot-candles. Special attention has been given to the relationship of walls, floors, and working surfaces to light.

The somber institutional tones of prewar days have given way to attractive interior decoration. When draperies are required, they are cheery and original. Great care is given to the color of upholstered chairs. Recently a large supply house has introduced a line of library tables in pastel colors.

Librarians have been famous for their efficient supervision and their control of noise, but this attitude is now a matter of past history. Sound absorbent ceilings have come in and the "hush" and "silence" signs have disappeared. In general, the large reading-rooms dominated by the supervisor's desk are also in disfavor. These areas are broken up by occasional bookshelves or other visual barriers. The supervisor is still there, but her chief role has been changed from patrol to one of assistance and guidance in the use of materials.

Naturally, these changes have not overtaken all college libraries, but the trend is unmistakable. There is common agreement among librarians on the importance of comfort to reading and study. A majority of college libraries have made important physical improvements in the past decade. In another ten years, nearly all should be largely transformed by these new concepts.

Of equal importance to physical comfort is a sense of freedom and acceptance in the library. In the past, college administrators as well as librarians have emphasized the "book-keeper" function as the most important responsibility. In his desire to be a good steward of college property, the librarian had developed the watchdog function to the detriment of reading interests. Consequently, he established elaborate rules requiring tedious identification when borrowing books, blocked off student access to most or all of the material, set up elaborate schedules of fines for sundry offenses, and in a score of ways introduced a regimentation and air of suspicion that has been a decided damper on the reading interests of generations of students.

Change has come more slowly in this area. Some control is obviously necessary. The income from fines is attractive to the budget-starved administrator. It is always tempting to solve a vexing problem by the expedient of a new rule. While nearly all small libraries have had stacks open for the use of all students, those of the large universities, with very few exceptions, have been closed to undergraduates. Since 1947 a number of the greatest libraries have opened their entire collections to all comers. Likewise, books put on reserve for course work have been gradually moved from behind counters to bookshelves around the room. A few bold institutions have abolished fines and use strong disciplinary action to enforce cooperation from those who neglect overdue notices. Some libraries have even flouted academic dignity by installing coke machines in entrance or corridor areas. This trend toward humanizing the library is slow, but it is definite. It is doing more than any other single innovation to make the life with books attractive and satisfying to young adults in their college years.[13]

Stimulating Reader Interest

The serious, study-motivated college student will range wide in his reading if he is given a good, easy-to-use book collection, relative freedom from restrictions, and comfortable and attractive study conditions. Guidance in his reading is desirable, but lack of guidance will not kill his reading interests. Unfortunately, a large percentage of our college students are not study-motivated to the degree we would wish. They need to be led into the life with books by individual counsel, by interest-stimulating programs, and by any stratagems that a fertile imagination can produce.

Teaching faculty and library administrator share responsibility for planning and executing the attack on the young mind which is

13. For a report on fundamental changes in one library from the attitude of book preservation to one of book use, see Arthur T. Hamlin, "Service Report from Pennsylvania," *College and Research Libraries*, XI (January, 1950), 63-68.

ignorant of or allergic to the wonders of the world of books. In the following discussion of some typical programs, the leadership has come from both sources. The important point to remember is that the library as the college book-center is the instrument of all programs. Ideally, librarian and classroom teacher work hand in hand with the techniques which produce intellectual curiosity, the thrist to know, and the satisfactions of mental growth.

Some years ago, Stephens College [14] began a program of taking library books to the students in their classrooms and dormitories. This practice has been adopted by some other institutions. The underlying theory is, of course, to take good books to the students and not to depend entirely on student interest to seek out literature in the library.

The Stephens librarians selected small collections of books especially suitable for individual classrooms devoted principally or entirely to certain subjects. The books circulate to the students from the classroom and are returned there. Obviously, the proximity of these books leads the teacher to mention them, recommend certain titles for specific needs, and discuss their contents. If the collection is well selected and the professor persuasive, few students can resist the urge to do a little reading that is not required for course purposes. A questionnaire distributed to Stephens' students produced almost unanimous approval of classroom libraries. Unfortunately, this practice has been followed by relatively few institutions. It deserves wider acceptance.

The dormitory library was not originated at Stephens and is found in sundry forms at many institutions. In its simple form the dormitory collection is a few hundred volumes drawn from the college library for indefinite loan to the residence hall. The books are carefully chosen for breadth of interest. A large proportion of them represent the better modern recreational reading. The University of Southern Illinois recently established residence-hall libraries of paper-bound titles. These collections are rotated each quarter. The libraries "include contemporary fiction, poetry, drama, biography, and popular nonfiction as well as material on religion, careers,

14. B. Lamar Johnson, *Vitalizing the College Library*. Chicago: American Library Association, 1939.

marriage and sex education, psychology, art, and homemaking." [15] Some dormitory libraries are open for only part of the day, but ideally the honor system should prevail and they should never be locked up. There will inevitably be some losses, but better a lost book than one unread.

A good many college libraries and museums have made prints and other art works available on long-term loan for student rooms, but very few have followed the Stephens practice of providing personal libraries. The objective is to establish the habit of a living environment in which books are important. Some years ago the students at Stephens were invited to recommend titles of books (not texts, reference books, or casual reading) "which you would like to have in your room for your personal use. It is suggested that this list consist of books which you would most like to own permanently—have in your home." [16] On the basis of student suggestions, some four hundred volumes were purchased for personal libraries. Students who desire these libraries first discuss their interests and college course work with a librarian. The volumes selected are charged for the duration of the school year. The library also loans small bookcases.

Many institutions may not have the funds to finance this type of personal library, but most college libraries contain a wealth of good literature in duplicate editions which could be available to students on long-term loan.

Although few colleges provide personal libraries on a loan basis, a great many institutions have sought to stimulate student personal libraries by annual competitions. [17] These contests may be limited as to total cost of the collection or number of items. There is great

15. Elizabeth O. Stone and Mary B. Melvin, "Paperbounds Go to College," *Library Journal*, LXXX (August, 1955), 1647.

16. Johnson, *op. cit.*, p. 65.

17. These home-library contests have received little publicity in professional literature. They take place on probably a majority of the campuses of this country. Some are conducted under library auspices, others by the English department, and a few by the student union, bookstore, or other college departments. See, for example, the annual contests at Colby Junior College, Birmingham-Southern, Swarthmore, Smith, University of Pennsylvania, and Wellesley.

variety in the nature of the personal library. Some must be built around a subject, others stress general reading and reference values. A few of the ivy-league institutions have contests emphasizing or limited to rare books.

These events are given all possible local publicity by posters, articles in the college paper, and classroom announcement. Prizes are awarded in cash or credit for the purchase of books. The winning libraries are placed on display. Whatever the local restrictions and stated objectives, these contests all have the central purpose of promoting the pleasure and pride of planning a collection and book ownership.

Another device directed toward the same end is the sale of duplicates to students. Not all library sales are motivated by educational objectives, of course, but some are strictly for this purpose and generate important interest in book ownership. The stock should be good and the prices low. The book sale reaches many students who do not compete in the personal library contest and is another device to develop recognition of the value of a personal library and the joy in its use.

A distressing number of colleges today have no bookstore worthy of the name on or near the campus, and for this serious omission the blame must be shared equally by college administrator, faculty, and librarian. The bookstore is essential to the development of young bookmen. If the intellectual climate is not sufficiently strong to attract a commercial bookseller, then the institution must dip into its own pocket to subsidize a bookstore. A great many institutions offer nothing better than a few cheap paper-bound displays and a bookstore limited to college texts and a lavish display of pennants, drinking glasses, and embossed stationery.

At a few institutions this need has been recognized and filled by the college library. Best known is the Bull's Head Bookshop at the University of North Carolina, which owes its origin largely to the initiative of a young English professor and is owned and operated by, and housed in, the university library. (A fine example of faculty-librarian co-operation.) This bookstore has comfortable chairs for readers, attractive displays of current literature, and plenty of rental copies. There are no textbooks, no bobbypins or pennants. Lengthy reading from current stock is encouraged. Somewhat similar facilities exist at Rockford and Vassar.[18]

Some libraries have limited their selling to inexpensive books. Several years ago Hamilton College set up a self-service, paper-back bookstore in the library. Here also the furniture is informal, the displays interesting, and supervision is nonexistent. Students browse at leisure and pay for their selections by dropping money in an open box. Skeptics will be surprised to learn that this Hamilton experiment has been a financial success.[19] Similar facilities exist at Beloit and probably other colleges.

Some tax-supported institutions face legal difficulties in operating library bookstores and limit themselves to displays of books. The University of Southern Illinois was a pioneer with its paper-back bookstore. Student selections are ordered and delivered by the library.[20] Queens College equipped its new library building for this same purpose, but each book on display carries a note as to what near-by bookstore carries it in stock. A full page is devoted to a discussion of the local bookstores in "Know Your Library," the student handbook at the University of California at Los Angeles.

In the last analysis, the library exists to put the right books into the hands of students and their teachers. Why must a sharp line be drawn between loan and purchase, especially when much of the best literature may be purchased in editions ranging in cost from 25 cents to $1.00? The library should always co-operate with the bookstore in promoting the sale of books. If there is no bookstore near by, the librarian has a responsibility to assist in the creation of one and to sell books in the library if necessary. Naturally, the motivation for sale must be education and not profit. Recently the Association of College and Reference Libraries, a division of the American Library Association, has stressed this responsibility, and the concept is winning some acceptance.

Nearly every college library does a good deal with exhibitions of books and manuscripts in order to publicize the collections and

18. Lyle, *op. cit.*, p. 241.

19. *Publishers' Weekly*, CLXIII (January 17, 1953), 211.

20. Stone and Melvin, *op. cit.*

particularly to stimulate broad social and cultural reading interests. An exhibition takes a great deal of work. Sometimes these are prepared by student groups or faculty members with special interest in the subject matter. At Brooklyn College [21] a number of exhibition cases are available to the departments of instruction and student groups. The local Shakespeare Club needs very little coaching or assistance to assemble an effective display on some aspect of its subject. Whenever possible, the exhibit should be accompanied by a few shelves of books available for loan on the same subject.

The exhibit is only one of a dozen devices to develop reading interests. Some libraries, such as those of the University of Pennsylvania and Massachusetts Institute of Technology, have regular programs of recorded music. Leading poets and stage celebrities are in demand for campus readings. Authors are eagerly sought for lectures on their own works or subjects on which they are authorities. Much of this type of extracurricular intellectual stimulation takes place in the library or is arranged by the librarian. Much of it is likewise provided by special university funds through one or another of the departments. The location of the special event and its sponsorship is of no concern; the important point is to capitalize on the interests thus created by making easily available a wealth of reading on the subject. Libraries sometimes take a truckload of books to the lecture or concert hall and circulate them at the door. Others set up special shelves and tables of books, with appropriate posters, in the entrance way or other prominent position, well before the event. The student whose interest is whetted by an approaching personal appearance of a Robert Frost cannot easily brush past a copy of the *Collected Poems*, which he could take along for the trouble of signing his name. This loan of one book may do a great deal toward developing an interest in modern poetry.

All libraries seek to stimulate reader interest by displaying dust jackets, by preparing special lists of readings on special subjects, by putting the new books together for a few weeks, and similar devices. Most of the practices used in public libraries to create reader interest are also found in colleges.

21. Rose Z. Sellers, "Exhibits Can Be Easy," *Wilson Library Bulletin*, XXIII (March, 1949), 526-27.

College librarians are well aware of the importance of providing students with individual counseling on their reading. Much of this guidance comes informally from faculty members in chance encounters in the bookstack or the reading room, as has been noted. The same give-and-take with students is the daily life of the library staff, but most of the requests for advice are made at library service desks. A few institutions, such as the Teachers College at Columbia University, have staff members whose principal assignment is to advise students with their reading. In a typical case, a student is required to read any one of thirty titles for a novel course. He has had a first choice in mind, but it has been charged out. He needs to talk to someone who knows many of the titles and can suggest special reasons for reading one or another. Should his instructor happen to be near by, all is fine; but probably the only help in sight is a librarian. In other cases, students are following up special interests which have no study connection. The need may be for recreational reading. The possibilities are endless. A versatile, quick mind and a very wide reading background are most important in advising students. The library fails in an important duty if it does not provide for this type of need.

A good many libraries use the so-called browsing room to make the life with books attractive to students. Here are found several thousand books carefully selected for their appeal to the general reader. The collection is usually balanced between recent and traditional material. There are likely to be one or two titles of T. S. Eliot, a selection of Hardy and Thackeray, a few well-illustrated volumes on modern painters, something on glass, pewter, or oriental rugs, as well as shelves of history and biography. Almost all browsing rooms are furnished comfortably, have a few prints or water colors, if wall space permits, and a rug or two for home atmosphere. Recreational reading is emphasized, study of any sort is forbidden, and books are not loaned for room use. Browsing rooms have been popular with students. The modern librarian attempts to create the same atmosphere, minus the restrictions on study, throughout the whole building. Where browsing rooms are lacking, most libraries have as a substitute some informal reading center or room where one will find a wide range of selected current literature either for home use or for reading on the spot in a comfortable chair.

Many larger college and university libraries are now organized into several principal segments, each one responsible for a broad subject, such as the social sciences or the humanities. In this one area are most or all of the books on the subject. Near by are the studies or stack carrells for professors. The library-staff members who are responsible for the collection have all had graduate study in the field, often teach a course or two, and are especially well qualified to help students in their use of material and to discuss reading needs. Libraries are thus often able to give counsel and advice of a very high caliber. Furthermore, this subject division helps librarian and student to become acquainted through long, often daily, association in the same reading room and obvious interest in the same subjects. The divisional plan, as it is called, draws librarian, teacher, and student into a closer working relationship, and this obviously promotes reading guidance and book talk.

A series of experimental programs to develop reading interests in college students has recently been planned by the Association of College and Reference Libraries. The proposal provides for cooperative effort by librarian, classroom teacher, and bookstore manager. The experimental programs are to be measured carefully for success or failure. It is hoped that this project will publicize the need for emphasis on student reading and point the way to the most effective operating procedures. The Association expects to seek funds in the near future to put these experiments into operation.

Developing Reading Habits

There is today very wide recognition of the importance of developing reading habits in young people while at school and college in order to have them continue a life with books in later years. This is equally a major concern of the National Book Committee, the American Book Publishers Council, the American Library Association, and various organizations of educators, college administrators, and booksellers.

The library shares with the faculty responsibility for many different types of semicurricular programs designed to develop student reading. At one institution a tutorial system leads the student to wide reading, largely of his own choice. At another institution it may be a plan of work for "honors" at graduation. Some of the experimental colleges such as Bard, Bennington, and Sarah Lawrence allow the student very wide selection and development of personal interests for college credits. Wilson College has a summer reading program which should be in subjects more or less untouched by the student in course work. These and many other programs are developing experienced, interested adult readers, and they all center in the college library. If the library and the faculty have jointly done a good job, these students will continue to read and think for themselves in later years. The test of such programs is not what is absorbed at the time but how long the interest is maintained after graduation.

The college student must budget a good deal of his time for attending and preparing for class. He may have a job; if not, he is almost certain to be involved in a sport, glee or dramatic club, religious group, and a few of the many other organized activities of college life. Add to these a few dates, inevitably a certain amount of social yak-yak, and the question arises as to how much time he has for reading. Certainly he has no time for general reading unless he brings to college a strong interest in books or unless his mind is sufficiently stimulated to make time for general reading. The library is responsible for providing the right books for most student interests and making them easy to find and convenient to borrow or purchase. The library staff assumes joint responsibility with faculty in stimulating reading interests sufficiently strong to compete for a large measure of student time. Many institutions have an intellectual climate sufficient to make confirmed readers of nearly all students; elsewhere reading students are a small minority. Reading cannot be legislated. The granting of course credits for reading is an artificial stimulation which is generally considered undesirable.

Many years ago Ralph Waldo Emerson recognized this problem and offered a solution:

Meantime the colleges, while they provide us with libraries, furnish no professor of books; and I think no chair is so much wanted. In a library we are surrounded by many hundreds of dear friends, but they are imprisoned by an enchanter in these paper and leathern boxes; and though they know us . . . they must not speak until spoken to; and as the enchanter has dressed them, like battalions of infantry, in coat and jacket of one cut, by the thousand and ten thousand, your chance of hitting on the right one is to be computated by the arithmetical rule of Permutation and Combination—not a choice out of three caskets, but out of half a million caskets, all alike." [22]

The modern ideal is for every librarian, faculty member, and administrative officer to be an official "Professor of Books." A recent study of reading at the school level [23] emphasizes that enthusiasm for reading is contagious. The teacher, the college professor, the librarian, and even the college president must be active, constant readers in order to be first-class Typhoid Marys, and the truly enthusiastic bookman will break down the resistance of the most skeptical collegians. The college library is generously supplied with books and has swept away most of the physical and clerical barriers between student and book collection. It has created a healthy working environment. Its principal future development lies in the developing of an atmosphere of contagion for ideas and book interests. In measure, as it succeeds, the nation is assured a majority of citizens who are constantly growing mentally and spiritually because of regular contact with the best that is written.

22. Ralph Waldo Emerson, *Works*, Vol. VII, pp. 191-92. Cambridge, Massachusetts: Harvard University Press, 1904.

23. Jean Grambs, *The Development of Lifetime Reading Habits*. New York: Published for National Book Committee by R. R. Bowker Co., 1954.

CHAPTER VII

The Use of Print in Adult Educational Agencies

CYRIL O. HOULE [1]

The educator of adults is concerned not so much with the process of reading as with its effect. He owes no loyalty to any one means of learning but must consider all of them as methods or devices to be used as needed, either singly or in combination. His central aim is to help people change themselves in desirable ways; and his concern with reading or any other process depends solely on its relative usefulness in producing the hoped-for result.

Considered even in these austere and demanding terms, however, reading is clearly the central and most important method of formal learning. The vast spread of adult education did not begin until the growth of the common schools had made most Americans literate. The other techniques of teaching, including the widely heralded methods of recent years, either incorporate the printed word or rely upon it to heighten their distinctive effects. So, too, do the newer and somewhat more glamorous forms of mass communication. One of the most fruitful fields of invention has been the duplication and spread of written materials. For all of these

1. The author of this chapter has had the benefit of the advice and criticism of the other members of the yearbook committee and of all the people whose names are listed below. The Center for the Study of Liberal Education for Adults generously served as host at a conference to discuss co-ordinated courses; the names of those present are designated with asterisks: Roger Axford, *George E. Barton, Jr., *Robert J. Blakely, Donald O. Bolander, D. Garron Brian, Glen Burch, James T. Carey, Frank S. Cellier, Veronica L. Conley, Paul H. Durrie, *Robert A. Goldwin, Morton Gordon, G. H. Griffiths, *C. R. Harrington, James Harrison, Bettie E. Houle, Martha C. Howard, *Ethel Kawin, *William J. Kimball, Malcolm S. Knowles, Harry L. Miller, Caroline G. Mitchell, *Hugh Moorhead, *Charles A. Nelson, Howard Nyberg, John Osman, Ralph J. Ramsey, Herman Richey, *John B. Schwertman, Ronald Shilen, Robertson Sillars, Peter Siegle, Elwin V. Svenson, *Ruth Warncke, and James Whipple. While everyone named tried to help the author, he alone is responsible for the final result.

reasons, reading remains, despite its competition, the most important form of communication other than talking, and print [2] is still the most flexible, the most widely available, the most adaptable, the least expensive, and the most indispensable tool of learning. It is appropriate, therefore, to examine directly the part which it has played in the modern growth of adult education.

The Spread of Universal Education

The growth began in the third decade of the present century. Morse Cartwright, one of the early architects of the movement, was fond of the sweeping pronouncement that, "Before the month of June, 1924, the term 'adult education' was not in use in the United States of America." He made that statement, among other places, in his major book,[3] and yet, later in that same book, he estimated that in 1924 there were already 14,881,500 persons participating with some regularity in activities which they regarded as educational.[4] Furthermore, chronicles of the three centuries of American life reveal countless earlier efforts which would seem to fit any acceptable definition of adult education. Cartwright was nonetheless correct in believing that he was dealing with both a new term and a new idea. Previously the many different institutional forms in which mature people learned or taught were all separate, each one with its own aims and its own independent status. In the 1920's, however, Cartwright and others realized that all these institutions, whatever their differences of purpose, tradition, or structure, embodied a common idea and sought a common end. New institutions did not need to be created in order to have an adult-educational movement. It was only necessary to bring existing efforts into closer and more fruitful contact with one another.

As this co-ordination began to take place, an even bolder idea came into the minds of many of the new pioneers. Americans had come to believe that education should be made available to all children. Why, then, should it not be made equally available to all

2. The term "print" is used throughout this chapter to signify all printed or duplicated forms of written language.

3. Morse Adams Cartwright, *Ten Years of Adult Education*, p. 3. New York: Macmillan Co., 1935.

4. *Ibid.*, p. 69.

adults? For milleniums, philosophers and poets had advanced the
idea that learning should be lifelong. A few, Thoreau among them,
had even suggested that all men should have equal opportunity to
win the rewards of knowledge. Why not try to achieve, as practical reality, an ideal which had previously been only a flight of
poetic imagination? The number of people involved in adult education was already large. Could not everyone be reached? The
pioneers of the mid-twenties decided to try.

Like most pioneers, they underestimated the task ahead of them.
They were swept away by their own conception of the importance
of adult education and assumed that it would have an equal attractiveness and appeal for everyone. They believed that the masses of
the people yearned for culture and were kept from it only by the
lack of opportunities to learn. They saw a bright promise in the
radio, the motion picture, the new forms of print, and the educational techniques which made use of freedom, informality, and
participation. Like all pioneers, they hoped for too much. Great
though their actual achievements were, their hopes were often
dashed by the stubborn desire of most people to keep on doing
things pretty much the same way they always had. It soon appeared
that adult education had no infallible magic to stir men's imagina-
tions, that the masses were not yearning for culture, and that, while
new forms of teaching greatly aided the processes of education, sustained and arduous application was still required to produce any
deep changes.

These pioneers of adult education did not examine the educational history of their own country to seek such guidance as it
might offer. They were, as a matter of fact, rather repelled by
the schools, considering them to be formal and stereotyped institutions, the very antithesis of the new and dynamic kinds of learning
which the era of adult education would launch. They took equality
of educational opportunity for granted, scarcely realizing how long
was the campaign which had carried this idea to common acceptance. Had they been closer students of the origins of the common
school system, they would have discovered that the earlier pioneers
who brought it into being faced virtually the same problems adult
educators were now encountering, even though the earlier focus of
education was on children, not adults. The sea was not as uncharted

as it appeared even though the earlier navigators had steered other kinds of ships. The supporters of the common school had achieved for children precisely the result which the proponents of adult education wanted so ardently to accomplish for adults. Perhaps the twentieth century might learn something from the nineteenth.

THE BEGINNINGS OF THE COMMON SCHOOL

In the 1820's, few Americans received more than a smattering of education. Both public and private schools existed, and the statute-books contained a few provisions which stated lofty, though largely unrealized, aspirations for public education. Most children, if they attended school at all, went for a few months a year for several years to an unattractive hovel often presided over by an old woman or a teen-aged youngster, whose primary attention was, of necessity, given to maintaining order. "In most of the old district schools," says their best known historian, Clifton Johnson,

> Little was imparted beyond a few bare rudiments, the teachers were often ignorant, and sometimes brutal, the methods mechanical and dreary. Notable men have come from "the little red school houses," but this was because of their own native energy and thrifty acquisitiveness, and was not due to any superlative virtues of the schools themselves.[5]

Even in the large urban centers, the condition of schools was far from good. Cubberley reports that in Chicago in 1853,

> There were 7 district schools, employing 34 teachers, and enrolling 3086 children, or an average of 91 children to the teacher. The schools at that time still were ungraded, and practically independent in methods, textbooks, and plan. They were also very insufficient in numbers, as they had been provided only in parts of the city where the demand for schools was strong enough to insure the voting of taxes. Thousands of children were being turned away because of lack of school facilities.[6]

The problems, in short, were similar to the difficulties which were to face the pioneers of adult education a hundred years later. Existing facilities had to be made better, they had to be co-ordinated, and they had to be extended to everyone. The idea of education

5. Clifton Johnson, *Old-Time Schools and School-Books*, p. 134. New York: Macmillan Co., 1904.

6. Ellwood P. Cubberley, *Public Education in the United States*, p. 238. Boston: Houghton Mifflin Co., 1919.

had to become a concrete reality supported by the people and made available to all. The money, the buildings, the physical resources, and (most important of all) the teachers and educational administrators had to be found. All of the whole complex system had to be integrated. The leaders of that day had to deal, as leaders always do, with the situation they had at hand; they could not wait for ideal conditions. The problems they dealt with were so vast that, even though the American school system has grown to great size, they still have not been finally solved.

THE ROLE OF THE TEXTBOOK

The story of the growth of the common schools has been told so often and so well that it needs no repetition here. In view of the theme of the present chapter, however, it is appropriate to point out the outstanding advance which was made by the development of the textbook. In the early decades of the nineteenth century, the schools used any pieces of print which came to hand, most frequently the *Bible*, the *Catechism*, and the *Psalter*.[7] A few textbooks were in existence but they were little known or used. John Howland, founder of the Providence school system, wrote in 1824:

> Up to this time I had never seen a grammar—a sorry confession for a school committeeman, some may think—but observing that *The Young Lady's Accidence* was in use in the Boston schools, I sent to the principal bookseller in that town and purchased one hundred copies for the use of ours.[8]

As the reformers began to agitate for the idea of free public schools for all, they found the textbook an elemental feature of their plan. It put a sound basis of knowledge at the disposal of even the most poorly trained teacher, it gave every student an instrument through which he could work at his own speed, it provided a structure for the activities of the classroom, and it established the basis for dividing the children into grades in terms of ability and maturity. These results were brought about by such books as Noah Webster's *Blue-backed Speller*, Warren Colburn's *Arithmetic*, and best-loved of all, William H. McGuffey's *Readers*. This latter series

7. Johnson, *op. cit.*, p. 265.

8. Cubberley, *op. cit.*, p. 220.

(the first volume of which was published in 1836) soon attained a dominant popularity which was to last for seventy-five years. The most conservative estimate of the total sale, up to 1920, was 122,000,000.[9] Since each copy was used over and over again, *McGuffey's Readers* achieved a mass use which is impressive even by modern standards.

With the gradual spread of the elementary school to reach almost all children, the secondary schools and the colleges began their own process of expansion. In 1890, they still adhered rigidly to the classical curriculum, with some grudging attention to modern languages and science. The number of children they served was very small, the secondary school reaching only about 7 per cent of the young people of secondary-school age. But the demands for education beyond the elementary school could not be denied, and the next sixty years witnessed a phenomenal growth which is still continuing. Today the secondary schools reach about 75 per cent of the young people of secondary-school age, despite the fact that the number of such young people has almost doubled.

Once again the full story of this second wave of expansion may be omitted, other than to point out that it could not have occurred without the diversification of the curriculum and the development of new textbooks. The classical curriculum was not capable of either interesting or serving more than a small part of the people. As the hordes of students flooded in, they demanded that old courses be adapted and new ones devised. The era of specialization was at hand and the old idea of the omnicompetent secondary-school or college teacher virtually disappeared. The textbook authors came to the rescue once again by developing a highly diversified stream of materials for use in both old and new courses. P. P. Claxton, the United States Commissioner of Education from 1911 to 1921, observed that, "Until the schools progress far beyond their present status, it will be essentially true that the children of the United States will go to school not to teachers but to books."[10] His comment was as true of the high school of that day as of the

---

9. *Textbooks in Education,* p. 45. New York: American Textbook Publishers Institute, 1949.

10. *Ibid.,* pp. 11-12.

elementary school, and it was not entirely without its application to college and university classrooms.

Throughout the history of American education, then, the textbook has been championed not necessarily as the ideal instrument for teaching but as the means whereby education could be provided for a very large number of people. Even in 1820, there were good schools, governesses, and tutors for fortunate children. The sons of the gentry went to Latin grammar schools or academies and then to small liberal-arts colleges, finishing up their formal study perhaps by a year or two in Europe. To extend such opportunities to everyone was a sheer impossibility. Only through the use of the one mass medium then available—the printed textbook—was mass education possible.

Similarly, the task which confronted the pioneers of adult education in 1924 was not the creation but the vast extension of learning. Adult education had always existed, even in the days before the spread of the elementary school. In 1820, the few people who were fortunate enough to be educated regarded their schooling as merely the first stage of their learning. They expected to continue their study throughout their lives. They read. They formed literary and philosophical societies. They built collections of objects which were later the nuclei of museums. They created discussion groups (most notably the lyceums) in which they met to talk together about books and the issues of the day. In 1820, education was clearly considered a lifelong pursuit, even though only a few people had a sustained opportunity to learn.

During the next century, in which the elementary and the secondary school were expanded so tremendously, some adults continued to study. Indeed, several movements of adult education during that period laid the foundations for much of the later growth. But as the emphasis on childhood education continued for generation after generation, the new groups who studied in the common school did not acquire the ancient belief in lifelong learning. They came to think of education as an attribute of childhood. When the idea of adult education was crystallized in the 1920's, it was considered a fresh and wonderful conception. Only a few of its ardent proponents realized how time-honored was the ideal which they set for themselves.

If adult education was to expand so greatly as to be, in effect, a third wave of educational advance, and if the idea of lifelong learning was to be achieved for all men, the old forms clearly would not be sufficient to meet the needs of the vast numbers who might hope to enrol. The gentleman's library, the literary and philosophical society, and the pursuit of amateur scholarship would continue as they always had, but they must be supplemented by countless other forms. Actually, by the 1920's, this supplementation was well under way or Cartwright would not have been able to count his total of almost 15,000,000 participants. But there was still a great difference between that figure (including many duplications) and anything like the record of saturation already achieved by the schools. The inventions to be used for adults could not, of course, be so simple as those which were developed for childhood education, where the chief aim was to build highly organized and articulated systems of a fairly unitary sort, serving students whose primary task was learning. Adults live diversified lives, and their education cannot be carried out in any single framework. Their education must ordinarily be fitted into the patterns of work, play, family, community, and social life which make up the primary concerns of adulthood.

On the other hand, the pioneers of adult education had certain great advantages. Although they knew little about the history of the great tradition of education in the United States, they benefited from it in many ways: in the relatively high level of literacy of the people, in the popular acceptance of education for youth as a desirable service of government, in the equalitarian idea that learning should be available for all youth, and in the knowledge of educational processes which had grown up during a hundred years of development. Furthermore, the media of mass communication were being developed very rapidly. There was little negative tradition to hold back progress.

Since 1924, the number of participants in adult education has steadily risen. Various estimates have been made, using roughly the definition adopted by Cartwright. In 1934, there were 22,311,000 persons involved. In 1950, there were 29,250,000. In 1955, there were 49,508,500.[11] The authors of all of these estimates warned their readers that these figures were imprecise, and yet, even if a substantial margin of error is allowed, the increase in numbers appears phenomenal.

The full story of this growth has not yet been told. The process of expansion is still in midcourse, and its historian cannot undertake his work until the main lines of development and the relative importance of various factors can be more clearly assessed than is possible at the present time. The central place which the development of reading materials occupied in each of the two previous periods of educational expansion should cause us, however, to focus our attention on this one question: Will the development of special materials for adults aid substantially the third great period of educational expansion?

Textbooks certainly will never occupy the central place with adults that they do in the education of children. In contrast to the schools, the organization of adult education is decentralized, and this tendency grows more marked every year. Agencies are greatly diversified in terms of purpose and function as well as in terms of local, state, and regional differences. There is no single major institutional form, as is true of elementary, secondary, and higher education. Furthermore the differences and divergences of adult educational institutions are cherished. Those people who are interested in health education, family-life education, religious education, safety education, and the other special fields have a dedication to their purposes. Those who work in the Co-operative Extension Service, the public schools, the universities, community centers, industrial training or union-education activities, and the countless other programs have an identification with the institutions with which they are affiliated. Even within a single agency, there are many differences, since programs must often be built around local needs and interests and the involved patterns of adult life. This complicated structure encourages and requires a complex, diversified group of materials rather than the simple pattern of content which the textbook provides.

11. Malcolm S. Knowles, "Adult Education in the United States," *Adult Education*, V (Winter, 1955), 76.

The Kinds of Print Which Adult Educational Agencies Use

What kinds of print, then, do adult educational agencies use to convey the understanding and information which their students wish to learn? The answer is, of course, that they use everything. It would be a very odd piece of print for which no instructional purpose could be found. As the whole field is examined, however, it becomes apparent that the materials tend to fall into several large and overlapping groups.

Specially published materials probably make up by far the largest volume. Each sponsoring organization, once it has achieved a sufficient size, usually goes into the business of producing its own print. Unions, churches, voluntary citizen organizations such as the Parent-Teacher Association or the League of Women Voters, the Co-operative Extension Service, and countless other agencies feel that they must build their own groups of materials, imbued with their own philosophies and points of view. Very often, too, these publishing programs are a source of revenue; they help support the organization.

Furthermore those who control many of the agencies of adult education are not content with nationally published materials. As soon as state or local programs grow large enough, each one begins to issue its own forms of print. The Co-operative Extension Service is an excellent case in point. The authorities in each state ordinarily believe that they must have many bulletins dealing with their own distinctive agricultural and homemaking problems to supplement the more general materials issued by the federal office.

Probably most of the specially prepared materials are merely informational in character, presenting the facts about some one subject. In addition, however, some institutions also provide co-ordinated materials of instruction tying together both content and teaching materials. Many churches, for example, have series of lesson plans for their adult Bible classes. Sometimes, too, a completely integrated book will be provided for local use as is done in the first-aid and life-saving courses of the American Red Cross and the leadership-training manuals of the Boy Scouts and Girl Scouts.

Textbooks prepared for children and young people are also

widely used, particularly in the more formal kinds of programs carried on by schools and universities. Often such use is entirely appropriate, particularly at the university level where the age difference between the adult and the student for whom the text was originally prepared is not very significant. Sometimes, however, the use of children's textbooks is so inappropriate as to be ludicrous— a muscular coal miner learning to read is seldom enthralled by the story of how Susy and her dog Skip spent a day in the country with grandmother. The use of such materials usually defeats the educational process completely, implying as it does that learning is a childish activity which an adult should be heartily ashamed to undertake.

Very few *special textbooks for adults* have been developed apart from those used within particular organizations and classified above as specially prepared materials. For the most part special texts are in the field of elementary English and Americanization, although the correspondence schools have a number of special texts for adults, particularly in vocational subjects. The publishers would, of course, be happy to develop special series designed for adults, but a textbook is economically feasible only when there is a large enrolment in a specific course. As we have seen, the extraordinary diversity of adult education makes it doubtful that special textbooks will ever play a very large role.

Government publications are widely used because of their low price, their availability, and their variety. Often materials not primarily intended for use by groups are adapted to that purpose.

Many organizations issue *sponsored materials* with the hope that they will be adopted and used by adult groups. The announcement of a workshop for teachers and administrators of adult educational activities will ordinarily bring far more letters from people who want to distribute copies of advertising or promotional pamphlets than it does from prospective students. Each of these materials is issued to advance some special interest of its sponsor. Sometimes this purpose is so broad and general as to raise no questions about the objectivity of the viewpoint. The Metropolitan Life Insurance Company is interested in the improvement of health, and the Household Finance Company in better family financial planning; the excellent materials which both produce are very widely used. Other kinds of sponsorship cause no problem, at least to a public which is inured to advertisements. For example, an adult class in cooking does not very much mind being told to use some particular brand of flour or cheese or ham, since what the students want are the recipes which go with such admonitions. Many sponsored materials advocate a point of view rather than a product, however, and therefore must be given a sharper scrutiny by the teacher who considers using them. The American Association of School Administrators has recently issued a brief guide [12] on how to select the best items from the flood which daily pours in upon anybody who has access to the minds of others.

General books and magazines, having been chiefly prepared for adult minds, are very widely adapted to educational uses. A nonfiction book or magazine article is, in effect, a lecture or a series of lectures in print. Ordinarily it has been prepared and is presented with far more care than the typical lecture. It can be read at the student's convenience, it can be reread as often as is necessary, it preserves the time of the group entirely for discussion, and it is inexpensive. These great advantages are so apparent that the idea of book-related discussion has been rediscovered again and again. The lyceum movement of the period from 1825 to 1840 and the Chautauqua reading-circles of the last quarter of the nineteenth century were both large-scale programs. There are many modern forms ranging all the way from the ever present annotated bibliography to the highly developed institution focused on this reading-and-discussion kind of education. Perhaps the best-known instance of the latter type was the School of Social Studies described by Powell.[13]

The magazine publishers, in particular, have promoted the use of their materials for education, largely as a public service and promotional device. It is not uncommon for a mass-circulation magazine to have an educational bureau which distributes reprints, prepares special pamphlets, organizes programs for clubs and other groups, publishes discussion guides and lesson outlines, and performs

12. *Choosing Free Materials for Use in the Schools.* Washington: American Association of School Administrators, 1955.

13. John Walker Powell, *Education for Maturity.* New York: Hermitage House, 1949.

other specialized services. A few of the book publishers have also become interested in the secondary use of their materials which is made by organized groups; perhaps the best example is the New American Library with its extensive series of inexpensive paper-bound books. Crohn has written a general account of the use of mass-produced print by adult educational agencies,[14] and a number of ideas for the stimulation of reading by individuals and groups is to be found in *The Wonderful World of Books*.[15] This latter publication grew out of a special conference on rural reading which was sponsored by the United States Department of Agriculture and the American Book Publishers' Council. This national conference and the later activities which it stimulated represent the most sustained attempt yet made to build a bridge between trade books and adult educational agencies.

The existence of the large potential market for books in adult educational groups has not escaped the attention of the commercial publishers. Their obvious temptation is to think by analogy and assume that this new market is like that for children's textbooks, where one sale may be sufficient for the distribution of a very large number of copies. Such thinking usually results in frustration. The agencies of adult education which can command large-scale audiences for a particular subject already have their own printing presses at work.

In the typical adult class or other group, materials are chosen from all of the foregoing categories in terms of the usual principles of selection: the objective of the instruction, the relative availability of the various items, the interest of the instructor and students, and the method used. Often in the weaving together of various items, *supplementary and integrative materials* need to be prepared. Correspondence-course syllabi and discussion guides are excellent examples of this form.

The Co-ordinated Course

Out of the adaptation and combination of existing materials for

14. Richard J. Crohn, "New Ways to Reading," *Adult Leadership*, II (January, 1954), 8-9, 28.

15. *The Wonderful World of Books*. Edited by Alfred Stefferud. New York: Houghton Mifflin Co., 1952.

the achievement of specific educational purposes, there has gradually grown a new educational idea which may, in time, prove to be as important for the mass development of adult education as the textbook was for the spread of the elementary and secondary schools. This idea is embodied in many different forms but, in essence, it is the attempt to construct a course in which an educational goal is defined, a specific content and method are selected and put in sequence, and a plan for securing and training leaders and extending the program to large numbers of participants is worked out. At its best, such a course goes far beyond the textbook in incorporating other media of communication than print (although print is still central) and in providing a far more complete and flexible integration of all of the component parts of the total educational process. The great present and potential significance of the co-ordinated course justify its close examination here, particularly since its development and operation raise many of the fundamental issues in the educational use of print and other media of communication.

The co-ordinated course did not have any single inventor; the idea came naturally and spontaneously to many different minds. Perhaps its development is but one aspect of the American genius for specialized merchandising. Certainly such frequently used terms as "canned courses" and "packaged programs" bring to mind the parallel of prefabrication (and sometimes predigestion) as well as slick and streamlined systems of distribution. Be that as it may, the courses have been very widely developed and used, as the citing of a few examples will indicate. The courses sponsored by the American Red Cross and the leadership-training programs of various youth agencies have already been mentioned. Industry has also made a wide use of co-ordinated courses: in the courses in job-instruction training and job-relations training, in trade association programs for employees in various kinds of jobs, in standardized induction activities for new workers, in courses conveying certain economic viewpoints,[16] and in training programs provided for the

16. For a sardonic review of the effort of corporations to communicate with their employees by co-ordinated courses and other means, *see:* William H. Whyte, Jr., *Is Anybody Listening?* New York: Simon & Schuster, 1952.

purchasers of specialized equipment such as sewing machines or complicated office equipment. The military services and the civilian departments of government, faced with the enormous training needs presented by World War II made extensive use of co-ordinated courses, standardizing and developing them to a far greater extent than had ever previously been the case.

A recent account of the experience in the armed forces presents a clear picture of both the logic and the process of building a co-ordinated course:

Those of us who prepared materials for the schools of the Armed Forces during World War II were continually faced with the fact that hurriedly trained instructors made uncountable errors of procedure. They went too fast or too slow. They forgot to introduce topics in a way that would motivate, or else they spent far too much time on anecdotes and building rapport. They introduced explanations which confused the student or even misstated facts. And so on. The solution widely adopted and regarded as highly successful was packaged training programs in which every possible judgment was anticipated for the instructor. Motivation at the start of a unit was supplied in careful dosage, often through a specially made film. Explanations were worked out with care, charts were provided in profusion so that inadequate blackboard technique would introduce no learning difficulties. In the most highly developed programs the instructor was told what questions to ask and what answers to accept. The basic view was that the instructor who followed the master plan religiously could not do a bad job of teaching.[17]

Just as every educator can give an eloquent dissertation on what is wrong with the textbook, so even the most casual observer can detect the weaknesses in "canned courses" and "packaged programs." The difficulties are almost entirely the problems which are always attached to mass distribution and use. There is no adequate accounting for local variation. The materials presented are so highly selected to be useful to the majority that they may not provide for the individual interest of the members of the group. The students may be given an oversimplified and, therefore, false picture of the ideas included. The teacher may become a slave to the demanding schedule of the program; if he is a poor teacher, he had

17. Lee J. Cronbach, *Text Materials in Modern Education*, p. 196. Urbana, Illinois: University of Illinois Press, 1955.

better do just what the course says he should, but if he is a good teacher, he may be seriously handicapped.

Some of these problems are inherent in the nature of any educational program which is constructed to reach a large audience in a short period of time. To some extent, too, they are present in any teaching which falls short of the superlative levels achieved by Socrates or Mark Hopkins. The difference is only one of degree, not kind. Realizing this fact, those who have constructed co-ordinated courses in recent years have given much thought to the methods of improving them. Since co-ordinated courses are usually developed by specific organizations to meet their own needs, their production is decentralized, and there is relatively little relationship among those who sponsor them. A review of the courses which have proliferated since the war, however, would reveal a steady improvement in them. An excellent example is the economic-education program developed by Sears Roebuck and Company. This course, entitled "The Story of Sears in America," consisted of a series of eight units, each of which was composed of a specially prepared film, a discussion leader's guide, a take-home pamphlet, and a comprehensive informational booklet. More than 71,000 discussion sessions were conducted by 2,600 discussion leaders for 200,000 employees, and the total cost of the program is estimated to have been more than six million dollars.[18]

AN INSTRUMENT OF LIBERAL ADULT EDUCATION

Throughout the years of growth of adult education there has been a constant concern on the part of some leaders for the development of more significant programs of liberal education. Toward the close of World War II, in which the co-ordinated courses had achieved such spectacular results, the question began to be raised as to whether this form of education could be used to achieve broader educational goals for a more general audience than had ever previously been the case.

Certainly the principles of adult liberal education would appear to be capable of expression in a co-ordinated course. The mature person should expect to take charge of his own education. He

18. Frank S. Cellier, *The Story of Sears in America*. New York: American Management Association, 1953.

should want to learn the best that has been thought or said or por-
trayed by those who have had the deepest insight into what he hopes
to learn. He should realize that many minds have preceded his along
the particular voyage of inquiry on which he is embarking and that
consequently he should try to secure the very best guidance as to
what he should read and in what order. To maintain his independence and vigor of viewpoint, however, he should use experts in both
content and method but never abdicate to them. The mature person
will often study independently, but he should also seek the stimulation of a group of like-minded people who, through discussion,
can bring their different backgrounds to bear on common problems
and thereby illuminate the understanding of everyone concerned.
This discussion is the joint responsibility of the whole group but
often it is desirable for at least one member to accept the special
duty of leadership to aid in achieving both focus and progression.
The mature person always evaluates a program of learning in terms
of the meaning it has for him and the group to which he belongs.
Finally, he expects that any given learning experience should provide him with the stimulus for further thinking, reading, and
participation.

One of the most sustained attempts to embody these principles
in co-ordinated courses was begun at the University of Chicago in
1944. The effort was started with the hope that a series of well-
constructed courses might play an important role in the expansion
of liberal education, becoming, as it were, a kind of "McGuffey's
Reader" of adult education. This attempt to design and spread new
courses has now been undertaken by many other organizations.
The work will be described in some detail here, not necessarily
because it is of paramount importance in the number of people
served or its eventual impact, but because, to date, it is the most
determined effort to construct and spread co-ordinated courses as
a way of providing liberal education for American adults.

The sequence of events began with the development of the
"Great Books" courses, first, for an experimental period at University College of the University of Chicago and, then, in a program
of national expansion through the work of the Great Books Foundation. Simultaneously a similar effort was being carried forward

by the Washington, D. C., Public Library.[19] The next program launched was designed to give its students a familiarity with certain aspects of foreign affairs. The American Foundation for Political Education was founded in 1947, and, in co-operation with the Chicago Council on Foreign Relations and the University of Chicago, began to offer its course on "World Politics." Later, under the auspices of the American Foundation for Political Education and various local sponsors, the program was taken to other cities. Eventually two new courses—"American Foreign Policy" and "Russian Foreign Policy"—were added.

In 1951, the Fund for Adult Education was founded. It adopted the idea of creating new courses and extending the use of these and other existent courses as a fundamental part of its work. It provided both the Great Books Foundation and the American Foundation for Political Education with funds to extend their work and also made it possible for other programs to be launched. The Association of University Evening Colleges was given a grant to develop a Center for the Study of Liberal Education for Adults; a large part of its effort has gone into the development of co-ordinated courses to be offered by evening colleges. The American Heritage Council was provided money to offer courses in American traditions in the state of Illinois. The University of Chicago was given a grant to set up a parent-education project; the course developed by this project is entitled "Parenthood in a Free Nation." The Fund itself early began its own work of developing a diversified range of courses, an effort which was greatly expanded in 1954. Among the courses which it is now offering are: "Economic Reasoning," prepared by the Brookings Institution; "You and Your Community," prepared by the American Community Project of New York University; "Ways of Mankind," "Ways to Justice," and "Jefferson and Our Times," all based on materials originally prepared for radio by the National Association of Educational Broadcasters; "Introduction to the Humanities," prepared by the humanities staff of the College of the University of Chicago; and "Great Men and Great Issues" and "World Affairs Are Your Affairs," both developed

19. John Powell, "One Step Nearer Leadership," *Library Journal*, LXXI (April 1, 1946), 443-49.

by the Fund for Adult Education with the assistance of various authorities.

Each of these many programs is operated on its own set of assumptions and in terms of its creators' conception of what was required. As a result, in more than ten years of experience, there has been a marked broadening of viewpoint, a sharper realization of the inherent strengths and weaknesses of the co-ordinated course, and the development of some issues about which there is substantial disagreement. Most of the programs, however, share certain important elements.

To begin, the sole concern of their sponsors is with education. The courses are not designed to achieve prescribed kinds of specific social action (as would be the case with the courses designed to train civilian defense workers) or to use education as an instrument to secure some other primary purpose (as when a trade union uses a course to build understanding and support for its established policies).

In all of the programs, the content to be taught is nonvocational in character. The purpose of the courses is to aid individuals and groups in their roles as citizens, parents, or seekers after liberal education.

In all cases, the sponsors are not concerned with building new administrative mechanisms but with using existing institutions and, in some cases, co-ordinated groups of local agencies. For example, a recent publication of the American Foundation for Political Education lists programs in 117 cities in 24 states, sponsored by 48 colleges and universities, 59 service organizations, 40 libraries, 20 world-affairs councils, 23 churches, 29 public school systems, and 51 women's organizations, adult-education councils, and others.[20]

The limitations inherent in mass distribution have been frankly faced. The central purpose in every case has been to give a large number of people a few basic concepts rather than to give a few people a large number of concepts. The general procedure may be sketched as follows:

20. *A Statement Concerning the American Foundation for Political Education*, pp. 20 ff. Chicago: American Foundation for Political Education, (19 S. LaSalle St.), n.d.

(a) Choose some broad topic or area of knowledge about which a large number of adults would like to know more.

(b) Analyze the topic in terms of its basic elements, the probable amount of time it can command from the busy adults to whom it is directed, and other relevant factors.

(c) Select or construct a series of readings and, where desirable, include such other materials as films, phonograph records, and pictures, which will convey the basic concepts.

(d) Arrange these materials in a series imposed by the discipline concerned.

(e) Develop a methodology of discussion leadership which is appropriate to the aim and materials.

(f) Identify the kinds of leaders who should be chosen for service in the program and the nature of the instruction they should receive.

(g) Test and revise the content and method with numerous groups until both have been sufficiently perfected to be generally useful.

(h) Provide mass distribution by making the materials available in large quantity, instructing a number of nonprofessional leaders, and securing effective sponsorship locally.

Although the general objective of any co-ordinated course can usually be stated fairly clearly, the more specific objectives always require a great deal of analysis. It is easy enough to say, for example, that one plans to introduce attentive American citizens to the general field of economic theory, but the decisions as to just what concepts should be selected for inclusion in such a program and just how they should be presented requires a whole series of difficult judgments. And when, in the testing of the course by experimental groups, new light is thrown on how many ideas it is possible to convey in the time available, substantial revisions of the sequence and content are ordinarily necessary. New instructional materials must be found or prepared, and sometimes new organizing principles must be used. These changes, in turn, frequently call for revisions in the specific aims of the course.

The objective of each course is most fundamentally stated in terms of the learning which it is intended to convey; thus, the chief test of a course in economics is whether its students learn that subject. As the number of co-ordinated courses has grown, however, at least three other more general goals have come to be accepted.

The first is to stimulate the participants to do more about their own continuing education than they have done in the past. Robert Redfield has defined an educated person as "one who is at work on his enlargement." [21] Too many adults either consider themselves already educated or believe that they are beyond the need or the capacity for education. Participation in a co-ordinated course gives them some opportunity to escape from the monotonous pattern of their lives. To them, as to Isaac D'Israeli, "The delight of opening a new pursuit, or a new course of reading, imparts the vivacity and novelty of youth even to old age." [22] The case was very well put by a student in one of the very first sessions of the "Great Books" class:

> I leave each class session feeling mentally aroused and eager for further reading. And the informal discussions and comparisons of opinions helped me a great deal. They were a gauge by which I would judge whether I'd gotten all I should have from my reading. Also, they inspired me to not only *read* books, but to *think* about them, in relation to the past, the present, and myself.[23]

The second general objective has been to counteract the stultifying influence of mass communication. In the society of the past, face-to-face contact and the influence of small groups and community participation were far more significant than they are today. The advent of the new forms of transportation and communication has removed the barriers of distance, but it has also broken down the diversified and intimate structure of social life and made possible the mass manipulation of opinion and the decreasing influence of the individual. Adult education is one of the most important counterbalances to the drift toward the mass man, since effective programs create forward-looking small groups, the members of which are interested in and significant to one another. Co-ordinated courses are particularly valuable in this respect because of their reliance on the discussion method in which all members of a group participate together.

21. Robert Redfield, *The Educational Experience*, p. 41. Pasadena, California: Fund for Adult Education, 1955.

22. Isaac D'Israeli, *The Literary Character*, Vol. II, pp. 235-36. London: Davison Whitefriars, 1822 (third edition).

23. Quoted in Cyril O. Houle, "What Adults Think of the Great Books," *School Review*, LIV (May, 1946), 278.

The third objective has to do with the development of leaders for our society. The experience of presiding over a co-ordinated course, of being for a time the first among equals in an exploration of an important topic, can have a significant influence on the development of community leaders.

To understand fully the problems involved in accomplishing the last two general goals, it is necessary to examine both the discussion process itself and the methods by which leaders of co-ordinated courses are selected and instructed.

From the beginning of the work on the "Great Books" program, method has always been considered of first importance. Lowell Martin, in his excellent description of the early days of that course, defined the method as follows:

> The educational objectives of book discussion groups are primarily two: training in the arts of communication (reading, speaking, and listening) and improvement of understanding of fundamental human problems. The method used to achieve these objectives is guided group reading of important books. The only formal teachers in the groups are the authors of the books; the discussion leaders mediate between the "teachers" and the "students" by creating those conditions under which constructive group thinking occurs. The technique has assumed a distinctive character involving intensive reading of relatively short and difficult passages prior to group meetings, closely controlled seminars in which irrelevance is the greatest sin and integrated group thinking the greatest virtue, and dependence by leaders on the Socratic method of questioning to direct discussions.[24]

The term "Socratic method" which was fairly common in the earlier days has since fallen into disuse, except in the "Great Books" program, chiefly because it has been found more satisfactory for lay leaders to occupy a less dominant role than they usually did when they were told to emulate the Greek sage. But the central concept which Martin presented is still essentially true. The leader is not a lecturer. Instead, he is a co-ordinator, stimulator, and guide. Some of the co-ordinated courses even incorporate the practice of using two simultaneous leaders so that each can prevent the other from lapsing into bad habits.

An appropriate term for the general method used might be

24. Lowell Martin, "Guided Group Reading as a Library Service: The Chicago Project," *Library Journal*, LXXI (May 15, 1946), 734.

"focused" discussion [25] since its distinctive feature is that the attention of the group is always directed toward some stimulus or experience which all of the members have in common. They have read a book, or seen a film or a picture, or heard a record. Now their task is to examine it together to be sure that they understand it, to determine whether what it says is true, and to consider its bearing on their own and their society's perplexities and problems. The common exploration of the material is led by one who is essentially of their own number and who never considers himself to be an expert on the subject under discussion. Nor is it his task to summarize or to "reach agreement" or to test the knowledge of others, since all such activities usually imply, though perhaps subtly, that he has a superior understanding of the material on which the group is focusing its attention. His duty is simple but sometimes very hard to perform; he must so conduct the discussion that the group and its individual members enlarge and deepen their own understanding of the subject under discussion.

As might be expected, perhaps the most controversial topic in the whole development of co-ordinated course programs has to do with the methods of selecting and instructing lay leaders. Some national and local sponsors have taken the position that leadership can only be undertaken by professionally equipped persons such as schoolteachers or college professors. Others have held that such persons are already too habituated to traditional forms of teaching to be able to adjust to the freer air of focused discussion.

Those who believe in using nonprofessional leaders agree fairly well on the kind of people they wish to select. They want intelligent citizens who are well adjusted socially, have a warm regard for people, an objective respect for facts, and a natural inclination for positions of leadership. Ordinarily, too, it is expected that a person who is to lead a given course shall first have taken it himself as a participant. There is, however, a very real disagreement about how such a person should be instructed for his task. Some hold that a program can be more successful if no special instruction is planned and provided, believing that it increases the distance be-

25. This term comes readily to mind because it somewhat parallels the procedure of the focused interview in which Robert Merton of Columbia University has been the pioneer.

tween the leader and the other members of the group and destroys the spirit of intimacy and co-operativeness. Others are convinced that the leader should go through an instructional program which is intimately and directly related to the particular co-ordinated course which he proposes to lead, arguing that, because of the specific emphasis of each course, an exact orientation to it is needed. Still others maintain that a generalized instructional program can prepare leaders for all courses, since the method to be used is essentially unitary; perhaps some special briefing is necessary for each course but not very much.

The settlement of such controversial issues as leadership instruction will be aided if the sponsors of the various co-ordinated courses continue to maintain their present objectivity of viewpoint. The necessity for testing each course exhaustively with experimental groups before it is released for general distribution, the assiduous collection of information concerning the success of the course (as measured chiefly by the opinions of participants and leaders), and the resulting revisions of content or methods of administration have served to make both national and local sponsors remarkably aware of the strengths and limitations of their work. The evaluative work done routinely by each of the national sponsors has shown a generally favorable response and a steadily enlarging group of participants.[26] Little exact research analyzing the effectiveness of the programs has been carried on, although the field is certainly one in which research is both possible and needed. An illustration of at least one kind of investigation is the study by Alexander Charters of the effect of the elementary Great Books course on the capacity of its participants to think logically. He demonstrated a positive relationship between the increase of this capacity and length of participation in the course, but he was not able to prove that this relationship was statistically significant, chiefly, he believed, because he could not carry on his study beyond the first year's program.[27]

26. The most comprehensive investigation is that made by the Great Books Foundation and reported in: *Great Books Under Discussion*. Chicago: Great Books Foundation, 1954.

27. Alexander N. Charters, *An Evaluation of the Development of Certain Aspects of the Ability to Think by Participation in an Adult Program*. Unpublished Doctor's dissertation, University of Chicago, 1948.

CRITICISMS OF CO-ORDINATED COURSES

Co-ordinated courses have been criticized on almost every conceivable ground, and the "Great Books" program has, in particular, been subjected to slashing attack.[28] Some of the objections have been concerned with the selection of content of the course itself or the administrative policies of the national or local sponsor. Each such objection must be met on its own specific terms. In some cases, however, more general criticisms of co-ordinated courses have been made because of a genuine misunderstanding of what they were intended to do. To argue, for example, that a two-semester university seminar can convey more facts about anthropology than a ten-session course on "Ways of Mankind" is to state the obvious. To compare lay and professional leaders by identical criteria with no regard to the appropriate tasks which can best be performed by each is to blur an important distinction. The proponents of the co-ordinated courses keep on repeating (rather wearily by now!) that they are dealing with a kind of education which has been deliberately constructed for mass use and for responsible adults. It should not be evaluated on any other terms. Some critics object to the very idea of mass education itself, believing that in this way knowledge is cheapened and made trivial and that the teaching resources of the country are dissipated. Such objections involve a fundamental difference in philosophy which does not relate any more to co-ordinated courses than to other attempts to spread to everyone the opportunity to learn.

Specific criticisms tend to follow the same patterns, and it may, therefore, somewhat illuminate the subject to summarize a few of them briefly, suggesting as well the rejoinders which are most frequently made.

Co-ordinated courses are superficial and trivial, dulling the edge of true learning and giving a crumb rather than a whole loaf. A little learning is a dangerous thing. To such a contention, perhaps the best answer is the one given by T. H. Huxley: Where is the man who knows so much that he is out of danger? The true parallel is not between co-ordinated courses and deep intensive study. It is

---

28. *See*, for example: Edward A. Fitzpatrick, *Great Books: Panacea or What?* Milwaukee: Bruce Publishing Co., 1952.

between co-ordinated courses and nothing at all. The introduction of an adult to an area of subject matter gives him a structural framework on which to fit his later study and observation. One who has taken a course in "American Foreign Policy" and has learned the fundamental issues with which it deals will have a continuing education on the front page of his newspaper every day. Having been sensitized to crucial terms and ideas, he will tend to have an aroused interest in the subject where previously his eye slid rapidly past any treatments of it. Furthermore, a large number of case studies show that co-ordinated courses often serve as the necessary introductions to more extensive study.

Adult education should be centered on the particular community or group and should be developed in terms of immediate needs and interests. In any comprehensive view of adult education, there should be room for both that education which focuses on the community and that which is directed toward the common concerns of people everywhere. Furthermore, the co-ordinated courses introduce many people to programs of continuing education, and the discussion method gives them a sense of participation. They are thereby encouraged to proceed into much more extensive community activity. At least one of the present courses has such participation as its specific goal.

Co-ordinated courses are too rigid and inflexible. The best adult education results when the teacher and group together explore a wide variety of materials, methods, and forms of organization, choosing the ones which appear most relevant. There is some truth in this contention. But this kind of educational program takes a high degree of skill, and it takes time. It is precisely because these two commodities are scarce that co-ordinated courses have been developed.

Co-ordinated courses are unnecessary. The knowledge is already widely available in books and other media. Anybody who really wants to learn can easily do so. This contention is partly true, but it places the full emphasis on content, ignoring the values which come from group participation, from the interaction of many minds focused on a common topic, and from the training in leadership which good courses provide. Furthermore, the course diminishes the austerity of approach to basic written materials. When "Great

Books" students are asked which authors they have liked the best, they ordinarily choose the Greeks; but very few of these same students would ever have opened books by Plato or Aristotle if they had not been encouraged to do so by the knowledge that the experience was being shared by a group of other congenial people no brighter and no more knowledgeable than themselves. The course also gives a sense of comprehensiveness, of the bird's-eye view which most people like to have before they begin more detailed study, just as the student of geography begins first with the globe. Finally, some media of communication (most notably the film) are difficult or impossible for an individual to use by himself.

Co-ordinated courses are fine, but one should be selective in using them, dropping some of the readings and adding others, using occasional lectures rather than discussion, shortening the number of sessions, and, in other ways, adjusting the course to the group. Here the proponent of a course is often in a real dilemma. He knows that such adjustment is often good when undertaken by an imaginative and highly prepared leader. But, since such leaders are still fairly rare, he has to insist on uniformity and say that the course must be conducted exactly as planned. He is at once accused of being rigid, dogmatic, and authoritarian. But—he answers—perhaps he really knows what will satisfy a local group better than its own sponsors do. After all, countless hours have been invested in the construction of the course by people familiar with the general principles and practices of adult education. Furthermore, the course has been tried out with many groups and adjusted in the light of the results of such trial. Its materials and its method have been chosen to complement one another and to produce the clearly defined result stated in the objective. It should not be changed except on the basis of equally careful thought and experience.

THE FUTURE OF THE CO-ORDINATED COURSE

The sponsors of co-ordinated courses feel that they have little difficulty in defending themselves on any of the points which have so far been mentioned. There are, however, a whole group of other questions for which answers are harder to find.

Can the number of courses be extended to encompass all fields of knowledge or are there some topics which are too complicated or too filled with tension to be left to lay leaders?

So far, the co-ordinated courses which are purely educational have not succeeded in reaching a really widespread audience nor one which is characterized by very much breadth of representation. Why? Has there not yet been enough time for a real trial? Is there a natural saturation point? Do courses of different sorts need to be shaped for other audiences, particularly those who have low reading ability or who are unwilling to do sustained reading? Does the failure lie in the fact that such courses have not yet been really adopted by either the public evening schools or the Co-operative Extension Service, the two largest agencies of adult education?

An allied question is simply: How are such courses to be paid for? A co-ordinated course which is sponsored to achieve some specific task can usually find funds in the budgets of those who want that task accomplished. The military, civilian defense, and industrial courses have few problems of finance. But what about the others? So far, the support has come from foundation grants, contributors, tuition fees, and unpaid service. Must these continue to be the chief sources? The textbooks were able to create mass movements in elementary and secondary education only because the primary costs of the schools were paid from the public purse. Must the same source be used if co-ordinated courses are indeed to become the "McGuffey Readers" of adult education? If so, some safeguards must be found against deadly uniformity. All of the other levels of education have private institutions which justify their existence on the basis of their special services, their freedom to experiment, their independence of viewpoint, and their maintenance of standards. It is greatly to be hoped that private institutions may find it possible to continue to serve these same broad functions in the field of adult education.

In the pressure for funds, will the courses be simplified into textbooks, accompanied by leaders' aids but omitting the training which is now a basic element? The Center for the Study of Liberal Education for Adults has been able to develop its courses in this form but only because it has dealt primarily with evening colleges where trained faculty members already exist. The decline of the courses into mere textbooks would be a most unhappy event unless it can be delayed until there are large numbers of trained leaders in the field.

This point leads to another fundamental question: Will co-ordinated courses serve their purpose only until trained and professionalized leadership is developed? Are they merely transitional? It would take a foolhardy man to answer, but it might be observed that, in spite of the extraordinary development of the schools and universities, textbooks are still with us. The most comprehensive account of textbooks produced in the past twenty-five years opens with the statement: "At the center of the present-day educational scene in America is the textbook. It takes a dominant place in the typical school from the first grade to the college." [29] The McGuffey readers are no longer used but only because they have been replaced by larger, more attractive, and more scientifically constructed texts. A recent examiner of textbooks found that he "couldn't compare the old with the new with much precision for there are at least a dozen new textbooks for every old one, and the names of subjects have changed." [30] At the end of his study, however, he concluded that "the modern ones are unquestionably superior to the old in almost every way." [31] The present versions of co-ordinated courses will certainly disappear, but probably only as they are replaced by better ones.

In summary, it may be said that the co-ordinated course embodies very basic beliefs about adult education: that the students are mature, that they can conduct their own education, that they will want to be aided by highly expert guidance, that they need to use the various media of communication in terms of the appropriate values of each, that they find learning more profitable in groups, and that the value of their education lies in the changes which it brings about in them. These beliefs must surely underlie any sound program of education for the mature; at least it is hard to see how contradictory principles can be defended. Some of the other principles on which co-ordinated courses are based are more contro-

29. Cronbach, *op. cit.*, p. 3.

30. Sloan Wilson, "Lures To Learn," *Saturday Review*, XXXVI (March 7, 1953), 13.

31. *Ibid.*, p. 62.

versial: the compression of the content, the indirect rather than the direct employment of expert teachers, the use of lay leaders, and the strict ordering of the stimuli presented to the learners. And yet if the aim of spreading understanding to many people is accepted as a desirable goal, these principles or something very like them must be used. In no other way can the democratic hope for universal adult education be achieved.

Conclusion

This chapter has dealt primarily with print as a means of mass communication and as a device for greatly extending the scope of the field of adult education. To the man who chiseled out inscriptions in stone or who laboriously copied a manuscript, the printing press came as a new instrument full of promise as it offered enlightenment to more people [32] or full of danger as it threatened to open the sacred mysteries of learning to vulgar eyes. The spread of print has had precisely those two effects and still does; and, if modern man has now come to esteem the promise more than he fears the danger, it is because his values have been shaped by his observation of the happy consequences of widespread reading. The other chapters of this yearbook have been concerned chiefly with the reading which individuals undertake on their own initiative, whereas this chapter has been devoted entirely to the way in which reading is organized, channeled, and motivated by purposeful adult educational activities, usually carried on by groups. In both cases, however, the underlying assumption is that reading is a means by which enjoyment and enlightenment may be carried to everyone.

But breadth is properly balanced by depth and here, too, reading performs a unique function for both individual and group. Now that the other forms of communication are receiving so much attention, the loyal adherents of books sometimes seem like the chiselers of stone and the copiers of manuscripts in being both attracted and repelled by the future possibilities. In the public mind, indeed, reading is considered the means for deep study as contrasted to the

---

32. Comenius, for example, believed that print made universal education possible, provided that an exact order of instruction were followed. The developer or analyst of co-ordinated courses will find *The Great Didactic* highly instructive.

sharper but briefer impact of the other media. As we have seen, the contrast is an artificial one because reading is so frequently combined fruitfully with the other media and each medium has its own distinctive values. Nonetheless, it is true that reading permits a depth of study which radio, the films, and television can achieve only under extraordinary circumstances. Many of the fifty million adults who are consciously attempting to gain enlightenment have gone far beyond the co-ordinated course in their search for understanding, and for such people the chief means of learning, whether they work alone or in groups, is print. Its value when used for this purpose has not been celebrated here, but only because it is so obvious and so readily accepted by everyone.

In the growth of adult education in this generation there are, in fact, two central tasks. One is to broaden the base of participation and the other is to increase the depth of learning of those who take part. Though the two may sometimes appear to be contradictory, they must, in fact, always be considered together. We want neither a broad-based but superficial movement nor one which is of great depth but available only to a few people. Everyone should be given both the opportunity to learn and the encouragement to learn as much as he will and can. In the accomplishment of both of these goals, the use of print plays a central and essential part.

CHAPTER VIII

How Books Get to Adult Readers

DAVID H. CLIFT

AND

DAN LACY

The reading of adults—whether they read, how much they read, and what they read—depends on many factors of skill, habit, and motivation. But it also depends in very great measure on what is conveniently available to them to read. About 9,500 new books and about 2,500 new editions of previously issued works are published annually in the book trade in the United States. Moreover, the book trade keeps in print some 100,000 different books. The network of arrangements by which these tens of thousands of separate books, emanating from hundreds of separate sources, find their way, or more often fail to find their way, to their potential users among the adult Americans in many thousands of communities throughout the country is one of the principal determinants of reading. One explanation, indeed, of the sad comparison of Americans with Britons and North Europeans as readers of books is doubtless the inadequate arrangements for the distribution of books in the United States as contrasted with the distribution both of books in those countries and of magazines and newspapers here. This difference in distribution methods has dictated a different pattern of the use of reading time and skills in this country.

The question, however, is not merely quantitative. In considering the social adequacy of adult reading, we need to inquire whether our arrangements for the publication and distribution of books produce and make conveniently and widely available a sufficient number of copies. We need to inquire, also, into the adequacy of those arrangements in terms of the extent and the quality of the range of choice as to reading matter which is really available to the citizen. It is not, in other words, solely a question of whether he has enough to read, but whether he has an adequate *choice* of what he wants to read from a sufficient variety of good books. To the extent that books serve a distinct social role as a means of varying and enriching the communications flow received through the mass media, the characteristics of the various distribution methods in terms of the enlargement or limitation of choice assumes a special importance.

There are published annually in the United States about 760 million copies, valued at 600 million dollars wholesale, of close to 12,000 different books. Of these, 230 million copies, valued at 211 million dollars and comprising 2,800 titles, are textbooks or children's books, including the mass-market juveniles, and are beyond our immediate concern. Another 45.6 million copies, valued at 36 million dollars (both figures approximate), are exported, offset by imports of 4 million copies of 1,500 titles. Our domestic distribution system thus has to deal annually with about 488 million copies of 9,200 new and reprinted titles in terms of their accessibility to 98 million adults throughout the United States, not to mention the 100,000 or so titles of prior years still in print and the many hundreds of thousands of titles useful but no longer in print with which libraries and antiquarian bookstores must concern themselves.

Channels of Distribution

THE LIBRARY

Early Aims and Services. The principal public institution through which this distribution is accomplished is, of course, the public library. So far as is known, there were twenty-nine public libraries in the thirteen American colonies in 1776. During the following one-hundred years, the library earned a place of considerable importance in the educational life of the country. The United States Bureau of Education felt impelled to make its thorough and, in many ways, monumental survey in order that the library's influence might be recognized and understood as a matter clearly within public interest. The 1876 report stated:

The influence of the librarian as an educator is rarely estimated by outside observers, and probably seldom fully realized by himself. Performing his duties independently of direct control as to their details, usually selecting the books that are to be purchased by the library and read by its patrons, often advising individual readers as to a proper course of reading and placing in their hands the books they are to read, and pursuing his own methods of administration generally without reference to those in use elsewhere, the librarian has silently, almost unconsciously, gained ascendancy over the habits of thought and literary tastes of a multitude of readers who find in the public library their only means of intellectual improvement. That educators should be able to know the direction and gauge the extent and results of this potential influence, and that librarians should not only understand their primary duties as purveyors of literary supplies to the people, but also realize their high privileges and responsibilities as teachers, are matters of great import in the interests of public education.[1]

The report offers much testimony on the vigor and future of this growing social agency. J. P. Quincy had no doubts about the high place the public library was to occupy in American life. He stated the convictions of a growing number of persons:

When Thomas Hobbes declared that democracy was only another name for an aristocracy of orators, he never conceived of a democracy which should be molded by the daily journal and the free library. To this latter agency we may hopefully look for the gradual deliverance of the people from the wiles of the rhetorician and stump orator, with their distorted fancies and one-sided collection of facts. As the varied intelligence which books can supply shall be more and more wisely assimilated, the essential elements of every political and social question may be confidently submitted to that instructed common sense upon which the founders of our government relied. Let us study to perfect the workings of this crowning department in our apparatus for popular education. Unlike all other public charities, the free library is equally generous to those who have and to those who lack. It cares as tenderly for the many as for the few, and removes some of those painful contrasts in human opportunity which all good men are anxious to rectify.[2]

While none would wish to quarrel with Mr. Quincy's hopes for the public library, one is struck by his classification of the library as one of the nation's "public charities." It is probably true that this viewpoint has accounted for much of the uphill fight which the public library has always faced in seeking its share of the tax

---

1. United States Bureau of Education, *Public Libraries in the United States of America: Their History, Condition, and Management,* Part I, p. xi. Washington: Government Printing Office, 1876.

2. United States Bureau of Education, *op. cit.,* p. 402.

dollar. For while the public library has become an accepted American institution, too few persons do much about extending it, supporting it, or using it. "Free" has too often meant free of concern and responsible support by the community.

Public libraries spread across the country in the years following 1876. The number grew from 3,682 in that year to 7,172 in 1948. Did its influence grow as the United States Bureau of Education predicted in 1876? The answers are mixed. In one thoughtful view, the library's full potential is far from realized. Berelson, in the Public Library Inquiry, concluded in 1949:

> From existing research it would appear that librarians individually have had little effect upon the reading tastes and interests of the adult public, who in their choice of reading are most widely influenced by their own personal interests, friends, reviews, and advertisements, and comparatively little by librarians. . . . Whether and how the library has influenced popular reading through its acquisition and promotion program is not known. From a nation-wide survey, it appears that the influence of the library and the librarians will be deepened more than broadened by the introduction of new services such as films, records, and group discussions; these new services appeal most to old friends of the public library.[3]

General data available from studies dealing with popular opinion and knowledge of the library indicated in 1949 [4] that "most people are satisfied with the public library. The major dissatisfaction centers upon inadequacy of the book collection. . . ." These studies also indicated "that the general public has little knowledge about the public library and its services and seems to regard the public library as a fine thing for the community to have—for other people to use."

The Public Library in 1955. Today there are about 7,500 public library systems in the country. The governmental units in which these exist have a total population of around 123 million persons. These library systems had, in 1950, upwards of 150 million books, more than 26 million borrowers, circulated over 404 million volumes

3. Bernard Berelson, *The Library's Public: A Report of the Public Library Inquiry*, p. 86. New York: Columbia University Press, 1949.

4. *Ibid.*, pp. 86-87.

annually, spent in excess of $115 million each year, and employed over 46 thousand persons.[5]

Books remain the prime staple in the library. However, when financial support allows and the librarian's sense of service permits, audio-visual materials are combined with books. Figures for 1950 show that the country's public libraries held 24,272 films, 52,523 microfilms, 201,582 slides and filmstrips, 320,660 sound recordings, and 8,062,186 photographs, pictures, and prints.

The public library has come to mean many things to different persons. To one, it is where he can find the classics and the great books. To another, it is where he can hope to find the best sellers. To the student, it may be a place for required schoolwork. For the club woman it may be the stock bin for a course of study. To the businessman, it can be a specialized collection of the many technical books, government regulations, and public opinion surveys to which he turns for ideas to run and improve his business. To the person with a hobby, it can offer much satisfaction. To the puzzle enthusiast, it has books that may help land him in the winner's circle.

What does the librarian consider the library to be? He has concluded that it is "a collection of materials suited in content and organization to the needs of a reading group. The American public library is a community agency containing the materials required by local residents to realize their potentialities as individuals and citizens, arranged and interpreted to facilitate use."[6] To meet its responsibilities fully, the library attempts to provide books and other materials to meet the reader's needs in education, information, aesthetic appreciations, research, and recreation.

The Library and the Adult Reader. Books, we have said, are basic in the library's efforts. How effective is the library in bringing books to the adult reader? Very effective in large metropolitan communities, less effective in small communities, notably deficient

---

5. Indicated by figures issued in *Public Library Statistics, 1950.* United States Department of Health, Education and Welfare. Office of Education Bulletin, 1953, No. 9. Washington: Government Printing Office, 1953.

6. American Library Association, Committee on Postwar Planning, *A National Plan for Public Library Service,* p. 4. Chicago: American Library Association, 1948.

in rural areas. It takes money, which the larger libraries are most apt to have. It takes professional skill, which the smaller libraries often lack. The possibilities are indicated by the funds reported available for book purchasing in a random selection of libraries of different sizes from the 1954 American Library Directory: Chicago, $468,889.00; Baltimore, $273,492.00; Boston, $250,023.00; Denver, $58,000.00; Los Angeles, $344,123.00; Bridgeport, Connecticut, $48,655.00; Canton, Ohio, $37,518.00; Kansas City, Kansas, $14,-000.00; Salt Lake City, Utah, $34,140.00; Alhambra, California, $14,261.00; Hoboken, New Jersey, $3,000.00; Port Arthur, Texas, $6,725.00; Georgetown, Delaware, $325.00; Woodbine, Iowa, $252.00; Hamilton, Missouri, $173.00; Milford, New York, $319.00; and Kingwood, West Virginia, $171.00.

The great range in size and support of public libraries brings about wide variations in the provision of books for the adult reader. In one city, he has a wide choice of good book materials available to him through the public library; in another, his choice is restricted. In one, he has expert guidance from the library's staff; in another, he's pretty much on his own.

Other chapters in this yearbook have indicated that "availability" of books is an important factor in reading. This section will deal with the general availability of books for the adult reader through the public library. It will not attempt to present examples of superior book provision on the part of many individual libraries. The elements of good library service, as practiced by many libraries in the country, are considered in chapter v.

A great deal can be learned from the operations and experiences of individual libraries. However, we are trying, in this section, to present something of the total picture, for the problems inherent in the availability of good books to all the people by means of the public library are not wholly local in nature. The implications and, in some measure, the solutions are national rather than local problems. Much study and research are needed to round out the picture. Existing statistics are incomplete. Only the barest of refined figures exist, and evaluative studies of the whole situation are few.

The reader is affected, first, by the extent to which public library service, whether good or poor, exists in his community and state.

The distribution of public library systems, by area and population served, is unequal, as Table 1 indicates.[7]

TABLE 1

DISTRIBUTION OF PUBLIC LIBRARY SYSTEMS BY AREA AND POPULATION SERVED

Region	States Included	Number of Public Library Systems	Population Served
East South Central	Alabama, Kentucky, Mississippi, Tennessee	177	7,054,691
West South Central	Arkansas, Louisiana, Oklahoma, Texas	213	8,731,971
Mountain	Arizona, Colorado, Idaho, Montana, Nevada, New Mexico, Utah, Wyoming	218	2,931,627
Pacific	California, Oregon, Washington	398	13,514,482
South Atlantic	Delaware, District of Columbia, Florida, Georgia, Maryland, North Carolina, South Carolina, Virginia, West Virginia	493	15,651,750
Middle Atlantic	New Jersey, New York, Pennsylvania	963	25,450,015
New England	Connecticut, Maine, Massachusetts, New Hampshire, Rhode Island, Vermont	1,010	8,092,789
West North Central	Iowa, Kansas, Minnesota, Missouri, Nebraska, North Dakota, South Dakota	1,254	9,174,409
East North Central	Illinois, Indiana, Michigan, Ohio, Wisconsin	1,302	24,363,996
	Totals	6,028	114,965,730

The Reader's Share of Books. How many books per capita should a library have if it is to meet the reading requirements of the community? Many librarians will be quick to state that the number is generally far in excess of what the library can provide. In an effort to assist libraries in this respect, the American Library Association, in 1943, formulated minimum standards on the number

7. These and many figures which follow are derived in one form or another from *Public Library Statistics,* 1950, *op. cit.* It should be noted that not all libraries responded to the Office of Education's request for information.

of books needed per capita.[8] Its recommendations are shown in Table 2.

TABLE 2

MINIMUM STANDARDS FOR NUMBER OF VOLUMES PER CAPITA IN A PUBLIC LIBRARY

Population of Library Area	Volumes per Capita	
6,000–10,000 .... 3.0	(up to a total of	25,000 volumes)
10,000–35,000 .... 2.5	(up to a total of	70,000 volumes)
35,000–100,000 .... 2.0	(up to a total of	175,000 volumes)
100,000–200,000 .... 1.75	(up to a total of	300,000 volumes)
200,000–1,000,000 .... 1.5	(up to a total of 1,000,000 volumes)	
Over 1,000,000 .... 1.0		

The per capita standard must be used with caution. Many factors, such as the age of the libraries, density of population, size of the geographical area, and the number of library-service outlets affect the value of this index. However, it is one indication of the general availability of books. It is of interest to examine the present national situation as to book holdings in relation to the above minimum standards. "In 1950," reports the United States Office of Education, "the public library systems in the cities with populations of 100,000 or more owned 1.07 books per capita; in the 50,000 to 99,999 group of cities they possessed 1.45 per capita." [9] Not all libraries in the country responded to the Office of Education's request for information. Basing the number of reporting libraries (6,028) upon the population served by those libraries (114,966,000), the Office found that these libraries had 1.24 volumes per capita. The corresponding figure for 1945, was 1.4, and for 1939 it was 1.3. The per capita figure for the entire population would have been much smaller. On the basis of these figures and remembering that the American Library Association's standard is a minimum one, the Office of Education concluded that "no improvement has taken place during the past 12 years in the per capita book holdings of public libraries."

There is wide variation among the states and regions in the

8. American Library Association, Committee on Postwar Planning, *Postwar Standards for Public Libraries*, p. 71. Chicago: American Library Association, 1943.

9. *Public Library Statistics, 1950, op. cit.*, pp. 7–8.

number of books available per person through the public library. Generally speaking, the various regions provide books per capita as follows: From one-half to one book per person in the East South Central, West South Central, and South Atlantic regions; from one to two books per person in the Mountain states, Pacific states, Middle Atlantic, West North Central, and East North Central regions; in New England, slightly more than two and a half books per person. These figures indicate that the reader's chances to get the book he needs from his public library depends a lot on where he lives. His chances are less if he lives in Tennessee; better if he lives in Mississippi. The former, through its public library systems, can provide only about one book for every three people, a ratio of .39; the latter has a book for each two persons (.54). To turn from the lowest books-per-capita region (East South Central) to the highest (New England), the reader in Vermont has four books (4.34) as his per capita share; in Connecticut he has two (2.08).

To further suggest the spread in book availability, imagine a modern-day Mark Twain voyaging down the Mississippi intent upon reading books rather than writing them. He must obtain his books from the public libraries of the states along the banks of the Mississippi as that river winds its way from Minnesota to the Gulf. When the Mississippi is small, his chances are better; as the river widens, his books become fewer. In the upper reaches, he finds the libraries supplying from one to two books per capita (from 1.09 in Illinois to 2.29 in Iowa). After the Mississippi and Ohio rivers join, he must satisfy himself with a more meager book diet (from .39 in Tennessee to .64 in Kentucky).

Money for Public Library Books. The number of books which a public library system is able to offer its readers is determined by the amount of money which the governing unit provides for that purpose. How well the library spends its book money is another matter. The financial support is affected by a number of factors, including the general maturity of the concept of the public library in the community; the recognition by the people of the community's need for informational, educational, and recreational services rendered through the books of the library; the initiative, public relations ability, and the resourcefulness of the librarian; and the ability of the library trustees to interpret the library's needs. As a norm for the support of public libraries, the American Library Association has recommended the following: $1.50 per capita for "minimum" service, $2.25 per capita for "good" service, and $3.00 per capita for "superior" service.[10]

Out of its funds, the library must pay salaries of the library and maintenance staff; purchase books, periodicals, and other library materials; bind and preserve those materials; and purchase equipment. What proportion of this expenditure should go for books? The standards for the different expenditures have been suggested by the American Library Association: "As a general norm applicable to many public libraries, the following proportions of expenditures may be suggested: 60 per cent for library salaries; 20 per cent for books, periodicals, and binding; and 20 per cent for other operating expenditures." [11]

The percentage of expenditures for books and periodicals has steadily decreased from 1939. The percentage for 1939 was 21.8; for 1945, 19.7; and for 1950, 18.5.[12] When these figures are related to the changes in the purchasing power of the dollar, the decline becomes all the more pronounced.

If a community were to provide the "minimum" support of $1.50 per person, and if the library then spent 20 per cent of this income for books, periodicals, and binding, it would be able to spend 30 cents per person for these items. (It should be mentioned here that a thorough revision of standards for public libraries is under way by the American Library Association. It is very likely that these new standards will emphasize qualitative rather than quantitative guides.) However, the present standard for "minimum" book provision is not met. The latest available per capita expenditures for books show the following when computed on a state-wide basis (figures for public libraries in 1950):

Eleven states spent from four to nine cents per person.
Fifteen states spent from ten to fourteen cents per person.

10. *A National Plan for Public Library Service, op. cit.*, p. 96.

11. *Ibid.*, pp. 101-2.

12. These figures are for expenditures for books and periodicals only, binding being excluded. It is clear, however, that the figure would be little increased by the addition of expenditures for binding.

Thirteen states spent from fifteen to nineteen cents per person. Ten states spent from twenty to twenty-three cents per person. (These figures include the District of Columbia.)

The per capita expenditures for books and periodicals by regions is shown in Table 3.

TABLE 3

PER CAPITA EXPENDITURES FOR BOOKS AND PERIODICALS, SHOWN BY REGIONS, FOR PUBLIC LIBRARIES IN 1950

Region	Per Capita Expenditure	Number of Persons Served by Region
East South Central.....................	5 cents	5,984,898
West South Central....................	9 cents	8,663,945
South Atlantic	10 cents	15,498,592
Middle Atlantic	13 cents	25,164,931
Mountain	15 cents	2,819,716
West North Central....................	17 cents	9,092,526
East North Central....................	18 cents	24,325,526
Pacific	19 cents	13,504,826
New England	21 cents	7,888,957
United States	15 cents	113,943,917

The public library systems of three states (New York, Ohio, and California) each spent over $1,000,000.00 for books and periodicals in 1950. Sixteen states (Vermont, Rhode Island, North Dakota, South Dakota, Delaware, West Virginia, Mississippi, Oklahoma, Montana, Idaho, Wyoming, Colorado, New Mexico, Arizona, and Nevada) spent under $100,000.00 each in the same year. Of these sixteen states, six (North Dakota, Delaware, Idaho, Wyoming, Arizona, and Nevada) spent under $50,000.00. New York, with a population of 12,706,718, expended roughly $400,000.00 more for books and periodicals than did the sixteen states included in the Mountain states, the West South Central states, and the East South Central states, which altogether served a population of over 20 million.

The larger public library systems of the country are able to purchase all, or so much, of the total publishing output each year as is needed. They can also provide duplicate copies of titles in order to meet the needs of many readers. None is able to build up a solid collection of research and retrospective materials in all fields of interest to its readers, but this need is met by interlibrary loan and the resources of the state library agency. The medium-sized library must be highly selective in the books it purchases with its limited funds; the small library, rigidly so. In the small library the acquisition of titles which the librarian believes to be the best additions to the library must be weighed against a popular demand for less desirable titles. Thus, the greatest difficulties are experienced by the smaller libraries, serving smaller communities, and supported less well because of the small share of the total tax money which can go to the library. There are a great many of these libraries. Analysts of library service have maintained that good library service is possible only if support is based on a reasonably large population group—normally at least 25,000 persons. The United States Office of Education report shows that 5,134 libraries, or 85.2 per cent of the 6,028 reporting, served population groups under 25,000; 57.6 per cent of all the public library systems reporting served population groups of under 5,000, and only 6.65 per cent served population groups of 50,000 and over.

Number of Adult Readers and the Circulation of Books. The number of persons who go to the library is one indication of its service to the adult reader. In 1950, the registered borrowers reported by 5,162 public library systems totaled 25,361,000. Of these, 50.6 per cent were designated as adult borrowers; 22.8 per cent of those registered were not broken down between adult and juvenile. The number of persons registering in public libraries has shown only a slight increase during the past twelve years and has not kept pace with the increase in the country's population. However, this figure is not in itself dismaying. Many services, such as furnishing reference works and materials used within the library, are not reflected in the number of persons registered.

The libraries reporting in 1950 show that adults accounted for the larger percentage of books circulated from all service points except bookmobiles, 52.5 per cent of the total as against 41.2 per cent for juveniles, with 6.34 per cent undistributed. Children were the heavier borrowers of books from bookmobiles. All told, the circulation per capita for the population served throughout the country amounted to 3.37 books per capita. Again, it must be noted that a very considerable amount of reading is done in the libraries themselves.

THE BOOKSTORE

Because of the large number of readers per copy, because of their extraordinary effectiveness in providing a wide reader choice, and because, as public institutions, they can be used to serve needs and areas which it would be impossible for commercial activities to attempt to serve, libraries play a role in the distribution of books for adult reading far beyond quantitative measurements. But in terms of the sheer number of books that reach readers, they do and can do only a part of the total job. For every book that goes into a public library, thirty go directly into the hands of the adult readers through commercial channels. (Each library book, of course, presumably finds many more readers than a book purchased by an individual.)

The backbone of this commercial distribution remains the retail bookstore. Statistics on the number, geographic distribution, and volume of sales of retail bookstores are distressingly inadequate. Part of this inadequacy arises from the difficulty in defining a "bookstore" and in separating sales of books from those of cards, stationery, records, and other items commonly sold in the same store. (Is a sporting-goods store which handles books on sports a bookstore? What of an office-supply house that sells dictionaries, etiquette books, and a half-dozen best-sellers?)

However, there are sufficient data to draw the picture of book-store distribution in broad outline. There are probably about 9,000 outlets of all kinds and sizes for hard-cover books in the United States, of which about half make an effort to handle new, non-specialized books. The R. R. Bowker Company's "selected" mailing includes 834 bookstores and 640 book departments of department stores. This means that there are about 1,500 bookstores in the United States that handle a sufficient number of books to justify relatively extensive mailings of circulars and other promotional material. Applying a more severe test, publishers who have endeavored to economize their sales costs have generally concluded that there are 400 to 500 bookstores in the United States justifying calls by salesmen. In other words, we may hazard the guess that for the 98 million adults in the United States there are about 500 good, adequately stocked bookstores; an additional 1,000 smaller stores attempting to offer a general book service; perhaps 3,000 other outlets offering at least the most popular new books; and perhaps another 4,000 small or highly specialized outlets making little if any effort to provide a general book service. The responsibility of providing an effective book service to the country rests primarily on the 1,500 in the first two classes mentioned.

These are disturbing figures. They are made more disturbing by three further considerations. One is that the bookstore network is not increasing; it is decreasing relatively to the total adult population, and relatively to the national income it is decreasing very rapidly. Moreover, the point of least growth or most rapid contraction is at the margin of bookstore service: the middle-sized town. Again there are no dependable statistics, but on the whole it would appear that a town of 10,000 people is less likely to have a bookstore today than a town of that size a generation ago. The failure of the bookstore distribution system to achieve significant growth in the boom years of the postwar period is indicative of what might occur in a less prosperous future.

The second additionally disturbing fact is the high degree of urban concentration of the limited number of bookstores that do exist. It has been estimated that 62.5 per cent of all bookstore sales are made in 25 cities which, even including their metropolitan areas, account for only 20 per cent of the population of the country. To approach the problem another way, though there are no precise statistics, it would be the common observation of the book trade that the very few really adequate bookstores outside of cities of 50,000 or more and their metropolitan areas are far more than offset by the absence of adequate bookstores in a great many cities of that size. Since 75 million people, or 47 per cent of the population of the United States, live outside such cities and their surrounding areas, it would be a very conservative estimate, indeed, that roughly half of the United States does not have access to even reasonably good bookstore service.

What is perhaps most dismaying of all is the tiny percentage of those in cities served by bookstores who make any sort of regular use of them. Here statistics are least adequate of all, but $2.00 per year per capita is considered a fairly good level of sales in a city well served by bookstores. This is the sale of one book per person about every other year. But of these a high proportion, perhaps half, are juveniles, cookbooks, dictionaries, and other reference books, and another large proportion are gifts. Adults' bookstore purchases of books for their own general reading certainly average far less than one every two to three years. We believe it would be the consensus of booksellers that almost all their sales of books for personal reading are made to not more than 1 per cent, or at most 2 per cent, of the people in the area served.

In summary, there are approximately 500 bookstores in the United States handling an adequately broad range of current materials. Another 1,000 handle a considerable number and are probably willing and equipped to "special-order" any book in print. Almost all of these are in cities of some size; their number is not growing appreciably; and even in the cities where they exist they find regular users among only a very small fraction of the residents. Among them they sell close to 125 million adult books a year, valued at about $250 million wholesale, or about 40 per cent of the total national output. They perform an indispensable, remarkably effective service in providing current books of their choice to a relatively small group of urban readers; but they are not able to give the average citizens of the country an opportunity to learn about or choose from the range of current book production.

The inadequacy of retail-bookstore outlets as a distribution device to the entire population has always been present and has historically resulted in a variety of other distribution methods. Through most of the nineteenth century, door-to-door "subscription" sale, usually in advance of publication, was perhaps the principal method of distribution. That form of selling survives today as a major distribution method, but the unit cost of sales is so high that it is now practical only for encyclopedias and other relatively expensive sets. Total sales in this category today are approximately $125 million a year. Geographic coverage is much more even; salesmen reach quite small towns, and certain subscription houses make a special effort to reach the rural market. Though a large part of this sales figure represents purchases of encyclopedias and other reference works by schools and libraries, subscription sales represent one of the major means by which books reach individual homes. The "standard sets" made available in this way provide a reading opportunity for many homes which would otherwise have almost none. But it is obviously not a feasible means of distributing current individual books.

The first really successful distribution mechanism for printed words in this country was created for magazines rather than books. It used two channels, both dependent upon the achievement of a nation-wide network of rapid railway communication. Cheap and rapid mail service came with the railroads, and the second-class postal-rate act of 1879 extended its benefits to magazines and newspapers at a flat nation-wide rate, well below cost. The mass-circulation national magazines, carried into homes—urban, village, and rural—throughout the country, became a possibility. The second channel was created by the news companies which provided reading matter for passengers in the stations and on the trains, and which laid the basis for the present newsstand distribution of magazines.

THE BOOK CLUB

Both of these magazine-distribution methods have been adopted for the use of books. The book club, though it does not enjoy a postal subsidy at all comparable to that of magazines, does combine the subscription method (of assuring a predetermined volume of sales) with the use of the postal service (as a means of reaching customers inaccessible through stores). Book clubs, in their contemporary form, began with the Book-of-the-Month Club in 1925 and the Literary Guild in 1926. Since that time they have grown rapidly in both size and number. There now are probably nearly a hundred book clubs, and, though their total volume of business cannot be precisely determined, it is certainly well over $75 million a year, and the number of volumes distributed is certainly over 50 million annually. Probably the volume of sales through book clubs approximates very roughly that through bookstores.

There can be no question but that book clubs have greatly extended the geographic availability of books. The regional pattern of strengths and weaknesses does not differ greatly from that of bookstore distribution. In the case of the Book-of-the-Month Club, in 1952, the New England states, with 6 per cent of the adult population, and the Southern states, with 20 per cent, each provided 10 per cent of the members. But the divergencies are not so great as in the case of bookstores even on a regional basis, and it is clear the clubs perform a substantial service in reaching small towns and rural areas served distantly, if at all, by bookstores. The Book-of-the-Month Club has made the assertion that it has never found a single one of the more than 40,000 post offices in the United States at which it has not had a member, and, though its search may not have been exhaustive, it is certain that the Club and similar groups have carried some books into thousands of communities with no other means of access to them. (There is little doubt, however, that the great majority of book-club members, as of other book users, is urban.)

Book clubs have also done much to acquaint the members with other books than their current selections. Almost all clubs publish a monthly newsletter or magazine describing new books of likely interest to the members. Books so reviewed can be ordered through the club, frequently, if they are "alternate selections," at a discount or with credit toward a book dividend. The Book-of-the-Month Club has stated that the 130 million books distributed during its first 25 years included 14,000 different titles. The extraordinary variety of book clubs now existing, embracing many specialties of interest and levels of taste, has also done much to broaden the range of choice available through book clubs. Of books published annually, probably 1,000 or more are distributed by one or another club.

The fact remains, however, that the whole economy of the book club depends on eliminating the unpredictability of sales which is inherent in the free choice of the reader. At the same time that there has been a broadening of the range of books offered to the reader through clubs, there has been a spectacular growth of clubs offering abridgments of books under terms that leave the reader little or no choice and that hence make possible a very low cost.

THE NEWSSTAND

The magazine method of distribution through newsstands has also been employed for inexpensive paper-bound books. Several earlier attempts of this sort met with only temporary success, but in the last ten years there has been an almost revolutionary increase in the distribution of books through this channel. The present era of inexpensive book production was initiated by Pocket Books, Inc., just before World War II. A great deal of experience in the manufacture of cheap books was gained by the book industry during the war in the production of pocket editions for the armed forces. When paper quotas were released after the war, the industry expanded with almost explosive rapidity. By 1953 more than a dozen publishers were issuing about 1,000 titles a year in paper-bound format, priced from 25 cents to 50 cents and distributed through magazine wholesalers. The sale of these books was enormous. In 1953 the total production was nearly 300 million copies, and sales were probably nearly 250 million. This is certainly well over half of all books bought for general reading, as opposed to textbooks or reference works.

The extraordinarily large volume of sales was undoubtedly based not merely on the lower price but also on the ubiquitous availability of the paper-bounds. The norm for magazine and small-book distribution is one outlet per thousand persons, and over much of the country this ratio is achieved. Paper-bound books are actively sold at more than 100,000 locations. Moreover, the newsstands and drug-stores and cigar counters at which they are sold are places to which people come in large numbers for other purposes, and the use of display racks forces books upon their attention. Where one has to seek out a bookstore to buy a hard-cover book, of which he has learned from some other source, he daily encounters paper-bound books ready-to-hand for purchase as he goes about his business. This distribution network, operating through more than a thousand independent wholesalers and through branches of the American News Company to the more than a hundred-thousand outlets, reaches into every village in the country. It has in some aspects revolutionized the geography of book distribution.

But it has not solved the other problem of the range of choice, of the availability not merely of "books" but of the particular book needed. Initially, books reprinted in paper-bound format were principally mysteries, westerns, and light romances; but the quality and range of materials published has now greatly improved. Substantial bodies of serious, even advanced, nonfiction are now reissued in this format, and the whole range of fiction with any potentiality of wide sale is represented. One now has no difficulty in finding a "good" book on almost any newsstand today.

The whole economy of paper-bound books rests, however, on

the pattern of magazine distribution. This involves a more or less automatic distribution at each step, the handling of a relatively limited number of titles, a minimum of "paperwork," and a rapid rotation of issues available as new numbers of magazines appear and last month's are recalled. On the average newsstand probably only fifty or a hundred titles are on sale at any one time, and any one title is likely to be there for only a very few weeks. Only rarely, of course, are there facilities for individual ordering. Though about a thousand titles are published annually and nearly five thousand are in print, the practical availability is confined to those displayed at any one place at any one time.

Efforts have been made to overcome this limitation. Books are now held in print longer. The recent appearance of R. R. Bowker Company's *Paper-bound Books in Print* gives the first effective bibliographical listing of paper-bound books. A number of book-stores, especially in large cities, maintain comprehensive stocks of paper-bound books in print, and special orders for quantities of books for classroom or library use are now generally possible. But this opportunity for wide personal selection does not operate gen-erally, and indeed it cannot, since it is precisely the avoidance of the costs of individual handling of single copies of particular titles that is a major—probably the major—factor in the low cost of the less expensive paper-bound books.

The recent appearance of paper-bound books usually retailing at 95 cents to $1.45 is quite a different phenomenon. They are dis-tributed through bookstores in the normal patterns and, except for price, are substantially similar in their problems of availability to hard-cover books.

DISTRIBUTION BY DIRECT MAIL

Finally, there is direct-mail sale as a means of book distribution. Three categories of mail sale should be considered. Many publishers make a specific effort to sell certain books directly to the consumer by mail instead of through bookstores. These are generally books of fairly wide popular appeal to groups not likely to patronize book-stores or specialized books of interest only to a small professional or hobby group who can be inexpensively reached through adver-tising in specialized journals or the use of select mailing lists. Though the volume of books sold in this way is substantial, in neither case do such mail-order-department promotions do much to increase the availability of general books. In the second place, almost all publishers, though they may not solicit them, are prepared to accept mail orders from individuals for any books on their list. This is most helpful to an active book user who reads reviews but is remote from an adequate bookstore, but it obviously does not provide that easy availability which enlarges book audiences. Finally, one or two of the major mail-order houses, as do a number of bookstores, make rather comprehensive efforts to sell books by mail through catalogues, and this undoubtedly does afford an opportunity to materially enlarge and widen the flow of books.

The Pattern of Book Availability

From this summary account, certain major characteristics of book availability in the United States are obvious. Perhaps foremost is the fact that those areas that are poor in libraries are also poor in all other opportunities to learn about, see, read, or acquire books. Almost without exception, the 27,000,000 people who are without public library service also lack convenient access to any bookstore and do not regularly see any newspaper or magazine that reviews current books at all comprehensively. The book poverty of these areas, comprising a high percentage of all rural America, has been mitigated, but only to a degree, by the newsstand distribution of paper-bound books and by book clubs. The rack of paper-bound books in the county-seat drugstore is far better than no books at all, but it is not nearly as large a rack nor does it have as wide a variety of good titles as the one in the corner drugstore in the city. And while the drugstore is on the nearest corner in the city, its rural equivalent is likely to be several miles from the farmhouse. Though adequate statistics are not available, it is reasonably certain that book-club membership is highest in the cities with the best libraries and bookstores and lowest in the rural areas with neither.

Beyond this 20 per cent of the people, whose lives are passed with almost no opportunity for contact with books, are the tens of millions who live in small towns or villages or more fortunate rural areas where there is at least some library service. They are the basis for the comfortable assurance that though 27 million Americans do not have library service, 130 million or more do. But for these tens of millions, the library service is likely to be very limited and the bookstores nonexistent or confined to a gift shop or stationery store handling a few dozen standard titles. Book-club membership is likely to be larger, but other sources of news about books almost as limited as in the remoter rural areas.

By and large, it is probably true that the residents of rural areas and of towns and cities of less than 25,000 in the United States rarely have a convenient means of learning about or seeing or choosing from anything like an adequate range of books; and those in rural areas and villages more often than not gravely lack opportunity for frequent contact with books at all. Even in large cities, books are relatively far less accessible than films or newspapers or magazines, not to mention broadcasts. This is the blunt set of facts that is a principal determinant of adult reading in this country, both quantitatively and qualitatively.

The implications for public policy are serious. Alone of the great media of communication, books combine the ability to convey extended and detailed discussion of a problem with entire freedom on the part of the consumer to choose from thousands of authors awaiting his attention. The characteristic pattern of the "mass media" is ephemeral communication from a single source to a very large audience who see or hear the same message simultaneously. This is an essential characteristic in a society that needs, as does ours, the prompt, widespread, and dependable dissemination of news. But it affords little opportunity for the thorough study of a problem, the publication of the specialized work that can command but a small audience, the expression of the dissident view, or the completion of the individual inquiry. It is the book that serves these ends, but it can serve them only to the degree that books are realistically available, that their existence is known, and that they are accumulated in stocks that can give readers an adequate range of choice to meet their varied and specialized needs.

It is, of course, not a matter merely of local but rather of national concern that so large a part of the total population of the country lacks this kind of opportunity. The decision of any national question—of foreign policy, for instance—depends as much on the ten million or more voters who have neither library nor bookstore to turn to (and who have probably not seen since school days a book seriously treating foreign policy) as it does on those who have access to full resources of information. As in all other aspects of education, national policy must of necessity address itself to those problems that have national consequences.

Problems and Answers

What are the steps that can be taken by organized effort to enlarge the availability of books to adult readers? These steps need to be aimed at three objectives:

1. Having more adequate collections of books available for public use through libraries and bookstores.
2. Bringing the services of bookstores and libraries closer to the daily activities of readers so that they encounter books in their normal comings and goings rather than having to seek them out in inconvenient locations.
3. Making effective arrangements for service by mail in those cases in which it is not practical to have an adequate stock of books available to the village or rural user.

With respect to the first, the number of bookstores in the United States probably cannot be markedly increased, particularly in smaller towns, until the level of book-buying in the country increases, for the present market serves only marginally to support the present array of bookstores. In part, this is a circular argument, because one reason for the meager sales of books in this country is the limited number of retail outlets, but the circle will probably have to be broken at other points. Bookstores will follow a market enlarged by the growth of libraries and book clubs and by better education, but they do not have the resources to pioneer in its creation.

On the other hand, there may be real promise in the improvement of the numerous outlets for paper-bound books so that they may more dependably offer a broad selection from among the rapidly increasing number and range of books appearing in this format. There has been already a considerable adaptation of the magazine distribution system to meet the special requirements of books, and further improvements seem likely.

It is primarily on the library, however, that society will have to rely for carrying an adequate book distribution system beyond the present limits, for their tax-supported base makes it possible for them to respond to social pressure without the limit of profit-and-loss calculations.

Better book distribution through the public library can be expected as libraries become more widespread, better recognized as community agencies, and more heavily used. The proponents of better and more extensive library service—librarians, library trustees, citizen groups, legislators—have been greatly concerned over the low rate of use which generally prevails throughout the country. They have been concerned over the quiet apathy which greets the library and its services. They realize that while the library has many deficiencies, it also has much to offer that is left unused. They believe in the great potential of the public library as an information center and as an instrument for adult education. Why, they ask, isn't the public library used more?

Part of the answer is that the potential user doesn't know about libraries. He has not been exposed to dynamic public library service. As a consequence, he does not often think of making use of the library. He does not spread word of its resources. He does not exert himself in its support. He is not inclined to get excited over the library's needs. The librarian, the library trustee, and lay supporters of the public library are aware of an encircling dilemma: If more funds were available for the support of public libraries, the values of good library service could be demonstrated. But good library service cannot be demonstrated without funds, and funds are hard to come by because good library service is unappreciated where it is unknown. The problem is how to break out of the circle.

Many ways have been tried. Many have been successful. Others have had a measure of success. The "library demonstration" has been particularly successful in bringing good library service to the attention of the people and causing them to want to have the service continued. The state of Louisiana is an example. Here a "demonstration" plan has been in existence for about thirty years. The plan is exactly what the name implies. The state library goes into a parish, sets up a library system of branch libraries and bookmobile service so that no one has to go too far for the books he wants and needs. During a trial period of a year, the state pays the greater part of the expenses. At the end of the demonstration period it becomes the responsibility of the parish to continue the service— if its people wish to continue to have books. They have—and the plan has been successful.

The "demonstration" idea is the main element in the library legislation now pending before the Congress of the United States. Proposals for federal aid to libraries have been before Congress repeatedly during the past decade. The Library Demonstration Bill was defeated in the House on March 9, 1950, by a vote of 161 to 164 after five hours of debate.

Throughout this chapter, the figures given have been related to "the population served," meaning generally the population reached by existing libraries. There is also an "unserved" population. This population is largely in rural areas and is estimated to be at least 27 million persons. These persons have no local library service. Four hundred of the 3,000 counties in the country do not have a public library within their borders.

Legislation to improve this situation has been before the Congress since 1946. Forty-two identical bills were introduced into the Eighty-fourth Congress during January, 1955, by members of both parties. Known as the Library Services Bill, this legislation sought to take books to rural areas lacking in library service. The Bill provided for $7,500,000 annually in federal funds for five years, this amount to be matched by the states. The states were to be given complete jurisdiction over the expenditures and could spend the funds in whatever ways seemed best calculated to promote books and other library services in unserved areas. The proponents of the legislation were firm in the belief that the states and localities would continue the library services provided by the five-year period of demonstration. The sponsors of the bill argued: [13]

1. The public library is one of the principal institutions of public education, which is basic to the maintenance of our American way of life.

13. *Educational Issues of Concern to the Eighty-fourth Congress.* A Report prepared in the Legislative Reference Service of the Library of Congress, March 17, 1955. (For the use of the Committee on Education and Labor, House of Representatives.)

2. There is a great need in the United States for further extension of public library service.
3. The provision of essential library services for all citizens is a major concern and partly a responsibility of the federal government.
4. In the past, Congress has recognized the need and established a precedent for federal promotion of nonfederal library services.
5. The pending library services bill would provide a wholly desirable and effective program of federal promotion of library services in the states.
6. The proposed legislation should be enacted now, for the need is urgent.

Relatively little argument unfavorable to the bill has appeared within the last ten years. Unfavorable views which were or could be expressed have been summarized as follows: [14]

1. The provision of public library services is a state and local concern.
2. Federal grants for public library services would add to the cost of federal government at a time when the national debt should be reduced.
3. If this measure is passed, it may become a permanent activity of the federal government.
4. There is no need for the requested federal aid.
5. The passage of this legislation might lead to federal control of libraries throughout the country.
6. Consideration of this bill should be postponed.

The individuals and organizations in favor of the legislation noted that while 27 million persons in this country were without local public library service, perhaps as many as 53 million had only inadequate service. Observing that the adult population of the United States twenty-five years of age and over had an average of only a little over ten years of formal schooling, they expressed the conviction that "this inadequate education of our people to meet the changing needs of the times, vocationally, technically, and culturally, points to an imperative need for public library service to assist in meeting the deficiencies." [15]

The conclusions reached by Mr. Berelson in 1949 on the public's interest in and use of the library were reported earlier in this chapter.

14. *Ibid.*

15. *Ibid.*, p. 28.

It is interesting and encouraging to note the testimony in this respect offered at the hearings on the Library Services Bill.[16]

The witnesses were users or potential users of the library and included legislators, businessmen, leaders in public affairs, educators, newspapermen, agricultural experts, housewives, and students. The testimony went always to the need for books:

Once the residents of these counties—and I am talking now about your rural counties that have never had library service—begin to use books, there will be a continuing desire for the education and for the recreation and inspirational value that they get from this service.—U.S. Representative in Congress.

Education is a lifelong process. It continues beyond grade school, beyond high school, and beyond college. This process is sometimes called adult education. But although there are many adult education programs throughout the country, not many appear in rural areas. . . . Where the opportunity for such self-education is not available, we should see that it is made possible through a more widespread and adequate library service.—A college president.

It has often been said that informed people are free people, are slow to panic, difficult to fool and enslave. And so it is good to know that this year Americans are thoughtfully turning the pages of 350 million books drawn from public libraries alone. Each goes out from its little niche in the treasure house and leaves its imprint on a free mind, and returns to its niche ready for the next American who wants to know. So long as this goes on, we can feel more sure of the strength and the wisdom and the freedom of America.—Quoted in the Hearings from a public interest advertisement in *Life* magazine.

Books and library materials are not static. They are alive and they give life and help to people. Books are the products of people, of their thoughts, hopes, ambitions, and skills. They can transmit past experience and knowledge and benefits to us both now and in the future. There is no substitute for them and there is not likely to be one.—U.S. Representative from Oklahoma.

. . . There must be some way out—some way to continue the educational growth of American citizens. And there is a way. That way is the public library. It is America's continuation school. . . . If the schools

16. *Federal Aid for Library Service in Rural Areas.* Hearings before a Subcommittee of the Committee on Education and Labor, House of Representatives, Eighty-fourth Congress, First Session, on Bills To Promote the Further Development of Public Library Service in Rural Areas. Hearings held at Washington, D.C., May 25, 26, and 27, 1955.

will only teach the reading habit, the library will educate the world. The public should be made to see that the library is a continuation school. While the library is useful and helpful, it has still not reached its maximum of helpfulness, and it cannot do so until the people themselves realize what it has to give them.—William Allen White, quoted at the Hearings.

The testimony offered in support of the bill showed a sincere belief in the desire of people to read. The values, benefits, and delights of reading, thought the witnesses, may have to be demonstrated just as good roads, fast automobiles, vacuum cleaners have to be demonstrated. They stressed the need in these times for an informed citizenry and the part books, and only books, can play in that process. They stressed the need for the equalization of educational opportunity through the library. And they came back time and again to the need for better-supported libraries. Figures were presented showing the per capita expenditure of state funds for various public services. These figures showed schools at $28.22, highways at $23.12, public welfare at $16.22, health and hospitals at $6.47, natural resources at $3.50, public safety at $2.67, employment administration at $1.20, airports at 37 cents—and libraries at six cents.

MAIL SERVICES

Book distribution systems, however, need to be enlarged not only extensively, into areas not served, but intensively, to groups not reached even in the cities and counties that have bookstores and libraries. Many studies have indicated that library use is affected to a surprising degree by the location of branches. A difference of even a few blocks may determine whether a service is really used or not. Dispersion of relatively small branches and the use of bookmobiles in cities have been sound responses to this situation. But libraries may be able to go farther in the way of deposits in factories or railroad or bus or airline terminals. Similarly, newsstand sale of books has indicated that availability as well as price is important to large sales. An aggressive bookstore might be able to expand sales considerably by the promotion of books more vigorously in places in which people gather in any case.

But even at best it is simply not possible to put a bookstore or a good library within convenient reach of everyone. It is a stubborn fact that many millions of people, for as long as we can foresee, will have to buy by mail the books they want or to borrow, through interlibrary loan, those which are beyond the resources of a modest county library collection. Industry or government policy has done much in the other media to equalize access to information in rural and small-town areas. Though the quality of newspapers varies tremendously, the national press services do much to provide universally available information. Network broadcasting results in the same radio and, in less degree, television programs being available almost everywhere. Most important of all, a flat and very low postal rate makes it as easy and cheap and nearly as quick to get a magazine in the remotest hamlet as in New York City. Free carriage of newspapers through the mails in the county in which they are published makes rural newspaper delivery cheap and easy in areas in which carrier delivery would be impossibly expensive.

Less has been done to achieve a similar equalization of opportunity to use books. The state library agencies have accomplished much here. At least forty-five states strengthen the resources of existing libraries, particularly small ones, through loans of collections of books. Many state agencies will make such loans to individuals if there is no local library to which they can turn. Libraries add to the availability of books through the well-established system of interlibrary loan. A danger, perhaps small, exists in both of these practices. Ironically enough, if the state agency does an excellent job in this respect, something may be lost in the way of local initiative.

Since mail service is expensive and, in economic terms, relatively unprofitable, publishers and bookstores have done less to cultivate this market aggressively except for highly specialized types of books. Though all bookstores and almost all publishers are glad to receive and fill mail orders, they can afford the expense of advertising by mail only for books especially likely to sell by mail, and only to people especially likely to buy them. In particular they cannot afford to advertise to precisely the markets that—from a social viewpoint—most need this service: the rural and village groups who have little other way to learn of books or to acquire them but who are not yet habituated to buying books. Nor can they afford to advertise in this way the kinds of books that most need it—those that would otherwise escape general attention.

It is clear that the provision of adequate mail service requires three things:

1. Consistent and vigorous effort at serving a group that has been on the margins of interest and service of both librarians and the book trade, including adequately stocked and staffed agencies (both libraries and booksellers to give the service).
2. Adequate means of giving news about available books.
3. Postal rates that, as in the case of magazines and newspapers, will encourage the service.

The profit margins of bookstores are not sufficient to permit them to undertake intensive efforts to develop new markets by mail, from which the returns may be limited for a long time. But such promotion, if it can help to develop a new market, may be of substantial benefit to the industry as a whole, and it may be possible to find ways in which publishers could join in helping to defray the cost of such promotion.

In view of the inadequacy both of reviewing services and of advertising to provide enough information about new books to stimulate potential readers to make good use of the resources that are available to them, a major effort is needed to provide a comprehensive, readable, popular guide to new books and new editions of general interest. One specific need is a free reviewing service, aimed especially at rural audiences, for use by weekly newspapers and farm organizations. But a general monthly review, aimed at catching the interest of the infrequent as well as the regular book-buyer or borrower, covering new books and containing articles describing books on particular subjects or for particular purposes (such as Christmas or graduation gifts) is needed. It might be supported by the book industry and intended for use by bookstores in mailing to their customers and potential customers, by libraries as a handout or as a mailing piece, and by rural or other organizations seeking to encourage reading among their members. It should be designed with great care, edited with great skill, and have all the resources of both the book industry and the library profession behind it to make it a practical and effective means of leading people to acquire and use books.

Further, a postal rate is required that will recognize the public interest in the genuinely national dissemination of information as it is already recognized in the postal rates applicable to newspapers and magazines. The library-loan rate is now at a suitably low level but is restricted in many annoying ways. On the other hand, the general book rate is well over three times as high as the applicable rate for reading matter in newspapers and magazines, though there would appear to be no justification either in cost or in social utility for such a differential.

Finally, in so far as a really vigorous effort to cultivate a new market outside the present distribution machinery is made by bookstores or wholesalers or mail order houses, the extra cost of this effort and the economic advantages of having an almost wholly new market added may need to be appropriately recognized in the discount structure or by some other means.

The book-distribution machinery has hitherto largely ignored or underemphasized whole segments of our population, both in geographic terms (rural and village populations) and in economic terms (wage earners, for example). In part, this was because the rural and village readers, at least, were difficult to serve because of their dispersion; in part, it was because the relative lack of means, leisure, and education made them a relatively unprofitable "market" for the bookseller and, in some degree, even for the librarian to cultivate. But today the rapid equalization of income, leisure, and education has opened a greatly wider potentiality for book use, which has been exploited effectively by neither libraries nor the book trade. And because opportunity, availability, and familiarity are lacking, the demand for books that might exist is not felt or effectively expressed. In devising the means of distribution that will reach this now-unserved audience is the great opportunity of the book world.

CHAPTER IX

Developing Readable Materials

EDGAR DALE

and

JEANNE S. CHALL

Some Problems in Communication

The aim of communication is to share ideas, information, attitudes, and skills. The sharing may be through direct imitation of an action or indirectly by words, pictures, and other symbols. In a simple society where specialized information is rare, everyone can talk to and learn from everyone else. But in today's specialized society we have reached a point where, as Robert M. Hutchins once put it, even our anatomists cannot talk to each other unless they happen to be working on the same part of the body.

The late Irwin Edman pointedly observed that:

Even philosophers get into the habit of talking only to each other, in a private professional language, gratuitously complicated and esoteric, unavailable to the generality of educated men [and] the seminal ideas of philosophers, historians, and scientists reach only after a long time-lag the large public more eager than we suspect for leading ideas, for the best that is being discovered and thought in the world. Meanwhile the general public is fed on the prejudices, conventions, and secondhand opinions of propagandists and entertainers. The gap between scholarship and the educated man outside the ranks of the professional scholarship is a wider chasm almost than that between the literate and the illiterate.[1]

Sometimes, unfortunately, the specialist has isolated himself intentionally. Crane Brinton points out, for example, that the humanists abandoned medieval Latin and deliberately revived a dead

---

1. Irwin Edman, "The Business of the Scholar," *Saturday Review of Literature*, XXXII (July 23, 1949), 20.

tongue, the kind of Latin Cicero and his fellows wrote. He says: "The humanists were . . . a small privileged group, not interested in a wide audience; some of them damned the printing press as the vulgarization of learning." [2]

The conflict between liberal and special education reflects this same problem of communication. Specialized knowledge is growing so rapidly that specialists learn only a small part of their specialty. Yet, the citizen faces and needs more general knowledge about the world. In the last ten years, for example, extended study of the Far East and of Africa has become increasingly important, but there has been no lessening of the need for understanding of other better-known parts of the world.

It settles nothing to say that information is so vast we cannot encompass it, that the best we can do is to get our ignorance better organized. As teachers of adults we must still ask: What of all this vast knowledge is most important? And then: How can we teach it? The first problem is one of the philosophy of education. The second is that of humanizing or popularizing knowledge. This is the problem for specialists in communication.

How can we humanize knowledge? How can we develop a citizen who shares important general ideas with other citizens yet also meets his specialized obligations? One way is through better printed materials. Radio, TV, and movies are also important, but print remains one of the major ways in which adults continue to learn.

If printed materials are to be a force in adult education, we must meet three conditions:

1. We must have books, articles, and pamphlets on important subjects prepared by able writers for the layman as well as the specialist.
2. We must make these materials physically available and psychologically acceptable. The book, pamphlet, or article must reach the potential reader and must be attractive enough so that he will try to read it. This is no simple task, since only one item in eight is usually read in the easily available newspaper.
3. The reader must understand what he reads. If he does not, he either quits or gets a confused idea of what the writer means.

2. Crane Brinton, *The Shaping of the Modern Mind*, p. 25. New York: New American Library, Mentor Book, 1953.

Certainly, if adults are to read wisely and well, they must have a wide variety of excellent reading materials from which to choose—some easy and some hard. Why is this true? First, the reading ability of adults varies greatly, with millions unable to read anything but the simplest writing. Second, we do not always read at the level we *can* read but tend to seek material that is easy for us. And finally, although we may each be specialists in one or two fields, we are laymen in all others. Hence, we need simple, nontechnical materials that can be assimilated easily.

How and What Adults Read

HOW WELL DO ADULTS READ?

Although data are limited, it is usually assumed that years of schooling correspond roughly with reading abilities. For example, a study of enlisted men in World War II revealed that, among adult illiterates in the armed forces, 97 per cent had attended school to some extent, more than 25 per cent had reached at least the seventh grade, and almost 5 per cent had been in school more than eight years. Yet they could not read fourth-grade material.[3] It is likely, however, that young people who have gone beyond the sixth or seventh grade might improve their reading somewhat in later years, while those who spent four years or less in school may lose some of their reading ability as they grow older.

Table 1 shows the years of schooling completed by persons

TABLE 1

YEARS OF SCHOOL COMPLETED FOR 87,675,000 PERSONS TWENTY-FIVE
YEARS AND OVER, 1950 CENSUS *

Years of School	Per Cent
Less than 5	10.9
5 and 6	9.2
7 and 8	27.1
9, 10, and 11	17.1
12	20.3
13, 14, and 15	7.2
16 and over	7.0
Not reported	2.2

* The cumulative percentages are as follows: 6.0, college graduates; 13.2, college graduates and some college; 33.5, high-school graduates or more; 50.6, some high school or more; 77.7, seven grades or more; 86.9, five grades or more.

3. Eli Ginzberg and Douglas W. Bray, *The Uneducated*, p. 81. New York: Columbia University Press, 1953.

twenty-five years of age and over, as reported in the 1950 census of population.[4] Note that 10.9 per cent had *less* than five years of schooling in 1950. When we add to this group the ones having five and six years of schooling, we have 20.1 per cent of our adults twenty-five years of age and over with six or less years of schooling.[5] Thus, materials at the seventh-grade level are probably too hard for one-fifth of our adult population. In numbers, over seventeen million adults would probably find such materials too hard for them.

Additional census data (not in table) concerning the nonwhite population show that in 1950, 62.2 per cent, or almost two-thirds had six or less years of school. Materials at the seventh-grade reading level may thus prove too hard for two out of three. We see why many Negroes and other disadvantaged groups are not very good customers for books and newspapers.

But won't the need for simple materials decline soon with the rise in educational attainment? It might lessen somewhat, since in April, 1950, our average (median) years of school completed was 9.3. This is a gain of almost a year from 8.4 years (median) in April, 1940. However, it will be a long time before we are a nation of high-school graduates. In 1950, only a little more than half of the approximately two million young men and women eighteen years of age in that year graduated from high school.

Now let us compare the above estimates of reading ability with estimates of the difficulty of reading materials. Are the reading abilities high enough to match the reading levels of available informative materials on child care, everyday economics, human relations, or world affairs? Probably not. More than thirty years ago, in *The Humanizing of Knowledge*, James Harvey Robinson contended that the available books on serious subjects were too difficult for the general reader and called for short, readable books. During the 1930's and 1940's the need for such materials was confirmed by the studies of Ojemann, Dale and Tyler, Gray and Leary, Bryson,

4. *United States Census of Population: 1950.* Special Report P-E No. 5B, p. 13. Washington: Government Printing Office.

5. *Ibid.*

and others.[6] There have also been several organized attempts to write simple materials. In spite of these efforts, however, Kempfer reported in 1950 from a survey of librarians and evening-school principals that the greatest shortage of reading material for adults is still below the sixth grade.

What about newspapers and magazines? Do they match the reading abilities of most adults? The earliest surveys of the difficulty of newspapers concluded that the important news was written above the level of a majority of newspaper readers. In fact, these dramatic findings spurred the readability campaign of the United Press with Robert Gunning as consultant and the Associated Press with Rudolf Flesch as consultant.[7]

The current magazines of any given time always show a rich variety of reading materials which range in reading difficulty from the standard for pulp fiction to that which is suitable for the scientific journals. However, even the pulp magazines—*True Confessions* and *Modern Romances*—are at about seventh-grade level. The *Reader's Digest* averages about eighth- to ninth-grade level. *Harper's* and *Atlantic Monthly* are more difficult—about tenth- to twelfth-grade level. In other words, most magazines, especially the ones that contain serious and informative materials, are beyond the reading ability of a large proportion of adults.

WHAT DO ADULTS READ?

Let us now match these estimates with the facts about readership in leading magazines. Table 2 lists these facts from information re-

6. Ralph Ojemann, "The Reading Ability of Parents and Factors Associated with Reading Difficulty of Parent-Education Materials," *Researches in Parent Education,* University of Iowa Studies in Child Welfare, VIII (March 1, 1934), 11-32.

Edgar Dale and Ralph W. Tyler, "A Study of the Factors Influencing the Difficulty of Reading Materials for Adults of Limited Reading Ability," *Library Quarterly,* IV (July, 1934), 384-412.

William S. Gray and Bernice E. Leary, *What Makes a Book Readable.* Chicago: University of Chicago Press, 1935.

Lyman Bryson, "Readability Laboratory," *Library Journal,* LXI (June 1, 1936), 455.

Homer Kempfer, "Simpler Reading Materials Needed for 50,000,000 Adults," *School Life,* XXXII (May, 1950), 115-27.

7. Rudolf Flesch, *The AP Writing Handbook.* New York: Associated Press, 1951.

ceived by the writers from the publishers of six popular periodicals.

This table indicates that persons with only an eighth-grade education scarcely read these magazines at all and that the bulk of the readers, even the readers of *Life* magazine, are high-school graduates or much higher. Evidently adults tend to read what is easy for them rather than types of material they can read only if they make the necessary effort.

TABLE 2

EDUCATIONAL LEVELS ACHIEVED BY READERS OF CERTAIN LEADING MAGAZINES

HIGHEST EDUCATIONAL LEVEL ACHIEVED BY READERS	PERCENTAGE DISTRIBUTION OF READERS CLASSIFIED BY EDUCATIONAL LEVEL ACHIEVED					
	Look	*Newsweek*	*Atlantic Monthly*	*Reporter*	*Time*	*Life*
College degree and above	*	35.3	63.9	68.5	40.9	*
Some college.....	23.2	25.7	21.8	16.8	27.1	45.2
High-school graduate	54.3	*	11.1	7.9	19.7	21.8
Some high school.	22.5**	34.1	2.0	3.8	7.1	13.5
Eighth grade or less	*	4.9	1.2	3.0	5.2	19.5

   * Figures unavailable.
   ** Includes grade school.
   Note: This table is to be read: 40.9 per cent of the readers of *Time* were listed as college graduates; 27.1 per cent had pursued college courses for a period of time but did not graduate.

As readers, we prefer informative and expository materials at a level where the intake of ideas is worth the effort expended. Only when highly motivated do we read difficult materials with any new ideas. Without high motivation such materials are ignored. However, most reading in the adult field is not done under the compulsion of high motivation. If the reading gets tough, the adult can quit. He may drop out of the "Great Books" course or may not read the rather difficult magazine to which he has subscribed. We see, then, that elevation in quality of reading, as in mountain climbing, can be secured by walking a longer distance on a gentle slope or a shorter distance on a steep slope. Many persons are not sufficiently motivated to read and reread the difficult materials which will help them reach the goal faster but are quite willing to take more time and reach the summit by easy stages. When it becomes important to read a book or article we may choose the steep slope. People who want to get rich on uranium are digging deep into books on geology.

If, therefore, we want a well-informed, literate population, we must have a variety of reading materials on many levels of difficulty. We need these to satisfy the able reader who wishes variation in difficulty level as well as to fill the need of the less able reader who wants the same variation within his range. We suggest the following broad classification of reading levels, all of which require informative and worth-while reading materials:

1. *The learning level* (Grades I, II, and III): Serious adult content must be used even on this level. This material is needed for the teaching of reading to native and foreign-born adults. It could also be used in the teaching of English as a foreign language outside the United States. At the present time, children's books are often used. Adult books on a learning level might follow some of the principles developed for children's graded readers. However, such books should not pattern themselves too strictly after children's beginning reading books. Adults can manage a higher idea load than children.

2. *The elementary level* (Grades IV, V, and VI): Materials at this level can be understood by about 80 per cent of the adult population. It would be easy reading for most adults who have completed the eighth grade. Serious, informative materials have been written at this level. See section (following in this chapter) on use of readability formulas.

3. *Junior high school level* (Grades VII, VIII, and IX): This is the standard, nontechnical reading level for the adult of average reading ability and is easy reading for the high-school graduate.

4. *High-school level* (Grades X, XI, and XII): Material at this level is fairly difficult reading for a large majority of the population, requiring motivation.

4. *College level* (Grades XIII, XIV, and XV): Difficult reading, suitable for specialists or for very highly motivated readers.

It should be pointed out that when we speak of something at the fifth-grade level we merely mean that it can be read by children or adults as far down as that level. Some articles, for example, will be at the seventh-eighth-grade level, e.g., Pearl Buck's "The Touch of Life." [8] This does not mean that it is at the maturity level of junior high school pupils. It means that it can be read satisfactorily by adults whose reading ability is rated at the junior high school level.

8. Pearl Buck, "The Touch of Life," *Atlantic Monthly*, CXCIV (November, 1954), 45-48.

Readability Formulas

Readability formulas are yardsticks for estimating the difficulty of written or oral communication. They are statistical devices based on those aspects of the communication process that most highly reflect the comprehension difficulty of the written or spoken message.

Since 1923, about thirty readability formulas have been devised. The books by Klare and Buck [9] and Chall [10] give complete references for all the formulas. Some of them are developed for measuring the difficulty of children's books; others, for adult materials. The most recently devised and widely used formulas—Lorge, [11] Flesch, [12] and Dale-Chall [13]—are used for both children's and adult reading materials. When sample passages from a book, article, speech, or script are analyzed for the kinds of words and sentences used, one can determine the approximate level of reading ability needed to understand the communication. Thus, if a book scores at seventh-grade level, it can probably be understood by people with reading ability of seventh grade or above. Those with less than seventh-grade reading ability will probably find the book too difficult. It should be remembered, of course, that a readability formula gives only an estimate or a prediction of difficulty. The true test of readability is whether it can actually be read by people with reading ability of seventh grade and above. This can be determined by actual testing of representative readers on portions of the book. The formula only analyzes elements in the reading or spoken material and makes predictions from them.

9. George R. Klare and Byron Buck, *Know Your Reader*. New York: Hermitage House, 1954.

10. Jeanne Chall, *Readability: An Appraisal of Research and Application*. Columbus: Ohio State University Press, (in press).

11. Irving Lorge, "Predicting Readability," *Teachers College Record*, XL (March, 1944), 404-19; and "The Lorge and Flesch Readability Formulae: A Correction," *School and Society*, LXVII (February 21, 1948), 141-42.

12. Rudolf Flesch, *How to Test Readability*. New York: Harper & Bros., 1949.

13. Edgar Dale and Jeanne S. Chall, "A Formula for Predicting Readability: Instructions," *Educational Research Bulletin*, XXVII (February, 1948), 37-54.

WHAT READABILITY FORMULAS MEASURE

What elements are measured by the formulas? On what is the predicted readability based? A careful study of the formulas disclosed only four kinds of elements used:

1. *Vocabulary:* All of the readability formulas contain a measure of vocabulary difficulty. Vocabulary difficulty is measured either by word length (Flesch, Farr-Jenkins-Paterson,[14] Gunning,[15]) or by rarity or unfamiliarity as determined by a particular word list (Gray-Leary, Lorge, Dale-Chall, Yoakam [16]). All measures of vocabulary difficulty correlate very highly, and using one in a formula is sufficient.

    In general, the greater the number of hard, rare, or long words, the more difficult the material is to understand. In readability formulas, vocabulary is the most important element and, hence, receives the most weight. The other elements listed below add to the prediction of difficulty, but they do not add much.

2. *Sentence structure:* This is the second most important element. All formulas that use more than one element, use a measure of sentence structure. It is usually measured by average sentence length. Since long sentences are usually complex, sentence length also indicates sentence complexity. In general, the harder the material, the higher the average sentence length.

3. *Idea density:* This has been measured indirectly by the number of prepositional phrases. In general, the more prepositional phrases, the higher the ideational content, and the more difficult the material. Prepositional phrases also contribute to sentence complexity as measured by average sentence length. Only the Gray-Leary and Lorge formulas use this element.

4. *Human interest:* Some formulas (Gray-Leary, Flesch Human Interest) have employed measures indicative of human interest or directness of approach, such as personal pronouns, proper names, nouns with gender, personal references. In general, the more personal references, the easier the material.

WHAT THE FORMULAS DO NOT MEASURE

Are these, then, the only elements that make books easy or

14. James N. Farr, J. J. Jenkins, and D. G. Paterson, "Simplification of Flesch Reading-Ease Formula," *Journal of Applied Psychology*, XXXV (October, 1951), 333-37.

15. Robert Gunning, *The Technique of Clear Writing.* New York: Mc-Graw-Hill Book Co., Inc., 1952.

16. Gerald A. Yoakam, "The Yoakam Readability Formula," *Basal Reading Instruction*, pp. 329-40. New York: McGraw-Hill Book Co., Inc., 1955.

difficult? Can we assume that hard or long words and long sentences tell most of the story of readability? Not exactly. Other important factors have been isolated but were not included in the readability formulas because they could not be measured reliably. Some of the factors overlooked by the major readability formulas follow:

1. *Conceptual difficulties.* Readability formulas overlook the possibility of conceptual or meaning difficulty in relatively common and short words. "To be or not to be, that is the question," is considered easy by every formula since all the words are short and within most lists of easy words. The word *strike* is considered easy whether it means "to deliver a blow," "to hit," "to miss a baseball," or "an act of quitting work." In short, none of the formulas gives adequate weight to the contextual meaning of the particular word; only the structure is considered.

The formulas also overlook difficulties inherent in combinations of relatively familiar words used in a rare or idiomatic sense, e.g., "to come by wealth," "to have a change of heart," "to bring to light."

The widely used vocabulary measures also fail to distinguish between different kinds of difficulties—concrete terms relatively unknown to the average adult (e.g., "velocipede," "fusilage," "counterpane") and those that are difficult because they are inherently abstract ("autocratic," "permissive," "correlation"). Both kinds of words would be considered hard by readability formulas, whether based on word lists or on word length. Yet, the words in the latter group are more difficult since they presuppose a higher level of abstract thinking.

Morriss and Holversen demonstrated that abstract conceptions are significantly related to difficulty. Their readability technique appraised the difficulty of words in context by classifying them, not on the basis of commonness or length, but in terms of their remoteness and nearness to the readers' experience.[17] It has, however, never been published nor could evidence of its use be found in the literature. More recently Flesch published a formula attempting to measure abstraction.[18] It appears rather complex, and, so far, no evidence of its use has been found.

2. *Organization.* Considerable evidence is accumulating on the influence of organization on the comprehension of expository material. This

---

17. Elizabeth C. Morriss and Dorothy Holversen, "Idea Analysis Technique." Unpublished manuscript, Teachers College, Columbia University, 1938. (Cited in Flesch's *Marks of Readable Style.*)

18. Rudolf Flesch, "Measuring the Level of Abstraction," *Journal of Applied Psychology,* XXXIV (December, 1950), 384-90.

evidence comes mainly from experiments designed to validate the effect of simplification through a reduction of readability scores. These studies seem to indicate that while lower readability scores result in greater reader comprehension or readership, as much, if not more, of the effect may be due to the reorganization of the material.[19] This point was first made by Lorge in his interpretation of the results of the Murphy split-run experiments.[20] Negligible effects on comprehension have often been found when changes in vocabulary and sentence structure were made without an accompanying change in organization. When organization was also changed, either through enumeration, anecdote, direct question-and-answer approach, or summary of main points, benefits were found.[21]

Recently, Carter studied the effect of three different ways of structuring controversial news stories. He found that "total comprehension of issues was increased by giving the reader a neutral orientation in the lead paragraph, followed by equal presentation of both sides, with issues divorced from names." The other two "structure-types" were merely rearrangements of the story. The Flesch reading-ease scores for the different versions were about equal.[22]

Related to organization and to conceptual difficulty is amplification of main ideas. Wilson found that adding detail through explanation and example aids comprehension.[23] There was an increase in comprehension although readability scores of the original and amplified versions were substantially the same.

3. *Content.* None of the formulas directly measures the nature of the content nor the reader's interest in it. Yet this factor was considered the most important aspect of readability of adult materials by the librarians, teachers, and publishers in the Gray and Leary survey.[24] Bernstein demonstrated recently the importance of interest for both reading speed and comprehension. She gave her teen-age readers stories which differed widely in adolescent interests according to research evidence. One was chosen for its action, suspense, clear

19. William Allen, "Readability of Instructional Film Commentary," *Journal of Applied Psychology*, XXXVI (June, 1952), 164-68.

20. Irving Lorge, "Readability Formulae: An Evaluation," *Elementary English*, XXVI (February, 1949), 86-95.

21. For other studies and examples, *see* Jeanne Chall, *op. cit.*

22. Richard F. Carter, "Writing Controversial Stories for Comprehension," *Journalism Quarterly*, XXXII (Summer, 1955), 319-28.

23. Mary C. Wilson, "The Effect of Amplifying Material upon Comprehension," *Journal of Experimental Education*, XIII (September, 1948), 5-8.

24. William S. Gray and Bernice E. Leary, *op. cit.*

style, and teen-age variety. The other was a long, wordy description. The two stories were equivalent in readability according to the Flesch, Lorge, and Dale-Chall formulas. The story containing the high-interest factors was understood better, read faster, and judged to be more interesting than the wordy selection, even though both stories had the same readability scores.[25]

The subject matter also influences the style of the material. Books on abstract, complicated subjects will be harder than those which discuss relatively simple, elementary ideas and events. Fiction is easier to read, in general, than nonfiction because it deals with more concrete actions. Nonfiction varies more and can approach the highly scientific and abstract.

An excellent review of studies of adult interests can be found in the book by Klare and Buck.[26]

4. *Format.* Such physical features of the text as the size and kind of type, leading, margins, and size and kind of illustrations have long been accepted as important in the appeal of reading materials and in their general effectiveness. These factors are not measured by any of the readability formulas. Paterson and Tinker [27] and Burtt [28] present summaries of research on the physical features most suitable for adults.

VALIDITY OF READABILITY FORMULAS

How valid are the formulas? How much confidence can be put in their use?

1. We can use a formula for estimating *relative* difficulty with considerable confidence. That is, when a formula is applied to a series of books that range in difficulty, it will tend to arrange the books in the same order as actual testing of the readers or judgment of experts. There is also considerable agreement among the formulas (particularly the Lorge, Flesch, and Dale-Chall) in assigning the same relative positions of difficulty. In short, a formula can tell whether one book is easier or harder than another.

2. With somewhat less confidence, we can say that because a book scores sixth-grade by a readability formula, it can be understood by

25. Margery R. Bernstein, "Relationship between Interest and Reading Comprehension." Unpublished Doctor's dissertation, Teachers College, Columbia University, 1953.

26. George R. Klare and Bryon Buck, *op. cit.*

27. D. G. Paterson and M. S. Tinker, *How To Make Type Readable.* New York: Harper & Bros., 1940.

28. Harold E. Burtt, "Typography and Readability," *Elementary English,* XXVI (April, 1949), 212-21.

sixth-graders. When the exact grade scores from formulas have been compared with reader comprehension and judgment of experts, there has been some disagreement. It is questionable, therefore, whether we can accept predicted difficulty as true difficulty. However, when a particular formula is used often, the user learns its pitfalls and can estimate whether it is inaccurate on a particular piece of communication.

The above generalizations about validity come from a study of the original standardization of the formulas and more recent studies attempting to validate the formulas. Most of them were based on children's reading.[29] A detailed summary of these studies, listed under the various formulas they were designed to validate, can be found in Chall's book.[30]

For adult materials, validation studies were concerned mainly with the effect of readability on readership. It should be noted that readership—how many readers read a given article—encompasses many more factors than the difficulty of the material (readability), and hence it is an imperfect criterion against which to validate readability formulas. In spite of this limitation, the following validation studies cited by Klare and Buck [31] show that easier stories did get more readers:

Daniel Starch . . . analyzed the copy of over 1,000 ads one-third page or larger over a period of three years. He found that the three ads that got read most were, according to Flesch's formula, comfortable reading for nearly 80 per cent of the population. The three that were read least, however, tested as comfortable reading for less than 35 per cent of the adult population.

Murphy,[32] editor of *Wallace's Farmer*, found that increasing the readability of articles could increase their readership as much as

29. David H. Russell and Henry R. Fea, "Validity of Six Readability Formulas as Measures of Juvenile Fiction," *Elementary School Journal*, LII (November, 1951), 136-44.

Edward Howard Latimer, "A Comparative Study of Recent Techniques for Judging Readability." Abstract of Doctor's dissertation, *University of Pittsburgh Bulletin*, XLIV (April, 1948), 1-11.

30. Jeanne Chall, *op. cit.*

31. George R. Klare and Byron Buck, *op. cit.*, p. 24.

32. Donald R. Murphy, "How Plain Talk Increases Readership 45 to 66 Per Cent," *Printer's Ink*, CCXX (September 19, 1947), 35-37.

18 to 66 per cent. Feld [33] found a 20 to 70 per cent increase. Schramm [34] noted that a readable style might well contribute to depth of readership as well (i.e., how many paragraphs into a story a reader will go). Swanson [35] followed this with a demonstration that it can increase depth by as much as 80 per cent. A further study (not published) showed a magazine's circulation to be affected by its readability, with increased sales following the month after a more readable issue and decreased sales after a less readable issue.

A more recent study by Swanson and Fox found that easier versions of articles do not increase readership or retention, although they do increase the reader's comprehension. They offered this hypothesis for the contradictory evidence on readership. When articles are already interesting, as these were, the simpler style does not add significantly to readership. However, when articles aren't as interesting, simplification will increase readership.[36]

A further word about the split-run technique used by Murphy. A split-run of *Wisconsin Agriculturist and Farm* was handled in this fashion: The harder half of the printing had a Flesch score of 37. It was read by 44 per cent of the men and 11 per cent of the women. The simplified copy used in the other half of the run had a Flesch score of 74 and was read by 54 per cent of the men and 23 per cent of the women. Based on a circulation of around 200,000 and a reader total of around 320,000, some 30,000 extra readers were picked up by the simpler copy.

We have run ten of these readability tests, and we have found that the trend is almost always toward the simple style. . . . This kind of readability test goes on the assumption that both pieces of copy are interesting and well done, that the only difference is the difference in syllable count and sentence length. . . . There is no substitute for good writing. But if you have two pieces of copy on the same subject, and

33. B. Feld, "Empirical Test Proves Clarity Adds Readers," *Editor and Publisher*, XXIV (1948), 81-88.

34. Wilbur Schramm, "Measuring Another Dimension of Newspaper Readership," *Journalism Quarterly*, XXIV (December, 1947), 293-306.

35. Charles E. Swanson, "Readability and Readership: A Controlled Experiment," *Journalism Quarterly*, XXV (December, 1948), 339-43.

36. Charles E. Swanson and Harland G. Fox, "Validity of Readability Formulas," *Journal of Applied Psychology*, XXXVII (April, 1953), 114-18.

if they are equally well written at different levels, then the one that uses the simpler words and the short sentences is going to come out ahead.[37]

Perhaps the increase in readers was at the expense of losing the abler readers? "Not so," says Mr. Murphy. "A breakdown showed results exactly the opposite of what you would expect. The simpler copy was scoring better with the high-school graduates than with the grade-school graduates."

Use and Interpretation of Readability Formulas

A readability formula tells us the relative difficulty or grade level of reading material—how hard it is. It does *not*, however, tell us how hard it *ought* to be. This will depend on whom we are trying to reach. We might, of course, say reading materials should be no *harder* than they need to be. Yet we must quickly add that they should be no *easier* than they need to be. If too hard, they will frustrate unnecessarily. If too easy, they will waste time, especially of the abler readers. Vernon's research on the intelligibility of British Broadcasts suggests that if a communication is too simple, it may reduce the level of interest of the more highly educated or the one who already knows a lot about a subject. They prefer to be "stretched" and resent what they regard as overpopularization. He writes: "This should be no surprise. An astonishingly large proportion of the adult population confines its reading to comic strips, the *Daily Mirror* and *Picture Post*, which are scorned by the well-educated." [38]

Our problem, therefore, in preparing materials for adults is to set the desired degree of hardness. We must remember that it will be difficult for some readers and easy for others. Thus, *Harper's* may offer little difficulty to the reader of this chapter. Yet, *Foreign Affairs* and *Partisan Review* might occasionally represent hard reading. Most adults who may read this chapter probably do a small

37. From a speech given by Donald R. Murphy, editor of *Wallace's Farmer* and *Iowa Homestead,* before the American Association of Agricultural College Editors, East Lansing, Michigan, July 13, 1954.

38. P. E. Vernon, *An Investigation into the Intelligibility of Educational Broadcasts,* p. 62. London: Audience Research Department, British Broadcasting Corporation, November, 1950.

amount of "hard" reading and a very large amount of "easy" reading. This "easy" reading may be in their own field or it may be the reading of materials which are at the tenth- to the twelfth-grade level. Easy reading is usually at least two to three grades below our top-ability level.

Here are comments on typical objections to the use of readability formulas:

1. *Why make all writing simple?* We do not intend to do so— it would be impossible anyway. We suggest only that writing be as clear as possible. Further, as noted above, no readability formula tells how hard any material *ought* to be; it tells how hard the material *is*. We could discover that the material is too easy as well as too hard. What we wish to do is to roughly match reading ability with reading material and provide a wide range of choice at the reading level of the individual. The adult who reads comfortably at the seventh-grade level may find tenth- or eleventh-grade levels too hard for him. We do, however, want some reading materials which are hard enough to challenge, but not so hard that they constantly frustrate.

2. *You can't write by a formula. Writing is an art which cannot be reduced to or circumscribed by a formula.* Formula-makers warn users that a high correlation between difficulty of reading and long, complex sentences or hard words does not prove that these are necessarily the *causes* of the difficulty. The long sentences and hard words in a particular article may be the result of the complex ideas. To shorten the sentences will not remove the reading difficulty.

Fine writing is certainly an art. Unfortunately, there are not enough artists to go around. Genius, whether in writing, in music, or whatever the field may be, is rare. Much reading material, therefore, must be written by artisans rather than by artists. Interestingly enough, the ablest writers are usually the ones most concerned about ways of improving their writing.

3. *Formulas are not exact.* It is true that a formula applied to material of known difficulty, e.g., philosophy, may give inaccurate scores. However, all formulas represent averages, and those responsible for formulas have indicated this limitation. Furthermore, the correlations rarely run above .70, indicating that there are factors

in the materials which the formula does not take into account. Nevertheless, formulas are exact enough to be useful as has been pointed out in the section on validity.

4. *Why bother with complicated formulas? Why not have able teachers, persons who know a great deal about writing and teaching, evaluate these materials?* Groups of able individuals, whether librarians or teachers, can make good predictions of reading difficulty. But you can get similar results quickly and inexpensively by using a formula. This is the whole point of readability formulas. They were developed so that books and manuscripts would not have to be tested out on the potential readers or need always to be evaluated by experts. Such estimates of difficulty take much longer and are quite expensive.

5. *Formulas do not measure important factors in comprehension.* This is a sound criticism and has been commented on. There are many questions for which we do not have suitable answers. What are the effects of more frequent summarizing, the numbering of points? What is the effect of increased use of questions and answers as in the interview techniques increasingly used in magazines like *U.S. News and World Report?* When does amplification really become dilution? When is rewriting merely translating and when does it become restructuring? Certainly, too, we need more thought and research on the problem of complexity of ideas. Which ideas are hard merely because of the limitations of words and thus are easily made intelligible by pictorial methods? And, which ideas are truly mature and complex?

Wilson Taylor's "Cloze Procedure" is a promising way of testing the difficulty of communication.[39] Taylor omits words (by a predetermined pattern) in a passage and asks readers to fill them in. He finds that passages on which the readers show good agreement on what the missing words should be are easier than those on which there is less agreement. He has compared the difficulty of selections by his procedure with the Flesch and Dale-Chall scores. For most materials, there is a high correlation. However, for selections from Gertrude Stein, James Joyce, and Erskine Caldwell, the cloze-procedure estimates made more sense than the formulas. These

39. Wilson L. Taylor, "Cloze Procedure: A New Tool for Measuring Readability," *Journalism Quarterly,* XXX (Fall, 1953), 415-33.

selections "fooled" the formulas since they used either short, hard words (fooling the Flesch formula) or used easy words in a rare sense (fooling the Dale-Chall formula).

It should be noted that Wilson's cloze procedure is not a readability formula since it requires representative readers. It is a very simple comprehension test that may prove an excellent way to check the predictions of the formulas and give additional insight into sources of difficulty.

6. *You can't simplify materials by just changing the hard words to easy ones or by shortening the sentences.* We agree and have partially discussed this problem above. Serra notes studies which show that merely rewriting material by using simpler words may not really make it simple.[40] If the difficulty of the material is due merely to hard words which have a simple equivalent, vocabulary simplification will help. But it will be that kind of simplification which merely is a one-to-one translation just as material written in a foreign language might be easily understood when translated. It will apply only to those materials where the words are hard but the ideas are easy. Thus the expression, "extinguish the illumination" is easily understood as "put out the light."

But some materials are not translatable in this degree. They must be reinterpreted. This reinterpretation may involve extensive amplification of concepts, it may involve a reduction in total load of concepts, and it may involve a rewriting of the material, not only in terms of its basic logical structure but also of its sentence structure. It is the maturity of the idea, not a simple translation factor that offers difficulty.

Clear Writing for All Readers

Norman Cousins pointed out in an editorial that:

An occupational failure in the education of advanced scholars is a tragic inability to use the English language for purposes of effective communication.

There is fear of simplicity lest one be thought simple; fear of clarity lest one be thought transparent; fear of lucidity lest one be thought glib.

---

40. Mary C. Serra, "Amplifying and Simplifying Instructional Materials: Effect on Comprehension," *Elementary School Journal*, LV (October, 1954), 77-81.

Along with this is the quaint but respectable notion that good scholarship requires academic jargon—interlarded and overlarded. Hence the love of the mouth-filling phrase and the worship of the polysyllables.

Scholars have failed to build a bridge to the very public they are anxious to serve. . . . They are apparently unaware that understanding is tied to communication.[41]

What should we do to improve scholarly writing for adults? Certainly we can reduce the jargon. Jargon often combines the lingo of a technical field with fanciful, involved, high-sounding circumlocutions.

Here is an example of educational jargon:

Attempts to evaluate and clarify a developmental approach to the major aspects of group life must be interpreted in the light of a critical appreciation of the creative role of our educational leadership.

Note this simple and effective introduction to an article on community education:

I stood on the edge of a cotton field. A few acres of red earth between me and the match-box houses of Mill Village. Rising behind these little gray dwellings, a backdrop of dark yellow factory buildings dominated the horizon.

The writer of jargon might have begun:

The folk patterns characteristic of a semirural southern environment provided the challenging sociological background for an experiment in school-community relationships.

Herman Struck of the English Department, Michigan State University, has criticized science writing, saying, "Sentences bulge like overfed matrons with unnecessary words that obscure a writer's ideas and weaken his emphasis." To strengthen one's writing, he advises converting the passive to the active voice. Here are some samples, with the original and Struck's edited version: [42]

---

41. Norman Cousins, "Completing the Scholar's Education," *Saturday Review of Literature*, XXXIII (September 2, 1950), 22.

42. Herman R. Struck, "Recommended Diet for Padded Writing," *Science*, CXIX (April 23, 1954), 522-25.

Original	Revision
Is of concern to	Concerns
There has been a tendency for	Has tended to
Have an ability to	Can
Gave careful consideration to	Considered carefully

Robert Gunning makes a similar point regarding the writing of technical reports, giving these and other examples: [43]

Original	Revision
A sharp decrease in profits was noted.	Profits decreased sharply.
Increases in sales of 10 per cent were obtained in July.	Sales increased 10 per cent in July.
Evaporation of the liquid takes place.	The liquid evaporates.

The reader may well say that there is nothing criticized here that recourse to Fowler won't cure. And he would be quite right. But unfortunately the problem still remains. In fact, the problem has been so great in recent years that the British government invited Sir Ernest Gowers to write *Plain Words* and the *ABC of Plain Words* as a guide for improving official English of government writers.[44] This year the United States government has issued a fifty-page booklet called *Plain Letters*, for government workers.

But what about the writing of science or history as a fine art? Mere editing of the sort noted above may reduce jargon, let the wind out of inflated writing, but it will not produce graceful prose. How can we, for example, get better writing of history?

Samuel Eliot Morison, noted professor of history at Harvard, offers these suggestions to young writers:

Keep the reader constantly in mind. You are not writing history for yourself or for the professors who (you may imagine) know more about it than you do. Assume that you are writing for intelligent people who know nothing about your particular subject but whom you wish

43. Robert Gunning, *op. cit.*, p. 306.

44. These pamphlets have recently been reprinted in one book: Sir Ernest Gowers, *Plain Words: Their ABC*. New York: Alfred A. Knopf, 1954.

to convince of its interest and significance. I once asked the late Senator Beveridge why his *Life of John Marshall,* despite its great length and scholarly apparatus, was so popular. He replied, "The trouble with you professors of history is that you write for each other. I write for people almost completely ignorant of American history, as I was when I began my research. . . . "

Use direct rather than indirect statements, the active rather than the passive voice, and make every sentence and paragraph an organic whole. Above all, if you are writing historical narrative, make it move. . . .(p. 9).

Do not be afraid to revise and rewrite. Reading aloud is a good test—historians' wives have to stand a lot of that! A candid friend who is not a historian and so represents the audience you are trying to reach, is perhaps the best "dog" to "try it on." Even if he has little critical sense, it is encouraging to have him stay awake. My good friend, Lucien Price, years ago listened with a pained expression to a bit of my early work. "Now, just what do you mean by that?" he asked after a long, involved, pedantic and quote-larded paragraph. I told him in words of one syllable, or perhaps two. "Fine!" said he, "I understand. Now, write that down and throw the other away!" . . .

The historian should have frequent recourse to the book of life. The richer his personal experience, the wider his human contacts, the more likely he is to effect a living contact with his audience. In writing, similes drawn from the current experience of this mechanical age rather than those rifled from the literary baggage of past eras are the ones that will go home to his reader. . . . (p. 10).

Bring all your knowledge of life to bear on everything that you write. Never let yourself bog down in pedantry and detail. Above all, *start* writing. Nothing is more pathetic than the "gonna" historian, who from graduate school on is always "gonna" write a magnum opus but never completes his research on the subject, and dies without anything to show for a lifetime's work (p. 8).[45]

It would help the cause of adult education if all historians wrote like Samuel Eliot Morison, Henry Commager, Charles A. Beard, or Carl Becker. It would be fine if our newspaper men wrote like Gerald W. Johnson, formerly of the *Baltimore Sun,* James Reston of the *New York Times,* or Richard Strout of the *Christian Science Monitor.* But even so, we must remember that about half of our population, the ones with less than ninth-grade education, would still not be able to read such articles with ease and comfort. What

45. Samuel Eliot Morison, *History as a Literary Art,* pp. 8-13 *passim.* Old South Leaflets, Series II, No. 1. Boston: Old South Association (Old South Meeting House).

about the reading materials for these adults who vote and make national policy the same as every other adult?

Finding and Writing Simple Reading Materials

What can we do for the large number of adults who read at the seventh-grade level or below? What about adults who are learning to read, who may not be able to get beyond the sixth-grade level in reading? What can we do for the 40 per cent of our youth who quit high school before they graduate? How can they develop a taste for good reading and the habit of doing it?

One approach is to provide a wide variety of materials at the reader's level of interest and ability. Many lists of books for such readers have been prepared, of which the following are excellent examples:

1. *A Bibliography of Reading Lists for Retarded Readers.* Compiled by Margaret Keyser Hill. State University of Iowa Bulletin 681. Iowa City, Iowa: State University of Iowa, 1953.
2. Anita E. Dunn, Mabel E. Jackman, Bernice C. Bush, and J. Roy Newton, *Fare for the Reluctant Reader.* Albany, New York: New York State College for Teachers, State University of New York, 1952 (revised).
3. *Books for Adult Beginners,* Grades I to VII. Compiled by Viola Wallace. Chicago: American Library Association, 1954.
4. Ruth Strang, Margaret Scoggin, and Christine Gilbert. *Gateway to Readable Books.* New York: H. W. Wilson Co., 1952 (revised).
5. Cloy S. Hobson and Oscar M. Haugh, *Materials for the Retarded Reader.* Issued by Adel F. Throckmorton, State Superintendent of Public Instruction, Topeka, Kansas, 1954.

Another approach is to face frankly the fact that we have millions of adults who need materials written at the sixth-grade level and sometimes below if they are to get in touch with important ideas in health, business, politics, and other fields. To summarily consign these adults to their television set or the motion-picture theater to get this information does not solve the problem and is an abdication of the real responsibility—preparing interesting reading materials for all adults, no matter what their reading level.

There have been several successful attempts during the past fifteen years to write materials for adults of limited and average reading ability. The most famous is the work of the Readability

Laboratory directed by Lyman Bryson at Teachers College, Columbia University. On a grant from the American Association for Adult Education, the Laboratory produced a set of serious, nonfiction books on economic, political, and social problems for the average adult. The authors were instructed in the principles of readability established by Bryson—lucidity, comprehensibility, and appeal.[46]

In 1939 Irving Lorge introduced readability measurement to government agencies at a seminar on "Evaluation of Government Information Services." At that time he presented his readability formula and suggested ways in which it could be used. By the mid-1940's, several government agencies were checking the readability of their publications, holding readability workshops, and setting up standards for their publications. Gladys Gallup and Amy Cowing of the Extension Service, Department of Agriculture, were pioneers in the "readability campaign." In 1945 a readability laboratory was organized to check the publications of the extension service and of other government agencies.[47]

During World War II, Paul Witty supervised an army program designed to teach illiterates and non-English-speaking servicemen to read. Filmstrips were used to begin the reading, and the next step was to use the *Army Reader*. This was supplemented by specially constructed bulletins, a weekly newsmap, and a monthly magazine. All used carefully controlled vocabulary. A second program made use of a reader, "Private Pete," written with a range of about 1,400 words grouped on four levels containing 283, 312, 384, and 411 words respectively.[48]

The Literacy Education Project, under the sponsorship of the Office of Education and the Carnegie Corporation, developed instructional materials suitable for adult-literacy programs. The

46. Lyman Bryson, "Readability Laboratory," *Library Journal*, LXI (June, 1936), 455. The set of books was entitled *The People's Library* and published by Macmillan Co.

47. Amy G. Cowing, "They Speak His Language," *Journal of Home Economics*, XXXI (1945), 487-89. *See also, Readability Unit Reports* (United States Department of Agriculture, Division of Field Studies and Training, Extension Service), and Amy G. Cowing, "Readability for Farm Families," *Land Policy Review*, X (Spring, 1947), 29-31.

48. Paul Witty, *Reading in Modern Education*, p. 198. New York: D. C. Heath & Co., 1949.

writers used readability principles and checked readability with the Lorge formula.[49]

Dr. Loyd W. Rowland, Director of the Louisiana Society for Mental Health, has developed and field-tested a series of monthly bulletins for a specialized public, the parents of first-born children. An illustrated character called "Pierre, the Pelican," a folk symbol for the stork, gives continuity from pamphlet to pamphlet. These widely used pamphlets are written at the sixth-grade level, a point where Dr. Rowland believes that he can adequately write any needed material. He finds the fourth-grade level too constricting and the eighth- or ninth-grade level too hard for many parents. Data on effectiveness of the series are presented in Edgewood Medical Monographs.[50]

Dale, under contract with the United States Armed Forces Institute, prepared a series of three adult readers at the fourth-, fifth-, and sixth-grade reading levels. The stories deal with human relations, personal business, physical and mental health, citizenship, vocational guidance, and recreation. *Stories for Today* (MC002) is available from the Government Printing Office; *Stories Worth Knowing* (MC003) is printed but not yet available; *New Flights in Reading* (MC004) is in press. Each reader includes 25 to 30 original or revised stories, all of which were tested in the field for interest and comprehension. Dale and Hager [51] have prepared a pamphlet, *Some Suggestions for Writing Health Materials*, which includes techniques they used in writing or revising health pamphlets prepared by the National Tuberculosis Association. Most of these pamphlets were written at the sixth- and seventh-grade level.

Another approach to providing readable materials is to simplify and abridge classics. Some say that this will make the classics avail-

49. Ambrose Caliver, "Literacy Education Project Draws to a Close," *School Life*, XXXII (February, 1950), 74-75. The readers are called "The Brown Family Series," published by Washington Educators Dispatch, 100 Garfield Avenue, New London, Connecticut.

50. *Edgewood Medical Monographs*, I (February, 1950), 150-62. Compiled and edited by Orin Ross Yost and Marion Manning Hiers (Orangeburg, South Carolina).

51. Edgar Dale and Hilda Hager, "Some Suggestions for Writing Health Materials." Prepared for National Tuberculosis Association. Available only from Bureau of Educational Research, Ohio State University, Columbus, Ohio.

able to readers who will otherwise never read them. The argument between those who wish to simplify and those who do not is one of values. When one simplifies, the story line is accentuated and descriptions and qualifications are reduced. The "Harvard Report," however, speaking for artful abridgment says:

> There is a need for versions of the great works cleared of unnecessary and unrewarding obstacles and made by abridgment and reflective editing more accessible to general readers. . . . Great books are being read increasingly in abridgments. If these are not made by scholars, they will be made by relatively incompetent hands. Only the scholar knows enough to distinguish the parts of Homer, Plato, the Old Testament, Bacon, Dante, Shakespeare, or Tolstoy which are essential to their value for contemporary general readers from the parts which concern only the special student. But the scholar, by his training, his competitive position, above all his professional ideal, is as a rule unconcerned with this problem. . . . How far this process of clarification or simplification should be carried is, if course, in every instance the prime question. Nothing but a fine awareness both of the material and of the reader's resources will answer it.[52]

Some Suggestions for Writers

Here are some questions that a writer might put to himself as he prepares materials for adults:

Audience and purpose:

1. For whom is my material prepared? For parents, union workers, business men? What is their reading level and background of experience? Have I written for them rather than for persons like myself?

2. What are the big ideas I am trying to put across and the main points under these ideas? Am I trying to change an attitude, convey information, or both? Is this material aimed to re-enforce an accepted idea or to get acceptance of a new one?

3. Does the material satisfactorily explain to the reader why and how the material will help him? Are there visual and verbal cues to catch initial interest?

How secured and used?

4. Where and how will readers get this material?

---

52. *General Education in a Free Society,* p. 114. Report of the Harvard University Committee on General Education. Cambridge, Massachusetts: Harvard University Press, 1945.

5. Will they see it "on the run" or will they have a chance to study it carefully, to read and reread?
6. Will they read this material independently or will there be planned instructional help?

Individualization.

7. Does my writing have a warm, friendly tone? A spirit of sharing? Have I been expressive rather than impressive?
8. If appropriate, have I written in the style of informal conversation?
9. Are the problems considered in terms of people rather than in terms of abstractions and technicalities?
10. Have I used concrete examples wherever I could? Do I usually go from the specific to the general, rather than in the reverse order?

Logic.

11. Is the material well organized? Visibly well mapped?
12. Are the ideas presented in logical order? Can the reader follow me easily step by step?
13. How many different ideas have I discussed? Are there too many?
14. Is the article too long? Does it require too much concentration over too long a period of time?
15. Is each idea really pertinent and essential to my main point?
16. Is each idea clearly developed and explained? Are there good transitions between different ideas?
17. Have I used enough explanatory material? Too much?

Breaking-up of material.

18. Are my sentences clear and quickly grasped? Have I overqualified my general statements?
19. Are my paragraphs short enough so that the reader won't get lost or bored?
20. Are important points made to stand out by effective typography?
21. Have I used subheads correctly? Where they direct a desired shift of reader attention? Where they add punch to the copy?
22. Have I used questions and answers effectively?

Vocabulary.

23. Have I used familiar terms whenever possible?
24. Have I omitted unnecessary technical terms? Avoided jargon and clichés? Explained the necessary hard or unusual terms?

Summarization.

25. Have I summarized the main points briefly and in the right places?
26. Have I repeated important information in different ways throughout?

Over-all view.

27. Is this material attractive or does it look like it would be uninteresting and difficult?
28. Does it provide for feed-back? Interaction? Invite help? Will I learn how effectively I have done the job?
29. Does it tell the reader just *how* to do the things he should do? Invite action?
30. Have I written and revised to a point where I can see no gain in further revision?

There are three ways to improve reading as a means of communication:

1. We can help the reader improve the skill, the efficiency, the understanding with which he reads.
2. Teachers of adults can learn to use texts and other teaching materials more effectively. They can learn when and how to supplement reading material with oral instruction, when to use other media.
3. Finally, and this is the theme of the chapter, we can improve the readability of our adult materials. We can make them more attractive through type and layout, more understandable by improving the quality of the writing, and more congenial and useful by matching reading difficulty with reading ability. Good writing makes good reading.

Classified Bibliography

REVIEW OF LITERATURE

BETTS, EMMETT A. "Readability: Its Application to the Elementary School," *Journal of Educational Research*, XLII (February, 1949), 438-59.

CHALL, JEANNE S. "This Business of Readability," *Educational Research Bulletin*, XXVI (January, 1947), 1-13.

DALE, EDGAR. "The Problem of Readability," *News Letter* (Bureau of Educational Research, Ohio State University), XIX (February, 1954), 1-4.

DALE, EDGAR, AND CHALL, JEANNE S. "The Concept of Readability," *Elementary English*, XXVI (January, 1949), 19-26.

GRAY, WILLIAM S. "Progress in the Study of Readability," *Elementary School Journal*, XLVII (May, 1947), 490-99.

HOTCHKISS, SANFORD N., and PATERSON, DONALD G. "Flesch Readability Reading List," *Personnel Psychology*, III (Autumn, 1950), 327-44.

KEARL, BRYAN. "A Closer Look at Readability Formulas," *Journalism Quarterly*, XXV (December, 1948), 344-48.

Readability. Edited by Edgar Dale. Chicago: National Conference on Research in English, 1949. (Reprinted from *Elementary English*, January to May, 1949.)

READABILITY FORMULAS

DELONG, VAUGHN R. "Primary Promotion by Reading Levels," *Elementary School Journal*, XXXVIII (May, 1938), 663-71.

DOLCH, EDWARD W. "Fact Burden and Reading Difficulty," *Elementary English Review*, XVI (April, 1939), 135-38.

————. *Problems in Reading*, chap. vi. Champaign, Illinois: Garrard Press, 1948.

————. "Vocabulary Burden," *Journal of Educational Research*, XVII (March, 1928), 170-83.

FARR, JAMES N., and JENKINS, JAMES. "Tables for Use with Flesch Readability Formulas," *Journal of Applied Psychology*, XXXIII (June, 1949), 275-78.

FLESCH, RUDOLF. "A New Readability Yardstick," *Journal of Applied Psychology*, XXXIII (June, 1948), 221-33.

————. *Marks of Readable Style*. Teachers College Contributions to Education No. 897. New York: Bureau of Publications, Teachers College, Columbia University, 1943.

FORBES, F. W., and COTTLE, W. C. "A New Method for Determining Readability of Standardized Tests," *Journal of Applied Psychology*, XXXVII (June, 1953), 185-90.

JOHNSON, GEORGE R. "An Objective Method of Determining Reading Difficulty," *Journal of Educational Research* XXI (April, 1930), 283-87.

KEBOCH, F. D. "Variability of Word Difficulty in Five American History Textbooks," *Journal of Educational Research*, XV (January, 1927), 22-26.

KLARE, GEORGE R. "A Table for Rapid Determination of Dale-Chall Readability Scores," *Educational Research Bulletin*, XXXI (February, 1952), 43-47.

LEWERENZ, ALFRED S. "Measurement of the Difficulty of Reading Materials," *Los Angeles Educational Research Bulletin*, VIII (March, 1929), 11-16.

LIVELY, BERTHA A., and PRESSEY, S. L. "A Method for Measuring the 'Vocabulary Burden' of Textbooks," *Administration and Supervision*, V (October, 1923), 389-98.

LORGE, IRVING. "Predicting Reading Difficulty of Selections for Children," *Elementary English Review*, XVI (October, 1939), 229-33.

McCLUSKY, HOWARD Y. " A Quantitative Analysis of the Difficulty of Reading Materials," *Journal of Educational Research*, XXVIII (December, 1934), 276-82.

PATTY, W. W., and PAINTER, W. I. "Improving Our Method of Selecting High-School Textbooks," *Journal of Educational Research*, XXIV (June, 1931), 23-32, and (September, 1931), 127-34.

SPACHE, GEORGE. "A New Readability Formula for Primary-Grade Reading Materials," *Elementary School Journal*, LIII (March, 1953), 410-13.

STONE, CLARENCE R. "Measures of Simplicity and Beginning Texts in Reading," *Journal of Educational Research*, XXXI (February, 1938), 447-50.

TWEDT, D. W. "A Table for Use with Flesch's Level of Abstraction Readability Formula," *Journal of Applied Psychology*, XXXV (June, 1951), 157-59.

VOGEL, MABEL, and WASHBURNE, CARLETON. " An Objective Method of Determining Grade Placement of Children's Reading Material," *Elementary School Journal*, XXVIII (January, 1928), 373-81.

WASHBURNE, CARLETON, and MORPHETT, MABEL V. "Grade Placement of Children's Books," *Elementary School Journal*, XXXVIII (January, 1938), 355-64.

WHEELER, L. R., and WHEELER, V. D. "Selecting Appropriate Reading Materials," *Elementary English*, XXV (December, 1948), 478-89.

WORD LISTS

CHALL, JEANNE, and DALE, EDGAR. "Familiarity of Selected Health Terms," *Educational Research Bulletin*, XXIX (November, 1950), 197-206.

COLE, LUELLA. *The Teacher's Handbook of Technical Vocabulary.* Bloomington, Illinois: Public School Publishing Co., 1940.

A COMBINED WORD LIST. Compiled by B. R. Buckingham and E. W. Dolch. Boston: Ginn & Co., 1936.

DALE, EDGAR. *Bibliography of Vocabulary Studies.* Columbus, Ohio: Bureau of Educational Research, Ohio State University, 1949.

———. "A Comparison of Two Word Lists," *Educational Research Bulletin,* X (December, 1931), 484-89.

DOLCH, E. W. "The First Thousand Words for Children's Reading," *Problems in Reading, op. cit.,* chap. x.

———. "The Use of Vocabulary Lists in Predicting Readability and in Developing Reading Materials," *Elementary English,* XXVI (March, 1949), 142-49, 177. Also in *Readability* (edited by Edgar Dale), *op. cit.,* 17-25.

GATES, ARTHUR I. *A List of Spelling Difficulties in 3,876 Words.* New York: Bureau of Publications, Teachers College, Columbia University, 1937.

———. *A Reading Vocabulary for Primary Grades.* New York: Bureau of Publications, Teachers College, Columbia University, 1935.

INTERNATIONAL KINDERGARTEN UNION CHILD STUDY COMMITTEE, *A Study of the Vocabulary of Children before Entering First Grade.* Washington: International Kindergarten Union, 1928.

LORGE, IRVING. "Word Lists as Background for Communication," *Teachers College Record,* LXV (May, 1944), 543-52.

LORGE, IRVING, and THORNDIKE, EDWARD L. *A Semantic Count of English Words.* New York: Institute of Educational Research, Teachers College, Columbia University, 1938.

RINSLAND, HENRY D. *A Basic Vocabulary of Elementary-School Children.* New York: Macmillan Co., 1945.

STONE, CLARENCE R. *Stone's Graded Vocabulary for Primary Reading.* St. Louis, Missouri: Webster Publishing Co., 1941.

THORNDIKE, EDWARD L., and LORGE, IRVING. *The Teacher's Word Book of 30,000 Words.* New York: Bureau of Publications, Teachers College, Columbia University, 1944.

RELIABILITY OF READABILITY TECHNIQUES

DOLCH, E. W. "Sampling of Reading Matter," *Journal of Educational Research,* XXII (October, 1930), 213-15.

DUNNETTE, MARVIN D., and MALONEY, PAUL W. "Factorial Analysis of the Original and Simplified Flesch Reading Ease Formulas," *Journal of Applied Psychology,* XXXVII (April, 1953), 107-10.

ELLIOTT, CATHERINE JANETTE. " A Critical Analysis of the Objective Method of Measuring Reading Difficulty," *Pittsburgh Schools,* XV (May-June, 1941), 201-9.

ENGLAND, GEORGE W.; THOMAS, MARGARET; and PATERSON, DONALD G. "Reliability of the Original and the Simplified Flesch Reading Ease Formulas," *Journal of Applied Psychology,* XXXVII (April, 1953), 111-13.

HAYES, PATRICIA M.; JENKINS, JAMES J.; and WALKER, BRADLEY J. "Reliability of the Flesch Readability Formulas," *Journal of Applied Psychology,* XXXIV (February, 1950), 22-26.

LEIFESTE, BERTHA V. "An Investigation of the Reliability of the Sampling of Reading Material," *Journal of Educational Research,* XXXVII (February, 1944), 441-50.

VALIDITY OF READABILITY TECHNIQUES

CHALL, JEANNE S., and DIAL, HAROLD E. "Predicting Listener Understanding and Interest in Newscasts," *Educational Research Bulletin*, XXVII (September, 1948), 141-53, 168.

CLARKE, LOIS KATHERINE. "The Effect on Comprehension of Simplification of Social Science Reading Material in a Second Grade." Unpublished Master's thesis, University of Iowa, 1933.

DiVESTA, FRANCIS J. "The Effect of Methods of Presentation and Examining Conditions on Student Achievement in a Correspondence Course," *Journal of Applied Psychology*, XXXVIII (August, 1954), 253-55.

FIGUREL, J. ALLEN. "Relative Difficulty of Reading Material for Ninth-Grade Literature," *Pittsburgh Schools*, XVI (January-February, 1942), 125-38.

FOSTER, CHARLOTTE. "The Effect upon Reading Comprehension of Paraphrasing Historical Material into Spoken and Written Vocabularies of Children." Unpublished Master's thesis, University of Iowa, 1931.

HACKMAN, RAY C., and KERSHNER, ALAN M. *The Determination of Criteria of Readability*. Technical Report for Contract NR 153-024 between the Office of Naval Research and the University of Maryland. College Park, Maryland: University of Maryland, n.d.

JACKMAN, MABEL E. "The Relations between Maturity of Content and Simplicity of Style in Selected Books of Fiction," *Library Quarterly*, XI (July, 1941), 302-27.

KLARE, GEORGE R.; MABRY, JAMES E.; and GUSTAFSON, LEVARL M. "The Relationship of Human Interest to Immediate Retention and to Acceptability of Technical Material," *Journal of Applied Psychology*, XXXIX (April, 1955), 92-95.

KUENEMAN, HUBERTEEN. "A Study of the Effect of Vocabulary Changes on Reading Comprehension in a Single Field." Unpublished Master's thesis, University of Iowa, 1931.

LORGE, IRVING, and KRUGLOV, LORRAINE. "The Relation between Merit of Written Expression and Intelligence," *Journal of Educational Research*, XLIV (March, 1951), 507-19.

——. "The Relationship between the Readability of Pupils' Compositions and Their Measured Intelligence," *Journal of Educational Research*, XLIII (February, 1950), 467-74.

LUDWIG, MERRITT C. "Hard Words and Human Interest: Their Effects on Readership," *Journalism Quarterly*, XXVI (June, 1949), 167-71.

LYMAN, H. B. "Flesch Count and Readership of Articles in a Midwestern Farm Paper," *Journal of Applied Psychology*, XXXIII (February, 1949), 78-80.

NOLTE, KARL FREDERICK. "Simplification of Vocabulary and Comprehension in Reading," *Elementary English Review*, XIV (April, 1937), 119-24, 146.

ROBINSON, FRANCIS P. "Comprehension Difficulty and Inspirational Value," *Journal of Genetic Psychology*, LVI (March, 1940), 53-65.

——. "The Effect of Language Style on Reading Performance," *Journal of Educational Psychology*, XXXVIII (March, 1947), 149-56.

SMITH, RUTH I. "An Investigation of the Readability of Recently Published History and Geography Textbooks and Related Materials for the Fourth Grade." Abstract of Doctoral Dissertation, *University of Pittsburgh Bulletin*, 1951, 521-27.

SWANSON, CHARLES E., and FOX, HARLAND G. "Validity of Readability Formulas," *Journal of Applied Psychology*, XXXVII (April, 1953), 114-18.

TUBBS, A. E. "Assessing the Suitability of Geography Textbooks," *Proceedings*, British Association for the Advancement of Science, 1950. Cited by P. E. Vernon, "An Investigation into the Intelligibility of Educational Broadcasts," pp. 17-18. London: British Broadcasting Corporation, November, 1950 (mimeographed).

WALTHER, CYRILLA. "The Reading Difficulty of Magazines," *School Review*, LI (February, 1943), 100-105.

WERT, JAMES E. "A Technique for Determining Levels of Group Reading," *Educational Research Bulletin*, XVI (May, 1937), 113-21.

YOUNG, JAMES R. "Understanding Radio News: The Effect of Style," *Journalism Quarterly*, XXVII (Winter, 1950), 19-23.

APPLICATIONS OF READABILITY IN ADULT EDUCATION

Books for Adult Beginners, Grades I to VII. Compiled by Viola Wallace. Chicago: American Library Association, 1954.

BRYSON, LYMAN. "What Are Readable Books?" *Educational Forum*, I (May, 1937), 397-402.

CLARKE, JAMES. "Readability: A Practical Problem," *Library Journal*, LXVI (May, 1941), 383-85.

EGAN, MARGARET. "An Experiment in Advisory Service and Graded Reading in the CCC Camps," *Library Quarterly*, VII (October, 1937), 471-91.

GUCKENHEIMER, S. N. "Readability of Pamphlets on International Relationships," *Educational Research Bulletin*, XXVI (December, 1947).

WHITE, DAVID M. "Are Our 'American Scriptures' Readable?" *School and Society*, LXVII (September 4, 1948), 154-55.

APPLICATIONS TO MASS MEDIA, INDUSTRY, AND GOVERNMENT

ABER, LEE A. "A Comparison of the Readability Levels of Broadcasts by Certain National and Local Newscasters." Unpublished Doctor's dissertation, University of Pittsburgh, 1953.

BURTON, PHILIP W., and SWANSON, CHARLES E. "Can Mass Audiences Read Institutional Advertising?" *Journalism Quarterly*, XXV (June, 1948), 145-50.

DAVIS, KEITH, and HOPKINS, JAMES O. "Readability of Employee Handbooks," *Personnel Psychology*, III (1950), 317-26.

ENGLAND, A. O. "Getting Your Message Across by Plain Talk," *Journal of Applied Psychology*, XXXIV (June, 1950), 182-85.

———. "Influence of 'Plain Talk' on AMC Communications," *Journal of Applied Psychology*, XXXV (December, 1951), 381-82.

FARR, JAMES N. "Readability and Interest Values in an Employee Handbook," *Journal of Applied Psychology*, XXXIV (February, 1950), 16-21.

FLESCH, RUDOLF. "How To Write Copy That Will Be Read," *Advertising and Selling*, XL (March, 1947), 113.

GETZLOE, LESTER. "U.S. Press Does Well in Foreign News Values, but Less Readable Than 1945," *The Ohio Newspaper* (Ohio State University), XXVIII (November, 1946), 1-5.

IRVINE, PAUL. "Plain Talk for Government Writers," *Public Personnel Review*, X (1949), 140-47.

KNAUFT, E. G. "Measured Changes in Acceptance of an Employee Publication," *Journal of Applied Psychology*, XXXV (June, 1951), 151-56.

LAMBIE, JAMES M., JR. "Financial Reports Can Be Written So People Can Understand Them," *Journal of Accountancy*, XIV (1947), 40.

LAUER, JEANNE, and PATERSON, D. G. "Readability of Union Contract," *Personnel*, XXVIII (1951), 3-7.

LOSTUTTER, MELVIN. "Some Critical Factors of Newspaper Readability," *Journalism Quarterly*, XXIV (December, 1947), 307-14.

PASHALIAN S., and CRISSEY, W. J. E. "How Readable Are Corporate Reports?" *Journal of Applied Psychology*, XXXIV (August, 1950), 244-48.

PATERSON, DONALD G. "Development of a General Information Sheet for Potential Applicants," *Personnel*, XXIV (March, 1948), 314-20.

PATERSON, DONALD G., and JENKINS, JAMES J. "Communication between Management and Workers," *Journal of Applied Psychology*, XXXII (February, 1948), 71-80.

PATERSON, DONALD G., and WALKER, BRADLEY J. "Experts Review NIEA Publications," *Reporting* (Official publication of International Council of Industrial Editors), II (November-December, 1949), 12-14.

——. "Readability and Human Interest of House Organs," *Personnel*, XXV (1949), 438-41.

RANEY, EDWARD T. "How Readable Is Your Employee Publication?" *Personnel Psychology*, II (1949), 437-59.

Readability in News Writing: Report on an Experiment by the United Press. New York: United Press Association, 1945.

"Reading, Writing, and Newspapers: A Special Issue," *Nieman Reports* (Cambridge, Massachusetts), IV (April, 1950).

SIEGEL, ARTHUR I., and SIEGEL, ESTELLE. "Flesch Readability Analysis of the Major Pre-election Speeches of Eisenhower and Stevenson," *Journal of Applied Psychology*, XXXVII (April, 1953), 105-10.

SILVEY, ROBERT. "The Intelligibility of Broadcast Talks," *Public Opinion Quarterly*, XV (Summer, 1951), 299-304.

TRINCHARD, KENDALL I., and CRISSEY, W. J. E. "Readability of Advertising and Editorial Copy in *Time* and *Newsweek*," *Journal of Applied Psychology*, XXXVI (June, 1952), 161-63.

WEARNE, D. "The Readability of House Magazines," *Bulletin of Industrial Psychology and Personnel Practice* (Melbourne, Australia), V (1949), 29-32.

UNITED STATES DEPARTMENT OF AGRICULTURE, DIVISION OF FIELD STUDIES AND TRAINING, EXTENSION SERVICE. *Readability Unit Reports.* Washington: Government Printing Office.

VANCURA, RUDOLPH H. "Flesch Readability Formula Applied to Television Programs," *Journal of Applied Psychology*, XXXIX (February, 1955), 47-48.

TESTS AND QUESTIONNAIRES AND OTHER APPLICATIONS

JOHNSON, R. H., and BOND, G. L. "Reading Ease of Commonly Used Tests," *Journal of Applied Psychology*, XXXIV (1950), 319-24.

KLARE, GEORGE R. "Understandability and Indefinite Answers to Public Opinion Questions," *International Journal of Opinion and Attitude Research*, IV (1950), 91-96.

MACKINNEY, ARTHUR C., and JENKINS, JAMES J. "Readability of Employee's Letters in Relation to Occupational Level," *Journal of Applied Psychology*, XXXVIII (February, 1954), 26-30.

MALONEY, PAUL W. "Reading Ease Scores for File's How Supervise?" *Journal of Applied Psychology*, XXXVI (August, 1952), 225-27.

NUKOLS, ROBERT C. "Verbi!" *International Journal of Opinion and Attitude Research*, III (1949-50), 575-86.

PATTY, W. W. "Reading Difficulty Differences of Health Knowledge Tests," *Research Quarterly*, XVI (October, 1945), 206-15.

PAYNE, STANLEY L. *The Art of Asking Questions.* Princeton, New Jersey: Princeton University Press, 1951.

STEFFLRE, BUFORD. "The Reading Difficulty of Interest Inventories," *Occupations*, (November, 1947), 95-96.

TERRIS, FAY. "Are Poll Questions Too Difficult? *Public Opinion Quarterly*, XIII (Summer, 1949), 314-19.

WYANT, ROWENA. "Voting Via the Senatorial Mailbag," *Public Opinion Quarterly*, V (Fall, 1941), 359-82.

PRINCIPLES OF READABILITY APPLIED TO WRITING

DALE, EDGAR, and CHALL, JEANNE S. "Techniques for Selecting and Writing Readable Materials," *Elementary English*, XXVI (May, 1949), 250-58; also in *Readability* (edited by Edgar Dale), *op. cit.*, pp. 36-44.

FLESCH, RUDOLF. *The Art of Plain Talk*. New York: Harper & Bros., 1946.

————. *The Art of Readable Writing*. New York: Harper & Bros., 1949.

MASTERSON, JAMES R., and PHILLIPS, WENDELL BROOKS. *Federal Prose: How To Write in and/or for Washington*. Chapel Hill, North Carolina: University of North Carolina Press, 1948.

STRANG, RUTH. "Principles of Readability Applied to Reporting Research," *Teachers College Record*, XLIX (1948), 449-51.

CHAPTER X

The Improvement of Reading Abilities

PAUL A. WITTY

It is possible for almost any adult to improve his reading both in rate and in comprehension.[1] In practice, most of us adopt a congenial pace in reading much below our actual capacity. And some of us read everything in the same way—a newspaper, a novel, or a conference report. In many cases, this is a snail's pace; in others it is a relatively slow rate that becomes habitual. There are, of course, large numbers of adults who read various types of material skilfully. Yet many of these people can improve their reading habits.

Individual and Group Differences in Rate of Reading

Great differences may be observed in any group. For example, the rates of reading textbook material in one of the writer's college classes varied from 140 to 750 words a minute. The young woman who read most rapidly was a very intelligent student, whose reading and study habits enabled her to assimilate a great amount of material in a very short time. Since she finished her assignments so quickly, her classmates thought she "never studied."

One of the slowest readers in this group was also bright, and he understood thoroughly the materials after he plodded through them. But he had to spend hours on each assignment. He was looked upon

---

1. Parts of this chapter have been adapted from the following articles by the writer: "Developing Better Reading Skills and Habits in High-School Pupils," *Bulletin of the National Association of Secondary-School Principals,* XXXVIII (December, 1954); "Evaluation of Methods and Devices To Improve Reading Rate and Comprehension," *Elementary English,* XXXI (May, 1954); "You Can Improve Your Reading," *Today's Health,* XXXI (November, 1953); and (in collaboration with Theodore Stolarz and William Cooper), "Some Results of a Remedial Reading Program for College Students," *School and Society,* LXXVI (December 13, 1952).

as a "grind," for he had time for little else but study. It was very difficult for him to keep up with his assignments.

Another member of the class, the slowest reader, never finished his assignments although he spent excessive amounts of time in this effort. Because his grades were low, he developed a feeling of incompetency and displayed anxiety over his chances of success in completing college.

One small group of students, including the girl who read 750 words per minute, read rapidly—with skill and understanding. There was little need for most of them to improve. Two students of this group, however, read very little except course requirements. They had not discovered that reading could be satisfying and rewarding.

The members of another rather large group within this class also read very little, since reading had always been a tedious process for them. Although they worked hard to read their assignments, they often left them unfinished, and they rarely turned to reading as a source of pleasure. They had not learned to read skilfully enough to enjoy the act of reading.

A condition similar to the one so strikingly revealed among these college students, is found generally among high-school students and in adult groups. For example, studies show a wide range in ability to read and a large amount of reading retardation in the modern high school. Thus, a study of 7,380 graduates from the eighth grade in one large city showed that 2,169 were reading at or below the sixth-grade level.[2] Other studies of high-school pupils reveal that, in many high schools, fully one-third of the pupils read poorly, and about 15 per cent are seriously retarded. In 1951, the following condition was reported as typical for high-school Freshmen: ". . . Two per cent of the pupils score below fourth-grade norms in reading ability, 30 per cent below the seventh-grade norms, and 48 per cent below the eighth-grade norms on tests."[3]

At the college level, too, many students need help in reading.

2. William Kottmeyer, "Improving Reading Instruction in the St. Louis Schools," *Elementary School Journal*, XLV (September, 1944), 34.

3. John DeBoer, Walter Kaulfers, and Helen R. Miller, *Teaching Secondary English*, p. 162. New York: McGraw-Hill Book Co., Inc., 1951.

Thus, Triggs [4] found that, in a large state university, 20 per cent of college Freshmen read at or below the eighth-grade norms. Many other students, of course, read so slowly that they could obtain little satisfaction or enjoyment from reading. Their range of ability was very great; and there were many able students who needed further guidance and direction in reading.

Need for Improvement in Reading Rate and Comprehension

It has been found that the average adult uses but very little of his actual capacity for rapid silent reading. Thus, among businessmen, lawyers, and even librarians and teachers, there is often a relatively low level of reading proficiency, i.e., an effortless pace is adopted which is not consonant with the numerous reading demands of life today.

The reading rate of the average adult is difficult to estimate. It is, of course, well known that the typical person reads at a rate far below his potentiality for rapid, assimilative reading. It has been estimated that most of us utilize only about 20 per cent of our capacity to read rapidly and intelligently. Certainly, it seems that most adults can improve their rate of reading various kinds of material. One group of college students changed their rates of reading relatively easy materials from an average of 250 to 480 words per minute; another group went up from an average of 300 to 450 words per minute. A group of businessmen and a group of lawyers improved 100 per cent. All these gains were made during short training periods. Not only did these groups increase their rate of reading the kind of material on which they were tested but they also improved their ability to read rapidly other types of printed matter. On the whole, comprehension scores were altered favorably.

There is, of course, a great need in modern life not merely to read rapidly but also to be able to adapt one's reading rate to various types of presentation—to the newspaper, the magazine, the scientific article, the legal document, the novel, and so on. Industry and the professions have their own publications and literature which require special proficiencies in reading.

4. Frances O. Triggs, *Remedial Reading: The Diagnosis and Correction of Reading Difficulties at the College Level.* Minneapolis: University of Minnesota Press, 1943.

Most of the members of these varied groups can improve their reading. But the needs in such groups differ in the same way as they do in the college class we described. For example, in one adult group there were several men students who at first read all materials in the same way. Others were excessively slow in reading technical materials. Still others read most things in a laborious way—almost word by word. And few of this group read widely. Not a single person made consistent use of the public library. Like many other adults, their reading consisted chiefly of the few vocational publications they were required to read, the daily newspaper, and, occasionally, a magazine article or a book.

Despite long-established reading habits and attitudes toward reading, most young people and adults can change their reading abilities and patterns so as to obtain greater satisfactions as well as to achieve greater skill in reading. Recognition of this fact has led to the establishment of reading-improvement programs in many schools and colleges today and, increasingly, to the formation of classes for business and professional people. Also, increasing numbers of people are seeking to improve their reading status independently. This endeavor is proving quite successful and is leading many adults to read more widely. Most of the participants in such programs not only improve their reading abilities but also gain in self-esteem arising from their awareness of increased competency for their work.

Amount and Nature of Reading among Different Groups

Many studies over the past twenty years have revealed the relatively small amount of reading (apart from textbook assignments) among high-school and college students. It is not surprising, then, to find that adults generally read little, although there are, of course, many exceptions. Thus, McMahan comments: "It is estimated that fewer than half of the people of the United States ever read a book; fewer than one-fifth of them ever buy a book." [5]

The small amount of reading done by the typical adult has been commented on frequently, and attention has usually centered on the fact that not more than 10 per cent of our adults can be considered

5. Allan McMahan, "Make Friends with Your Bookseller," *The Wonderful World of Books*, p. 226. A Mentor Book, edited by Alfred Stefferud. New York: New American Library of World Literature, Inc., 1952,

"readers" of library books. Certainly there are many factors which contribute to the relatively small amount of reading carried on by adults. It is obvious, of course, that poor reading habits alone do not account entirely or even largely for the above condition. For it has been shown that many adults do not have ready access to public libraries. Leigh has offered the following explanation:

We have seen that public libraries in the United States have been organized as municipal services, that they are dependent on local initiative for their creation and on local tax sources for their support. The result is that half of the incorporated places are too small or too poor to have any public library, and two-thirds of the people in the unincorporated areas are equally without direct library service.[6]

Closely associated with the problem of availability of books is interest in reading. Many schools are attempting to develop a more general and lasting interest in reading by establishing elementary-school libraries and by extending secondary-school library facilities. Moreover, there is a growing tendency to initiate developmental reading programs designed to satisfy students' interests and meet their needs and hence to lead them to enjoy reading and to read widely. School people generally recognize the validity of the following statement by Norvell: "To increase reading skill, promote the reading habit, and produce a generation of book lovers there is no other factor so powerful as interest."[7]

There is heartening evidence that the effort to improve the reading ability of high-school students is generally successful and that many pupils are now reading more effectively. In a recently published book, Simpson[8] describes a number of such newly developed high-school programs, providing evidence of their success.

There is evidence, too, that many adults are reading more today than ever before. One factor leading to more extensive reading is the publication of inexpensive, paper-bound books. Thus, reading

6. Robert D. Leigh, *The Public Library in the United States*, p. 227. The General Report of the Public Library Inquiry. New York: Columbia University Press, 1950.

7. George W. Norvell, "Some Results of a Twelve-Year Study of Children's Reading Interests," *English Journal*, XXXV (December, 1946), 536.

8. Elizabeth Simpson, *Helping High-School Students Read Better*. Chicago: Science Research Associates, Inc., 1954.

material has become more accessible to many adults, as is illustrated by the following report:

A Midwesterner wrote me recently: "I am a housewife who lives in a small town where the only entertainment is a movie that changes once a week. If you knew how bored I get looking after two small children, doing housework, and seeing the same old neighbors day after day, you'd understand what a godsend your inexpensive books have been. I never knew that books could be so interesting, but I'm proud of the library of your books that I'm building—for the first time in my life." [9]

Additional evidence of a growing interest in reading is found in the increased participation by adults in book clubs, "great books" discussions, and courses designed to improve reading ability.

Speed of Reading—Its Importance and Control

The widespread interest today in improving speed of reading has led to some exaggerated claims concerning the importance of rate of reading and the efficacy of depending primarily upon machines, devices, and routine exercises in efforts to improve adult reading. Hence, it is desirable to inquire: Are reading speed and comprehension associated closely? Is it possible that increase in speed in reading will bring a correlated increase in comprehension? Should reading programs be limited primarily to the use of devices to be employed with a relatively small number of practice materials? What are some characteristics of desirable and efficient programs?

Interest in increasing speed of reading was evident in the professional literature of education from 1920 to 1930, when studies showed the possibility of improving speed of reading in relatively short periods of time. In these early studies, gains were reported also in the test scores of comprehension. In some of the reports, it was assumed that rate of reading was a rather general acquisition that transferred to the reading of many kinds of material. Accordingly, improvement in rate of reading was thought to influence favorably a student's performance and his grades in many school subjects.

From 1925 to 1930, several noteworthy attempts were made to improve rate and comprehension in college classes. In the writer's

9. Richard J. Crohn, "Good Reading for the Millions," *The Wonderful World of Books, op. cit.,* p. 203.

courses in educational psychology offered at that time in the University of Kansas, the students (many of whom were teachers) considered the possibility of improving their own reading rate and comprehension. By simple procedures, they observed the characteristics of eye movements in reading. For example, a mirror was placed on the left side of mimeographed pages which one student read silently and then aloud as another noted in the mirror the number of fixation pauses, the regressions, and the nature of the return sweeps of the eye from the end of one line to the beginning of the next one. Then the relationship of eye movement to efficient reading of various kinds of materials was discussed. Early in the semester all students started a reading-improvement program. They were given help in understanding the new vocabulary and the unfamiliar concepts found in instructional materials. And they read their own assignments in terms of various purposes such as: to answer questions, to note details, and to follow directions. Each student arranged to spend three 30-minute periods each week in the reading practice. After every period, he made a summary or an outline of the materials read. He was encouraged to do extensive reading, too, and to attempt at all times to improve his understanding as well as his rate of reading. It was suggested that additional periods be set aside for practice in reading other materials.

The results of standard and informal tests, given at the beginning and at the end of the semester, were compared. Most of the students made marked gains. The average increase in rate was about 50 per cent during the single semester. Comprehension, too, was favorably affected. Although these gains were considered important, it was recognized that the improvement applied chiefly to the reading of materials in the field of educational psychology. It was suggested, therefore, that the students attempt to make further gains in other fields. This work was continued during the second semester, and increased attention was given to wide reading. The students who participated in this program gave unmistakable evidence of general improvement in reading proficiency and in their attitude toward reading.

DEVELOPMENT OF DEVICES FOR CONTROLLING RATE OF READING

Knowledge of the fact that almost every adult can improve his speed of reading has been disseminated as business firms have publicized devices for studying and controlling eye movement. In efforts to control eye movement, simple flash cards have been replaced by other types of tachistoscopes (mechanical devices for exposing materials at different speeds). One of the most widely known of these devices is the metronoscope—a cumbersome triple-shuttered tachistoscope—which exposes successively three segments of a line of large print. Rather optimistic claims were set forth for this device when it first appeared.

Interest in eye movement in relationship to reading has resulted in the making of other types of tachistoscope such as the "Reading Accelerator," the "Flashmeter," and the *Harvard Reading Films*. The "Reading Accelerator" is a device through which the reading of a page in a book is controlled by a shutter which is lowered mechanically to expose successive lines of print. A somewhat similar device is known as the "Reading Rate Controller." The Flashmeter is an instrument by which different kinds of material may be exposed upon a screen at varying speeds. Films, too, have been designed to encourage the student to increase his speed of reading. In using these devices, the speed of exposure of different kinds of material may be controlled and advanced as progress warrants.

The use of such instruments has become a feature of "accelerated reading programs." Speer [10] emphasizes the current demand for such programs and points out that, although schools have for many years been concerned about remedial and developmental reading, accelerated reading has been largely neglected. He writes:

Accelerated reading using a variety of instruments has as its main emphasis the development of more rapid and efficient reading, while at the same time effective comprehension or understanding is retained.

Accelerated reading is not a method of teaching reading independent of the usual methods, but is an auxilliary approach used with those who have already acquired the basic skills. It is being included more and more as a part of the total reading program to aid those who are not working to the level of their potential capacity but who are not otherwise regarded as having reading problems.

10. George S. Speer, "Using Mechanical Devices Can Increase Speed of Reading," *Nation's Schools*, XLVIII (October, 1951), 45-48.

Speer points to the gradual development of reading instruments and their value in "accelerated reading programs." Devices of various kinds are generally found in reading centers and clinics today.

RENEWED INTEREST IN DEVICES FOR CONTROLLING READING RATE

Within the past few years, magazine and newspaper articles have described again and again the success of programs designed to accelerate reading. And educational periodicals have contained accounts of the nature and amount of improvement associated with the use of instruments and devices.

Accelerated programs have proved unusually successful with adult groups, as have other efforts to improve the efficiency of their reading. In *Business Week* (April 5, 1952), it was reported that a program of reading improvement, utilizing the facilities of the University of Pittsburgh, resulted in attracting groups of businessmen who made unusual progress. Similarly, according to this article, the Foundation for Better Reading in Chicago has attracted various groups of businessmen to its courses. The president of Reading Laboratory, a New York "reading clinic," is quoted as follows:

Some clients begin reading at from 150 to 200 words a minute. Others can do as well as 300 to 500. The average is about 250. With individual equipment each can work at his own pace toward the goal of 650-700 words per minute. Some of the pupils go way beyond that. A Chicago lawyer set a foundation record of 3,750 words.[11]

These articles illustrate the demand at the present time among adult groups for programs in reading improvement. And the articles reflect another fact of significance. Most people adopt a way of reading that is far below the level in speed and comprehension at which they might read with pleasure and efficiency. The gains made in programs designed to improve reading ability show that this pace can be greatly altered by practice. Undoubtedly, accelerated reading programs have brought gains in speed of reading as measured by the tests employed. But it is well to inquire whether such gains are really worth while, and whether one is justified in concluding that very large gains in rate of reading carry with them correlated improvement in comprehension.

11. "Fast Reading Courses Take Executives Back to School," *Business Week,* April 5, 1952, pp. 78-80.

ADJUSTMENT OF SPEED TO PURPOSE AND TO MATERIALS

In 1939, the writer, in collaboration with Kopel, warned against excessive emphasis on speed of reading.[12] The reason for the exercise of caution in this respect is the well-known fact that the good reader cultivates different techniques for reading different kinds of material and is able to apply the techniques as they are needed. The poor reader, on the other hand, is often unable to make such adjustments readily. The point should be emphasized too, that reading rate does not depend upon a single capacity; instead, it should be regarded as an aggregate of abilities which one employs selectively in reading different types of material. Consequently a desirable program of reading improvement must provide opportunities for increasing speed in reading various types of material. Important also is the development of the ability to decide upon and to use effectively the most appropriate rates with the different presentations being read. Finally, consideration must be given to the importance of interest, difficulty of material, and familiarity with the concepts presented as factors influencing both rate and comprehension. In fact, rate of reading has little value *per se.*

Similar convictions have been expressed by other investigators. For example, McKee writes:

Speed in itself has no value. Every pupil should learn to adjust his speed of reading to the purpose for which he is reading and to the difficulty of the material at hand. He should have several speeds, each to be used as needed.[13]

Carrillo and Sheldon have made the following observation:

The mature reader is the adaptable, versatile reader; he should be able to adapt his rate of reading to the purpose with which he approaches the printed page, and to the difficulty of the material. The goal is understanding at an adequate level.[14]

It is clear, then, that reading rate will vary with the type of reading one does. Therefore, one should not expect that a *general* rate

12. Paul A. Witty and David Kopel, *Reading and the Educative Process.* Boston: Ginn & Co., 1939.

13. Paul McKee, *The Teaching of Reading in the Elementary School*, p. 110. Boston: Houghton Mifflin Co., 1948.

14. Lawrence W. Carrillo and William D. Sheldon, "The Flexibility of Reading Rate," *Journal of Educational Psychology*, XLIII (May, 1952), 300.

of reading should be established which will apply in many or most situations.

Limitations in Tests of Rate and Comprehension

High relationship between speed and comprehension have often been cited and fallacious assumptions have been drawn from these reports. For example, it is sometimes assumed that a causal relationship exists between reading rate and comprehension. This, of course, does not necessarily follow. Moreover, the high coefficients of correlation reported may, in themselves, be misleading for they are sometimes based on the use of tests that are of doubtful validity. The size of a coefficient of correlation has been influenced in some studies by the types of material read and by the procedures used to measure reading speed and comprehension. Standard tests of reading speed are obviously limited to the particular kinds of material covered. The materials included in such tests are frequently inadequate samples of the kinds of material people read or need to read. Moreover, the tests are often too short to afford reliable measures of speed. A much larger and more varied amount of reading material is needed than that found in many standard tests if one is to measure rate of reading validly. Important, too, is the type of material used in tests of reading comprehension.

One of the most obvious limitations of comprehension tests is the fact that they are "timed," thus introducing the element of speed during the measurement of comprehension. Preston and Botel attempted to check the hypothesis that "when reading comprehension is tested under 'untimed' conditions, rate and quality of reading are unrelated." After testing 32 students in a class at the University of Pennsylvania, they concluded:

> The correlation of rate and *timed* comprehension yields the statistically significant coefficient of .48. The correlation between rate and untimed comprehension yields the coefficient of .20—not statistically significant. Since untimed comprehension is the "purer" comprehension score, we conclude there was little relationship between rate and comprehension. It is clear that the usual procedure for measuring comprehension is untenable. It errs in its measurement of comprehension by designating as "comprehension" what is in reality partly speed.[15]

15. Ralph C. Preston and Morton Botel, "Reading Comprehension Tested under Timed and Untimed Conditions," *School and Society*, LXXIV (August 4, 1951), 71.

It seems, from studies such as Preston and Botel's, that faulty or inadequate testing devices and procedures have led to some doubtful conclusions about the close relation between reading rate and comprehension. Several other studies support this conclusion. For example, on the basis of three rate-of-reading scores made by elementary-school pupils on a test "of ability to read and think about that which was read," Shores and Husbands suggested the following hypothesis:

> The relationship between speed of reading and comprehension depends to a large extent upon the purpose set for the reading and upon the nature of the reading material. With some purposes and some materials, fast readers are the best readers. With other purposes and materials, the best readers will read as slowly or even more slowly than the inefficient readers.[16]

Perhaps the following comment from a recently published book on reading represents a fair evaluation of the relationship between speed and comprehension in reading.

> When speed and comprehension are tested on similar passages within the reader's educational experience, a positive relationship between independent measurement of rate of reading and comprehension may be expected.[17]

In many types of reading there is some truth to the statement that the more rapidly a person reads, the more he will comprehend. Yet, one should expect variability in the individual's speed and comprehension in reading different kinds of material. And since most persons can make marked gains in improving their reading efficiency and can become proficient in adjusting their speed to suit their purposes for reading and the types of material read, it is desirable to initiate reading-improvement programs.

The Use of Devices in Various Groups

We have seen that most people can improve their rate as well as their understanding in reading various kinds of material. How is

---

16. J. Harlan Shores and Kenneth L. Husbands, "Are Fast Readers the Best Readers?" *Elementary English,* XXVII (January, 1950), 57.

17. Ruth Strang, C. R. McCullough, and Arthur E. Traxler. *Problems in the Improvement of Reading,* p. 71. New York: McGraw-Hill Book Co., Inc., 1955 (second edition).

improvement most effectively accomplished? Is the use of a tachistoscope or a reading accelerator recommended? Let us again examine the literature which has contained a number of accounts of
"speed reading" courses in high schools and in college classes as well
as for adult groups.

In some of these reports, commercial tachistoscopes have been
employed; in others, simpler approaches have been used. An unusual procedure is described in one article in which the speed of
reading is increased without the use of mechanical devices. The
author asserts that about one hundred pages of relatively simple
reading material are sufficient for a year's instruction in reading.
The time required is about two ten-minute sessions a week. In
the early practice periods, emphasis is placed on speed, and the
students are instructed to disregard comprehension:

> The drill itself is quite simple. Give the students about five seconds'
> warning, let them read for a minute, ask them to count the words they
> have read, and ask them to report the results. They may call off the
> number of words read, estimate how much they understood, or raise their
> hands if they read more than at a designated speed. Books are collected
> and regular class begins. This drill is repeated some fifty times during
> the year until four-fifths of the class have so overlearned the silent read-
> ing skill that they use it automatically where it is appropriate.[18]

Andrews reports that, after two months of this type of practice,
his class members read at speeds varying from 250 to 1,000 words
per minute; they are ready then to vary their speeds. Practice is
given, and, after the third month, speed alone is seldom emphasized;
adaptability of speed to purpose continues to be the important
emphasis.

A somewhat different procedure is recommended by another
teacher. It involves the use of the "flashreader"—a device covering
and concealing several lines of print.

According to this writer, "Flashreader training supplies variety
and collects enthusiasm. In conjunction with other aspects of the
reading program, it seems to justify the 200-minute role it plays in
the production of rapid readers." Perhaps the most important aspect
of this approach is its value in interesting the students in improving

---

18. Joe W. Andrews, "An Approach to Speed Reading," *English Journal*,
XLI (September, 1952), 352.

their reading. The writer claims that "the motivation of the class is wooed, won, and held." [19] Great gains are reported by the use of this approach.

VALUE OF DEVICES DESIGNED TO IMPROVE READING SPEED

The foregoing statements illustrate reports in which claims are made for different approaches designed to "accelerate reading." Such reports often include enthusiastic endorsements of commercial machines. Occasionally, however, one encounters an experimenter who questions the value of one or more of the devices. Such an attitude is expressed in an article by Manolakes,[20] whose experiment was conducted with a class of adults. The subjects for his investigation were officers in the Marine Corps supply schools. They were divided into experimental and control groups. "The variable element within their instruction was the exclusion of tachistoscopic training from the program of the experimental group, and the extension of instruction in vocabulary and comprehension skills."

The investigator reports that significant differences were not found between the groups in "the reduction of the number of fixations, the increase of the span of recognition, the reduction of regressive movements, or reduction of the duration of fixations." There was a significant difference in reading rate at the conclusion of the training program, but this difference favored the experimental group.

This study leads one to recall somewhat similar conclusions from other experiments. Thus, Gates has pointed out another weakness in the use of devices to improve reading rate.

While such a machine may have some value for demonstration purposes, it does not really teach the pupil to read as he should read in a normal situation and forces him to learn adjustments that do not exist when he sits down to read a book by himself. Unfortunately, no book has been made as yet which will conveniently flash the phrases one after another as the mechanical apparatus does. He may learn to read "thought

---

19. Alan Snyder, "The Flashreader in the Reading Laboratory," *English Journal*, XLI (May, 1952), 269.

20. George Manolakes, "The Effects of Tachistoscopic Training in an Adult Reading Program," *Journal of Applied Psychology*, XXXVI (December, 1952), 410-12.

units" when the machine forces them upon him but will read a book in quite another way. Another popular pacing machine requires the teacher or pupil to place a book under a metal covering, turn on the motor, and then try to keep reading the lines as the metal shutter moves down the page covering line after line. This calls for a less artificial departure from the natural situation than the preceding gadget, but the same effect can be obtained better and with less distraction without the machine. All the pupil needs is a piece of cardboard which he himself moves down the page at a pace to suit his ability. He can force the pace as he desires; he can make it faster or slower or skip back and repeat a line as needed. Every such device—mechanical or other—should be appraised in terms of the extent to which it introduces artificial factors, distorts the natural process, lacks proper flexibility and adaptability to the reader's needs.[21]

We have examined some studies which have led authorities in reading to recommend caution in the use of mechanical devices. Yet there is a place, many people believe, for such devices in programs for young people and adults. In the high school, pupils may derive enhanced interest from the use of devices such as the Reading Accelerator. That such devices are necessary for conducting a successful program has not been demonstrated. At the high-school and college levels, as well as with adult groups, they may become a factor, if judiciously used, in fostering interest and zeal for learning.[22] It is clear, however, that at every level of instruction they are not the essential item in fostering improved reading. The chief requirements for effective reading programs are: clear objectives, careful diagnosis of each student's needs, a variety of books and reading materials, high motivation, and sufficient time to enable the student to develop skills in reading in accord with his most pressing needs. Many students will, of course, require exercises to increase their speed of reading. The aim of this endeavor should be to develop a capacity to adjust one's method and rate of reading to different demands. The objectives for pupils will vary with the

21. Arthur I. Gates, *Teaching Reading*, p. 26. What Research Says to the Teacher, No. 1. Department of Classroom Teachers and American Educational Research Association of the National Education Association. Washington: National Education Association, 1953.

22. Paul Witty, Theodore Stolarz, and William Cooper, "Some Results of a Remedial Reading Program for College Students," *School and Society*, LXXVI (December 13, 1952), 376-80.

types of material to be read as well as with the individual differences.

Characteristics of Effective Reading Programs

In recent years there has been considerable criticism of the effectiveness of reading instruction. Some of the criticisms, it appears, are justified, despite the fact that our schools are doing, on the whole, an effective job in teaching reading—better perhaps than at any time in the past. Moreover, this result is achieved in spite of mounting enrolments and the distracting influence of TV, radio, motion pictures, and the comic magazines—all bidding for the student's leisure, a situation that did not exist in previous generations. However, a great need exists in many high schools today for the provision of experiences in reading of heightened interest and of a sufficiently diversified nature to meet the needs of the various reading levels of the students in regular classes. There is need, too, for an even more efficient program of reading instruction and for the application of established principles of instruction. For we do know how to teach reading. The fact was demonstrated during World War II.[23] Special training units were organized to give functionally illiterate and non-English-speaking men the academic training they needed to become useful soldiers.[24] In these units they took part in an educational program characterized by (*a*) definite objectives, (*b*) high motive and interest, (*c*) careful testing and grouping of the students, (*d*) the use of functional methods and materials in small classes, (*e*) provision for vocabulary development, (*f*) wide application of visual aids, (*g*) hygienic conditions insuring a sense of security and general well-being, (*h*) possibilities of small successes at the start, and steady, satisfying progress as the course went on, and (*i*) the use of thoroughly trained, enthusiastic instructors.

By participating in this program, functionally illiterate and non-English-speaking men were able to acquire the reading skills needed in the army in a period of eight weeks. There are significant implications in this work. In the first place, it is evident that illiteracy

23. For an account of this work, see Paul Witty, *Reading in Modern Education.* Boston: D. C. Heath & Co., 1949.

24. "Functional" illiteracy referred to the condition of men who could not read and understand simply written accounts such as those found in *The Soldier's Handbook.* On tests, these men scored below the fifth-grade norms.

need not continue to be a great social problem in America. But it does continue—almost unchecked. A comprehensive educational program for illiterate adults is necessary to correct this condition. One phase of it should be carried on in the armed forces so that potentially good soldiers would not be rejected. In addition, a nation-wide civilian program should be inaugurated. In both programs for functionally illiterate adults, the instructional techniques employed so effectively during World War II might be utilized to great advantage. But our schools have an additional and a more important obligation, namely, to teach reading to all children and youth so efficiently that functional illiteracy will be virtually unknown among the adult populations of the future. The emphasis in this chapter on the importance of both remedial and developmental reading programs is in keeping with W. S. Gray's conclusion in chapter ii that "the nature of the reading competence of any generation of adults is determined to a large extent by the kind and amount of instruction given when they were in school." We must give every youth an opportunity to learn to read with ease, effectiveness, and pleasure. Such skill and enjoyment in reading will also help him make his greatest contribution as an adult.

Developmental Programs for High-School Students

Reading programs in superior high schools are commonly identified as either remedial or developmental. It is probable that increased numbers of remedial programs will be initiated to care for the very large numbers of young people who, in recent years, have been taught in elementary-school classes of exceedingly high enrolments and who are now entering high schools. But there is need for junior and senior high schools to establish developmental programs also. To some degree, every high-school teacher should be considered a teacher of reading; as such, he should seek to cultivate the reading skills appropriate to his subject field. Some stimulating practices have been developed in our high schools. For example, to foster developmental reading, one school system utilizes the services of a reading consultant who has played an important role in leading other teachers to become interested, informed, and co-operative in seeking reading improvement. One outstanding result of this practice is a change in the attitudes of the teachers.

Today the attitude of high-school teachers toward reading has greatly changed. . . . They are beginning to teach the skills of reading. . . . The teacher accepts his responsibility to teach the reading skills pertinent to his subject. Some are even experimenting with grouping pupils into a class according to reading level. All are working toward increasing the pupils' proficiency in reading. Reading as a tool has taken its rightful place in the total curriculum of the high school. . . . The teaching of reading is a new process for many secondary-school teachers. They can still learn much from the procedures and techniques used in the elementary school.

.   .   .   .

By working on a continuous program such as is being established in many school systems, the elementary teachers become more aware of the pupils' reading needs in the secondary school. And equally important, the secondary-school teacher becomes aware that he must carry on the development of reading skills begun by the elementary school.[25]

In developmental programs for high-school pupils, extensive use is made of films, filmstrips, and other aids such as the tape or wire recorder. For example, the reading program in the Evanston (Illinois) Township High School is introduced through the film, *Better Reading*. The Reading Accelerator and the Flashmeter are employed only as motivating devices. Filmstrips have proved effective in building vocabulary. Also, a textbook [26] is used in the reading-improvement program. The following description sets forth some features of this work:

A full-time reading consultant has been appointed and has been given ample time and diversified materials for use with individuals. One of the major purposes of the program is to encourage the improvement of reading within every classroom rather than merely to offer remedial services. This developmental program has emphasized four types of instruction to improve reading: (1) remedial classes as substitutes for freshman English, (2) skill classes for upper-classmen, (3) individual diagnostic work for students having special problems, and (4) emphasis upon growth in reading in all classrooms.

.   .   .   .

To co-ordinate the reading program with the regular English course [for example], units on grammar and social topics were included.

25. David L. Shepherd, "Secondary Teacher Views Elementary-School Reading," *Grade Teacher*, LXXI (November, 1953), 86 and 91.

26. Paul A. Witty, *How to Become a Better Reader*. Chicago: Science Research Associates, 1953.

Shakespeare recordings were employed to familiarize the group with plays such as *The Merchant of Venice*. Enthusiastic discussions, dramatizations, and question-and-answer panels made these plays interesting to students who otherwise might not have enjoyed them.

.   .   .   .

More important, perhaps, than the reading gains made by these groups was the students' change in attitude toward reading. Practice and knowledge of efficient reading skills stimulated interest and prepared students to attack assignments in other classes. This led to a change in attitude toward reading in the different subject areas, as well as to improvement in the mental health of the students. It is the purpose of the school's reading committee to promote a school-wide acceptance of this type of reading instruction and to establish developmental conditions for reading and learning activities within the classrooms of all the content fields.[27]

Reading-Improvement Programs for College Students and for Adult Groups

At the college level, remedial programs have proved very successful in improving both reading rate and comprehension. At Northwestern University, students judged to need help in reading are carefully screened and are given a systematic program of instruction.[28] Careful study is made of the students and their problems, and needs are classified. The following characteristics of the members of one group of students suggest the problems faced in providing a helpful program for them:

1. They adopted a very slow, uneven rate of reading for most materials.
2. They lacked the ability to adjust their rate of reading to different types of material or to their immediate purpose for reading.
3. They were more successful in reading very short passages than in getting the meaning from longer presentations.
4. They lacked accuracy in reading. They comprehended little of the materials read and, in many cases, gained a false impression.
5. They lacked the ability to concentrate upon difficult materials and frequently were unable to complete their assignments in a reasonable amount of time.

27. Phyllis Bland, "Adjusting Instruction to Individual Differences in Grades Ten to Fourteen," *Improving Reading in All Curriculum Areas*, pp. 44-45. Compiled and edited by William S. Gray. Supplementary Educational Monograph, No. 76, November, 1952. Chicago: University of Chicago Press, 1952.

28. Witty, Stolarz, and Cooper, *op. cit.*

6. They had poorer-than-average vocabulary scores. They lacked an understanding of the precise meanings of many words. They were weak in "specialized vocabularies."
7. They did very little leisure reading.
8. They lacked the ability to comprehend important details in many types of presentations.
9. They were unable to organize materials read and to present the facts in concise outline form.
10. They read uncritically and were unable to discern contradictions or inconsistencies in many presentations.

In an effort to meet the varied needs of these college students, rather comprehensive programs of individual and group work were planned for them. The following activities were featured:

1. *Rapid reading of fairly easy, interesting materials.* The selections which the students read at first were short stories or magazine articles of eighth- or ninth-grade difficulty. The Reading Accelerator was used in practice periods.
2. *Leisure reading.* An inventory was used to ascertain the areas of greatest interest to each student. Appropriate reading materials of suitable difficulty were read in accord with any particular interest. In addition, some students chose to read novels that they had planned to read "some day," and others read nonfiction ranging in type from legal cases and mechanical manuals to popular biographies.
3. *Speed-reading practice.* Periods for practice in rapid reading each day in addition to the time for the reading program were arranged for each student. Records of rate and comprehension were kept by the student in his daily effort to improve speed and comprehension.
4. *Training in recognizing short phrases on the tachistoscope.* This practice was designed to encourage rapid recognition of groups of words. Two or three students worked with the tachistoscope while the rest of the group was occupied with other activities. This training was limited to about ten minutes per day. Most of the students became very proficient in this skill and discontinued practice after a few weeks.
5. *Vocabulary building.* Exercises were planned to enable students to obtain the meanings of unfamiliar words from their context. Students also kept records of new words encountered in various types of reading. The importance of vocabulary in each subject area was stressed throughout the program, and students kept lists of key words and their meanings. These lists were frequently reviewed and related to assignments and to textbook reading.
6. *Attack on specific reading skills.* In reading assignments as well as in the use of manuals, emphasis was placed upon exercises to facilitate

the mastery of important reading skills such as skimming, reading for details, getting the general thought of paragraphs, and critical reading. Competent advisers aided students in the exercise of discrimination in the selection of materials and in the choice of the method to be used in reading. They learned to select materials for skimming, for precise reading, for leisure reading, and for other purposes.

7. *Frequent individual conferences.* Particular problems and needs of the students were studied, and materials and methods to overcome difficulties were discussed in individual conferences.

8. *Help in reading textbooks.* Students were taught to interpret graphs, illustrations, and charts, and the special vocabulary of each subject was studied.

Gains Made in Reading-Improvement Programs

The results of this program were gratifying. Test-retest scores showed that marked gains had been made. Percentile gains were large. But even more important, gains were revealed in the students' ability and inclination to read widely and in various fields. The students gave unmistakable evidence that they had gained greatly in reading ability and that they had come to enjoy reading.

A remarkable gain was made, of course, in rate of reading. The average rate (for relatively easy materials) at the beginning of the program was 272 words a minute. After the program was completed the students read the same type of materials at an average rate of 474 words a minute. There was, of course, great variability in the gains made by individual students. However, every student improved in reading rate and some of the gains were very large. Comprehension scores also tended to improve.

Several programs have proved successful in meeting the needs of various adult groups. One of these was devised at Northwestern University for men attending a Traffic Institute. The program is similar in many respects to the one just described for college students. Essentially the same procedures and materials were employed with additional attention given to reading the areas studied in the Traffic Institute and to materials selected to satisfy the special interests and needs of these men. This program, like the others, has led to remarkable change in reading ability and in attitude toward reading.

The extent to which gains in reading rate and comprehension persist and influence grades in school and affect other aspects of behavior are unsettled issues. Some studies have revealed little or no relationship between the completion of a reading-improvement course and grades. Other recent studies have shown slightly better grades for groups of students who complete such courses. Many of these studies have conspicuous limitations in the procedures employed for making comparisons. A very careful recent study of seventy-four University of Michigan students who, as Freshmen, took part in a reading-improvement course were compared during sixty weeks with a control group not taking such a course. Certain gains, such as a tendency for a larger percentage of the experimental group to remain in college, were noted. The writers of this article conclude: "Significant superiority in academic status (increasing with time) is demonstrated by experimental subjects over both control and representative freshmen subjects when study and examination skills are emphasized during the training period." [29]

The results of some studies emphasize the importance of attitude in determining whether students will continue to use the skills developed during reading-improvement programs. The development of a desire to read widely should be one of the objectives of such a program. Of course, much depends upon whether the individual will use his newly found reading skills. Shores has suggested that if "you are an average reader you can read an average book at the rate of 300 words a minute," but that "you cannot maintain that average . . . unless you read regularly every day." He emphasizes the importance of systematic reading programs:

> Each of us must find our own 15-minute period each day. . . . The only requirement is the will to read. With it you can find the 15 minutes no matter how busy the day. And you must have the book at hand. . . . [In this way] . . . you will read half a book a week, 2 books a month, 20 a year, and 1,000 or more in a reading lifetime. It's an easy way to become well read.[30]

Naturally, the most effective way of improving reading ability is to enrol in a remedial course such as those given for adults in regular schools and colleges or in evening classes. If this is im-

29. Donald E. P. Smith and Roger L. Wood, "Reading Improvement and College Grades: A Follow-up," *Journal of Educational Psychology*, XLVI (March, 1955), 158.

30. Louis Shores, "How To Find Time To Read," *The Wonderful World of Books, op. cit.*, 77-78.

possible, anyone who really wants to improve may devise his own program. In order to start efficiently, he must set aside a time, perhaps 30 minutes or more daily, for undisturbed practice. He should begin by testing his rate of reading different kinds of material. A number of magazines provide such tests on their articles. Also, appropriate tests for adults will be found in *How To Become a Better Reader.*[31] This book contains testing and progress records to measure and guide improvement in skill. It also stresses the use of materials which lead to enjoyment of reading.

After obtaining measures of his reading rate and comprehension, the student should seek to read easy materials as rapidly as he can. After each period of practice, he should record his rate and try to summarize or outline each selection he has read. At first he should select stories he can complete in 30 or 40 minutes. He should read each story rapidly and make a summary. Then he should reread each selection to ascertain how well he has understood it. Gradually the difficulty of materials should be increased; practice should be continued and records kept. The beginner will want to start his practice by reading short stories—the easy kind such as may be found in booklets published by the *Reader's Digest.* Then he should turn to other types of materials—biography, scientific accounts, "solid" books or articles, and reports he has wanted to read for his personal pleasure or to increase his effectiveness on the job. He should record his improvement in reading different kinds of material. In his quest for appropriate and varied materials he should consult the librarian in the public library and should start a program of reading for enjoyment. *The Wonderful World of Books* contains many excellent suggestions for such reading.[32]

Systematic practice accompanied by wide reading will lead to improvement. But the extent of improvement depends upon the student's desire to improve and his consistency and zeal in following a schedule. If he really desires to improve, he usually can do so. It will require sustained effort, for it is difficult to break down old habits and establish new patterns. But the effort is worth while, since the person who learns to read rapidly and well has opened the doors to the world's storehouse of information and pleasure in books.

31. Paul A. Witty, *How To Become a Better Reader, op. cit.*

32. *Op cit.*

Index

CONSTITUTION AND BY-LAWS
OF
THE NATIONAL SOCIETY FOR THE
STUDY OF EDUCATION

(As adopted May, 1944, and amended June, 1945, and February, 1949)

ARTICLE I

NAME

The name of this corporation shall be "The National Society for the Study of Education," an Illinois corporation not for profit.

ARTICLE II

PURPOSES

Its purposes are to carry on the investigation of educational problems, to publish the results of same, and to promote their discussion.

The corporation also has such powers as are now, or may hereafter be, granted by the General Not For Profit Corporation Act of the State of Illinois.

ARTICLE III

OFFICES

The corporation shall have and continuously maintain in this state a registered office and a registered agent whose office is identical with such registered office, and may have other offices within or without the State of Illinois as the Board of Directors may from time to time determine.

ARTICLE IV

MEMBERSHIP

Section 1. *Classes.* There shall be two classes of members—active and honorary. The qualifications and rights of the members of such classes shall be as follows:

(*a*) Any person who is desirous of promoting the purposes of this corporation is eligible to active membership and shall become such on payment of dues as prescribed.

(*b*) Active members shall be entitled to vote, to participate in discussion, and, subject to the conditions set forth in Article V, to hold office.

(*c*) Honorary members shall be entitled to all the privileges of active members, with the exception of voting and holding office, and shall be exempt from the payment of dues. A person may be elected to honorary membership by vote of the active members of the corporation on nomination by the Board of Directors.

(*d*) Any active member of the Society may, at any time after reaching the age of sixty, become a life member on payment of the aggregate amount of the regular annual dues for th? period of life expectancy, as determined by standard actuarial tables, such membership to entitle the member to receive all yearbooks and to enjoy all other privileges of active membership in the Society for the lifetime of the member.

Section 2. *Termination of Membership.*

(*a*) The Board of Directors by affirmative vote of two-thirds of the members of the Board may suspend or expel a member for cause after appropriate hearing.

(*b*) Termination of membership for nonpayment of dues shall become effective as provided in Article XIV.

Section 3. *Reinstatement.* The Board of Directors may by the affirmation vote of two-thirds of the members of the Board reinstate a former member whose membership was previously terminated for cause other than nonpayment of dues.

Section 4. *Transfer of Membership.* Membership in this corporation is not transferable or assignable.

ARTICLE V

BOARD OF DIRECTORS

Section 1. *General Powers.* The business and affairs of the corporation shall be managed by its Board of Directors. It shall appoint the Chairman and Vice-Chairman of the Board of Directors, the Secretary-Treasurer, and Members of the Council. It may appoint a member to fill any vacancy on the Board until such vacancy shall have been filled by election as provided in Section 3 of this Article.

Section 2. *Number, Tenure, and Qualifications.* The Board of Directors shall consist of seven members, namely, six to be elected by the members of the corporation, and th? Secretary-Treasurer to be the seventh member. Only active members who have contributed to the Yearbook shall be eligible for election to serve as directors. A member who has been elected for a full term of three years as director and has not attended at least two-thirds of the meetings duly called and held during that term shall not be eligible for election again before the fifth annual election after the expiration of the term for which he was first elected. No member who has been elected for two full terms as director in immediate succession shall be elected a director for a term next succeeding. This provision shall not apply to the Secretary-Treasurer who is appointed by the Board of Directors. Each director shall hold office for the term for which he is elected or appointed and until his successor shall have been selected and qualified. Directors need not be residents of Illinois.

Section 3. *Election.*

(*a*) The directors named in the Articles of Incorporation shall hold office until their successors shall have been duly selected and shall have qualified.

Thereafter, two directors shall be elected annually to serve three years, beginning March first after their election. If, at the time of any annual election, a vacancy exists in the Board of Directors, a director shall be elected at such election to fill such vacancy.

(b) Elections of directors shall be held by ballots sent by United States mail as follows: A nominating ballot together with a list of members eligible to be directors shall be mailed by the Secretary-Treasurer to all active members of the corporation in October. From such list, the active members shall nominate on such ballot one eligible member for each of the two regular terms and for any vacancy to be filled and return such ballots to the office of the Secretary-Treasurer within twenty-one days after said date of mailing by the Secretary-Treasurer. The Secretary-Treasurer shall prepare an election ballot and place thereon in alphabetical order the names of persons equal to three times the number of offices to be filled, these persons to be those who received the highest number of votes on the nominating ballot, provided, however, that not more than one person connected with a given institution or agency shall be named on such final ballot, the person so named to be the one receiving the highest vote on the nominating ballot. Such election ballot shall be mailed by the Secretary-Treasurer to all active members in November next succeeding. The active members shall vote thereon for one member for each such office. Election ballots must be in the office of the Secretary-Treasurer within twenty-one days after the said date of mailing by the Secretary-Treasurer. The ballots shall be counted by the Secretary-Treasurer, or by an election committee, if any, appointed by the Board. The two members receiving the highest number of votes shall be declared elected for the regular term and the member or members receiving the next highest number of votes shall be declared elected for any vacancy or vacancies to be filled.

Section 4. *Regular Meetings.* A regular annual meeting of the Board of Directors shall be held, without other notice than this by-law, at the same place and as nearly as possible on the same date as the annual meeting of the corporation. The Board of Directors may provide the time and place, either within or without the State of Illinois, for the holding of additional regular meetings of the Board.

Section 5. *Special Meetings.* Special meetings of the Board of Directors may be called by or at the request of the Chairman or a majority of the directors. Such special meetings shall be held at the office of the corporation unless a majority of the directors agree upon a different place for such meetings.

Section 6. *Notice.* Notice of any special meeting of the Board of Directors shall be given at least fifteen days previously thereto by written notice delivered personally or mailed to each director at his business address, or by telegram. If mailed, such notice shall be deemed to be delivered when deposited in the United States mail in a sealed envelope so addressed, with postage thereon prepaid. If notice be given by telegram, such notice shall be deemed to be delivered when the telegram is delivered to the telegraph company. Any director may waive notice of any meeting. The attendance of a director at any meeting shall constitute a waiver of notice of such meeting, except where a director attends a meeting for the express purpose of objecting to the transaction of any business because the meeting is not lawfully called or convened. Neither the business to be transacted at, nor the purpose of, any regular or special meeting of the Board need be specified in the notice or waiver of notice of such meeting.

Section 7. *Quorum.* A majority of the Board of Directors shall constitute a quorum for the transaction of business at any meeting of the Board, provided, that if less than a majority of the directors are present at said meeting, a majority of the directors present may adjourn the meeting from time to time without further notice.

Section 8. *Manner of Acting.* The act of the majority of the directors present at a meeting at which a quorum is present shall be the act of the Board of Directors, except where otherwise provided by law or by these by-laws.

ARTICLE VI

THE COUNCIL

Section 1. *Appointment.* The Council shall consist of the Board of Directors, the Chairmen of the corporation's Yearbook and Research Committees, and such other active members of the corporation as the Board of Directors may appoint.

Section 2. *Duties.* The duties of the Council shall be to further the objects of the corporation by assisting the Board of Directors in planning and carrying forward the educational undertakings of the corporation.

ARTICLE VII

OFFICERS

Section 1. *Officers.* The officers of the corporation shall be a Chairman of the Board of Directors, a Vice-Chairman of the Board of Directors, and a Secretary-Treasurer. The Board of Directors, by resolution, may create additional offices. Any two or more offices may be held by the same person, except the offices of Chairman and Secretary-Treasurer.

Section 2. *Election and Term of Office.* The officers of the corporation shall be elected annually by the Board of Directors at the annual regular meeting of the Board of Directors, provided, however, that the Secretary-Treasurer may be elected for a term longer than one year. If the election of officers shall not be held at such meeting, such election shall be held as soon thereafter as conveniently may be. Vacancies may be filled or new offices created and filled at any meeting of the Board of Directors. Each officer shall hold office until his successor shall have been duly elected and shall have qualified or until his death or until he shall resign or shall have been removed in the manner hereinafter provided.

Section 3. *Removal.* Any officer or agent elected or appointed by the Board of Directors may be removed by the Board of Directors whenever in its judgment the best interests of the corporation would be served thereby, but such removal shall be without prejudice to the contract rights, if any, of the person so removed.

Section 4. *Chairman of the Board of Directors.* The Chairman of the Board of Directors shall be the principal officer of the corporation. He shall preside at all meetings of the members of the Board of Directors, shall perform all duties incident to the office of Chairman of the Board of Directors and such other duties as may be prescribed by the Board of Directors from time to time.

Section 5. *Vice-Chairman of the Board of Directors.* In the absence of the Chairman of the Board of Directors or in the event of his inability or refusal to act, the Vice-Chairman of the Board of Directors shall perform the duties of the Chairman of the Board of Directors, and when so acting, shall have all the powers of and be subject to all the restrictions upon the Chairman of the Board of Directors. Any Vice-Chairman of the Board of Directors shall perform such other duties as from time to time may be assigned to him by the Board of Directors.

Section 6. *Secretary-Treasurer.* The Secretary-Treasurer shall be the managing executive officer of the corporation. He shall: (a) keep the minutes of the meetings of the members and of the Board of Directors in one or more books provided for that purpose; (b) see that all notices are duly given in accordance with the provisions of these by-laws or as required by law; (c) be custodian of the corporate records and of the seal of the corporation and see that the seal of the corporation is affixed to all documents, the execution of which on behalf of the corporation under its seal is duly authorized in accordance with the provisions of these by-laws; (d) keep a register of the postoffice address of each member as furnished to the secretary-treasurer by such member; (e) in general perform all duties incident to the office of secretary and such other duties as from time to time may be assigned to him by the Chairman of the Board of Directors or by the Board of Directors. He shall also: (1) have charge and custody of and be responsible for all funds and securities of the corporation; receive and give receipts for moneys due and payable to the corporation from any source whatsoever, and deposit all such moneys in the name of the corporation in such banks, trust companies or other depositories as shall be selected in accordance with the provisions of Article XI of these by-laws; (2) in general perform all the duties incident to the office of Treasurer and such other duties as from time to time may be assigned to him by the Chairman of the Board of Directors or by the Board of Directors. The Secretary-Treasurer shall give a bond for the faithful discharge of his duties in such sum and with such surety or sureties as the Board of Directors shall determine, said bond to be placed in the custody of the Chairman of the Board of Directors.

ARTICLE VIII

COMMITTEES

The Board of Directors, by appropriate resolution duly passed, may create and appoint such committees for such purposes and periods of time as it may deem advisable.

ARTICLE IX

PUBLICATIONS

Section 1. The corporation shall publish *The Yearbook of the National Society for the Study of Education*, such supplements thereto, and such other materials as the Board of Directors may provide for.

Section 2. *Names of Members.* The names of the active and honorary members shall be printed in the Yearbook.

ARTICLE X

ANNUAL MEETINGS

The corporation shall hold its annual meetings at the time and place of the Annual Meeting of the American Association of School Administrators of the National Education Association. Other meetings may be held when authorized by the corporation or by the Board of Directors.

ARTICLE XI

CONTRACTS, CHECKS, DEPOSITS, AND GIFTS

Section 1. *Contracts.* The Board of Directors may authorize any officer or officers, agent or agents of the corporation, in addition to the officers so authorized by these by-laws to enter into any contract or execute and deliver any instrument in the name of and on behalf of the corporation and such authority may be general or confined to specific instances.

Section 2. *Checks, drafts, etc.* All checks, drafts, or other orders for the payment of money, notes, or other evidences of indebtedness issued in the name of the corporation, shall be signed by such officer or officers, agent or agents of the corporation and in such manner as shall from time to time be determined by resolution of the Board of Directors. In the absence of such determination of the Board of Directors, such instruments shall be signed by the Secretary-Treasurer.

Section 3. *Deposits.* All funds of the corporation shall be deposited from time to time to the credit of the corporation in such banks, trust companies, or other depositories as the Board of Directors may select.

Section 4. *Gifts.* The Board of Directors may accept on behalf of the corporation any contribution, gift, bequest, or device for the general purposes or for any special purpose of the corporation.

ARTICLE XII

BOOKS AND RECORDS

The corporation shall keep correct and complete books and records of account and shall also keep minutes of the proceedings of its members, Board of Directors, and committees having any of the authority of the Board of Directors, and shall keep at the registered or principal office a record giving the names and addresses of the members entitled to vote. All books and records of the corporation may be inspected by any member or his agent or attorney for any proper purpose at any reasonable time.

ARTICLE XIII

FISCAL YEAR

The fiscal year of the corporation shall begin on the first day of July in each year and end on the last day of June of the following year.

ARTICLE XIV

DUES

Section 1. *Annual Dues.* The annual dues for active members of the Society shall be determined by vote of the Board of Directors at a regular meeting duly called and held.

Section 2. *Election Fee.* An election fee of $1.00 shall be paid in advance by each applicant for active membership.

Section 3. *Payment of Dues.* Dues for each calendar year shall be payable in advance on or before the first day of January of that year. Notice of dues for the ensuing year shall be mailed to members at the time set for mailing the primary ballots.

Section 4. *Default and Termination of Membership.* Annual membership shall terminate automatically for those members whose dues remain unpaid after the first day of January of each year. Members so in default will be reinstated on payment of the annual dues plus a reinstatement fee of fifty cents.

ARTICLE XV

SEAL

The Board of Directors shall provide a corporate seal which shall be in the form of a circle and shall have inscribed thereon the name of the corporation and the words "Corporate Seal, Illinois."

Article XVI

WAIVER OF NOTICE

Whenever any notice whatever is required to be given under the provision of the General Not For Profit Corporation Act of Illinois or under the provisions of the Articles of Incorporation or the by-laws of the corporation, a waiver thereof in writing signed by the person or persons entitled to such notice, whether before or after the time stated therein, shall be deemed equivalent to the giving of such notice.

Article XVII

AMENDMENTS

Section 1. *Amendments by Directors.* The constitution and by-laws may be altered or amended at any meeting of the Board of Directors duly called and held, provided that an affirmative vote of at least five directors shall be required for such action.

Section 2. *Amendments by Members.* By petition of twenty-five or more active members duly filed with the Secretary-Treasurer, a proposal to amend the constitution and by-laws shall be submitted to all active members by United States mail together with ballots on which the members shall vote for or against the proposal. Such ballots shall be returned by United States mail to the office of the Secretary-Treasurer within twenty-one days after date of mailing of the proposal and ballots by the Secretary-Treasurer. The Secretary-Treasurer or a committee appointed by the Board of Directors for that purpose shall count the ballots and advise the members of the result. A vote in favor of such proposal by two-thirds of the members voting thereon shall be required for adoption of such amendment.

MINUTES OF THE ST. LOUIS MEETING
OF THE SOCIETY

FEBRUARY 26, 1955

This report describes the program presented by the Society at one of the three regional conferences of the American Association of School Administrators. In addition to the conference at St. Louis, similar meetings were scheduled by the Association for Denver and Cleveland. The two volumes of the Society's yearbook for 1955 were presented at each of the three conferences, the programs of the three meetings dealing with the same topics and the speakers being selected from the region in which the city is located. In each city, the Society's program was presented in a joint session with the American Association of School Administrators and the American Educational Research Asociation.

As a departure from previous practice, the discussion of the two volumes of the yearbook was conducted in the Saturday night session only, the time of the session being divided equally between the two subjects to be discussed. The plan was adopted by the Board of Directors for this year because of the smaller attendance at the regional conferences and is not to be employed in the years when the convention of school administrators is held in Atlantic City.

The St. Louis meeting was held in the Crystal Room of the Jefferson Hotel. Professor Paul A. Witty, Chairman of the Society's Board of Directors, was the presiding officer at this session, and the following program was presented.

Part I: MODERN PHILOSOPHIES AND EDUCATION

INTRODUCING THE YEARBOOK

Edgar Dale, Professor of Education, Ohio State University, Columbus, Ohio; Member of the Yearbook Committee

EVALUATION OF THE YEARBOOK

Robert J. Henle, S.J., Dean of the Graduate School, St. Louis University, St. Louis, Missouri

INFORMAL DISCUSSION

Part II: MENTAL HEALTH IN MODERN EDUCATION

INTRODUCING THE YEARBOOK

Paul A. Witty, Professor of Education, Northwestern University, Evanston, Illinois; Chairman of the Yearbook Committee

EVALUATING THE YEARBOOK

Kenneth Lund, Director, Child Study Bureau, Chicago Public Schools, Chicago, Illinois

INFORMAL DISCUSSION

SYNOPSIS OF THE PROCEEDINGS OF THE BOARD OF DIRECTORS OF THE SOCIETY FOR 1955

1. Meeting of February 26 at St. Louis

The Board of Directors met at the Jefferson Hotel, the following members being present: Brownell, Corey, Dale, Melby, Olson, Witty (*Chairman*), and Henry (*Secretary*).

1. The Secretary reported that the November election of members of the Board of Directors resulted in the re-election of Mr. Witty for a second term and the election of Professor T. R. McConnell of the University of California, each for the three-year period beginning March 1, 1955.

2. Officers of the Board of Directors for the year ending February 29, 1956, were chosen as follows: Mr. Melby, Chairman; Mr. Olson, Vice-chairman; Mr. Henry, Secretary.

3. Mr. Brownell reported on the status of the yearbook on the public junior college, explaining that the yearbook committee's review of the contributors' manuscripts at their October meeting resulted in the elimination of certain duplications and a better integration of the text of the volume as a whole. It was the expectation of the committee that the April first deadline for completion of the yearbook will be met.

4. Mr. Dale reported that arrangements for preparation of one of the chapters of the yearbook on adult reading are not yet made. Satisfactory progress has been reported on other chapters.

5. Mr. Brownell presented the communication of Professor Clifford Froelich of the University of California regarding a possible yearbook on personnel services. Interest of members of the Board in further consideration of this suggestion was clearly manifest in the discussion of the topic, and the Secretary was instructed to request Professor Froelich to prepare a formal proposal covering the content of an appropriate yearbook on this topic for consideration by the Board of Directors at its meeting in May.

6. Professor Preston was present at the invitation of the Board of Directors for the purpose of explaining his recommendations regarding a prospective yearbook on the social studies at the elementary-school level. The members of the Board approved the plans for this yearbook, selected the members of the yearbook committee, and appropriated funds for expenses incident to the work of the committee. It was agreed that the yearbook on the social studies should be prepared in time for publication in 1957.

7. Mr. Corey reported that two important chapters for the yearbook on inservice education had been assigned since the last meeting of the Board. These chapters deal with (1) the development of inservice education and (2) the implications of this yearbook for preservice education. Plans for the preparation of the manuscripts for all chapters are completed.

II. MEETING OF MAY 21-22 AT CHICAGO

The Board of Directors met at the Congress Hotel, the following members being present: Corey, Dale, McConnell, Melby (*Chairman*), Olson, Witty, and Henry (*Secretary*).

1. The Secretary presented reports of the committee chairmen on the present status of Parts I and II of the Fifty-fifth Yearbook. Part I, *The Public Junior College*, was reported as being completed except for some revisions requested by the yearbook committee in three of the chapters. All chapters of Part II, *Adult Reading*, were reported as being allocated to selected contributors with good prospect of being available for printing in time for publication in January, 1956.

2. Professor Preston, chairman of the Society's committee on the social studies in the elementary school, and Superintendent Oberholtzer of Denver, member of that committee, met with the Board of Directors for discussion of the committee's plans for the preparation of the yearbook. Mr. Preston explained the progress of arrangements for the assignment of chapters and the preparation of chapter outlines. Mr. Oberholtzer described certain features of the social-studies program in the Denver school system, emphasizing procedures for ascertaining citizen reaction to the results of social-studies teaching in the schools and for acquainting the classroom teachers with the implications of adult evaluations of the school program.

3. Dr. Paul L. Dressel's proposal for a yearbook on the subject of "integration in and through education" was reviewed by the Board. It was decided to request Dr. Dressel to formulate a more definite presentation of the content and organization of such a yearbook and submit the revised plan to the Board for consideration at the Autumn meeting.

4. The Secretary presented a list of topics previously discussed at meetings of the Board of Directors which had not been accepted as suitable and timely topics for yearbooks. Mr. Witty expressed the opinion that a yearbook on the education of gifted children would be appropriate at this time because of a heightening interest in the subject with reference to the problem of equality of opportunity in education and to the emphasis on the cultural and economic implications of the need for trained leadership in these areas. The Board requested Mr. Witty to draft a proposal for a yearbook in the area specified and to present the proposal for consideration at the next meeting.

5. Additional subjects for future consideration included "the role of the group" in relation to learning situations prevailing in organized programs of education. Mr. Olson was requested to report on this problem at the autumn meeting. Mr. Melby was requested to prepare a statement expressing his views on the subject of "educational policy," with reference especially to the content of formal education. Mr. Corey and Mr. Melby were requested to make some inquiries regarding the possible value of a future yearbook on international programs of education.

III. Meeting of October 15-16 at Chicago

The Board of Directors met at the Congress Hotel, the following members being present: Corey, Dale, McConnell, Melby (*Chairman*), Olson, Witty, and Henry (*Secretary*).

1. The secretary reported that plans for the two programs to be presented at Atlantic City have been completed. It is customary for copies of these to be mailed in January to all members of the Society. In keeping with a suggestion previously offered, it was agreed that the Secretary should send along with the announcements of the two programs a request that members of the Society submit suggestions for possible yearbooks to be published within the next four or five years.

2. Mr. Corey described the status of the yearbook on inservice education, explaining that several chapter manuscripts have been presented to him and others will be available in good time. The meeting of the committee for discussion of the manuscripts will be held November 4 to 6.

3. Dr. Dressel was present at this meeting for the discussion of his proposal for a yearbook on the subject of integration, which proposal had been mailed to members of the Board of Directors for examination in advance of the meeting. Pursuant to this conference, the Board requested Dr. Dressel to invite several persons who are conversant with the problems of integration to a conference for possible clarification of the proposed plan of such a yearbook and an evaluation of the probable desirability of a new publication on this subject. An appropriation for reimbursement of conference participants for expenses incurred was authorized.

4. Professor Preston reported that the committee's work on the yearbook on social studies was progressing according to schedule.

5. The Board invited Professor Havighurst of the University of Chicago to prepare a proposal for a yearbook on the education of gifted children and to recommend persons for appointment as members of the committee for such a yearbook.

6. The Board authorized an appropriation for the expenses of a conference for discussion of the subject of cultural communication as a possible subject for a yearbook. Mr. Corey and Mr. Melby were requested to conduct this conference.

7. An appropriation was authorized for expenses of a conference on group dynamics, Mr. Olson being requested to conduct the conference.

REPORT OF THE TREASURER OF THE SOCIETY

1954-55

RECEIPTS AND DISBURSEMENTS

Receipts

Membership dues	$15,506.86
Sale of yearbooks	30,054.55
Interest and dividends on securities	512.70
Miscellaneous	572.73
Advance on securities maturing in 1955-56	2,500.00
	$49,146.84

Disbursements

Yearbooks:

Manufacturing	$ 9,895.90
Reprinting	20,472.55
Preparation	2,062.49
Meetings of Society and Board of Directors	2,374.63

Secretary's Office:

Editorial, secretarial, and clerical service	9,979.73
Supplies	2,863.83
Telephone and telegraph	61.87
Miscellaneous	784.96
	$48,495.96

Cash at beginning of year	$ 1,779.56
Excess of receipts over disbursements	650.88
Balance at end of year	$ 2,430.44

xiii

STATEMENT OF CASH AND SECURITIES

As of June 30, 1955

Cash

University National Bank, Chicago, Illinois—
Checking account ....$ 2,430.44

Securities

Bonds: Cost

$17,700 U.S. of America Savings Bonds, Series "G", 2½%
due 12 years from issue date........................ 17,700.00
$1,000 dated September 1, 1943
$1,500 dated February 1, 1944
$2,700 dated May 1, 1944
$2,000 dated February 1, 1945
$1,000 dated April 1, 1945
$4,500 dated December 1, 1945
$5,000 dated February 1, 1949

Stock:

27 shares First National Bank of Boston, Capital Stock.... 1,035.75

Total securities $18,735.75

Total assets $21,166.19

MEMBERS OF THE NATIONAL SOCIETY FOR THE STUDY OF EDUCATION

(This list includes all persons enrolled November 20, 1955, whether for 1955 or 1956. Asterisk (*) indicates Life Members of the Society.)

ACTIVE MEMBERS

Aarestad, Amanda B., Elem. Educ., State Teachers College, Winona, Minn.
Aaron, Ira E., College of Education, University of Georgia, Athens, Ga.
Abarcar, Gudelia M., 705 South Sixth St., Champaign, Ill.
Abate, Harry, Principal, Niagara Street School. Niagara Falls, N.Y.
Abbott, Samuel Lee, Jr., Plymouth Tchrs. College, Plymouth, N.H.
Abel, Frederick P., University of Minnesota High School, Minneapolis, Minn.
Abelson, Harold H., College of the City of New York, New York, N.Y.
Abernethy, Ethel M., Queens College, Charlotte, N.C.
Abraham, Willard, Arizona State College, Tempe, Ariz.
Abrahamson, Stephen, Sch. of Educ., Univ. of Buffalo, Buffalo, N.Y.
Acharlu, K. S., 1404/4 Temple Rd., Bangalore 3, Mysore State, India
Adams, Mrs. Daisy Trice, Principal, Charles Sumner School, Kansas City, Mo.
Adams, Robert G., Principal, Lincoln School, Oakland, Calif.
Addelston, Lorraine W., Principal, Public School 89, Queens, Elmhurst, N.Y.
Addicott, Irwin O., Fresno State College, Fresno, Calif.
Adelaide Marie, Sister, Our Lady of the Lake College, San Antonio, Tex.
Adell, James C., Bureau of Educ. Research, Bd. of Educ., Cleveland, Ohio
Aden, Robert C., Dept. of Educ., Bethel College, McKenzie, Tenn.
Adler, Alfred, Dept. of Educ., Brooklyn College, Brooklyn, N.Y.
Adlerblum, Yetta, 535 West 110th St., New York, N.Y.
Adolphsen, Louis John, Albert Lea Senior High School, Albert Lea, Minn.
Agnes, Mother, Marymount College, New York, N.Y.
Agnes de St. Louis, F.S.E., Sister, Annhurst College, Putnam, Conn.
Ahlstrom, Adele, Sch. of Nursing, Univ. of Pittsburgh, Pittsburgh, Pa.
Ahmann. J. Stanley, Sch. of Educ., Cornell University, Ithaca, N.Y.
Akeret, Robert, 102 West 93rd St., New York, N.Y.
Alawi, A. H., Dept. of Educ., Univ. of Peshawar, Peshawar, West Pakistan
Albin, Floyd B., Oregon College of Education, Monmouth, Ore.
Albright, Frank S., Supv., Secondary Education, Public Schools. Gary, Ind.
Albright, M. Arline, Milwaukee County Soc. for Mental Health, Milwaukee, Wis.
Alcorn, Marvin D., San Diego State College, San Diego, Calif.
Aldrich, Frederic D., 1054 Greyton Road, Cleveland Heights, Ohio
Alexander, Jean H., Col. of Educ., University of Minnesota, Minneapolis, Minn.
Alexander, William M., School of Educ., Univ. of Miami, Coral Gables, Fla.
Allen, Beatrice Ona, Principal, Waters Elementary School, Chicago, Ill.
Allen, D. W., Assoc. Supt., Ohio State Reformatory, Mansfield, Ohio
Allen, Edward E., Supv. Principal of Schools, Akron, N.Y.
Allen, James Robert, Curriculum Consultant, Public Schools, Louisville, Ky.
Allen, Ross L., State University Teachers College, Cortland, N.Y.
Allman, Reva White, Dept. of Educ., Alabama State College, Montgomery, Ala.
Almcrantz. Mrs. Georgia. Box 87, Marseilles, Ill.
Alpren, Morton, Tchrs. College, Temple University, Philadelphia, Pa.
Alston, Melvin O., Florida Agric. and Mech. University, Tallahassee, Fla.
Alsup, Robert F., 1712 Farmers Ave., Murray, Ky.
Alt, Pauline M., Teachers Col. of Connecticut, New Britain, Conn.
Altena, Juul V. R., Gustavus Adolphus College. St. Peter, Minn.
Amar, Wesley F., 8036 S. Green St., Chicago, Ill.
Ambellan, Frederick, Public Schools, North Babylon, L.I., N.Y.
Amberson, Jean D., Home Econ. Bldg., Pa. State Col., State College, Pa.

Ambrose, Luther M., USOM, c/o American Embassy, Bangkok, Thailand
Amos, Robert T., Howard University, Washington, D.C.
Amundson, Carl L., Long Beach State College, Long Beach, Calif.
Anderson, Carl L., P.O. Box 1023, Denver, Colo.
Anderson, Ernest M., Kansas State Teachers College, Pittsburg, Kan.
Anderson, G. Lester, Dean, University of Buffalo, Buffalo, N.Y.
Anderson, Harold A., Dept. of Educ., Univ. of Chicago, Chicago, Ill.
Anderson, Harold H., 340 Wildwood Ave., East Lansing, Mich.
Anderson, Harry D., Supt., Maine Township High School, Des Plaines, Ill.
Anderson, Howard R., 2140 East Ave., Rochester, N.Y.
Anderson, John E., Inst. of Child Welfare, Univ. of Minn., Minneapolis, Minn.
Anderson, Kenneth E., Dean, Sch. of Educ., Univ. of Kansas, Lawrence, Kan.
Anderson, Linnea M., Minot State Tchrs. College, Minot, N.D.
Anderson, Marion, Ginn & Company, Boston, Mass.
Anderson, Paul S., San Diego County Schls., San Diego, Calif.
Anderson, Philip S., State Teachers College, River Falls, Wis.
Anderson, Robert H., Lawrence Hall, Harvard University, Cambridge, Mass.
Anderson, Rodney, Northern Illinois State Tchrs. Col., DeKalb, Ill.
Anderson, Stuart A., Eastern Illinois State Tchrs. Col., Charleston, Ill.
Anderson, Vernon E., School of Educ., Univ. of Connecticut, Storrs, Conn.
Anderson, Walter A., Sch. of Educ., New York University, New York, N.Y.
Anderson, William F., Jr., University of Alabama, University, Ala.
Anderson, William H., Prin., Smiley Junior High School, Denver, Colo.
Anderson, William P., Teachers College, Columbia University, New York, N.Y.
Andes, J. D., Dir., Elem. Educ., Richmond Schools, Richmond. Calif.
Andregg, Neal B., Provost Marshal General's School, Camp Gordon, Ga.
Andrews, Mrs. Elizabeth, Sam Houston State Tchrs. College, Huntsville, Tex.
Angell, George W., Pres., State Univ. Teachers College, Plattsburg, N.Y.
Angelo, Rev. Mark V., 600 Sound View Ave., New York, N.Y.
Anna Clare, Sister, College of St. Rose, Albany, N.Y.
Ansel, James O., Western Michigan College of Education, Kalamazoo, Mich.
Antell, Henry, 120 Kenilworth Pl., Brooklyn, N.Y.
Antonacci, Robert J., Wayne University, Detroit, Mich.
Apple, Joe A., San Diego State College, San Diego, Calif.
Applegate, Stanley A., Curric. Serv. Center, Plandome Rd. Sch., Manhasset, N.Y.
Appleton, David, Superintendent of Schools, Conway, N.H.
Aramvalarthanathan, M., Tchrs. Col., S.R.K.M., Vidyalaya, Coimbatore Dist.,
    Madras State, South India
Arbuckle, Dugald S., Sch. of Educ., Boston University, Boston, Mass.
Archer, Clifford P., Col. of Educ., Univ. of Minnesota, Minneapolis, Minn.
Armstrong, Grace, State Teachers College, Mankato, Minn.
Armstrong, Hubert C., Claremont Graduate School, Claremont, Calif.
Armstrong, V. L., 1906 Ullrich, Austin, Tex.
Arnaud, E. E., Supt., Edgewood School District, San Antonio, Tex.
Arnesen, Arthur E., Supv., Curriculum and Research, Salt Lake City, Utah
Arnold, Earl A., North Texas State College, Denton, Tex.
Arnold, Mabel, Dept. of Educ., Earlham College, Richmond, Ind.
Arnstein, George E., *NEA Journal*, 1201 Sixteenth St., N.W., Washington, D.C.
Arny, Clara Brown, University Farm, Univ. of Minnesota, St. Paul, Minn.
Arsenian, Seth, Springfield College, Springfield, Mass.
Artley, A. Sterl, School of Educ., Univ. of Missouri. Columbia, Mo.
Arveson, R. G., Superintendent of Schools, Leeds, N.D.
Ashbaugh, Ernest J., Miami University, Oxford, Ohio
Ashe, Robert W., Superintendent, Union High School District, Glendale, Ariz.
Ashland, Homer B., Superintendent of Schools, Rutland, Vt.
Atkinson, William N., Pres., Jackson Junior College, Jackson, Mich.
Auble, Donavon, Western College for Women, Oxford, Ohio
Aukerman, Robert C., University of Rhode Island, Kingston, R.I.
Austin, David B., Teachers College, Columbia University, New York, N.Y.
Austin, Glenn, Arizona State College, Tempe, Ariz.
Austin, Mary C., Western Reserve University, Cleveland, Ohio

Ausubel, D. P., Bur. of Research & Serv., Univ. of Illinois, Champaign, Ill.
Avegno, T. Sylvia, Supv., Student Teachers, Fordham Univ., New York, N.Y.
Ayer, Jean, 2 Little Point St., Essex, Conn.
Ayer, Joseph C., Cincinnati Public Schools, Cincinnati, Ohio

Baar, Lincoln F., Asst. Prin., Junior High School 117, Bronx, New York, N.Y.
Babcock, George Thomas. *Deceased.*
Bach, Jacob O., Southern Illinois University, Carbondale, Ill.
Bachman, Mrs. Nina S., Teachers College, Temple Univ., Philadelphia, Pa.
Bachman, Ralph V., Principal, South High School, Salt Lake City, Utah
Bacon, Francis L., Sch. of Educ., Univ. of California, Los Angeles, Calif.
Bacon, William P., Air Command and Staff Col., Maxwell Air Force Base, Ala.
Bahn, Lorene A., 32 South Elm Ave., Webster Groves, Mo.
Bailer, Joseph R., Dept. of Educ., Western Maryland College, Westminster, Md.
Bailey, Donald W., Sacramento State College, Sacramento, Calif.
Bailey, Dwight L., Western Illinois State Teachers College, Macomb, Ill.
Bailey, Edna W., School of Educ., Univ. of California, Berkeley, Calif.
Bailey, Francis L., President, State Teachers College, Gorham, Me.
Bailey, Lucile, Principal, Wm. T. Machan School, Phoenix, Ariz.
Bair, Medill, Supv. Principal, Pennsbury Schools, Fallsington, Pa.
Baker, Harry J., Dir., Psych. Clinic, Detroit Public Schools, Detroit, Mich.
Baker, Harry L., Head, Dept. of Educ. & Psy., State College, Manhattan, Kan.
Baker, James F., Sch. of Educ., Boston University, Boston, Mass.
Bakst, Henry J., Sch. of Medicine, Boston University, Boston, Mass.
Baldwin, Robert D., West Virginia University, Morgantown, W.Va.
Baldwin, Rollin, 125 Riverside Dr., New York, N.Y.
Balian, Arthur, Southern Colony and Training School, Union Grove, Wis.
Ballantine, Francis A., Dept. of Educ., San Diego State Col., San Diego, Calif.
Baller, Warren R., University of Nebraska, Lincoln, Neb.
Ballou, Stephen V., Div. of Educ., Fresno State College, Fresno, Calif.
Balyeat, F. A., University of Oklahoma, Norman, Okla.
Bancroft, Roger W., State University Tchrs. College, Cortland, N.Y.
Bannan, Louis I., S.J., University of Santa Clara, Santa Clara, Calif.
Banner, Carolyn, Critic Teacher, Langston University, Langston, Okla.
Bantel, Edward A., 420 West 118th St., New York, N.Y.
Barbato, Lewis, Dir., Student Health, Univ. of Denver, Denver, Colo.
Barber, Anson B., Superintendent of Schools, Attleboro, Mass.
Barber, Joseph E., Bureau of Naval Personnel, Washington, D.C.
Barbour, Helen F., New Mexico Col. of Agric. and Mech. Arts, State College, N.M.
Barden, John G., Appalachian State College, Boone, N.C.
Barlow, Melvin L., State Dept. of Educ., Univ. of Calif., Los Angeles, Calif.
Barnard, J. Darrell, Sch. of Educ., New York University, New York, N.Y.
Barnard, William H., Dept. of Educ., Miss. State Col., State College, Miss.
Barnes, Cyrus W., 625 Eastern Ave., Greenville, Ill.
Barnes, Fred P., Col. of Educ., University of Illinois, Urbana, Ill.
Barnett, George, Sch. of Educ., Boston University, Boston, Mass.
Barnett, Glenn E., Col. of Educ., University of Texas, Austin, Tex.
Barnett, Robert G., 2414 W. Whitton Ave., Pheonix, Ariz.
Barnhiser, Mrs. Armand O., Patterson School, Dayton, Ohio
Barr, Charlotte A., 4950 South Archer Avenue, Chicago, Ill.
Barrie, Margaret J., Principal, Lincoln School, Hawthorne, N.J.
Barros, Rev. Raymond, S.J., Catholic Univ. of Valparaiso, Valparaiso, Chile
Barry, Florence G., Adjustment Teacher, Lawson Elem. School, Chicago, Ill.
Barry, Robert F., Board of Education, Rochester, N.Y.
Bartels, Isabella, 3024 Fairway Drive, Dayton, Ohio
Barth, Rev. Pius J., Chm., Bd. of Trustees, Quincy College, Quincy, Ill.
Bartlett, Roland O., Principal, Westmount Sr. High School, Westmount, Que.
Barton, George E., University of Chicago, Chicago, Ill.
Bass, Floyd L., Div. of Educ., LeMoyne College, Memphis, Tenn.
Bash, Abraham, 135-01 228th Street, Laurelton, N.Y.

Batchelder, Howard T., Dept. of Educ., Indiana University, Bloomington, Ind.
Bate, Elsa B., Central Michigan College, Mt. Pleasant, Mich.
Bateman, E. Allen, Supt. of Public Instruction, Salt Lake City, Utah
Bateman, Jessie W., Box 3025, T.S.C.W. Sta., Denton, Tex.
Batha, Robert, Principal, Junior-Senior High School, Chester, Calif.
Battle, J. A., Florida Southern College, Lakeland, Fla.
Battle, John A., 77 Polo Road, Great Neck, N.Y.
Bauer, Joseph, Dept. of Philosophy, Mission House College, Plymouth, Wis.
Baum, Paul B., LaVerne College, LaVerne, Calif.
Bauman, F. A., Supt., San Benito County High School, Hollister, Calif.
Baumgartner, Reuben A., Senior High School, Freeport, Ill.
Baxter, Marlin B., Moline Public Schools, Moline, Ill.
Bay, James C., West Virginia Wesleyan College, Buckhannon, W. Va.
Beadle, Laurena A., Dean of Women, Drury College, Springfield, Mo.
Beadles, William T., Dean, Illinois Wesleyan Univ., Bloomington, Ill.
Beahm, W. I., Prin., Donegal High School, Mount Joy, Pa.
Beall, Ross H., Dept. of Educ., University of Tulsa, Tulsa, Okla.
Beamer, George C., North Texas State College, Denton, Tex.
Beams, Howard L., Psych. Dept., University of Pittsburgh, Pittsburgh, Pa.
Bear, David E., 3226 Brown St., Alton, Ill.
Beard, Richard L., Sch. of Educ., Univ. of North Carolina, Chapel Hill, N.C.
Beare, Robert S., General Motors Institute, Flint, Mich.
Beattie, Alfred W., Supt., Allegheny County Schools, Pittsburgh, Pa.
Beatty, Dorothy M., 403 North Linn St., Iowa City, Iowa
Beatty, Walcott H., 30 Tapia Dr., San Francisco, Calif.
Beaubier, Edward W., 4603 Fifty-sixth St., San Diego, Calif.
Beauchamp, George A., School of Educ., Northwestern Univ., Evanston, Ill.
Beauchamp, Mary, New York University, New York, N.Y.
Beaumont, Urville J., Prin., Tenney High School, Methuen, Mass.
Beaver, Eugene H., Prin., James R. Doolittle School, Chicago, Ill.
Bebb, Aldon M., Kansas State Teachers College, Pittsburg, Kan.
Bebb, Randall R., Iowa State Tchrs. College, Cedar Falls, Iowa
Bebell, Clifford, School of Educ., University of Denver, Denver, Colo.
Bechtel, Blair B., Moorestown High School, Moorestown, N.J.
Beck, Alfred D., N.Y.C. Board of Educ., New York City, N.Y.
Beck, John M., Chicago Teachers College, Chicago, Ill.
Beck, Norman W., Superintendent, Monroe County Schools, Waterloo, Ill.
Beck, Ralph Lea, Bowling Green State University, Bowling Green, Ohio
Becker, Harry A., Superintendent of Schools, Norwalk, Conn.
Becker, Millie, 8012 Ellis Ave., Chicago, Ill.
Becker, Philip, Prin., Wm. E. Grady Vocational High School, Brooklyn, N.Y.
Bedell, Ralph, South Pacific Com., Pentagon Anse Vata, Noumea, New Caledonia
Beecher, Robert H., Canal Zone Jr. College, LaBoca Branch, Balboa, Canal Zone
Beechy, Atlee, 5532 Emerson Ave., Worthington, Ohio
Beery, Althea, Supv., Elem. Educ., Public Schools, Cincinnati, Ohio
Beery, John R., Dean, Sch. of Educ., University of Miami, Coral Gables, Fla.
Behrens, Herman D., Dept. of Educ., State Teachers College, Oneonta, N.Y.
Behrens, Minnie S., Elem. Educ. Dept., East Texas Tchrs. Col., Commerce, Tex.
Beilin, Harry, 2744 Bedford Ave., Brooklyn, N.Y.
Beiser, M. J., Superintendent of Schools, Eaton Rapids, Mich.
Belcher, Eddie W., Div. of Curric., Louisville Public Schls., Louisville, Ky.
Belding, Robert E., Educ. Dept., Parsons College, Fairfield, Iowa
Belford, Lee A., Dept. of Religious Educ., New York University, New York, N.Y.
Bell, Dorothy M., President, Bradford Junior College, Bradford, Mass.
Bell, Keith A., Psych. and Educ. Dept., Cascade College, Portland, Ore.
Bell, Millard D., Superintendent, School Dist. 39, Wilmette, Ill.
Bell, R. W., Principal, Jenkintown High School, Jenkintown, Pa.
Bell, Robert M., Prin., Pulaski Elementary School, Chicago, Ill.
Bellack, Arno A., Teachers College, Columbia University, New York, N.Y.
Bellenger, Joseph C., West Contra Costa Junior College, Richmond, Calif.
Bellis, Bertha, McMurry Lab. School, State Tchrs. College, DeKalb, Ill.

Belshe, Francis B., Dept. of Educ., Illinois State Normal Univ., Normal, Ill.
Benben, John S., Northern Ill. State Tchrs. College, DeKalb, Ill.
Bennett, Chester C., Boston University, Boston, Mass.
Bennett, Robert, Supv. Prin., Greene Central School, Greene, N.Y.
Bennion, Hugh C., Dean of Faculty, Ricks College, Rexburg, Idaho
Bentley, Harold, Director, Worcester Junior College, Worcester, Mass.
Benz, H. E., Col. of Educ., Ohio University, Athens, Ohio
Beran, D. L., Col. of Educ., Drake University, Des Moines, Iowa
Berg, Selmer H., Superintendent of Schools, Oakland, Calif.
Berge, Marvin L., Asst. Superintendent of Schools, Elgin, Ill.
Bergesen, B. E., 180 Nassau St., Princeton, N.J.
Bergum, Gordon B., 120 Second Avenue S.E., Little Falls, Minn.
Berkson, I. B., 39 Claremont Avenue, New York, N.Y.
Berlin, Pearl W., Dept. of Phys. Educ., Univ. of Michigan, Ann Arbor, Mich.
Berman, Samuel, Prin., FitzSimons Junior High School, Philadelphia, Pa.
Bern, Henry A., Inst. of Educ. Research, Indiana University, Bloomington, Ind.
Bernard, Alpha E., State Teachers College, Clarion, Pa.
Bernard, Harold W., Portland State Extension Center, Portland, Ore.
Berning, Emanuel F., 972 McLean Ave., St. Paul, Minn.
Bernstein, Abbot A., 14-24 Chandler Dr., Fair Lawn, N.J.
Bernstein, Louis, Prin., Junior High School 29, Brooklyn, N.Y.
Bernstein, Norma Louise, Claymount Gardens, Claymount, Del.
Berson, Mrs. Philomena M., Asst. Prin., Public School 125, New York, N.Y.
Bertermann, Helen A., Prin., L. M. Schiel School, Cincinnati, Ohio
Berthold, Charles A., Prin., Clifton High School, Clifton, N.J.
Bertness, Henry J., 2419-29th Ave. South, Minneapolis, Minn.
Bertrand, John R., Dean, Col. of Agric., Univ. of Nevada, Reno, Nev.
Best, H. R., Supt. of Schools, Cranford, N.J.
Bethel, Hollie, Dept. of Educ., University of Omaha, Omaha, Neb.
Betts, Emmett A., 830 Chauncey Road, Penn Valley, Narberth, Pa.
Beverly, Mrs. Austin C., Prin., Spicer Demonstration School, Akron, Ohio
Beyer, Evelyn, Dir., Nursery School, Smith College, Northampton, Mass.
Beyer, Fred C., County Superintendent of Schools, Modesto, Calif.
Bickel, L. G., Dean, Concordia Teachers College, Seward, Neb.
Bieber, Ida P., 7357 Cornell Ave., University City, Mo.
Biemesderfer, D. L., State Teachers College, Millersville, Penn.
Biester, Lillian L., Arizona State College, Flagstaff, Ariz.
Bigelow, M. A., Prin., Franklin and Brookside Schools, Bloomfield, N.J.
Bigelow, Roy G., Div. of Educ. & Psych., Miss. Southern Col., Hattiesburg, Miss.
Biggy, M. Virginia, 227 Independence Drive, Chestnut Hill, Mass.
Bilhorn, J. Chester, 3846 North Kedvale Avenue, Chicago, Ill.
Billett, Roy O., School of Educ., Boston University, Boston, Mass.
Billig, Florence Grace, Col. of Educ., Wayne University, Detroit, Mich.
Bills, Mark W., Superintendent of Schools, Kansas City, Mo.
Bilterman, Kathryn S., San Diego State College, San Diego, Calif.
Binford, George H., Principal, Central High School, Charlotte Courthouse, Va.
Bird, Charles A., 23 Fraser Pl., Hastings on Hudson, N.Y.
Birkmaier, Emma, Univ. High School, Univ. of Minnesota, Minneapolis, Minn.
Birmingham, Sister Digna, College of St. Scholastica, Duluth, Minn.
Bishop, C. L., Chm., Dept. of Educ., State Tchrs. College, Cedar Falls, Iowa
Bishop, S. D., Principal, Community High School, West Chicago, Ill.
Bixler, Lorin, Dept. of Educ., Muskingum College, New Concord, Ohio
Bixler, Ray H., Dept. of Psych., Univ. of Louisville, Louisville, Ky.
Bjork, A. J., University of North Dakota, Grand Forks, N.D.
Black, E. H., Superintendent, LaMarque Independent School, LaMarque, Tex.
Black, H. B., Prin., Signal Hill School, East St. Louis, Ill.
Black, Leo P., Department of Public Instruction, Lincoln, Neb.
Black, Millard H., Box 294, San Diego, Calif.
Blackburn, Cleo W., Exec. Dir., Flanner House, Indianapolis, Ind.
Blackburn, Clifford S., Superintendent of Schools, North Little Rock, Ark.
Blaha, M. Jay, Curric. Co-ord., Los Angeles County Schools., Los Angeles, Calif.

Blair, Lois C., State Teachers College, Indiana, Pa.
Blake, Paul C., Superintendent of Schools, Eddyville, Iowa
Blanchard, B. Everhard, Plymouth Teachers College, Plymouth, N.H.
Blanton, Roy R., Jr., Sch. of Educ., Indiana University, Bloomington, Ind.
Bliesmer, Emery P., Col. of Educ., University of Texas, Austin, Tex.
Bligh, Harold F., Dept. of Educ., Hobart College, Geneva, N.Y.
Blisard, Thomas J., Newark Col. of Engineering, Newark, N.J.
Blodgett, Darrell R., Superintendent of Schools, Wheaton, Ill.
Blommers, Paul, Col. of Educ., State University of Iowa, Iowa City, Iowa
Blood, Don F., West. Washington Col. of Education, Bellingham, Wash.
Bloore, J. Stephen, Sch. of Educ., New York University, New York, N.Y.
Blyth, Donald J., Principal, Brainard Elementary School, Chicago, Ill.
Boardman, Charles W., Col. of Educ., Univ. of Minnesota, Minneapolis, Minn.
Boeck, Clarence H., Col. of Educ., Univ. of Minnesota, Minneapolis, Minn.
Boehm, Charles H., County Superintendent of Schools, Doylestown, Pa.
Bogle, Frank P., Superintendent of Schools, Morristown, N.J.
Boland, Michael P., St. Joseph's College, Philadelphia, Pa.
Bole, Lyman W., Superintendent of Schools, Springfield, Vt.
Bole, Rita L., President, Lyndon Teachers College, Lyndon Center, Vt.
Bolinger, Mrs. Elizabeth, 2924 East Fifth St., Long Beach, Calif.
* Bolton, Frederick E., University of Washington, Seattle, Wash.
Bond, G. W., Louisiana Polytechnic Institute, Ruston, La.
Bond, George W., State Teachers College, New Paltz, N.Y.
Bond, Guy L., Col. of Educ., Univ. of Minnesota, Minneapolis, Minn.
Bond, Jesse A., Dir., Tchr. Trg., Univ. of California, Los Angeles, Calif.
Bone, Margaretta, Mansfield State Teachers College, Mansfield, Pa.
Bonsall, Marcella Ryser, 137 Warwick Pl., South Pasadena, Calif.
Booker, Ivan A., Div. of Press and Radio Rela., N.E.A., Washington, D.C.
Booker, Nancy, Sydney Teachers College, Newtown, New South Wales, Australia
Bookwalter, Karl W., Sch. of Educ., Indiana University, Bloomington, Ind.
Boren, James H., Arlington State College, Arlington, Tex.
Boros, Arnold L., 396 East 170th St., New York, N.Y.
Bossier, Antonia M., 1661 North Roman St., New Orleans, La.
Bossing, Nelson L., Col. of Educ., Univ. of Minnesota, Minneapolis, Minn.
Bottrell, Harold R., Col. of Educ., University of Houston, Houston, Tex.
Bouchard, John B., State Teachers College, Fredonia, N.Y.
Bowen, Hilliard A., Sch. of Educ., Tenn. A. & I. State Univ., Nashville, Tenn.
Bowers, Norman D., Div. of Tchr. Educ., San Jose State College, San Jose, Calif.
Bowersox, Catherine, Bowling Green State University, Bowling Green, Ohio
Bowyer, Vernon O., 225 Millbridge Rd., Riverside, Ill.
Boyd, Elizabeth Marie, 4146 West 63rd St., Los Angeles, Calif.
Boyd, Fred, Box 247, Leachville, Ark.
Boyd, G. R., Dean, State Teachers College, Troy, Ala.
Boyd, Laurence E., Sch. of Educ., Atlanta University, Atlanta, Ga.
Boyd, Robert D., Laboratory Schls., University of Chicago, Chicago, Ill.
Boydston, Robert S., West Contra Costa Junior College, Richmond, Calif.
Bracken, John L., 7530 Maryland Ave., Clayton 5, Mo.
Brackett, Lee, Drake University, Des Moines, Iowa
Bradfield, James M., Sacramento State College, Sacramento, Calif.
Bradley, Mrs. Muriel O., Iowa State Teachers College, Cedar Falls, Iowa
Bradley, Raymond J., Chm., Div. of Educ., Macalester College, St. Paul, Minn.
Brady, Elizabeth H., Los Angeles State College, Los Angeles, Calif.
Braem, William A. F., CMU, Box 199, OMS Hq., Lackland Air Force Base, Tex.
Bragdon, Clifford Richardson, Dept. of Educ., Smith College, Northampton,
    Mass.
Bragdon, Helen D., Genl. Dir., American Assn. of Univ. Women, Washington, D.C.
Brandenburg, K. C., 110 Pine Avenue, Long Beach, Calif.
Brandon, Mrs. Bertha M., Waco Public Schools, Waco, Tex.
Brandt, Willard J., Wisconsin State College, Milwaukee, Wis.
Branom, Frederick K., Chicago Teachers College, Chicago, Ill.
Branom, Wayne T., Superintendent of Schools, Hillside, N.J.

Brasted, F. Kenneth, Pres., University of Dallas, Dallas, Tex.
Bratton, J. Wesley, Dean, Long Beach State College, Long Beach, Calif.
Brechbill, Henry, Dept. of Educ., University of Maryland, College Park, Md.
Breen, Lelwyn C., Territorial College of Guam, Agana, Guam
Brennan, A. F., Prin., Regina Regional High School, Corner Brook, Newfoundland
Brennan, Thomas G., Superintendent, Catholic Schools, Saginaw, Mich.
Bretz, Frank H., Dean of Students, Univ. of Dubuque, Dubuque, Iowa
Brewer, Karl M., Superintendent of Schools, DuBois, Pa.
Brewer, Wenonah G., Indiana State Teachers College, Terre Haute, Ind.
Brickman, Benjamin, Dept. of Educ., Brooklyn College, Brooklyn, N.Y.
Brickman, William W., Dept. of Educ., New York University, New York, N.Y.
Brieland, Donald, Dir., Eliz. McCormick Mem. Fund, 155 E. Ohio St., Chicago, Ill.
Briggs, Charles C., Dept. of Educ., San Diego State College, San Diego, Calif.
Briggs, Elmer H., Prin., Murrell Dobbins Voc.-Tech. Sch., Philadelphia, Pa.
Bright, O. T., Jr., Superintendent of Schools, Lake Bluff, Ill.
Brimley, Ralph F. W., Supt., Forsyth County Schools, Winston-Salem, N.C.
Brink, William G., School of Educ., Northwestern University, Evanston, Ill.
Brinkley, Sterling G., 1197 Emory Dr., N.E., Atlanta, Ga.
Brinkman, A. John, 9929 S. Maplewood Ave., Chicago, Ill.
Brish, William M., Superintendent, Washington County Schls., Hagerstown, Md.
Brislawn, Maurice J., Prin., Monticello Junior High School, Longview, Wash.
Bristol, Benton K., Pennsylvania State University, University Park, Pa.
Bristow, W. H., Dir., Bur. Cur. Res., NYC Bd. of Educ., 130 W. 55 St., New York, N.Y.
Bristow, William H., Dir. of Bureau of Curriculum Research, New York, N.Y.
Britt, S. S., Jr., Wofford College, Spartanburg, S.C.
Britton, Edward C., 1429 El Tejon Way, Sacramento, Calif.
Britton, Ernest R., Superintendent of Schools, Midland, Mich.
Broening, Angela M., Dir. of Publications, Public Schls., Baltimore, Md.
Bronson, Moses L., 104 West 70th St., New York, N.Y.
Brooks, John J., Dir., New Lincoln School, New York, N.Y.
Brooks, Mary B., Georgia State College for Women, Milledgeville, Ga.
Brostoff, Theodore M., Hunington Park High School, Hunington Park, Calif.
Brougher, John F., Principal, Woodrow Wilson High School, Washington, D.C.
Brown, Alma J., 6301 West 78th St., Overland Park, Kan.
Brown, Cynthiana E., Univ. Elem. Schl., Univ. of Calif., Los Angeles, Calif.
Brown, Donald R., Dept. of Psych., Bryn Mawr College, Bryn Mawr, Pa.
Brown, Francis J., 2500 Que St., N.W., Washington, D.C.
Brown, Francis W., 1804 N. Winona Blvd., Hollywood, Calif.
Brown, Gerald W., Los Angeles State College, Los Angeles, Calif.
Brown, Sister Gertrude Ann, Briar Cliff College, Sioux City, Iowa
Brown, Grant, Editor-in-Chief, American Book Co., New York, N.Y.
Brown, Harold N., Sch. of Educ., University of Nevada, Reno, Nev.
Brown, Hugh S., Pennsylvania State University, University Park, Pa.
Brown, I. C., Prin., Perrin-Thomas School, Columbia, S.C.
Brown, Josephine H., State Teachers College, Bowie, Md.
Brown, Kenneth R., Dir. of Research, Calif. Tchrs. Assn., San Francisco, Calif.
Brown, Leland P., Superintendent of Schools, Olympia, Wash.
Brown, Mrs. Marjorie Dowling, Manual Arts High School, Los Angeles, Calif.
Brown, Milton W., Superintendent of Schools, West Orange, N.J.
Brown, Nicholas C., Box 81, Emory, Va.
Brown, Thomas J., Hofstra College, Hempstead, N.Y.
Brown, William H., Dir., Bur. of Educ. Research, North Carolina Col., Durham, N.C.
Browne, Kenneth A., Dean of Instruction, State Teachers College, Towson, Md.
Browne, Rose Butler, North Carolina College, Durham, N.C.
Brownell, S. M., U.S. Commissioner of Education, Washington, D.C.
Brownell, W. A., Dean, Schl. of Educ., Univ. of California, Berkeley, Calif.
Browning, Roy W., Dir., Placement & Stud. Activ., Phillips Univ., Enid, Okla.
Bruce, Aldon J., Supt. Eliza Community School, Illinois City, Ill.

Bruce, Thor W., Auditor, Bd. of Education, St. Louis, Mo.
Bruce, William C., Editor, Bruce Publishing Co., Milwaukee, Wis.
* Bruck, John P., 218 Potters Corners Road, Buffalo, N.Y.
Brueckner, Leo J., Col. of Educ., Univ. of Minnesota, Minneapolis. Minn.
Brugger, Jeanne, Guidance Dir., Harcum Junior College, Bryn Mawr, Pa.
Brumbaugh, A. J., Southern Regional Education Board, Atlanta, Ga.
Brunner, Henry S., Head, Dept. of Agr. Educ., Penn. State Univ., University
    Park, Pa.
Brunner, Howard B., Supv. Principal of Schools, Scotch Plains, N.J.
Brunson, Mrs. DeWitt, Ellis Avenue School, Orangeburg, S.C.
Bryan, Ray, Head, Dept. of Voc. Educ., Iowa State College, Ames, Iowa
Bryant, Hayden C., Dir., Teacher Educ., Mercer University, Macon, Ga.
Bryant, Ira B., Prin., Booker T. Washington High School, Houston, Tex.
Bryant, Spurgeon Q., Alabama State College, Montgomery, Ala.
Bryner, James R., Superintendent of Schools, North College Hill, Ohio
Buchanan, Alfred K., 538 Leesburg Pike, Falls Church, Va.
Buchanan, James H., Kansas State Teachers College, Emporia, Kan.
Buchanan, Paul G., 195 Neponset Ave., Dorchester, Mass.
Buckingham, Guy E., Division of Educ., Allegheny College, Meadville, Pa.
Buckley, J. L., Superintendent of Schools, Lockhart, Tex.
Buckner, W. N., Armstrong Tech. High School, Washington, D.C.
Buda, Mrs. Mary C., Prin., Lafayette High School, Brooklyn, N.Y.
Bueker, A. H., Superintendent of Schools. Marshall. Mo.
Buelke, John A., Western Michigan College, Kalamazoo, Mich.
Bull, Stanley, 134 W. Whitman Dr., College Place, Wash.
Bullock, Harrison, 354 Quintora St., San Francisco, Calif.
Bullock. W. J., Superintendent of Schools, Kannapolis, N.C.
Bunch, Marion E., Washington University, St. Louis, Mo.
Bunker, James G., Superintendent, Secondary Schools, Coalinga, Calif.
Burch. Robert L., Ginn and Company, Boston. Mass.
Burdick, Richard L., Carroll College, Waukesha, Wis.
Burdine, D. I., Prairie View A. & M. College, Prairie View, Tex.
Burg, Ruth M., 502 Walnut St., Allentown, Pa.
Burgess. Thomas C., Psych. Dept., Oregon State College, Corvallis, Ore.
Burgdahl, Mrs. Lucile B., Southeastern Louisiana College, Hammond, La.
Burgdorf, Otto P., 314 East 196th St., New York, N.Y.
Burk, R. Burdett, Long Beach State College, Long Beach, Calif.
Burke, Arvid J., New York State Teachers Assn., Albany, N.Y.
Burke, Gladys, 244 Outlook Ave., Youngstown, Ohio
Burke, Henry R., 16 Oaklandvale Ave., Saugus, Mass.
Burke, Louis, 5391A Prince of Wales Ave., Montreal, Quebec, Canada
Burke, Mother Margaret, Pres., Barat Col. of the Sacred Heart, Lake Forest, Ill.
Burkhardt, Allen P., President, Norfolk Junior College, Norfolk, Neb.
Burlingame, Anna Louise, Principal. Ray School. Chicago. Ill.
Burnett, Lewie W., Col. of Educ., University of Toledo, Toledo, Ohio
Burnham, Archer L., Nebraska State Teachers Assn., Lincoln, Neb.
Burnham, Reba, Col. of Educ., University of Georgia, Athens, Ga.
Burns, Robert L., 1063 Palisade Ave., Palisade, N.J.
Buros, Francis C., Asst. Superintendent of Schools. White Plains, N.Y.
Burr, Elbert W., Monsanto Chemical Co., 1700 So. Second St., St. Louis, Mo.
Burrell, Anna P., State College for Teachers, Buffalo, N.Y.
Burrows, Alvina Treut, 117 Nassau Ave., Manhasset, N.Y.
Burt, Lucile, Principal, Lincoln School, Fond du Lac, Wis.
Burt, Millard P., Chm., Dept. of Educ., Atlantic Christian Col., Wilson, N.C.
Burton, Floyd H., Superintendent of Schools, Humble, Tex.
Burton, W. H. *Deceased.*
Burton, William H., 3512 Willamette Ave., Corvallis, Ore.
Bush, Clifford L., Western Reserve University, Cleveland, Ohio
Bussell, Lyell, Prin., Stevenson Elementary School, Muncie, Ind.
Buswell, G. T., School of Educ., University of California, Berkeley, Calif.
Buswell, Margaret M., Iowa State Teachers College, Cedar Falls, Iowa

Butler, Judson R., Dean, Boston Univ. Col. of Gen. Education, Boston, Mass.
Butler, Warren N., Superintendent of Schools, Maywood, N.J.
Butorac, Frank G., 700 So. State St., Ann Arbor, Mich.
Butterweck, Joseph S., Dir., Div. of Sec. Educ., Temple Univ., Philadelphia, Pa.
Butts, Franklin A., Principal, Clinton School, Poughkeepsie, N.Y.
Butts. R. Freeman, Teachers College. Columbia University, New York, N.Y.
Buvus, S. T., Sch. of Music, University of Wisconsin, Madison, Wis.
Buyse, R., School of Educ., University of Louvain, Tournai, Belgium
Byerly, Carl L., Dir. of Special Serv., School Dist., Clayton. Mo.
Byram, Harold M., Michigan State University, East Lansing, Mich.
Byrne, Richard Hill, Col. of Educ., University of Maryland, College Park, Md.

Caccavo, Emil, J-2, University Apartments, Newark, Del.
Cafasso, Orlando V., 21 Locust St., Everett, Mass.
Caird, Mrs. Florence B.. Prin., J. A. Sexton School, Chicago, Ill.
Caldwell, O. K., Prin., Fostoria High School, Fostoria, Ohio
Callaway, Byron, Illinois State Normal University, Normal, Ill.
Calvin, James S., Head, Dept. of Psych., Univ. of Kentucky, Lexington, Ky.
Cambron, Emmett F.. North Texas State College. Denton, Tex.
Cameron, Walter C.. Principal, Lincoln Junior High School, Framingham, Mass.
Campbell. R. F.. College of Educ.. Ohio State University, Columbus, Ohio
Cannon, W. E., School of Educ., Univ. of Southern California, Los Angeles, Calif.
Canuteson. Richard, State Teachers College, Brockport. N.Y.
Capehart, Bertis E., Superintendent of Schools, Oak Ridge, Tenn.
Cappa, Dan, Dir., Elem. Instr., City Schools, Santa Barbara, Calif.
Capps, Mrs. Marian P., State A. & M. College. Orangeburg, S.C.
Carbaugh. Gaile A.. Dir.. Holcomb Campus Sch.. Teachers Colelge. Geneseo, N.Y.
Cardwell, Robert H., Prin., Park Junior High School, Knoxville, Tenn.
Carey, Justin P., 110 Echo Ave., New Rochelle, N.Y.
Carlson, C. E., Superintendent of Schools, Ramsay. Mich.
Carlson, Clara H.. Principal, Elementary School, Elmont, N.Y.
Carlson, Evelyn F.. Principal, DuSable High School, Chicago, Ill.
Carlson, Ruth Kearney, 1718 LeRoy Ave., Berkeley, Calif.
Carlson, Stanley C., 821 N. Hagadorn Road, East Lansing, Mich.
Carlson. Thorsten R., Prin., Lab. Sch.. San Diego State Col.. San Diego, Calif.
Carmichael, Omer. Superintendent of Schools. Louisville, Ky.
Carnes, Earl F., University of Southern California, Los Angeles, Calif.
Carpenter, H. D., Dept. of Educ., Grambling College, Grambling, La.
Carpenter. W. W., Dept. of Educ.. University of Missouri, Columbia, Mo.
Carper, M. L., Superintendent of Schools, Martinsville, Va.
Carr, Edwin R., Col. of Educ., University of Colorado, Boulder. Colo.
Carr. John W., Jr.. Sch. of Educ.. Duke University, Durham. N.C.
Carrithers, Lura M., Wisconsin State College. Milwaukee, Wis.
Carroll. John B., Grad. Sch. of Educ.. Harvard University, Cambridge. Mass.
Carroll, John S.. Educ. Dir., Great Commonwealth Fdn., Lubbock, Tex.
Carson, Arthur L., 156 Fifth Ave., New York. N.Y.
Carson, Robert S., 3811 O'Hara St., Pittsburgh, Pa.
Carstater, Eugene D., Rte. 1, Falls Church, Va.
Carter, Gordon, Supt., Bellington School Dist. 501, Bellingham, Wash.
Carter, Harold D.. Sch. of Educ., University of California. Berkeley, Calif.
Carter, Richard C., Elem. Prin., Public Schools, Fairbanks, Alaska
Carter, R. L., Head, Dept. of Educ.. Stetson University, De Land, Fla.
Carter, Ruby, Dir. of Child Study, Harlan, Ky.
Carter, W. R.. Dept. of Educ., University of Missouri, Columbia, Mo.
Casale, Mary R., 1555 Mohawk St., Utica, N.Y.
Casenas, Lourdes Maria, Box 267, Rogers Center, Indiana Univ., Bloomington, Ind.
Caskey, Helen C., Tchrs. Col., University of Cincinnati, Cincinnati, Ohio
Caspers, Earl M., Hanau American Elementary School, Hanau, Germany
Cassidy, Rosalind, University of California. Los Angeles. Calif.
Caswell, Hollis L., President, Teachers College, Columbia Univ., New York, N.Y.

Caughran, Alex M., University of Maine, Orono, Me.
Cavan, Jordan, Dept. of Education, Rockford College, Rockford, Ill.
Cawthon, John A., Louisiana Polytechnic Inst., Ruston, La.
Cayne, Bernard S., 77 Trowbridge St., Cambridge, Mass.
Center, Aaron M., 922 Queen Ave., North, Minneapolis, Minn.
Centi, Paul J., 68 Tehama St., Brooklyn, N.Y.
Chadderdon, Hester, Iowa State College, Ames, Iowa
Chall, Jeanne, 218 East 12th St., New York, N.Y.
Chalmers, James F., Principal, High School, Perth Amboy, N.J.
Chamberlin, R. G., Principal, Rufus King High School, Milwaukee, Wis.
Chambers, W. Max. President. Central State College, Edmond, Okla.
Champlin, George R., Supt., Windham Schools, Willimantic, Conn.
Chandler, Charles C., 137 Bogue St., East Lansing, Mich.
Chandler, H. E., Dept. of Educ., University of Kansas, Lawrence, Kan.
Chandler, J. R., East Central State College, Ada, Okla.
Chang, Jen-chi, Claflin College, Orangeburg, S.C.
Chao, Sankey C., Claflin College, Orangeburg, S.C.
Chapman, Catherine, Weatherford College, Weatherford, Tex.
Chappell, S. G., Superintendent of Schools, Wilson, N.C.
Charles, William L., Principal, Southside School, Jacksonville, Fla.
Charnock, Leonard W. H., Eureka College, Eureka, Ill.
Charry, Lawrence, 5746 N. Camac St., Philadelphia, Pa.
Charters, Alexander N., University College, Syracuse Univ., Syracuse, N.Y.
Chase, Francis S., Dept. of Educ., University of Chicago, Chicago, Ill.
Chase, W. Linwood, Sch. of Educ., Boston University, Boston, Mass.
Chauncey, Marlin R., Oklahoma Agric. and Mech. College, Stillwater, Okla.
Cheek, N. A., Principal, W. G. Pearson Elementary School, Durham, N.C.
Cheeks, L. E., 213 McFarland St., Kerrville, Tex.
Chenault, R. N., Principal, Warner School, Nashville, Tenn.
Cherry, J. H., Asst. Supt., Joliet Township H. S. & Jr. Col., Joliet, Ill.
Cherry, Ralph W., University of Texas, Austin, Tex.
Chiappetta, Michael, Dept. of Educ., Penn. State Univ., University Park, Pa.
Chidester, Albert J., Head Education Dept., Berea College, Berea, Ky.
Chievitz, Gene L., Box 127, University P.O. Sta., Albuquerque, N.M.
Childress, Jack R., Dir., Univ. Col., Northwestern University, Chicago, Ill.
Chipman, R. S., Superintendent of Schools, Coalville, Utah
Choate, Ernest A., Principal, Roosevelt Jr. High School, Philadelphia, Pa.
Christensen, Arnold M., Long Beach State Col., Long Beach, Calif.
Christian, Mary R., Principal, Riverview Elem. Sch., Daytona Beach, Fla.
Christman, Paul S., Supervising Principal, Schuylkill Haven, Pa.
Chudler, Albert A., 11422 Washington Pl., Los Angeles, Calif.
Churchill, Ray L., Principal, Harrison Elementary School, Cedar Rapids, Iowa
Chute, Oscar M., 1606 Colfax Ave., Evanston, Ill.
Ciklic, Peter, Loyola Univ. of Los Angeles, Los Angeles, Calif.
Cioffii, Joseph M., 123 Palisade Ave., Garfield, N.J.
Clara Francis, Sister, Nazareth College. Louisville, Ky.
Clark, Mrs. C. Esmer Knudson, 2274 Cedar St., Berkeley, Calif.
Clark, Catherine, Middle Tennessee State College, Murfreesboro, Tenn.
Clark, Elmer J., Indiana State Teachers College, Terre Haute, Ind.
Clark, F. B., Dist. Superintendent of Schools, Athens, N.Y.
Clark, Francis E., St. Olaf College, Northfield, Minn.
Clark, John F., Superintendent of Schools, Dist. 45, Villa Park, Ill.
Clark, Stephen C., Dept. of Psych., Los Angeles State College, Los Angeles, Calif.
Clark, Woodrow Wilson, Box 1, University, Miss.
Clarke, Eunice A., Teachers College, Temple University, Philadelphia, Pa.
Clarke, L. Katherine, Prin., Meramec School, Clayton, Mo.
Clarke, Stanley C. T., University of Alberta, Edmonton, Alba.
Clayton, Thomas E., Dept. of Educ., Temple University, Philadelphia, Pa.
Cleeton, Kenneth, Dir., Summer Ses., Col. of William and Mary, Williamsburg, Va.

Cleland, Donald L., School of Educ., University of Pittsburgh, Pittsburgh, Pa.
Cleveland, E. D., Superintendent of Schools, Palestine, Tex.
Clewell, Geraldine, Texas Technological College, Lubbock, Tex.
Clifford, Paul I., Sch. of Educ., Atlanta University, Atlanta, Ga.
Clift, Virgil Alfred, 3501 Greenwood Ave., Louisville, Ky.
Clifton, L. L., Dean, Oklahoma City University, Oklahoma City, Okla.
Cline, Don Courtney, 1016 S. Orange Grove Ave., Los Angeles, Calif.
Cline, William Rodney, Louisiana State University, Baton Rouge, La.
Clodfelter, C. R., 900 Rindie St., Irving, Tex.
Cloues, Paul, Submaster, Harvard School, Charlestown, Mass.
Clouthier, Raymond P., Dept. of Educ., Lewis College, Lockport, Ill.
Clugston, Herbert A., Dean, State Teachers College, St. Cloud, Minn.
Clymer, T. W., Col. of Educ., University of Minnesota, Minneapolis, Minn.
Cobb, J. E., Indiana State Tchrs. College, Terre Haute, Ind.
Cochran, J. Chester, Dept. of Educ., Univ. of Houston, Houston, Tex.
Codwell, John E., Principal, Phillis Wheatley High School, Houston, Tex.
Cody, Martha Ballard, Col. of Educ., University of Florida, Gainesville, Fla.
Coetzee, J. Christian, University College, Potchefstroom, South Africa
Cofell, William L., St. John's University, Collegeville, Minn.
Coffey, Hubert S., Psych. Dept., University of California, Berkeley, Calif.
Coffin, Robert F., 202 Stone Hall, Cornell University, Ithaca, N.Y.
Cohen, George, 1450 Jesup Ave., New York, N.Y.
Cohen, Saris, 825 West End Ave., New York, N.Y.
Cohen, Victor, 256 Federal St., Greenfield, Mass.
Cohler, Milton J., Prin., Sullivan High School, Chicago, Ill.
Colbath, Edwin H., Bur. of Cur. Res., NYC Bd. of Educ., 130 W. 55th St., New
    York, N.Y.
Colburn, A. B., Vice-Prin., Everett Senior High School, Everett, Wash.
Cole, Glenn A., Dept. of Educ., University of Arkansas, Fayetteville, Ark.
Cole, Mary I., Western Kentucky State College, Bowling Green, Ky.
Coleman, F. Basil, 435 W. 119th St., New York, N.Y.
Coleman, Mary Elizabeth, Dept. of Educ., Univ. of Penn., Philadelphia, Pa.
Collette, Mabel, Supv. of Prim. Educ., State Dept. of Educ., Baton Rouge, La.
Collings, Miller R., Wayne University, Detroit, Mich.
Collins, Carrie Lee, Radford College, Radford, Va.
Collins, Ralph C., 177 Harvey St., Eugene, Ore.
Conaway, Mrs. Freda Y. Dir., Elem. Educ., State Col., West Liberty, W.Va.
Conaway, Winifred V., Bowling Green State University, Bowling Green, Ohio
Conchessa, Sister, College of St. Benedict, St. Joseph, Minn.
Condon, Jean F., 23 Roosevelt Rd., Weymouth, Mass.
Conley, William H., Marquette University, Milwaukee, Wis.
Connell, John T., Superintendent, Butler County Schls., Butler, Pa.
Connelly, George W., 6201 S. Richmond St., Chicago, Ill.
Conrath, Cecilia, 2305 Federal Office Bldg., Kansas City, Mo.
Conway, Marie M., 4925 Saul St., Philadelphia, Pa.
Cook, Raymond M., Dean, Chicago Teachers College, Chicago, Ill.
Cook, Ruth Cathlyn, Supv. Lab. Sch., State Teachers College, Mankato, Minn.
Cook, Walter W., Col. of Educ., University of Minnesota, Minneapolis, Minn.
Coon, Beulah I., U. S. Office of Education, Washington, D.C.
Coon, W. Edwin, Prin., Academy High School, Erie, Pa.
Cooper, Bernice, Peabody Hall, University of Georgia, Athens, Ga.
Cooper, George H., 2813 Washington Blvd., Chicago, Ill.
Cooper, James W., Principal, High School, Pleasantville, Iowa
Cooper, J. Louis, University of Connecticut, Storrs, Conn.
Cooper, Lewis B., Texas Technological College, Lubbock, Tex.
Cooper, Shirley, American Assn. of School Administrators, Washington, D.C.
Corbally, John E., Dept. of Educ., University of Washington, Seattle, Wash.
Corcoran, Mary, 211 Burton Hall, Univ. of Minnesota, Minneapolis, Minn.
Corey, Stephen M., Teachers College, Columbia University, New York, N.Y.
Cornell, Francis G., 551 Fifth Ave., New York, N.Y.
Cornish, Dale, 5770 Dudley St., Arvada, Colo.

Corrigan, A. B., Sch. of Educ., Gonzaga University, Spokane, Wash.
Corrothers, Thomasine, Dept. of Educ., Miner Teachers Col., Washington, D.C.
Cory, N. Durward, Superintendent of Schools, Rochester, Minn.
Cossa, John A., Dean, Dept. of Educ., Manhattan College, New York, N.Y.
Coster, J. K., Div. of Educ., Purdue University, Lafayette, Ind.
Cotter, Katharine C., Dept. of Educ., Boston College, Osterville, Mass
Couch, Paul E., Arkansas State College, State College, Ark.
Coules, John, Psych. Dept., Univ. of New Hampshire, Durham, N.H.
Coulson, John R., Principal, A. O. Sexton School, Chicago, Ill.
Courter, Claude V., Superintendent of Schools, Cincinnati, Ohio
* Courtis, S. A., 9110 Dwight Ave., Detroit, Mich.
Cousins, E. H., 8 Upper Sandringham Ave., Jamaica, British West Indies
Covell, Merle O., Head, Dept. of Educ., Kansas Wesleyan Univ., Salina, Kan.
Cowan, William A., San Francisco State College, San Francisco, Calif.
Cox, David R., Dean of Men, Carbon College, Price, Utah
Cox, Edith Clare, 117 Central Ave., Shelby, Mont.
Cox, Edwin A., Superintendent of Schools, Stratford, Conn.
Cox, Johnnye V., University of Georgia, Athens, Ga.
Coxe, W. W., Educ. Research Div., State Educ. Dept., Albany, N.Y.
Crackel, Verne E., Superintendent, Will County Schools, Joliet, Ill.
Cragen, Mrs. Dorothy Clora, County Supt. of Schools, Independence, Calif.
*Craig, Gerald S., Teachers College, Columbia University, New York, N.Y.
Craig, Isabel, Read. and Study Clinic, Indiana Univ., Bloomington, Ind.
Craig, Robert C., Amer. Inst. for Research, 410 Amberson Ave., Pittsburgh, Pa.
Cramer, Beatrice E., Post Road Junior High School, White Plains, N.Y.
Craven, Gus J., Dept. of Educ., Austin College, Sherman, Tex.
Crawford, C. C., University of Southern California, Los Angeles, Calif.
Crawford, J. R., Sch. of Educ., University of Maine, Orono, Me.
Crawford, Robert T., Lewis County Schools, Weston, W.Va.
Crawford, T. James, Sch. of Business, Indiana University, Bloomington, Ind.
Crawshaw, Clyde, Superintendent of Schools, Marseilles, Ill.
Creswell, Mrs. Rowena C., Prin., A. & M. Cons. Elem. Sch., College Station, Tex.
Crocker, Richard F., Jr., Superintendent of Schools, Caribou, Me.
Crook, Robert B., Dept. of Educ., Queens College, Flushing, N.Y.
Cross, C. Willard, Superintendent of Schools, Faribault, Minn.
Cross, Charles H., Dir., Univ. Trg. Sch., Univ. of Arkansas, Fayetteville, Ark.
Crosson, Robert Henry, 226 East Sixth St., Pittsburg, Calif.
Crow, Lester D., Brooklyn College, Brooklyn, N.Y.
Crowlie, Mrs. Leone B., 215 W. Minnehaha Parkway, Minneapolis, Minn.
Crull, Howard D., Superintendent of Schools, Port Huron, Mich.
Crum, Clyde E., Div. of Educ., San Diego State College, San Diego, Calif.
Crumb, Frederick W., President, Potsdam State Teachers Col., Potsdam, N.Y.
Crunden, Mrs. Marjorie Morse, 30 Porter Place, Montclair, N.J.
Crutchley, Susan Delano, P.O. Box 1014, Southampton, L.I., N.Y.
Crutsinger, George M., Howard Payne College, Brownwood, Tex.
Cruz, Emilio Ramos, Direccion de Educacion Federal, Mexicali, Bajo California,
 Mexico
Culmer, Mabel, Clinics Bldg., Indiana University, Bloomington, Ind.
Culver, Wallace W., 4816—69th Pl., Hyattsville, Md.
Cumbee, Carroll F., Col. of Educ., Universty of Florida, Gainesville, Fla.
Cummings, Matthew G., 131 Kensington Ave., Jersey City, N.J.
Cummins, L. Ross, Dept. of Educ. & Psych., Bates College, Lewiston, Me.
Cunliffe, R. B., Sch. of Educ., Rutgers University, New Brunswick, N.J.
Cunningham, Daniel F., Superintendent of Catholic Schools, Chicago, Ill.
Cunningham, Harry A., Dept. of Biol., Kent State University, Kent, Ohio
Cunningham, J., Cossitt Library, Memphis, Tenn.
Cunningham, Myron, Col. of Educ., University of Florida, Gainesville, Fla.
Cunningham, W. F., University of Notre Dame, Notre Dame, Ind.
Currie, Caroline, Lunt Bldg., Northwestern University, Evanston, Ill.
Curry, Guy A., Assoc. Dir., Ark. Experiment in Tchr. Educ., Little Rock, Ark.
Curtin, James R., Col. of Educ., University of Minnesota, Minneapolis, Minn.

Curtin, James T., Supt., Diocesan High Schools, 4371 Lindell Blvd., St. Louis, Mo.
Curtin, Wylma R., 1908 Erie St., Hyattsville, Md.
Curtis, E. Louise, Macalester College, St. Paul, Minn.
Curtis, H. A., Florida State University, Tallahassee, Fla.
Curtis, James E., San Jose State College, San Jose, Calif.
Curtis, Russell W., Janesville Public Schools, Janesville, Wis.
Cutts, Warren G., Jr., Dept. of Educ., Kent State University, Kent, Ohio

Dabney, Lillian G., Dir., Stud. Tchg., Coppin State Tchrs. Col., Washington, D.C.
Dabney, Richard S., State Department of Education, Jefferson City, Mo.
Dahnke, Harold L., Box 257, Okemos, Mich.
Dale, Arbie Myron, Sch. of Commerce, New York Univ., New York, N.Y.
Dale, Edgar, Col. of Educ., Ohio State University, Columbus, Ohio
Dallmann, Martha, Dept. of Educ., Ohio Wesleyan University, Delaware, Ohio
Dameron, Vernon, Dir. of Educ., Henry Ford Museum, Dearborn, Mich.
D'Amico, Charles C., 233 W. Bank St., Albion, N.Y.
Daniel, J. McT., University of South Carolina, Columbia, S.C.
Daniel, Theodora H., 127 Circular St., Saratoga Springs, N.Y.
Daniels, Paul R., 7700A Wagner Way, Elkins Park, Pa.
Darcy, Natalie T., Dept. of Educ., Brooklyn College, Brooklyn, N.Y.
Darden, William J., College of the Pacific, Stockton, Calif.
Darke, R. A., 508 East South Temple, Salt Lake City, Utah
Darling, C. Douglas, 5 Central Ave., Ithaca, N.Y.
Darnall, James D., Superintendent of Schools, Geneseo, Ill.
Darnell, Myra C., 207 West 37th St., Vancouver, Wash.
Darnell, Robert E., Frank Phillips College, Borger, Tex.
Darroch, Frank W., 27 Princeton Rd., Toronto, Ontario, Canada
Davidson, Mrs. Evelyn K., Kent State University, Kent, Ohio
Davidson, Lewis, Prin., Knox College, Spaldings, Jamaica, B.W.I.
Davies, Daniel R., Teachers College, Columbia University, New York, N.Y.
Davies, J. Leonard, East Hall, State University of Iowa, Iowa City, Iowa
Davies, Mrs. Lillian S., Curric. Consult., Rich Twp. High Sch., Park Forest, Ill.
Davis, Alice M., Sch. of Educ., Michigan State Univ., East Lansing, Mich.
Davis, Alonzo J., Dean, Sch. of Educ., Tuskegee Institute, Tuskegee, Ala.
Davis, Courtland V., 184 North Bridge St., Somerville, N.J.
Davis, David C., 556 Sanborn, Winona, Minn.
Davis, Dwight M., Dean, Moline Community College, Moline, Ill.
Davis, Floyd A., Supt. of Schools, Knoxville, Iowa
Davis, H. Curtis, Asst. Supt., Unified School District, San Jose, Calif.
Davis, Ira C., University of Wisconsin, Madison, Wis.
Davis, James M., Dir., International Center, Univ. of Michigan, Ann Arbor, Mich.
Davis, J. Pinckney, Prin., Haut Gap High Sch., John's Island, Charleston, S.C.
Davis, Joseph H., Normandy Junior High School, University City, Mo.
Davis, Louie Reid, P.O. Box 1211, University of Alabama, University, Ala.
Davis, Milton J., Principal, Gurnee Grade School, Gurnee, Ill.
Davis, Mrs. Nina Preot, Louise S. McGhee School, New Orleans, La.
Davis, Paul F., Prin., Manatee County High School, Bradenton, Fla.
Davis, Warren C., Rochester Inst. of Technology, Rochester, N.Y.
Dawe, Helen C., Sch. of H.E., University of Wisconsin, Madison, Wis.
Dawson, Dan T., Dept. of Educ., Stanford University, Stanford, Calif.
Dawson, W. Read, Sch. of Educ., Baylor University, Waco, Texas
Day, James F., Dept. of Educ., Texas Western College, El Paso, Tex.
Dear, R. Ernest, Supt. of Schools, Ironwood, Mich.
Deardorff, Ray E., Exec. Head, Ottawa Hills High School, Toledo, Ohio
DeBernardis, Amo, Supv., Audio-visual Educ., Public Schools, Portland, Ore.
Debin, Louis, Junior High School, Brooklyn, N.Y.
DeBoer, John J., Col. of Educ., University of Illinois, Urbana, Ill.
Debus, Raymond L., 666 Malabar Rd., Maroubra, N.S.W., Australia

DeCamp, Mrs. Hazel N., Essex County Voc. & Tech. High School, Bloomfield, N.J.
Decker, Fred J., Admin. Asst., N. Y. State Tchrs. Retirement Sys., Albany, N.Y.
Deer, George H., Col. of Educ., Louisiana State University, Baton Rouge, La.
DeHaven, Sula M., Junior High School, Martinsburg, W.Va.
DeJung, John E., 121 College Pl., Syracuse, N.Y.
DeKock, Henry C., Col. of Educ., State Univ. of Iowa, Iowa City, Iowa
DeKoker, Mary, Bur. of Child Study, Board of Educ., Chicago, Ill.
DeMand, J. W., Dept. of Educ.. Kansas State College, Manhattan. Kan.
Della-Piana, Gabriel M., Oak Terrace Elem. School, Highwood, Ill.
DeLong, Arthur R., Michigan State University, East Lansing, Mich.
Denecke, Marie G., University of Maryland, College Park, Md.
DePoister, W. Marshon, Dean, William Woods College, Fulton, Mo.
Derby, Orlo L., 370 Kunitomi, Okayamashi, Japan
DeRidder, Lawrence M., Col. of Educ., University of Tennessee, Knoxville, Tenn.
DeVeau, Burton W., Chm., Dept. of Agr., Ohio University, Athens, Ohio
*DeVoss, James C., 5336 Greenside Dr., San Jose, Calif.
Devor, J. W., Dept. of Educ.. Asbury College, Wilmore, Ky.
Dewine, Henry A., United Theological Seminary, Dayton, Ohio
Dexter, William A., Superintendent of Schools. Easthampton, Mass.
Deyell, J. Douglas, Master, Provincial Tchrs. Col., North Bay, Ontario
D'Heurle, Adma, 5727 Dorchester Ave., Chicago, Ill.
Dickerson, James L., Prin., University Demonstration School, Athens, Ga.
Diederich. A. F., 922 South Detroit St.. Los Angeles, Calif.
Diffley, Jerome, 133 Howard Hall, Notre Dame, Ind.
DiGiacinto, Rose D., 68 Pilgrim Ave., Yonkers, N.Y.
DiLeonarde, Joseph H., Principal, Hendricks School, Chicago, Ill.
Dilley, Norman E., Col. of Educ., Ohio University, Athens, Ohio
Dillinger, Claude. Illinois State Normal University, Normal, Ill.
Dillon, Frances H., State Teachers College, Moorhead, Minn.
Dimberg, David J., Dir., Audio-visual Educ., Public Schools, Shorewood, Wis.
Dimond, Stanley E., University of Michigan, Ann Arbor, Mich.
Di Napoli, Peter J., Principal, Public School 90, New York, N.Y.
Dingus, Lona G.. H.O.W. Staff Quarters 20, Kingsport, Tenn.
Dittmer, Daniel G.. Research Psychol., United States Air Force, Alexandria, Va.
Dixon, James T., 5329 North Wayne Ave., Chicago, Ill.
Dixon, W. Robert, School of Educ., University of Michigan, Ann Arbor, Mich.
Dobriansky, Lev E., Georgetown University, Washington, D.C.
Dodds, J. H., 1630 Alabama Dr., Urbana, Ill.
Doi, James I., P.O. Box 1616, Santa Fe, N.M.
Dolan, Francis, Superintendent, LaSalle-Peru Twp. High School, LaSalle, Ill.
Dolch, E. W.. Col. of Educ.. University of Illinois. Urbana, Ill.
Domian, O. E., 2641 Joppa Ave., St. Louis Park, Minn.
Dominick. Leo H.. Superintendent of Schools, International Falls, Minn.
Dominy, Mrs. Mildred, Educ. Div., State Univ. Tchrs. College, Plattsburgh, N.Y.
Donchion, Peter, 568 Student Center, Wayne University, Detroit, Mich.
Donner, Arvin N., Dir.. Col. of Educ., Univ. of Houston, Houston, Tex.
Donohue, Francis J.. Pres., St. Mary of the Plains College, Dodge City, Kan.
Donovan, Charles F., Dean, Sch. of Educ., Boston Col., Chestnut Hill, Mass.
Dooley, Helen, 2243 Kenilworth Ave., Los Angeles, Calif.
Dorsinville, Fritz, 1184 River Road Dorm., Ohio State Univ., Columbus, Ohio
Doster, Osie, Dorsey High School. Miami, Fla.
Doten, George W., 305 Faculty Court, Canton, N.Y.
Dotson, John A.. Dean. Col. of Educ.. University of Georgia, Athens, Ga.
Douglas, Lillian N., 919 Hillary St., New Orleans, La.
Douglass, H. R.. Dir.. Col. of Educ.. University of Colorado, Boulder. Colo.
Douglass, Malcolm P., Claremont Graduate School, Claremont, Calif.
Dowling, Thomas I.. Supt.. Greenwood City Schools, Greenwood, S.C.
Downer, Effie M.. Dept. of Education, Wayne University, Detroit, Mich.
Doyle, Andrew McCormick, Chm., Dept. of Educ., St. Vincent Coll., Latrobe, Pa.

Drag, Francis L., Asst. Supt. of Schls., San Diego, Calif.
Dragositz, Anna, 39-80 52nd St., Woodside, L.I., N.Y.
Drake, Richard M., University of Kansas City, Kansas City, Mo.
Dransfield, J. Edgar, Deerhaven Road, Oakland, N.J.
Draper, Edgar M., Dept. of Educ., Univ. of Washington, Seattle, Wash.
Dreier, William H., Dept. of Educ., Iowa State Teachers Col., Cedar Falls, Iowa
Dreikurs, Rudolf, 6 North Michigan Ave., Chicago, Ill.
Dressel, Paul L., Board of Examiners, Mich. State Col., East Lansing, Mich.
Driggs, Don F., Alabama Polytechnic Institute, Auburn, Ala.
Drobka, Frank J., Dept. of Educ., Catholic Univ. of America, Washington, D.C.
Drotter, Stephen J., Principal, Community High School, Fort Kent, Me.
Drummond, Harold D., George Peabody College for Teachers, Nashville, Tenn.
Duce, Hugh M., 2460 Lyon St., San Francisco, Calif.
Duffey, Robert V., 611 Sheffield Dr., Springfield, Pa.
Dunathan, Homer, University of Toledo, Toledo, Ohio
Duncan, Neal, Principal, Hyde Park High School, Chicago, Ill.
Dunham, Lance, 3609 North 4th Ave., Phoenix, Ariz.
Dunham, Ralph E., Middle Tennessee State College, Murfreesboro, Tenn.
Dunigan, David R., College of the Holy Cross, Worcester, Mass.
Dunkel, Harold B., Dept. of Education, University of Chicago, Chicago, Ill.
Dunkle, Maurice Albert, Supt., Calvert County Schools, Prince Frederick, Md.
Dunlap, E. T., Pres., Eastern Okla. A. & M. College, Wilburton, Okla.
Dunlop, G. M., Chm., Div. of Educ. Psych., Univ. of Alberta, Edmonton,
    Alberta
Dunn, Minnie, Alabama College, Montevallo, Ala.
Dunne, Joseph G., Headmaster, St. John's Preparatory School, Brooklyn, N.Y.
Dunning, Charles W., Van Nuys Junior High School, Burbank, Calif.
Dunsmore, Philo C., 121 Southard, Toledo, Ohio
Dupee, C. W., State Teachers College, East Stroudsburg, Pa.
Durant, Adrian J., Jr., State Department of Education, Jefferson City, Mo.
Durante, Spencer E., Principal, Carver High School, Mount Olive, N.C.
Durflinger, Glenn W., Santa Barbara College, Santa Barbara, Calif.
Durost, Walter, Dir., Test Service and Advisement Center, Dunbarton, N.H.
Durr, William K., Col. of Educ., Michigan State Univ., East Lansing, Mich.
Durrell, Donald D., Sch. of Educ., Boston University, Boston, Mass.
Dwyer, Roy E., 120 N.W. 9th St., Gainesville, Fla.
Dyde, W. F., Dean, University of Colorado, Boulder, Colo.
Dyer, Frank E., Delano Jt. Union High School, Delano, Calif.
Dyer, Mercedes H., Washington Missionary College, Takoma Park, Md.
Dykes, Mrs. Alma, 1418 East St., Reading, Ohio

Eads, Charles V., Principal, Lamar Elem. School, Amarillo, Tex.
Eads, Laura K., 141 Joralemon St., Brooklyn, N.Y.
Early, Margaret J., Sch. of Educ., Syracuse University, Syracuse, N.Y.
Early, William A., 208 Bull St., Savannah, Ga.
Early, William L., Keene Teachers College, Keene, N.H.
Eash, Maurice J., 3527 Washington St., Gary, Ind.
Eason, Leo A., Dept. of Educ., Washington University, St. Louis, Mo.
Eastburn, L. A., President, Arizona State College, Flagstaff, Ariz.
Easterly, Rev. Frederick J., Dean, Tchrs. Col., St. John's Univ., Brooklyn, N.Y.
Ebel, Robert L., Dir., Univ. Exam. Serv., State Univ. of Iowa, Iowa City, Iowa
Eberle, August William, Sch. of Educ., Indiana University, Bloomington, Ind.
Eberman, Paul W., Sch. of Educ., Univ. of Wisconsin, Madison, Wis.
Echols, J. W., Dept. of Educ., Prairie View A. & M. Col., Prairie View, Tex.
Eckelberry, R. H., Bur. of Educ. Research, Ohio State Univ., Columbus, Ohio
Eckert, Ruth E., Col. of Educ., Univ. of Minnesota, Minneapolis, Minn.
Eckhardt, John W., 2914 Sunset Ave., Bakersfield, Calif.
Eckles, H. R., Principal, Robert E. Lee School, Richmond, Va.
Eddy, Theo. V., Superintendent of Schools, St. Clair, Mich.
Edgar, Brother Julius, F.S.C., Dean of Studies, St. Mary's Col., Winona, Minn.
Edgar, Robert W., Queens College, Flushing, N.Y.

Edgerton, D. R., Superintendent, Sch. Dist. 110, Overland Park, Kan.
Edick, Helen M., Hartford Seminary Foundation, Hartford, Conn.
Edie, John W., Principal, Gundlach School, St. Louis, Mo.
Edmiston, R. W., Dir. of Extension, Miami University, Oxford, Ohio
Edson, William H., Col. of Educ., Univ. of Minnesota, Minneapolis, Minn.
Edwards, Arthur U., Eastern Illinois State College, Charleston, Ill.
Edwards, G. N., Inspector of Schools, Stratford, Ont.
Edwards, Marcia, Col. of Educ., University of Minnesota, Minneapolis, Minn.
Edwards, Seth Carlyle, Pres., Cuthington Col. & Div. Sch., Monrovia, Liberia
Edwards, T. Bentley, Sch. of Educ., University of California, Berkeley, Calif.
Edwards, William B., Superintendent of Schools, Lakewood, Ohio
Egan, Rev. Bro. John M., Iona College, New Rochelle, N.Y.
Egdorf, M. F., Superintendent of Schools, Garden City, N.Y.
Ehlers, Henry J., Duluth Branch, Univ. of Minnesota, Duluth, Minn.
Ehrenfeld, A., 50 West Ninety-sixth Street, New York, N.Y.
Ehrlich, Emanuel, 622 East Twentieth St., New York, N.Y.
Einolf, W. L., Birchrunville, Pa.
Eisen, Agnes, Dept. of Educ., Ohio University, Athens, Ohio
Eiserer, Paul E., Teachers College, Columbia University, New York, N.Y.
Ekstrom, Lena, Elem. Supv., Public Schools, Buchanan, Mich.
Elder, Ruth E., Dept. of Elem. Educ., Univ. of Oklahoma, Norman, Okla.
Eller, William, Reading Clinic, Col. of Educ., Univ. of Iowa, Iowa City, Iowa
Ellerbrook, Louis William, Stephen F. Austin State Col., Nacogdoches, Tex.
Ellingson, Mark, Rochester Institute of Technology, Rochester, N.Y.
Elliott, Allan R., Colorado State College of Education, Greeley, Colo.
Elliott, Lloyd H., Stone Hall, Cornell Univ., Ithaca, N.Y.
Ellis, Frederick E., University of Minnesota, Col. of Educ., Minneapolis, Minn.
Ellis, G. Gordon, Sch. of Educ., Univ. of North Carolina, Chapel Hill, N.C.
Ellis, Robert L., 6362 West Sixth St., Los Angeles, Calif.
Elmer, Mrs. Marion Short, 20 Belmont Street, Buffalo, N.Y.
Elsbree, Harold M., Prof. of Education, State Teachers Col., New Paltz, N.Y.
Ely, Donald P., State University Teachers College, New Paltz, N.Y.
Engbretson, William E., 604 West Walnut St., Kalamazoo, Mich.
Engelhardt, Jack E., 617 Emmett St., Battle Creek, Mich.
Engelhardt, N. L., 331 West 250th St., Riverdale, New York, N.Y.
Engels, Bernice, Supv., Elementary Education, Gary, Ind.
English, John W., 26720 North River Park Dr., Inkster, Mich.
Epstein, Bertram, City College of New York, New York, N.Y.
Erdman, Robert L., Wisconsin State College, Milwaukee, Wis.
Erickson, Carlton W. H., Audio-visual Center, Univ. of Connecticut, Storrs, Conn.
Erickson, Gerald M., 1100 East 78th St., Richfield, Minn.
Erickson, Harley E., Dept. of Educ., Wisconsin State College, Superior, Wis.
Erskine, Mildred R., 2096 Watson Ave., St. Paul, Minn.
Ersoff, Samuel, Sch. of Educ., University of Miami, Coral Gables, Fla.
Ervin, John B., Chairman, Educ. Div., Stowe Teachers College, St. Louis, Mo.
Ervin, William B., 1 Midland Place, Newark, N.J.
Erzinger, John F., 6600 North Campbell Ave., Chicago, Ill.
Eskridge, T. J., Jr., Dept. of Educ. & Psych., Newberry College, Newberry, S.C.
Eson, Morris E., New York State College for Teachers, Albany, N.Y.
Estvan, Frank J., School of Educ., Univ. of Wis., Madison, Wis.
Eugenia Marie, Sister, R.S.M., Mercy College, Detroit, Mich.
Eulalia, Sister, Cathedral Academy, Syracuse, N.Y.
Eurich, Alvin C., 655 Madison Ave., New York, N.Y.
Evans, Douglas V., Herndon High School, Herndon, Va.
Evans, Edgar Ernest, Albama State College, Montgomery, Ala.
Evans, Evan E., Exec. Dir., Nat'l Aviation Educ. Council, Washington, D.C.
Evans, Howard R., Dean, Col. of Educ., University of Akron, Akron, Ohio
Evans, J. H., Principal, Oshkosh High School, Oshkosh, Wis.
Evans, John C., Asst. Superintendent of Schools, Ogden, Utah
Evans, Ralph F., Head, Dept. of Educ., Fresno State College, Fresno, Calif.
Evenden, E. S., Teachers College, Columbia University, New York, N.Y.

Evenson, Warren L., Prin., Central High School, Fargo, N.D.
Everett, Millard S., Oklahoma A. & M., College, Stillwater, Okla.
Ewing, Parmer L., Superintendent of Schools, Buffalo, N.Y.
Eyman, R. L., Dean, Sch. of Educ., Florida State Univ., Tallahassee, Fla.
Ezer, Melvin, 35 Mora St., Dorchester, Mass.

Fahey, George L., University of Pittsburgh, Pittsburgh, Pa.
Falk, Conrad, Conception Seminary, Conception, Mo.
Falk, Philip H., Superintendent of Schools, Madison, Wis.
Fall, Charles R., University of Buffalo, Buffalo, N.Y.
Farber, Evan Ira, Main Library, Emory University, Ga.
Farber, Nathan, Escambia County Child Guid. Clinic, Pensacola, Fla.
Fargen, Jerome, Dept. of Educ., University of Notre Dame, Notre Dame, Ind.
Farley, H. Kent, Oregon College of Education, Monmouth, Ore.
Farley, John A., University of Detroit, Detroit, Mich.
Farmer, Floyd M., Prin., Wichita High School, Wichita, Kan.
Farnsworth, R. Earl, Principal, Senior High School, Fort Smith, Ark.
Fasan, Walter R., 7736 Sangamon St., Chicago, Ill.
Fattu, Nicholas, 921 Sheridan Drive, Bloomington, Ind.
Fawcett, Harold P., Ohio State University, Columbus, Ohio
Fawley, Paul C., Col. of Educ., University of Utah, Salt Lake City, Utah
Fay, Leo C., School of Education, Indiana University, Bloomington, Ind.
Fea, Henry Robert, University of Washington, Seattle, Wash.
Fee, Mary, McPherson College, McPherson, Kan.
Feelhaver, Carl T., Supt. of Schools, Ft. Dodge, Iowa
Feingold, S. Norman, Exec. Dir., Jewish Voc. Service, Boston, Mass.
Fell, E. E., Principal, East High School, Youngstown, Ohio
Fellbaum, E. H., Superintendent of Schools, Helena, Mont.
Feller, Dan, 9951-B Robbins Dr., Beverly Hills, Calif.
Feltman, Irene, No. Illinois State Teachers College, DeKalb, Ill.
Fergen, Geraldine K., Sch. of Educ., University of Missouri, Columbia, Mo.
Ferguson, W. Stewart, 3748 Maplewood Ave., Venice, Calif.
Feroze, Hyat, Kabal Road, Sialkot Cantt, Pakistan
Ferran, Rose M., Dir., Elem. Grades, Public Schools, New Orleans, La.
Ferraro, Charles D., 14611 Clifton Blvd., Lakewood, Ohio
Ferrier, William Kenneth, 6517 S.W. 35th Ave., Portland, Ore.
Ficken, Clarence E., Vice Pres. & Dean, Ohio Wesleyan Univ., Delaware, Ohio
Fickes, James A., State Teachers College, Towson, Md.
Fiedler, E. L., Superintendent of Schools, Abilene, Kan.
Fielder, Gordon W., Michigan State Normal College, Ypsilanti, Mich.
Fields, Clarence J., Coppin State Teachers College, Baltimore, Md.
Fields, Ralph R., Teachers College, Columbia University, New York, N.Y.
Fielstra, Clarence, Sch. of Educ., University of California, Los Angeles, Calif.
Fierman, Morton C., 600 Howard St., Burlingame, Calif.
Figurel, J. Allen, 2321 Walton Ave., Pittsburgh, Pa.
Finch, F. H., Col. of Educ., University of Illinois, Urbana, Ill.
Finck, Edgar M., Dickinson College, Carlisle, Pa.
Findley, Warren G., Educational Testing Service, Princeton, N.J.
Fink, Paul S., 31 South Penn St., Allentown, Pa.
Fink, Stuart D., Prin., Trg. Sch., No. Illinois State Teachers Col., DeKalb, Ill.
Fischoff, Ephraim, Dir., B'nai B'rith Hillel Foundation, Berkeley, Calif.
Fish, Allan, Supv. Prin., Oakwood Public Schools, Oakville, Ontario
Fishback, Woodson W., Southern Illinois University, Carbondale, Ill.
Fisher, Helen H., 41 West 72nd St., New York 23, N.Y.
Fisher, James A., Boston University Junior College, 688 Boylston, Boston, Mass.
Fisher, Joseph T., Hastings College, Hastings, Neb.
Fisher, Lawrence A., 515 Lincoln St., Ripon, Wis.
Fisher, Marie R., Supv. Tests and Meas., Dept. of Educ., St. Paul, Minn.
Fisk, Robert S., Dean, Sch. of Educ., University of Buffalo, Buffalo, N.Y.
Fitz, John Allen, 301 S. Gill St., University Park, Pa.
Fitzgerald, Edward J., Superintendent of Schools, Bristol, R.I.

Fitzgerald, James A., Sch. of Educ., Fordham University, New York, N.Y.
Fitzgerald, J. C., Dir., Audio-visual Center, Okla. A. & M. Col., Stillwater, Okla.
Fitzgerald, N. E., Dean, Col. of Educ., Univ. of Tennessee, Knoxville, Tenn.
Flaherty, Rev. J. L., Superintendent, Diocesan Schools, Richmond, Va.
Flamand, Ruth K., 72 Goldenridge Dr., Levittown, Pa.
Flamme, Wayne H., Principal, Junior High School, Antigo, Wis.
Flanagan, John C., Dir., Amer. Inst. for Research, 410 Amberson, Pittsburgh, Pa.
Flanders, Ned A., Col. of Educ., Univ. of Minnesota, Minneapolis, Minn.
Fleck, Henrietta, Chm., Home Econ. Dept., New York Univ., New York, N.Y.
Fleming, C. M., Inst. of Educ., University of London, London, England
Fleming, Harold D., Chm., Div. of Educ., State Tchrs. College, Bemidji, Minn.
Fleming, Ola, Atlantic Christian College, Wilson, N.C.
Fleming, Robert S., Sch. of Educ., New York University, New York, N.Y.
Flesher, Marie A., 6 Old Armory, Ohio State University, Columbus, Ohio
Flesher, William R., Sch. of Educ., Ohio State University, Columbus, Ohio
Fligor, R. J., Southern Illinois University, Carbondale, Ill.
Flinton, Edgar W., New York State College for Teachers, Albany, N.Y.
Flores, Vetal, Box 160, Bronte, Tex.
Flores, Mrs. Zella K., Western Montana College of Education, Dillon, Mont.
Flournoy, Frances, Dept. of Curric. and Instr., Univ. of Texas, Austin, Tex.
Flower, G. E., Canadian Educ. Assn., 206 Huron St., Toronto, Ont.
Flynn, F. E., College of St. Thomas, St. Paul, Minn.
Focht, James R., Education Dept., State Teachers College, Salisbury, Md.
Folger, D. F., Chm., Div. of Tchr. Educ., State Col. for Women, Milledgeville, Ga.
Fonacier, Andres Medina, Ilocos Norte Normal School, Laoag, Ilocos Norte,
     Philippines
Foote, Lawrence E., Superintendent, Allen County Schls., Fort Wayne, Ind.
Foran, Thomas G., Catholic University of America, Washington, D.C.
Forcinelli, Joseph, 2500 Benvenue Ave., Berkeley, Calif.
Ford, Edmund A., 1326 South Center, Terre Haute, Ind.
Ford, Henry W., Div. of Educ., Hofstra College, Hempstead, N.Y.
Ford, Paul L., Illinois Children's Hospital, Chicago, Ill.
Ford, Roxana R., Sch. of Home Econ., Univ. of Minnesota, St. Paul, Minn.
Fordyce, W. G., Superintendent of Schools, Euclid, Ohio
Fornaciari, Earl F., 6616 South Normal Blvd., Chicago, Ill.
Forner, James A., Walled Lake Consolidated Schls., Walled Lake, Mich.
Forney, E. B., Ginn & Company, 1932 Princeton Ave., St. Paul, Minn.
Forrester, Gertrude, 71 Overpeck Ave., Ridgefield Park, N.J.
Forsdale, Louis, Teachers College, Columbia University, New York, N.Y.
Foshay, Arthur W., Bur. of Educ. Research, Ohio State Univ., Columbus, Ohio
Fossieck, Theodore H., Principal, Milne School of Practice, Albany, N.Y.
Foster, Frank C., Sch. of Educ., University of Maine, Orono, Me.
Foster, Harry K., State Teachers College, Fredonia, N.Y.
Foster, Inez, Asst. Supt., Elem. Div., Public Schools, San Antonio, Tex.
Fougner, Herbert M., Whittier College, Whittier, Calif.
Fowlkes, John Guy, Dean, Sch. of Educ., Univ. of Wisconsin, Madison, Wis.
Fox, Rev. Charles, Oratory School, Summit, N.J.
Fox, Robert S., Univ. Elem. Sch., Univ. of Michigan, Ann Arbor, Mich.
Fox, William H., Sch. of Educ., Indiana University, Bloomington, Ind.
Frank, William P., 1234 S. Garfield Ave., Alhambra, Calif.
Franklin, J. E. 1602 Cooper St., Commerce, Tex.
Franz, Evelyn B., State Teachers College, Trenton, N.J.
Franzblau, Abraham N., Dean, Hebrew Union Sch. of Educ. & Sacred Music,
     New York, N.Y.
Franzen, Carl G. F., Indiana University, Bloomington, Ind.
Fraser, Dorothy McClure, City College, New York, N.Y.
Fraser, Margaret A., Read. Clinic, University of Pennsylvania, Philadelphia, Pa.
Frasier, George Willard, Sch. of Educ., Stanford University, Stanford, Calif.
Frazier, James R., Superintendent of Schools, Okmulgee, Okla.
Frederick, Orie I., Western Mich. Col. of Educ., Kalamazoo, Mich.
Frederick, Robert W., Jr., Fairleigh Dickinson College, Rutherford, N.J.

Freeman, Frank N., Dean Emeritus, Univ. of Calif., Berkeley, Calif.
Freeman, Frank S., Morrill Hall, Cornell University, Ithaca, N.Y.
Freeman, Kenneth, State Univ. Teachers College, Geneseo, N.Y.
Freeman, M. Herbert, New Jersey State Teachers College, Paterson, N.J.
Freeman, Ruges Richmond, Jr., 4582 Aldine St., St. Louis, Mo.
French, Lois M., 98 Alexander Ave., Nutley, N.J.
French, William M., Muhlenberg College, Allentown, Pa.
Fretwell, Elbert K., Jr., Teachers College, Columbia University, New York, N.Y.
Fretz, Floyd C., Superintendent of Schools, Bradford, Pa.
Freund, Evelyn, 5954 Guilford, Detroit, Mich.
Frick, Herman L., Dept. of Educ., Florida State University, Tallahassee, Fla.
Friedman, Bertha B., Dept. of Educ., Queens College, Flushing, N.Y.
Fristoe, Dewey, Superintendent of Schools, Flossmoor, Ill.
Fristoe, Wallace H., Prin., Kelvyn Park High School, Chicago, Ill.
Fritzsche, Bertha M., Mississippi Southern College, Hattiesburg, Miss.
Froelich, Gustav J., Bur. of Inst. Res., Univ. of Illinois, Urbana, Ill.
Frost, Norman, George Peabody College for Teachers, Nashville, Tenn.
Frost, S. E., Jr., Dept. of Educ., Brooklyn College, Brooklyn, N.Y.
Frutchey, Fred P., Ext. Serv., U. S. Dept. of Agriculture, Washington, D.C.
Fry, Clements C., Box 1505-A, Yale Station, New Haven, Conn.
Frye, C. L., Superintendent of Schools, Huntington, Utah
Fuglaar, Ollie B., Head, Dept. of Educ., Louisiana College, Pineville, La.
Fullager, William A., Col. of Educ., Univ. of Florida, Gainesville, Fla.
Fuller, Harvey, Superintendent of Schools, Wethersfield, Conn.
Fuller, John J., State Teachers College, Winona, Minn.
Fullerton, Craig K., Asst. Superintendent of Schools, Greeley, Colo.
Fullmer, C. E., Principal, Wadsworth Elem. School, Chicago, Ill.
Fullmer, David C. , Asst. Supt., Catholic Schools, Chicago, Ill.
Fulton, W. R., Educ. Materials Serv., Univ. of Oklahoma, Norman, Okla.
Fults, Anna Carol, Southern Illinois University, Carbondale, Ill.
Fults, Dan A., Central Missouri State College, Warrensburg, Mo.
Futch, Olivia, Dept. of Educ., Furman University, Greenville, S.C.

Gabbard, Hazel F., U. S. Office of Education, Washington. D.C.
Gabel, O. J., Northern Illinois State College, DeKalb, Ill.
Gabler, Earl R., Sch. of Educ., New York University, New York, N.Y.
Gabriel, A., Jr., 197 Avon Ave., San Lorenzo, Calif.
Gahlib, Hanna, River Road Dorm., Ohio State University, Columbus, Ohio
Gaither, F. F., Dir., Tchr. Educ., Univ. of Oklahoma, Norman, Okla.
Gale, Ann, Principal, Edison School, Chicago, Ill.
Gallagher, James J., Dept. of Educ., University of Illinois, Urbana, Ill.
Gallagher, Sister M. Muriel, Mount Mercy College, Pittsburgh, Pa.
Gallen, Albert A., Reading Consult., West Chester Public Schls., West Chester, Pa.
Galloway, O. F., Head, Dept. of Educ., MacMurray Col., Jacksonville, Ill.
Gambrill, Bessie Lee, Dept. of Educ., Yale University, New Haven, Conn.
Gamelin, F. C., 610 Grove St., Austin, Minn.
Gammon, Delore, Asst. Supt. in chg. Elem. Educ., Public Schools, Wichita, Kan.
Gardner, E. Claude, Registrar, Freed-Hardeman College, Henderson, Tenn.
Gardner, Leonard, Dept. of Educ., University of Tulsa, Tulsa, Okla.
Garinger, Elmer H., Superintendent of Schools, Charlotte, N.C.
Garlin, R. E., Dept. of Educ., Texas Technological College, Lubbock, Tex.
Garnett, Ray L., Wisconsin State College, River Falls, Wis.
Garrett, Charles G., 2 Ruth Street, Hammond, Ind.
Garrison. Karl C., College of Educ., University of Georgia, Athens, Ga.
Gastwirth, Paul, Principal, Berriman Junior High School, Brooklyn, N.Y.
Gates, Arthur I., Teachers College, Columbia University, New York, N.Y.
Gates, Charles D., East High Annex and School 14, Rochester, N.Y.
Gates, Mrs. Grace W., Supv., Elementary Education. Clarence, N.Y.
Gates, Mary Frances, Michigan State Normal College, Ypsilanti, Mich.
Gauerke, Warren E., Dept. of Teacher Educ., Emory University, Ga.
Gauger, Paul W., Sch. of Educ., University of Wisconsin, Madison, Wis.

Gega, Peter C., Educ. Dept., San Diego State College, San Diego, Calif.
Geiger, C. Vincent, Superintendent of Schools, Verona, N.J.
Gemeinhardt, William C., Col. of Educ., Univ. of Minnesota, Minneapolis, Minn.
Gentleman, Florence L., Prin., Barton Elem. School, Chicago, Ill.
Gentry, George H., Supt. of Schls., Pres., Lee Jr. Col., Baytown, Tex.
Gentry, Ira A., Jr., Tennessee A. & I. State University, Nashville, Tenn.
Geoghegan, Sister Barbara, Col. of Mt. St. Joseph-on-the-Ohio, Mt. St. Joseph, O.
George, Walter E. C., Edmund Ezra Day Hall, Cornell University, Ithaca, N.Y.
Georgesen, Sigrid, Principal, Park Point School, Duluth, Minn.
Georgiades, William, Whittier Union High School Dist., Whittier, Calif.
Gerberich, J. R., Dir., Bur. of Educ. Research, Univ. of Conn., Storrs, Conn.
Gerlach, Vernon, Bethany Lutheran College, Mankato, Minn.
Gerletti, John D., University of Southern California, Los Angeles, Calif.
Gernert, H. F., Jr., 522 North 24th St., Allentown, Pa.
Gesling, Martha M., Bowling Green State Univ., Bowling Green, Ohio
Gesslein, Charles H., 1120 College St., Davenport, Iowa
Getzels, J. W., Dept. of Educ., University of Chicago, Chicago, Ill.
Gholson, G. James, Prin., Fairmont Heights High School, Washington, D.C.
Gibson, Walter E., Prin., Lafayette School, Lincoln Park, Mich.
Gibbons, Joseph H., Superintendent of Schools, Stoughton, Mass.
Gibbs, E. Delmar, College of Puget Sound, Tacoma, Wash.
Gibson, Mrs. Kathryn S., Prairie View A. & M. College, Prairie View, Tex.
Gibson, Mrs. Norma, 902 South Manhattan Place, Los Angeles, Calif.
Gibson, Walter V. B., Principal, Elementary School, East Tallahassee, Ala.
Gignilliat, Arthur M., Dir., Armstrong Evening College, Savannah, Ga.
Gilbert, Floyd O., State Teachers College, St. Cloud, Minn.
Gilbert, Harry B., Bur. of Child Guidance, New York City Schls., New York, N.Y.
Gilbert, Luther C., Sch. of Educ., University of California, Berkeley, Calif.
Gilburne, Lester C., 305 Linden Blvd., Brooklyn, N.Y.
Giles, LeRoy H., Dean of Students, Carthage College, Carthage, Ill.
Gill, Bernard I., Librarian, State Teachers College, Moorhead, Minn.
Gilland, Thomas M., Dir. of Trg., State Teachers College, California, Pa.
Gillaspie, Howard H., Westfield Union Free High School, Westfield, Wis.
Gillet, Harry O., 7401 Luella Ave., Chicago, Ill.
Gillham, Vera M., Principal, Horace Mann School, Minneapolis, Minn.
Gilligan, Michael B., State Teachers College, Jersey City, N.J.
Gilmore, John V., 236 Bay State Rd., Boston, Mass.
Ginsburg, Mrs. Sadie D., Johns Hopkins University, Baltimore, Md.
Gjerde, Clayton M., San Diego State College, San Diego, Calif.
Glasow, Ogden L., Western Illinois State College, Macomb, Ill.
Gleason, Gerald T., Sch. of Educ., University of Wisconsin, Madison, Wis.
Glenn, J. Curtis, Chicago Teachers College, Chicago, Ill.
Glennon, Vincent J., Sch. of Educ., Syracuse University, Syracuse, N.Y.
Glock, Marvin D., Bur. of Educ. Research, Cornell University, Ithaca, N.Y.
Glogau, Arthur H., Dean of Men, Oregon College of Education, Monmouth, Ore.
Gluesing, Eugene C., Bagley High School, Bagley, Minn.
Gobetz, Wallace, 540 East 22nd St., Brooklyn, N.Y.
Godfrey, Mary E., State Board of Education, Richmond, Va.
Godfrey, Maurice L., 73 Barrington Ave., Toronto, Ont.
Godfrey, Rollin E., 504 East Lake Dr., Greensboro, N.C.
Godwin, Wendell, Superintendent of Schools, Topeka, Kan.
Goff, Mrs. Arnold E., Forest Grove, Ore.
Goldberg, Nathan, 75-47 196th Street, Flushing, N.Y.
Golder, Grace M., 52 Hillhouse Ave., Yale Sta., New Haven, Conn.
Goldhammer, Keith, 747 Marion St., Palo Alto, Calif.
Goldner, Ralph H., Dept. of Educ., State Univ. Teachers College, Fredonia, N.Y.
Goltry, Keith, Dean, Dept. of Educ., Parsons College, Fairfield, Iowa
Gomon, Neal S., Nebraska State Teachers College, Peru, Neb.
Good, Carter V., University of Cincinnati, Cincinnati, Ohio
Good, Warren R., Prin., Alfred I. DuPont Elem. School, Wilmington, Del.
Goodlad, John I., Emory University, Emory, Ga.

Goodside, Samuel, Supv., Ramaz Lower School, New York, N.Y.
Goodwill, Glen T., Superintendent, City School District, Monterey, Calif.
Goossen, Carl V., Prin., Univ. Elem. Sch., Univ. of Minn., Minneapolis, Minn.
Gordon, Ira J., Inst. for Child Study, Univ. of Maryland, College Park, Md.
Gordon, Jerome, 6659 Belmar Avenue, Reseda, Calif.
Gordon, Ted, 317 North Lucerne, Los Angeles, Calif.
Gorman, Burton W., Kent State University, Kent, Ohio
Gorman, Frank H., University of Omaha, Omaha, Neb.
Gorman, William J., Registrar, St. John's Prep. School, Brooklyn, N.Y.
Goslin, Willard E., George Peabody College, Nashville, Tenn.
Gossard, Paul, Superintendent of Schools, Quincy, Mass.
Gould, George, University of Pittsburgh, Pittsburgh, Pa.
Gourley, David, Superintendent of Schools, Salt Lake City, Utah
Graber, Eldon W., Head. Dept. of Educ., Bethel College, North Newton, Kan.
Grace, Alonzo G., Jr., Trinity College, Hartford, Conn.
Grace, H. T., Florida Southern College, Lakeland, Fla.
Grady, Joseph E., St. Bernard's Seminary, Rochester, N.Y.
Graebner, Oliver E., Valparaiso University, Valparaiso, Indiana
Graetz Ralph, Butler University, Indianapolis, Ind.
Graff, George E., Supt., Rural Educ., State Dept. of Educ., Rockville, Conn.
Graff, Orin B., Dept. of Sch. Adm. & Supv., Univ. of Tenn., Knoxville, Tenn.
Graff, Willard J., Superintendent of Schools, Springfield, Mo.
Graffam, Donald T., Dickinson College, Carlisle, Pa.
Graham, Cassin F., 127 North Mayfield Ave., Chicago, Ill.
Graham, Mattie, Supv., Elem. Educ., Troy, N.Y.
Graham, Willis Gayer, Rt. 1, Harrah, Wash.
Grams, Armin, Psych. Dept., Wisconsin State College, LaCrosse, Wis.
Grant, Edward H., Northern New Mexico Normal School, El Rito, N.M.
Grant, Eugene B., Northern Illinois State College, DeKalb, Ill.
Grant, Lester J., Superintendent of Schools, Decatur, Ill.
Granzow, Kent R., 1117 South York St., Denver, Colo.
Grau, Mary L., Supv., Elementary Educ., Montgomery County, Towson, Md.
Grau, R. T., Director of Curriculum, Public Schools, Clinton, Iowa
Graves, Elizabeth K., Haviland Court, Stamford, Conn.
Graves, Linwood D., Morris Brown College, Atlanta, Ga.
Gray, Archie L., University Station, Grand Forks, N.D.
* Gray, William S., Dept. of Educ., University of Chicago, Chicago, Ill.
Graybeal, Lyman B., Colorado State College of Education, Greeley, Colo.
Green, Harold W., Utah School for the Blind, Ogden, Utah
Greenberg, Joseph, Principal, Public School 238, Brooklyn, N.Y.
Greene, Charles E., 1844 Venus Dr., Sacramento, Calif.
Greene, Ellen F., Dept. of Educ., Fisk University, Nashville, Tenn.
Greene, Harry A., Ext. Div., State University of Iowa, Iowa City, Iowa
Greene, Maxine, Sch. of Educ., New York University, New York, N.Y.
Greene, Mrs. Minnie S., Southwest Texas Junior College, Uvalde, Tex.
Greenfield, Curtis O., Principal, Percy L. Julian School, Phoenix, Ariz.
Greenwood, Edward D., Menninger Clinic, Topeka, Kan.
Greenwood, Roy, Broome County Technical Institute, Binghampton, N.Y.
Gregg, Russell T., Dept. of Educ., Univ. of Wisconsin, Madison, Wis.
Gribble, S. C., Washington University, St. Louis, Mo.
Griffin, Lee H., Ginn and Company, Chicago, Ill.
Griffin, Margaret T., Principal, Warner Elementary School, Springfield, Mass.
* Griffin, Margery M., 5778 DeGiverville, St. Louis, Mo.
Griffin, Robert J., 612 Albermarle St., El Cerrito, Calif.
Griffith, Coleman R., University of Illinois, Urbana, Ill.
Griffiths, Daniel E., New York State College for Teachers, Albany, N.Y.
Griffiths, Ruth, Plymouth Teachers College, Plymouth, N.H.
Grim, Paul R., Col. of Educ., University of Minnesota, Minneapolis, Minn.
Grispino, J. A., Marist Col. and Seminary, Framingham Centre, Mass.
Grissinger, James A., Chm., Dept. of Speech, Otterbein Col., Westerville, Ohio
Gritzner, Leland J., Elem. Prin., Public Schools, Osage, Iowa

Grizzard, Mabel Youree, 711 West Main, Waxahachie, Tex.
* Grizzell, E. D., Dean, Sch. of Educ., Univ. of Pennsylvania, Philadelphia, Pa.
Groenke, Paul H., Box 287, Howard Lake, Minn.
Groesbeck, Lue, State Dept. of Instruction, Salt Lake City, Utah
Groff, Frank E., Reg. Supt., New Hope-Solebury Jt. Sch. Dist., New Hope, Pa.
Grogan, M. Lucille, 7638 South Wood St., Chicago, Ill.
Gronlund, Norman E., Col. of Educ., University of Illinois, Urbana, Ill.
Grose, Robert F., Psych. Dept., Amherst College, Amherst, Mass.
Gross, Marie L., Principal, Central School, Evanston, Ill.
Gross, Neal, Harvard University, 20 Oxford St., Cambridge, Mass.
Gross, Richard Edmund, Sch. of Educ., Stanford University, Stanford, Calif.
Gross, Robert Dean, Sacramento State College, Sacramento, Calif.
Grossnickle, Foster E., State Teachers College, Jersey City, N.J.
Grotke, Earl M., University of Southern California, Los Angeles, Calif.
Grout, W. Stuart, Illinois State Normal University, Normal, Ill.
Grubbs, Hazel A., 1230 Amsterdam Ave., New York, N.Y.
Gruber, Frederick C., University of Pennsylvania, Philadelphia, Pa.
Gruenberg, Benjamin C., 100 Central Park South, New York, N.Y.
Grundemann, Norma M., 3617 North 13th St., Milwaukee, Wis.
Guess, George T., Principal, Picadome Elementary School, Lexington, Ky.
Gumm, Boyce L., Box 103, Athens, W.Va.
Gunn, Henry M., Supt. of Schools, Palo Alto, Calif.
Gurr, Muriel N., 1725 Orrington Ave., Evanston, Ill.
Guss, Carolyn, Audio-visual Center, Indiana University, Bloomington, Ind.
Gussner, William S., Superintendent of Schools, Jamestown, N.D.
Gustin, Margaret, Elem. Supv., State Dept. of Educ., Unionville, Conn.
Guy, George Vance, Portland State College, Portland, Ore.
Gwynn, J. Minor, University of North Carolina, Chapel Hill, N.C.

Haaby, Lawrence O., Dept. of Educ., Univ. of Tennessee, Knoxville, Tenn.
Haas, Raoul R., Dir., No. Side Branch, Chicago Tchrs. Col., Chicago, Ill.
Haas, Richard J., Jr., 424 S. Summit St., Bowling Green, Ohio
Hackenberg, J. L., Superintendent of Schools, Shamokin, Pa.
Hadley, J. H., Superintendent of Schools, Tuscaloosa, Ala.
Hadley, S. Trevor, State Teachers College, Indiana, Pa.
Haefner, Alfred E., Dean, Wartburg College, Waverly, Iowa
Hager, Walter E., Pres., Dist. of Columbia Tchrs. College, Washington, D.C.
Hagerman, Helen L., State Univ. College for Teachers, Buffalo, N.Y.
Haggerty, Helen Ruth, Adj. Gen'ls. Office, Dept. of the Army, Washington, D.C.
Haggerty, William J., Pres., State University Tchrs. College, New Paltz, N.Y.
Hagman, Harlan L., Dean, Col. of Educ., Drake University, Des Moines, Iowa
Hahn, Albert R., Clinical Psychologist, V. A. Hospital, Madison, Wis.
Haight, Wilbur T., Guidance Counselor, Milford High School, Milford, Del.
Haimbach, David, 4738 Kendall Dr., Corpus Christi, Tex.
Halberg, Anna D., District of Columbia Tchrs. College, Washington, D.C.
Halbert, Bernice, Eastern Texas Baptist College, Marshall, Tex.
Hale, Gifford G., State Teachers College, Newark, N.J.
Haley, Gerald J., Principal, Medill Elem. School, Chicago, Ill.
Hall, Barbara C., 10 Agassiz St., Cambridge, Mass.
Hall, James A., Superintendent of Schools, Port Washington, N.Y.
Hall, J. E., Jackson College, Jackson, Miss.
Hall, Katherine H., San Jose State College, San Jose, Calif.
Hall, M. E., Sch. of Music, Northern Texas State College, Denton, Tex.
Hall, Ralph H., Audio-visual Center, Kent State University, Kent, Ohio
Hall, Robert King, Trng. Dept., Arabian Am. Oil Co., Dhahran, Saudi Arabia
Hall, Roy M., University of Texas, Austin, Tex.
Hall, Ruel, County Superintendent of Schools, Kankakee, Ill.
Hall, William F., Pennsylvania State University, University Park, Pa.
Hall, William Frank, Dir., Child Study Serv., Elem. Dist. 1, Phoenix, Ariz.
Ham, John E., Jr., Submaster, Deering High School, Portland, Me.
Hamalainen, Arthur E., Principal, Plandome Road School, Manhasset, N.Y.

Hamilton, Mrs. Charles W., Jr., Dept. of Educ., Creighton Univ., Omaha, Neb.
Hamilton, Holmes, Acting Supt. of Schools, Forest Park, Ill.
Hamilton, Homer H.. P.O. Box 9222. Dallas. Tex.
Hammer, Irwin A., Western Washington College of Education, Bellingham, Wash.
Hammock, Robert C., University of Alabama, University, Ala.
Hand, Harold C., Col. of Educ., University of Illinois, Urbana, Ill.
Hanitchak, John Joseph, Sch. of Educ., Univ. of Kansas City, Kansas City, Mo.
Hanna, Lavone A., San Francisco State College, San Francisco, Calif.
Hanna, Paul R., Dept. of Educ., Stanford University. Stanford, Calif.
Hanscom, James H., 90-20 52nd Ave., Elmhurst, N.Y.
Hansen, Abner L., Florida Southern College, Lakeland, Fla.
Hansen, Carl W., Teachers College, University of Cincinnati, Cincinnati, Ohio
Hansen, Einar A., Col. of Educ.. Ohio University, Athens. Ohio
Hansen, G. G., Supt., Huntley Project Schools, Worden, Mont.
Hansen, Helge E., University of Minnesota, Minneapolis, Minn.
Hansen, R. G., Asst. Supt., Elem. Educ., Public Schools, St. Paul, Minn.
Hansen, W. C., President, Wisconsin State College, Stevens Point, Wis.
Hanson, E. H., Superintendent of Schools, Rock Island, Ill.
Hanson, Gordon C.. University of Wichita, Wichita, Kan.
Hanson, John W., Michigan State University, East Lansing, Mich.
Hao. Peter T. Y.. 165 East 88th St.. New York. N.Y.
Harap, Henry, George Peabody College for Teachers, Nashville, Tenn.
Harbaugh. John W.. Sch. of Educ.. Univ. of Pittsburgh. Pittsburgh, Pa.
Harbin, Calvin E., Fort Hays Kansas State College, Hays, Kan.
Harbo, L. S., Superintendent of Schools. Austin. Minn.
Hardesty, Cecil D.. Supt. of County Schools, San Diego, Calif.
Hardgrove. Mrs. Clarence E., Northern Ill. State Teachers Col., DeKalb, Ill.
Harding, Vilas E., Dir., Leota School for Girls, Evansville, Wis.
Hare, H. Frank, Dist. Superintendent of Schools, Phoenixville, Pa.
Haring, Norris G., Dept. of Spec. Educ., Syracuse University, Syracuse, N.Y.
Harman, Matilda E., Principal. Lincoln School, Spring Valley. Ill.
Harnack, Robert S., Sch. of Educ., University of Buffalo, Buffalo, N.Y.
* Harney. Julia C.. 302 Pavonia Ave.. Jersey City, N.J.
Harney, Paul J., University of San Francisco, San Francisco, Calif.
Harney, Thomas E.. Superintendent of Schools, Dunkirk. N.Y.
Harnly, Paul W., Asst. Supt. in chg. Sec. Educ., Public Schools, Wichita, Kan.
Harper, George Leslie, Supv. Prin.. Person County High School. Roxbard, N.C.
Harper, James R. W., Box 128, Baylor University Sta., Waco, Tex.
Harper, Robert S., College Examiner, Knox College, Galesburg, Ill.
Harrington, E. Ross, Dir. of Educ., Richland Sch. Dist., Shafter, Calif.
Harrington, Johns H., Los Angeles City College, Los Angeles, Calif.
Harris, Albert J.. Dir., Educ. Clinic. Queens College, Flushing, N.Y.
Harris, Ben M., Lafayette School, Lafayette, Calif.
Harris, Chester W., Sch. of Educ., University of Wisconsin, Madison, Wis.
Harris, Dale B.. Inst. of Child Welfare. Univ. of Minn., Minneapolis, Minn.
Harris, Paul, Dir. of Art Educ., City Schools, Waukegan, Ill.
Harris, Raymond P., Sch. of Educ., Univ. of North Dakota, Grand Forks, N.D.
Harris, Ruby Dean, Agric. Extension Serv., Univ. of California, Berkeley, Calif.
Harris, Theodore L., Sch. of Educ., Univ. of Wisconsin, Madison, Wis.
Harris, Wylie V., Supt.. Westwood View School, Kansas City. Kan.
Harrison. George R., Head, Dept. of Elem. Educ., Bradley Univ., Peoria. Ill.
Harry. David P., Jr., Grad. Sch. Western Reserve University, Cleveland. Ohio
Harshbarger. Jake, U.S. Naval Admin. Unit, Box 6, Navy No. 935, FPO, San Francisco, Calif.
Harshman, Floyd E., Otterbein College, Westerville, Ohio
Hartman. A. L.. Principal, Edgemont and Watchung Schls.. Upper Montclair, N.J.
Hartsell, Horace C., Texas Technological College, Lubbock, Tex.
Hartsfield, Loy. Dept. of Educ., University of Houston, Houston. Tex.
Hartshorn, Herbert E., Dir., Elem. Educ., Edina-Morningside Sch., Minneapolis, Minn.
Hartstein, Jacob I., Dean, Grad. Sch., Long Island University, Brooklyn, N.Y.

Hartung, Helene, 2549 Decatur Ave., New York, N.Y.
Hartung, Maurice L., Dept. of Educ., University of Chicago, Chicago, Ill.
Harvey, A. D., Asst. Supt. of Schools, Kingsville, Tex.
Haskew, Laurence D., Col. of Educ., University of Texas, Austin, Tex.
Hasman, Richard H., 27 High Rock Ave., Saratoga Springs, N.Y.
Hass, C. Glen, Assoc. Supt., Arlington County Public Schls., Arlington, Va.
Hassel, Carl W., Coordinator of Curric., Central Schools, Liverpool, N.Y.
Hatch, Robert C., Supv., State Dept. of Education, Montgomery, Ala.
Hatchett, Ethel L., Dept. of Educ., Hardin-Simmons University, Abilene, Tex.
Hatfill, H. A., Supt. of Schools, Paris, Ill.
Haupt, George W., State Teachers College, Glassboro, N.J.
Hauser, L. J., Superintendent of Schools, Dist. No. 96, Riverside, Ill.
Haverland, Elizabeth R., State School of Science, Wahpeton, N.D.
Havighurst, Robert J., Dept. of Educ., University of Chicago, Chicago, Ill.
Hawes, Homer H., Head, Dept. of Educ., Park College, Parkville, Mo.
Hawley, Ray C., Superintendent of County Schools, Ottawa, Ill.
Haws, Nina, Principal, Riverside Elementary School, Wichita, Kan.
Hay, Louis, 140 Clarkson Ave., Brooklyn, N.Y.
Hayden, Alice H., Dir., Educ. Research, Univ. of Washington, Seattle, Wash.
Hayes, Dale K., Dir. of Research, American Sch. Pub. Corp., New York, N.Y.
Hayes, Denis A., Supt., Paterson Diocesan Schools, Paterson, N.J.
Hayes, Paul C., Superintendent of Schools, Sharonville, Ohio
Haynes, Hubert C., Dept. of Psych., East Carolina College, Greenville, N.C.
Hayward, Orville B., Principal, George Rogers Clark School, Whiting, Ind.
Hayward, W. George, Prin., Stockton and Eastern Schls., East Orange, N.J.
Hazen, Oliver M., Superintendent, District No. 403, Renton, Wash.
Heald, James E., 1534 Brookside, Waukegan, Ill.
Healy, Mary, 8459 Dante Ave., Chicago, Ill.
Hearn, Arthur C., Sch. of Educ., University of Oregon, Eugene, Ore.
Hearne, William P., Prin., Gage Park High School, Chicago, Ill.
Hecht, Irvin Sulo, Prin., Girls High School, Brooklyn, N.Y.
Heck, Theodore, Head, Dept. of Educ., St. Meinrad Seminary, St. Meinrad, Ind.
Hecker, Izora, 1486 Woodrow, Wichita, Kan.
Heding, Howard W., 617 Baltzell St., Madison, Wis.
Hedrick, E. H., Superintendent of City Schools, Medford, Ore.
Heer, A. L., Dir. of Student Teaching, Kent, Ohio
Heffernan, Helen, State Department of Education, Sacramento, Calif.
Hegman, M. Marian, 322 South Ave., Medina, N.Y.
Heilman, Arthur, Dept. of Educ., University of Oklahoma, Norman, Okla.
Heinen, Henrietta E., 817 Diversey Parkway, Chicago, Ill.
Heisner, H. Fred, Superintendent of Schools, Redlands, Calif.
Heist, Paul, 131 North 23rd Street, Corvallis, Ore.
Helding, Dorothy W., Principal, Washington School, Evanston, Ill.
Helen Jean, Sister, S.L., Head, Educ. Dept., Webster College, Webster Groves, Mo.
Hellman, Walter, Asst. Supt. of Schools, Fairfield, Conn.
* Helms, W. T., Supt. of Schools, Richmond, Calif.
Hemington, Mrs. Mabel G., Chicago Teachers College, Chicago, Ill.
Hemingway, William C., New Concord, Ohio
Henderer, M. Donaldson, 4304 Whittier Rd., Wilmington 2, Del.
Henderson, Kenneth B., Col. of Educ., University of Illinois, Urbana, Ill.
Henderson, Margaret G., 212 West Healey St., Champaign, Ill.
Henderson, Richard Lee, Agnes Scott College, Decatur, Ga.
Hendricks, F. W., Superintendent of Schools, Kirkwood, Mo.
Hendrickson, Gordon, University of Cincinnati, Cincinnati, Ohio
Hendrix, Herschel, Dept. of Educ., Upper Iowa University, Fayette, Iowa
Hendrix, Holbert H., Prin., University Elem. School, Athens, Ohio
Hengesbach, Alice R., Supv., Willoughby-Eastlake Schools, Willoughby, Ohio
Henle, R. J., Dean, Grad. Sch., St. Louis University, St. Louis, Mo.
Henry, Edna L., Dept. of Educ., Roosevelt University, Chicago, Ill.
Henry, Mrs. Helga B., Pasadena College, Pasadena, Calif.
* Henry, Nelson B., Dept. of Educ., University of Chicago, Chicago, Ill.

Hensley, Iven Howe, Stephen F. Austin State College, Nacogdoches, Tex.
Henzlik, Frank E., Dean, Teachers College, Univ. of Nebraska, Lincoln, Neb.
Herchek, Michel, Dir., Kent State University School, Kent, Ohio
Hereford, Karl T., Res. Dir., American School Publ. Corp., New York, N.Y.
Herge, Henry C., Dean, Sch. of Educ., Rutgers University, New Brunswick, N.J.
Herr, Ross, District Supt., Chicago Public Schools, Chicago, Ill.
Herr, William A., Principal, H. F. Grebey Mem. Jr. High Sch., Hazelton, Pa.
Herrick, Theral T., Dir. of Curric., Public Schools, Kalamazoo, Mich.
Herrick, Virgil E., Sch. of Educ., University of Wisconsin, Madison, Wis.
Herriott, M. E., Prin., Airport Junior High School, Los Angeles, Calif.
Hertzberg, Oscar E., State Teachers College, Buffalo, N.Y.
Hertzler, Silas, Goshen College, Goshen, Ind.
Hess, Clarke F., Marshall College, Huntington, W.Va.
Hess, Glenn C., Supv. Prin., Richland Township Public Schools, Johnstown, Pa.
Hetzel, Walter L., Superintendent of Schools, Decorah, Iowa
Hibbs, M. Gregg, Jr., Supt., Red Bank Senior High School, Red Bank, N.J.
Hickerson, J. Allen, New Haven State Teachers College, New Haven, Conn.
Hickey, Philip J., Superintendent of Inst., Public Schools, St. Louis, Mo.
Hickman, Clara, Principal, Rose Lees Hardy School, Washington, D.C.
Hickox, Edward J., 500 Alden Street, Springfield, Mass.
Hicks, Mrs. Aline B., Booker T. Washington High School, Norfolk, Va.
Hicks, Samuel I., Superintendent of Schools, Pearl River, N.Y.
Hicks, Victor H., Dir., Stud. Tchg., East Central State College, Ada, Okla.
Hicks, William Vernon, Michigan State University, East Lansing, Mich.
Hidy, Mrs. Elizabeth Willson, Box 287, Gila Bend, Ariz.
Hieronymus, A. N., Col. of Educ., State Univ. of Iowa, Iowa City, Iowa
Hieronymus, W. P., Wagner College, Staten Island, N.Y.
Higgins, Gordon H., Prin., Public School No. 6, Buffalo, N.Y.
Hilgard, Ernest R., Graduate Division, Stanford University, Stanford, Calif.
Hill, Alberta D., University of Connecticut, Storrs, Conn.
Hill, Edwin H., 2628 Cathedral of Learning, Univ. of Pittsburgh, Pittsburgh, Pa.
Hill, Elizabeth F., Bur. of Child Study, Chicago Public Schools, Chicago, Ill.
Hill, George E., Ohio University, Athens, Ohio
Hill, Guy H., Dir., H.S. Co-op., Mich. State Univ., East Lansing, Mich.
Hill, J. Levan, 124 South College Dr., Bowling Green, Ohio
Hill, Joseph K., State Univ. of N.Y. College of Medicine, Syracuse, N.Y.
Hill, Mrs. Margaret Ford, 32 South Patterson Ave., Santa Barbara, Calif.
Hill, William F., Box 41, Baylor University Station, Waco, Tex.
Hillestad, Mildred, 1000 University Ave., S.E., Minneapolis, Minn.
Hilliard, George H., Western Michigan College, Kalamazoo, Mich.
Hillier, Elizabeth C., Pennsylvania State University, University Park, Pa.
Himler, Leonard E., 1225 Fair Oaks Pkwy., Ann Arbor, Mich.
Himmele, Irvin H., Asst. Superintendent of Schools, Buffalo, N.Y.
Hinds, Lillian Ruth, Dir., Remed. Read., Bd. of Education, Shaker Heights, Ohio
Hines, Clarence, Superintendent of Schools, Eugene, Ore.
Hinrichs, Gerard, Sch. of Educ., St. Bonaventure Univ., St. Bonaventure, N.Y.
Hinton, Bobbie Ruth, Howard Payne College, Brownwood, Tex.
Hitchcock, William L., Col. of Educ., University of Georgia, Athens, Ga.
Hites, Christopher, 2201 Roseland Ave., Royal Oak, Mich.
Hixon, Lawrence, Dir., Stud. Tchg., Cornell University, Ithaca, N.Y.
Hobbie, Katherine E., State Teachers College, Oneonta, N.Y.
Hobson, Cloy S., Dir., Curriculum Lab., Univ. of Kansas, Lawrence, Kan.
Hockett, John A., Sch. of Educ., University of Calif., Los Angeles, Calif.
Hodge, Mrs. Rose M., Mississippi Vocational College, Itta Bena, Miss.
Hodges, James H., Principal, Kendall School, Tulsa, Okla.
Hodgkins, George W., 1832 Biltmore St., N.W., Washington, D.C.
Hodgson, Paul M., Head, Agr. Educ. Dept., University of Delaware, Newark, Del.
Hoech, Arthur A., Supt., Ritenour Consolidated School Dist., Overland, Mo.
Hoeft, Norman R., Adm. Asst., Board of Education, Springfield, Mo.
Hoffman, Charles L., Principal, East High School, Waterloo, Iowa
Hofstetter, George, 821 South Fifth St., West, Missoula, Mont.

Holden, Ruby, Dept. of Educ., Roosevelt University, Chicago, Ill.
Holdsworth, Willie, Div. of Ext., University of Texas, Austin, Tex.
Hollaway, Otto, Alabama Polytechnic Institute, Auburn, Ala.
Holliday, Jay N., Dist. Superintendent, North Ridge, Calif.
Hollingsworth, Henry T., Superintendent of Schools, Bloomfield, N.J.
Holloway, D. H., Principal, Westport High School, Kansas City, Mo.
Holloway, George L., 19462 Hatton St., Reseda, Calif.
Holmblade, Amy Jean, Home Econ. Bldg., Michigan State Univ., East Lansing, Mich.
Holmes, Chester W., Superintendent of Schools, Malden, Mass.
Holmes, Daniel L., Supervising Principal, North District, Braintree, Mass.
Holmes, Jack A., Sch. of Educ., University of California, Berkeley, Calif.
Holmes, Jay William, 350 Castlewood, Dayton, Ohio
Holmes, Keith D., East Carolina College, Greenville, N.C.
Holmgren, Marvin E., State Teachers College, St. Cloud, Minn.
Holmquist, Emily, 245 Melwood St., Pittsburgh, Pa.
Holmstedt, Raleigh W., President, Indiana State Tchrs. Col., Terre Haute, Ind.
Holroyd, Flora E., Kansas State Teachers College, Pittsburg, Kan.
Holstein, Louise V., 7130 South Union Ave., Chicago, Ill.
Holstein, Marion F., 7130 South Union Ave., Chicago, Ill.
Holston, M. J., 1128 Valley Dr., Borger, Tex.
Holt, Helen J., University of Toledo, Toledo, Ohio
Holterman, Mrs. Helen E., 124 Breese Terrace, Madison, Wis.
Holtz, H. Arnold, Macalester College, St. Paul, Minn.
Holwerda, Raymond, Prin., Holland Christian High School, Holland, Mich.
Homer, Francis R., 4800 Conshohocken Ave., Philadelphia, Pa.
Hong, Howard, Dept. of Philosophy, St. Olaf College, Northfield, Minn.
Hood, Carl, Michigan State Normal College, Ypsilanti, Mich.
Hood, Edwin Morris, 101 Old Mamaroneck Rd., White Plains, N.Y.
Hooper, George J., Sidney Lanier and Eisenhower Schools, Tulsa, Okla.
Hoover, Elmer B., Dept. of Educ., Elizabethtown College, Elizabethtown, Pa.
Hoppes, William C., Northern Mich. College of Education, Marquette, Mich.
Horn, Ernest, Prof. Emeritus of Educ., State Univ. of Iowa, Iowa City, Iowa
Horn, Thomas D., Dept. of Curric., University of Texas, Austin, Tex.
Hornback, Charles A., Prin., Sch. of Tchr. Educ., State College, Eau Claire, Wis.
Horsman, Ralph D., Superintendent, Mt. Lebanon Public Schools, Pittsburgh, Pa.
Horwich, Frances R., Essex House, 160 Central Park South, New York, N.Y.
Hosinski, Leona, 1221 North Brookfield, South Bend, Ind.
Hoskins, G. C., Southern Methodist University, Dallas, Tex.
Hosmer, Oscar H., Prin., Lab. School, New Mexico Western Col., Silver City, N. M.
Hostetter, Marie M., Library School, University of Illinois, Urbana, Ill.
Hottenstein, Gerald G., Supt., Montgomery County Schls., Norristown, Pa.
Houlahan, F. J., Catholic University of America, Washington, D.C.
Houle, Cyril O., Dept. of Educ., University of Chicago, Chicago, Ill.
House, Ralph W., State Teachers College, Kirksville, Mo.
Houston, James, Jr., Paterson State Teachers College, Paterson, N.J.
Hovell, Frank, Southern Texas Junior College, Houston, Tex.
Hovet, Kenneth O., University of Maryland, College Park, Md.
Hovland, C. W., Chm., Dept. of Philos., Oregon State College, Corvallis, Ore.
Howard, Alexander H., Jr., Cen. Wash. College of Educ., Ellensburg, Wash.
Howard, Daniel D., Dean, Pestalozzi-Froebel Teachers College, Chicago, Ill.
Howard, George, Chm., Dept. of Sch. Adm., Univ. of Alabama, University, Ala.
Howard, Glenn W., Queens College, Flushing, N.Y.
Howard, Homer, Philos. and Educ. Depts., Radford College, Radford, Va.
Howard, J. E., Principal, DeMun Elementary School, Clayton, Mo.
Howard, John A., Pres., Palos Verdes College, Rolling Hills, Calif.
Howd, M Curtis, Principal, Burris Lab. School, Muncie, Ind.
Howe, Elliot C., Elem. Trng. Sch., Brigham Young University, Provo, Utah
Howe, Henry W., Dept. of History and Pol. Sci., Alma College, Alma, Mich.
Howe, Joseph W., Superintendent of Schools, Burlington, N.J.

Howe, Walter A., Secy., Dept. of Educ., Cen. Union Conf. of S.D.A., Lincoln, Neb.
Hoyle, Dorothy, Dept. of Educ., Temple University, Philadelphia, Pa.
Hoyt, Carlyle G., Superintendent of Schools, Fairfield, Conn.
Hoyt, Cyril J., Bur. of Educ. Res., Univ. of Minnesota, Minneapolis, Minn.
Hoyt, Guy M., Assoc. Supt., Los Angeles City Schools, Los Angeles, Calif.
Hoyt, N. Deming, Dept. of Educ., Smith College, Northampton, Mass.
Hubbard, Frank W., Dir. of Research, National Educ. Assn., Washington, D.C.
Hubbard, Mary K., 2 Longfellow Dr., New Hartford, N.Y.
Hubbard, O. S., County Superintendent of Schools, San Jose, Calif.
Huber, Frederick, Dean of Men, Orange Coast College, Costa Mesa, Calif.
Hucksoll, William J., 3510 Woodlea Ave., Baltimore, Md.
Huddleston, Lonnie D., Dept. of Educ., University of Oklahoma, Norman, Okla.
Hudelson, Earl, Col. of Educ., West Virginia Univ., Morgantown, W.Va.
Huebner, Dwayne E., Dept. of Educ., Northern Illinois State College, DeKalb, Ill.
Huebner, Mildred H., Western Reserve University, Cleveland, Ohio
Huelsman, Charles B., Jr., 120 East Chestnut St., Oxford, Ohio
Hufford, G. N., Superintendent of Schools, Joliet, Ill.
Hufziger, Otto C., 290 Liberty St., Terrace 11, Pontiac, Mich.
Hughes, McDonald, Principal, Industrial High School, Tuscaloosa, Ala.
Hughes, Ray O., Deermont Hotel, St. Petersburg, Fla.
Hughes, Vergil H., Div. of Tchr. Educ., San Jose State College, San Jose, Calif.
Hughson, Arthur, 470 Ocean Ave., Brooklyn, N.Y.
Hullfish, H. Gordon, Sch. of Educ., Ohio State University, Columbus, Ohio
Hult, Esther, Iowa State Teachers College, Cedar Falls, Iowa
Hummel, Edward J., Deputy Supt. of Schools, Beverly Hills, Calif.
Hunscher, Helen A., Home Econ. Dept., Western Reserve Univ., Cleveland, Ohio
Hunt, Andrew W., Chairman, Dept. of Educ., McMurry College, Abilene, Tex.
Hunt, Herold C., Under Secy., Dept. of Health, Educ. and Welfare, Washington, D. C.
Hunt, Jacob T., University of North Carolina, Chapel Hill, N.C.
Hunt, Lyman C., Jr., Pennsylvania State University, University Park, Pa.
Hunt, William A., Dept. of Psych., Northwestern University, Evanston, Ill.
Hunter, Eugenia, Women's College, Univ. of North Carolina, Greensboro, N.C.
Hunter, James J., Jr., San Diego State College, San Diego, Calif.
Hunter, Lavinia, Western Kentucky State College, Bowling Green, Ky.
Hunter, Mrs. L. L., Curr. Cons., Wichita Pub. Schls., Wichita, Kan.
Hunter, Robert W., Southern University, Baton Rouge, La.
* Huntington, Albert H., 736 Fairview Ave., Webster Groves, Mo.
Huntington, Elizabeth A., 151 Vose Ave., South Orange, N.J.
Hupp, James L., West Virginia Wesleyan College, Buckhannon, W.Va.
Hurlburt, Allan S., State Dept. of Public Instruction, Raleigh, N.C.
Hurst, Theodore W., 14347 University Ave., Dolton, Ill.
Huss, Francis G., Dir., Lansdale Vocational School, Lansdale, Pa.
Husted, Inez M., Dir., Special Educ., Luzerne County, Wilkes-Barre, Pa.
Hutaff, Lucile W., Bowman Gray School of Medicine, Winston-Salem, N.C.
Hutchins, Clayton D., United States Office of Education, Washington, D.C.
Hutchins, Margaret, Head, Dept. of H.E., Cornell University, Ithaca, N.Y.
Hutchison, James M., 4231 West Fifty-ninth St., Los Angeles, Calif.
Hutson, P. W., University of Pittsburgh, Pittsburgh, Pa.
Hyde, Edith I., Phys. Educ. Dept., Univ. of California, Los Angeles, Calif.
Hyde, Eva Louise, Principal, Collegio Bennett, Rio de Janeiro, Brazil
Hyder, Gretchen, East Tennessee State College, Johnson City, Tenn.

Imhoff, Myrtle M., Long Beach State College, Long Beach, Calif.
Inabnit, Darrell James, 32 Sherman Terrace, Madison, Wis.
Ingebritson, Kasper I., Humboldt State College, Arcata, Calif.
Ingersoll, George S., Math. Dept., Mira Costa High Sch., Manhattan Beach, Calif.
Ingles, Edwin T., 1018 Hackberry St., Modesto, Calif.
Inlow, Gail M., Sch. of Educ., Northwestern University, Evanston, Ill.

Ireland, Dwight B., Superintendent of Schools, Birmingham, Mich.
Ireland, Everett W., Superintendent of Schools, Somerville, Mass.
Irene, Elizabeth, Sister, Dean, Sacred Heart Tchr. Trg. School, Groton, Mass.
Irish, Mrs. Betty H., Santa Barbara Col., Univ. of Calif., Santa Barbara, Calif.
Irving, J. Lee, Bluefield State College, Bluefield, W.Va.
Isaacs, Ann F., 409 Clinton Spring Ave., Cincinnati, Ohio
Isley, Thurston, William Jewell College, Liberty, Mo.
Ivins, George H., Dept. of Educ., Roosevelt University, Chicago, Ill.

Jackson, Frank M., Supt., Tom Green County Schools, San Angelo, Tex.
Jackson, Lowell M., Dir., Inf. and Educ. Sec., APO 74, c/o P.M., San Francisco, Calif.
Jackson, Stanley E., 415 You Street, N.W., Washington, D.C.
Jacob, Philip E., Dir., Summer School, Univ. of Penn., Philadelphia, Pa.
Jacobs, Ralph L., Dept. of Educ., Univ. of Cincinnati, Cincinnati, Ohio
Jacobs, Robert, U.S.A. Operations Mission to Ethiopia, c/o 806 Connecticut Ave., N.W., Washington 25, D.C.
Jacobson, Paul B., Dean, Sch. of Educ., University of Oregon, Eugene, Ore.
Jaeger, Alan Warren, 1425 Mar Vista Ave., Pasadena, Calif.
Jaeger, Herman F., Superintendent of Schools, Pasco, Wash.
James, Bro. Adelbert, F.S.C., Head, Educ. Dept., Manhattan Col., New York, N.Y.
James, Mrs. Bernice O., Central High School, Galveston, Tex.
James, Carl A., Superintendent of Schools, Concordia, Kan.
James, Newton Elder, 4611 Zane Ave., North, Minneapolis, Minn.
James, Preston A., Chm., Dept. of Geog., Syracuse University, Syracuse, N.Y.
James, Virginia White, University of Alabama, University, Ala.
James, W. Raymond, State Teachers College, Plattsburgh, N.Y.
Jamrich, John X., Dean, Doane College, Crete, Neb.
Jansen, William, Superintendent, New York City Schools, Brooklyn, N.Y.
Jarboe, Everett E., Dept. of Educ., North Texas State College, Denton, Tex.
Jarman, B. H., George Washington University, Washington, D.C.
Jelinek, James J., Sch. of Educ., Arizona State College, Tempe, Ariz.
Jemison, Margaret, Emory University, Emory, Ga.
Jenkins, Martin D., President, Morgan State College, Baltimore, Md.
Jenkins, T. C., Dir., Elem. Educ., Franklin College, Franklin, Ind.
Jensen, G. E., Grinnell College, Grinnell, Iowa
Jensen, Grant W., Principal, Shafter High School, Shafter, Calif.
Jensen, Harry T., San Jose State College, San Jose, Calif.
Jensen, Louis B., 12 Hamilton Place, Garden City, N.Y.
Jenson, Howard A., Superintendent of Schools, Litchfield, Minn.
Jenson, T. J., Superintendent of Schools, Shorewood, Wis.
Jessee, Mrs. Mabel C., Beattyville, Ky.
Jex, Frank B., Dept. of Educ. Psych., Univ. of Utah, Salt Lake City, Utah
Johnshoy, Howard G., 720 Shellbark Rd., Muncie, Ind.
Johnson, B. Lamar, Sch. of Educ., Univ. of California, Los Angeles, Calif.
Johnson, Carl E., 420 N. Elmhurst Ave., Mt. Prospect, Ill.
Johnson, Charles E., 2316 Colfax Ave., South, Minneapolis, Minn.
Johnson, Charles E., Sch. of Educ., Univ. of Kansas, Lawrence, Kan.
Johnson, Charles W., Teachers College, Univ. of Cincinnati, Cincinnati, Ohio
Johnson, DeWayne B., 740 Walker Ave., Ashland, Ore.
Johnson, Dorothy C., 3416 Wall Ave., Richmond, Calif.
Johnson, Douglas Andrew, 14568 Ashton Rd., Detroit, Mich.
Johnson, Eleanor M., American Education Publications, Middletown, Conn.
Johnson, Eric H., Illinois Curric. Program, Univ. of Illinois, Urbana, Ill.
Johnson, Evelyn Lawlah, Soc. Sci. Dept., North Carolina College, Durham, N.C.
Johnson, Gladys Viola, 3229 Fourth Ave., South, Great Falls, Mont.
Johnson, G. Orville, Sch. of Educ., Syracuse University, Syracuse, N.Y.
Johnson, Harry C., Duluth Branch, Univ. of Minnesota, Duluth, Minn.
Johnson, Harry O., Supt., Livonia Twp. Sch. Dist., 11411 Ingram, Livonia, Mich.
Johnson, J. B., Superintendent of Schools, Alton, Ill.
Johnson, Leslie W., Superintendent of Schools, Sheboygan, Wis.

Johnson, Loaz W., Dir. of Educ., Butte County Schools, Oroville, Calif.
Johnson, Lois V., Los Angeles State College, Los Angeles, Calif.
Johnson, Mrs. Marjorie S., Supv., Read. Clinic, Lab. Sch., Philadelphia, Pa.
Johnson, Mauritz, Jr., New York State College for Teachers, Albany, N.Y.
Johnson, Palmer O., Col. of Educ., Univ. of Minnesota, Minneapolis, Minn.
Johnson, Paul L., Pres., Jacksonville Jr. Col., Jacksonville, Fla.
Johnson, Ray W., Supt., Riverside County Schools, Riverside, Calif.
Johnson, Robert K., 913 Nelbar St., Middletown, Ohio
Johnson, Robert L., Curric. Coord., Public Schools, New Richmond, Wis.
Johnson, Roberta A. E., Dept. of Educ., Univ. of Rochester, Rochester, N.Y.
*Johnson, Roy Ivan, 1725 N.W. Sixth Ave., Gainesville, Fla.
Johnson, Theodore D., 8914 Lamon, Skokie, Ill.
Johnson, Theodore E., University of Buffalo, Buffalo, N.Y.
Johnson, Walter F., Michigan State University, East Lansing, Mich.
Johnston, Aaron Montgomery, University of Tennessee, Knoxville, Tenn.
Johnston, Edgar G., Wayne University, Detroit, Mich.
Johnston, Lillian B., 184 Coloma St., Placerville, Calif.
Johnston, Marion R., Long Beach State College, Long Beach, Calif.
Johnston, Mildred R., State Teachers College, Jacksonville, Ala.
Johnston, Ruth V., 125 Owre Hall, Univ. of Minnesota, Minneapolis, Minn.
Johnstone, Oliver P., Long Beach State College, Long Beach, Calif.
Joll, Leonard W., State Department of Education, Hartford, Conn.
Jonas, Richard O., University of Houston, Houston, Tex.
Jonas, Russell E., President, Black Hills Teachers College, Spearfish, S.D.
Jones, A. Quinn, 1013 N.W. Seventh Ave., Gainesville, Fla.
Jones, Aaron E., President, Carbon College, Price, Utah
Jones, Alfred, 522 West End Ave., New York, N.Y.
* Jones, Arthur J., University of Pennsylvania, Philadelphia, Pa.
Jones, C. E., Superintendent, Public Schools, Beloit, Wis.
Jones, C. H., Jr., Superintendent of Schools, Nevada, Mo.
Jones, Dilys M., 30 Waller St., Wilkes-Barre, Pa.
Jones, Dixie M., Union University, Jackson, Tenn.
Jones, Elvet Glyn, University of Minnesota, Minneapolis, Minn.
* Jones, Mrs. E. P., Bethune-Cookman College, Daytona Beach, Fla.
Jones, Harold E., Dir., Inst. of Child Wel., Univ. of Calif., Berkeley, Calif.
Jones, Howard R., School of Educ., Univ. of Michigan, Ann Arbor, Mich.
Jones, James Joseph, Sch. of Educ., Univ. of Virginia, Charlottesville, Va.
Jones, Kenneth G., Oswego State Teachers College, Oswego, N.Y.
Jones, Mrs. Lillian W., Box 172, Olmito, Tex.
Jones, Lloyd M., Pennsylvania State University, University Park, Pa.
Jones, Lyman L., Southeastern College, Hammond, La.
Jones, Richard N., Pennsylvania State University, University Park, Pa.
Jones, Vernon, Clark University, Worcester, Mass.
Jones, Vyron Lloyd, Principal, Fontanet High School, Fontanet, Ind.
Jones, Wendell P., Maryland State Teachers College, Bowie, Md.
Jones, W. Mitchell, Dean of Men, West Texas State College, Canyon, Tex.
Jordan, A. B., Central High School, St. Louis, Mo.
Jordan, Edward Thomas, Spec. Educ. Clinic, State Tchrs. Col., Terre Haute, Ind.
Jordan, Floyd, Co-ord. of Atlanta Area Tchr. Educ. Serv., Emory Univ., Ga.
Jordan, Howard, Jr., Dean, Sch. of Educ., So. Car. State Col., Orangeburg, S.C.
Jordan, Lawrence V., West Virginia State College, Institute, W.Va.
Judenfriend, Harold, 23 Pleasant St., Colchester, Conn.
Judge, Virgil H., Superintendent of Schools, Matoon, Ill.
Julstrom, Eva, 7647 Colfax Ave., Chicago, Ill.
Jung, Christian, Sch. of Educ., Indiana University, Bloomington, Ind.
Junge, Charlotte W., College of Educ., Wayne University, Detroit, Mich.
Junge, Ruby M., Michigan State College, East Lansing, Mich.
Juola, Arvo E., Sch. of Educ., University of Wisconsin, Madison, Mis.
Jurgens, Ernst F., Wisconsin State College, River Falls, Wis.
Justman, Joseph, Bur. of Research, Board of Educ., Brooklyn, N.Y.

Kaar, Mrs. Galeta M., Principal, Peabody Elementary School, Chicago, Ill.

Kaback, Goldie Ruth, Sch. of Educ., City College, New York, N.Y.
Kaemmerlen, John T., Superintendent of Schools, Hudson, N.Y.
Kalin, E. S., Dir., Isidore Newman School, New Orleans, La.
Kallen, H. M., 66 West Twelfth St., New York, N.Y.
Kalupa, Mrs. Marie, 2527 South Thirteenth St., Milwaukee, Wis.
Kandyba, Bernard S., 2536 East 83rd St., Chicago, Ill.
Kant, Louise E., Junear, Wis.
Kaplan, Louis, Univ. Col., University of Southern Calif., Los Angeles, Calif.
Karason, Halldor C., Western Washington College of Education, Bellingham, Wash.
Kardatzke, Carl, Anderson College, Anderson, Ind.
Karrel, Oscar, Boys' Dept., Lord and Taylor, New York, N.Y.
Kasdon, Lawrence, Department of Public Instruction, Honolulu, Hawaii.
Kata, Joseph J., Principal, Red Bank Valley High School, New Bethlehem, Pa.
Katz, Joseph, Faculty of Education, Winnipeg, Manitoba, Canada
Katz, Melvyn Myron, 2094 Smith Street, Merrick, Long Island, N.Y.
Katzenelbogen, Solomon, Sch. of Med., George Washington Univ., Washington, D. C.
Kauffman, Merle M., Dir. of Curric., Public Schools, Peoria, Ill.
Kauth, William M., Dept. of Math., Fordson High School, Dearborn, Mich.
Kavanaugh, J. Keith, 157 Birch St., Park Forest, Ill.
Kawin, Ethel, Plaisance Hotel, Chicago, Ill.
Kearney, Leo I., Fordham University, New York, N.Y.
Kearney, Nolan C., Asst. Supt., Res. & Curric., Dept. of Educa., St. Paul, Minn.
Keefauver, Lloyd C., Dist. Supt., Gettysburg Jt. Sch. System, Gettysburg, Pa.
Keenan, Robert C., Dist. Superintendent, Elem. Schools, Chicago, Ill.
Keene, Charles J., Jr., Tennessee Polytechnic Institute, Cookeville, Tenn.
Keener, Orrin L., Box 1068, Berea College, Berea, Ky.
* Keller, Franklin J., Principal, Metropolitan Voc. High Sch., New York, N.Y.
Keller, Fred L., Tarkio College, Tarkio, Mo.
Keller, Raymond E., 1503 Rochester Ave., Iowa City, Iowa
Keller, Robert J., Educ. Research Office, Univ. of Minn., Minneapolis, Minn.
Keller, William E., Supv. Prin., Williamsville, N.Y.
Kelley, Beaman, Dir. of Inst., Harnett County Schools, Lillington, N.C.
Kelley, Claude, North Texas State College, Denton, Tex.
Kelley, Janet A., Dept. of Educ., City College, New York, N.Y.
Kelley, Victor H., University of Arizona, Tucson, Ariz.
Kelley, William F., Dean, Col. of Arts and Sci., Creighton Univ., Omaha, Neb.
Kellogg, E. G., Supt. of Schools, West Allis, Wis.
Kelly, Edward J., Colorado State College of Education, Greeley, Colo.
Kelly, Mrs. Erma P., Principal, Capital Hill School, Little Rock, Ark.
Kelsey, Roger R., Registrar, Kansas State Teachers College, Emporia, Kan.
Kemp, Edward L., Sch. of Educ., New York University, New York, N.Y.
Kennard, Andrew J., Texas State University, Houston, Tex.
Kent, Walter, Principal, Mentone School, Mentone, Ind.
Kephart, John E., Wheaton College, Wheaton, Ill.
Keppel, Francis, Dean, Grad. Sch. of Educ., Harvard University, Cambridge, Mass.
Kerbow, A. L., University of Houston, Houston, Tex.
Kerr, Everett F., Superintendent of Elem. Schools, Blue Island, Ill.
Kescharmrus, Boonyun, Mack Hall, Ohio State University, Columbus, Ohio
Kesselring, Ralph, Principal, Anglo-Chinese School, Ipoh, Malaya
Keston, Morton J., Psych. Dept., Univ. of New Mexico, Albuquerque, N. M.
Kettelkamp, Gilbert C., College of Educ., Univ. of Illinois, Urbana, Ill.
Keucher, Rev. Werner G., Pres., Baptist Missionary Train. Sch., Chicago, Ill.
Kiah, Calvin L., Chm., Dept. of Educ., Savannah State College, Savannah, Ga.
Kiely, Margaret, Dean, Queens College, Flushing, N.Y.
Kies, Michael S., Supt. of County Schools, Milwaukee, Wis.
Kilbourn, Robert W., Central Michigan College of Education, Mt. Pleasant, Mich.
* Kilpatrick, William H., Teachers College, Columbia University, New York, N.Y.
Kilzer, L. R., Col. of Educ., University of Wyoming, Laramie, Wyo.

Kim, Ok Soon, International House, University of Chicago, Chicago, Ill.
Kincer, Charles L., Supv., Rural Sch. Improv. Proj., Berea Col., Pine Mountain, Ky.
Kindred, Leslie W., Temple University, Philadelphia, Pa.
King, John R., East Bakersfield High School, Bakersfield, Calif.
King, Kenneth E., 1136 South Swall Dr., Los Angeles, Calif.
King, Kent H., Nebraska State Teachers College, Peru, Neb.
King, Lloyd W., Exec. Secy., Amer. Textbook Publ. Inst., New York, N.Y.
King, Thomas C., Dean, Col. of Educ. & Nurs., Univ. of Vermont, Burlington, Vt.
Kinget, G. Marion, Michigan State University, East Lansing, Mich.
Kingham, Harry W., Prin., Senior High School and Jr. College, Burlington, Iowa
Kingston, Albert James, Jr., A. & M. College of Texas, College Station, Tex.
Kinsella, John J., Sch. of Educ., New York University, New York, N.Y.
Kinsellar, Frances M., 28 Emerson Rd., Watertown, Mass.
Kinsman, Kephas Albert, Long Beach State Col., Long Beach, Calif.
Kinzer, John R., Dept. of Psych., Ohio State University, Columbus, Ohio
Kirch, Mrs. Minnie B., 2553 Ocean Parkway, Brooklyn, N.Y.
Kirk, Samuel A., Col. of Educ., University of Illinois, Urbana, Ill.
Kirkland, J. Bryant, Sch. of Educ., North Carolina State College, Raleigh, N.C.
Kirkpatrick, J. E., University of Tulsa, Tulsa, Okla.
Kirkpatrick, Lawrence A., New Mexico Highlands University, Las Vegas, N.M.
Klausmeier, Herbert J., School of Educ., Univ. of Wis., Madison, Wis.
Kleinpell, E. H., President, Wisconsin State College, River Falls, Wis.
Klopfer, Leopold E., Harvard University, Cambridge, Mass.
Knapp, M. L., Superintendent of Schools, Michigan City, Ind.
Kneller, George F., Sch. of Educ., University of California, Los Angeles, Calif.
Knight, Reginald R., Prin., Roosevelt Junior High School, Bellflower, Calif.
Knoblauch, A. L., Moorhead State Teachers College, Moorhead, Minn.
Knower, Franklin H., Ohio State University, Columbus, Ohio
Knox, J. H., Superintendent, City Schools, Salisbury, N.C.
Knox, William F., Central Missouri State Teachers College, Warrensburg, Mo.
Knuti, Leo L., Montana State College, Bozeman, Mont.
Koch, H. C., University of Michigan, Ann Arbor, Mich.
Koch, Helen L., 1374 East Fifty-seventh Street, Chicago, Ill.
Koch, Wayne S., University of New Hampshire, Durham, N.H.
Koehler, Susanne M., Dept. of Educ., Kent State University, Kent, Ohio
Koehring, Dorothy, Iowa State Teachers College, Cedar Falls, Iowa
Koerber, Walter F., Jarvis School for Boys, Toronto, Ontario, Canada
Kohs, Samuel C., 620 Plymouth Way, Burlingame, Calif.
Kolesnik, Walter B., Dept. of Educ., University of Wisconsin, Madison, Wis.
Koos, Leonard V., Dept. of Educ., University of Chicago, Chicago, Ill.
Kopel, David, Chicago Teachers College, Chicago, Ill.
Korb, O. J., Superintendent of Schools, East Cleveland, Ohio
Korntheuer, G. A., Concordia High School, Fort Wayne, Ind.
Kough, Blachford, 1003 North Leavitt Street, Chicago, Ill.
Kov, Arnold C., Principal, Jackson School, Waukegan, Ill.
Kozak, Andrew V., Concord College, Athens, W.Va.
Kozlowski, Leokadya J., 7911 North McNulty Ave., Canoga Park, Calif.
Kraeft, Walter O., Concordia Teachers College, River Forest, Ill.
Kraft, Milton Edward, Earlham College, Richmond, Ind.
Kraus, Howard F., Principal, Louis Barrett School, Belmont, Calif.
Krautle, Hilda E., 3599 Werk Road, Cincinnati, Ohio
Kravetz, Nathan, 438 North Curson Ave., Los Angeles, Calif.
Kravetz, Sol., 1357½ South Cloverdale Ave., Los Angeles, Calif.
Kreitlow, Burton W., Dept. of Educ., Univ. of Wisconsin, Madison, Wis.
Kress, Roy A., Jr., Shady Brook Schls., Richardson, Tex.
Kriebel, John A., 106 West Highland Ave., Langhorne, Pa.
Kroenke, Richard G., Dir., Elem. Educ., Valparaiso University, Valparaiso, Ind.
Krueger, Lawrence, Supt., Pittsfield Sch. Dist. No. 9, Ann Arbor, Mich.
Krug, Edward, Sch. of Educ., University of Wisconsin, Madison, Wis.
Krug, Helen Esther, Defiance College, Defiance, Ohio

Krumboltz, Mrs. Helen B., University of Minnesota, Minneapolis, Minn.
Kruse, Samuel Andrew, State Teachers College, Cape Girardeau, Mo.
Kubik, Edmund J., Principal, Owen School, Chicago, Ill.
Kuehner, Kenneth G., Coker College, Hartsville, S.C.
Kuhnen, Mrs. Mildred, 2106 Park Ave., Chico, Calif.
Kullman, N. E., Jr., State University Teachers College, Plattsburgh, N.Y.
Kulp, A. M., Deceased.
Kulp, Claude L., Rand Hall, Cornell University, Ithaca, N.Y.
Kurtz, Alton R., Head, Dept. of Educ., Defiance College, Defiance, Ohio
Kurtz, John J., Inst. for Child Study, Univ. of Maryland, College Park, Md.
Kutz, Frederick B., Principal, Newark High School, Newark, Del.
Kutz, R. M., Hanover College, Hanover, Ind.
Kvaraceus, W. C., Sch. of Educ., Boston University, Boston, Mass.
Kyle, C. J. M., Div. Supt. of Schools, Orange County, Orange, Va.
Kyte, George C., Sch. of Educ., University of California, Berkeley, Calif.

LaBrant, Lou, University of Kansas City, Kansas City, Mo.
Lackey, Guy A., Sch. of Educ., Oklahoma A. & M. College, Stillwater, Okla.
Lafferty, Charles W., Superintendent of Schools, Atchison, Kan.
Lafferty, H. M., East Texas State Teachers College, Commerce, Tex.
LaForce, Charles L., Principal, Pope Elem. School, Chicago, Ill.
Laidlaw, John Laidlaw Brothers, River Forest, Ill.
Laird, Byron F., Indiana University, Jeffersonville, Ind.
Laird, Dorothy S., Col. of Educ., University of Florida, Gainesville, Fla.
Lake, Barbara, Sch. of Educ., Fordham University, New York, N.Y.
Lambert, Hazel M., Arkansas Teachers College, Conway, Ark.
Lambert, Pierre D., Sch. of Educ., Boston College, Chestnut Hill, Mass.
Lampkin, Richard H., State University Col. for Teachers, Buffalo, N.Y.
Lancaster, Christine, Keene Teachers College, Keene, N.H.
Landskov, N. L., Mississippi Southern College, Hattiesburg, Miss.
Lane, Elizabeth Miller, 4390 Hyland Ave., Dayton, Ohio
Lane, Frank T., State Teachers College, Brockport, N.Y.
Lane, John J., Principal, Coolidge Junior High School, Natick, Mass.
Langbell, Delmar P., Superintendent of Schools, Kalispell, Mont.
Lange, Phil C., Teachers College, Columbia Univ., New York, N.Y.
Langenbach, Louise, Government Center, c/o Co. Supt. of Schls., Placerville, Calif.
Langeveld, M. J., Dir., Educ. Inst., State's University, Utrecht, Holland
Langford, James A., California State Polytechnic Col., San Luis Obispo, Calif.
Langston, R. G., Los Angeles State College, Los Angeles, Calif.
Langwith, J. E., Superintendent of Schools, Terrell, Tex.
Lanier, Vincent, University of Southern California, Los Angeles, Calif.
Lanmon, J. M., Box 41, Clinton, Miss.
Lann, Frank R., 1245 Seminary Ave., Oakland, Calif.
Lant, Kenneth A., Principal, Jericho School, Jericho, N.Y.
Lantz, Donald L., 1541 Timberlake Rd., St. Paul, Minn.
Lanz, Anna D., Prin., Burbank Elem. School, Chicago, Ill.
Lapham, P. C., Deceased.
LaPoe, James L., Sch. of Educ., Rutgers University, New Brunswick, N.J.
Laramy, William J., Principal, Haverford Jr. High School, Havertown, Pa.
Larsen, Arthur Hoff, Illinois State Normal University, Normal, Ill.
Larson, Clint, Delta, Utah
Larson, Eleanore E., 602 East White St., Champaign, Ill.
Larson, Ira E., Principal, Osage High School, Osage, Iowa
Larson, Irene M., Board of Education Office, Green Bay, Wis.
Larson, L. C., Dir., Audio-visual Center, Indiana University, Bloomington, Ind.
Larson, R. H., Dir. of Indian Educ., State Dept. of Educ., St. Paul, Minn.
Larson, Rolf W., Sch. of Educ., University of Connecticut, Storrs, Conn.
Lass, Abraham H., Principal, New Utrecht High School, Brooklyn, N.Y.
Lassanske, Paul A., 35 W. 26th St., Bayonne, N.J.
Laub, Norman A., Prin., Junior and Senior High School, Northampton, Pa.
Lauby, Cecilia J., Illinois State Normal University, Normal, Ill.

Lauderbach, J. C., Superintendent of Schools, Chula Vista, Calif.
Laughlin, Butler, 7401 Bennett Ave., Chicago, Ill.
Laughlin, Hugh D., Ohio State University, Columbus, Ohio
Laughlin, Sam M., Head, Dept. of Elem. Educ., Univ. of Utah, Salt Lake City, Utah
Lauria, Joseph L., 13601 Sherman Way, Van Nuys, Calif.
Laurier, Blaise V., 1145 ouest, rue Saint-Viateur, Montreal, Quebec
Lavell, Robert J., Prin., Washington Junior High School, Cincinnati, Ohio
Law, Reuben D., Church College of Hawaii, Laie, Oahu, Hawaii
Lawhead, Victor B., Ball State Teachers College, Muncie, Ind.
Lawrence, Clayton G., Dir., Tchr. Educ., Marion College, Marion, Ind.
Lawrence, Raymond W., 614 East Wooster St., Bowling Green, Ohio
Lawrence, R. J., Supt., Bullock County Bd. of Educ., Union Springs, Ala.
Lawrence, Richard E., Assoc. Secy., A.A.C.T.E., 11 Elm St., Oneonta, N.Y.
Lawson, Burtis Carl, Dept. of Educ., Purdue University, Lafayette, Ind.
Lazar, May, Bur. of Research, Board of Educ., Brooklyn, N.Y.
Leach, Kent W., Sch. of Educ., University of Michigan, Ann Arbor, Mich.
Leach, Marian Edith, 744 Albemarle St., El Cerrito, Calif.
Leaf, Curtis T., University of Dubuque, Dubuque, Iowa
Leahy, Dorothy M., Dept. of H.E., Univ. of California, Los Angeles, Calif.
Lean, Arthur E., Sch. of Educ., University of Michigan, Ann Arbor, Mich.
Lear, Milton John, Prin., Children's Corner, Inc., Los Angeles, Calif.
Leavell, Ullin W., Dept. of Educ., University of Virginia, Charlottesville, Va.
Leavitt, Howard B., Northern Illinois State Tchrs. College, DeKalb, Ill.
Leavitt, Jerome, Portland State College, Portland, Ore.
Lee, Charles A., Washington University, St. Louis, Mo.
Lee, Floyd, Principal, Wheeler Elementary School, Oklahoma City, Okla.
Lee, Harold Fletcher, Dept. of Educ., Lincoln Univ., Jefferson City, Mo.
Lee, Howard D., Principal, Atwater School, Shorewood, Wis.
Lee, John J., Dean, Col. of Educ., Wayne University, Detroit, Mich.
Leeds, Don S., 612 Argyle Rd., Brooklyn, N. Y.
Leese, Joseph, State College for Teachers, Albany, N.Y.
Lefever, D. W., University of Southern California, Los Angeles, Calif.
Lefkowitz, Abraham, Prin., Samuel J. Tilden High School, Brooklyn, N.Y.
Leggett, Stanton, 221 West 57th St., New York, N. Y.
Lehman, Harvey C., Ohio University, Athens, Ohio
Lehmann, Charles F., Sch. of Educ., University of Michigan, Ann Arbor, Mich.
Lehmann, Irvin J., Sch. of Educ., University of Wisconsin, Madison, Wis.
Leib, Joseph A., 2386 Knapp Dr., Rahway, N. J.
Leichtweis, Charles F., University of Detroit, Detroit, Mich.
Leiman, Harold I., Prin., Hebrew Inst. of Long Island, Far Rockaway, N.Y.
Leister, Leroy L., Willimantic State Teachers College, Willimantic, Conn.
Lenaghan, Cletus A., Dir. of Educ., Conn. School for Boys, Meriden, Conn.
Lennon, Lawrence J., Head, Dept. of Educ., Univ. of Scranton, Scranton, Pa.
Leonard, Sally, Southeastern State College, Durant, Okla.
Lerner, Joseph S., Dir. of Trng., Arizona Children's Colony, Coolidge, Ariz.
Lessenberry, D. D., University of Pittsburgh, Pittsburgh, Pa.
Letson, J. W., Superintendent of Schools, Bessemer, Ala.
Letton, Mildred C., Lab. School, University of Chicago, Chicago, Ill.
Levin, Edward S., 125 College Place, Syracuse, N. Y.
Levine, M., Principal, Public School 111, Long Island City, New York, N.Y.
Levit, Martin, University of Kansas City, Kansas City, Mo.
Levy, Carrie B., 1369 East Hyde Park Blvd., Chicago, Ill.
Levy, Sidney, 1205 Avenue R, Brooklyn, N. Y.
Lewis, Carleton Kenneth, Box 443, Route 1, Annandale, Va.
Lewis, Dora S., Chm., Home Econ. Dept., Hunter College, New York, N. Y.
Lewis, Dwight Paul, General Elem. Consultant, County Schools, Riverside, Calif.
Lewis, Elizabeth V., Dept. of Educ., Huntingdon College, Montgomery, Ala.
Lewis, Gertrude M., U.S. Office of Education, Washington, D. C.
Lewis, Maurice S., 325 East 15th St., Tempe, Ariz.
Lewis, Mrs. M. E., Head, Dept. of Educ., Mary Allen College, Crockett, Tex.

Lewis, Philip, Chm., Dept. of Educ., Chicago Tchrs. College, Chicago, Ill.
Lichtenberger, J. F., Principal, Wenonah School, Minneapolis, Minn.
Liddle, Gordon P., Consult., Quincy Youth Develop. Commission, Quincy, Ill.
Lieberman, Myron, Dept. of Educ., University of Oklahoma, Norman, Okla.
Lifton, Eli, Principal Public School 2, Brooklyn, N.Y.
Liggitt, Earle O., District Superintendent, Public Schools, Munhall, Pa.
* Lincoln, Edward A., Thompson Street, Halifax, Mass.
Lindberg, Lucile, Sch. of Educ., Queens College, Flushing, N. Y.
Lindemann, Erich, Psychiatrist-in-Chief, Mass. General Hospital, Boston, Mass.
Lindgren, Henry Clay, San Francisco State College, San Francisco, Calif.
Lindvall, C. Mauritz, Sch. of Educ., University of Pittsburgh, Pittsburgh, Pa.
Lino, Frank D., Principal, Volta School, Chicago, Ill.
Linthicum, J. B., Dir. of Instr., Albuquerque Public Schls., Albuquerque, N.M.
Lippincott, Janet L., Dept. of Educ., University of Chicago, Chicago, Ill.
Lipsky, Celia, Asst. Prin., John Ericsson Junior High School, Brooklyn, N.Y.
Little, Mrs. Evelyn Steel, Mills College, Oakland, Calif.
Little, Evert T., c/o American Embassy, Addis Aboba, Ethopia, Africa
Little, Lawrence C., Sch. of Educ., Univ. of Pittsburgh, Pittsburgh, Pa.
Littlefield, Lucille J., State Teachers College, Indiana, Pa.
Littlepage, H. S., Superintendent of Schools, Carlinville, Ill.
Litzky, Leo, West Side High School, Newark, N.Y.
Livingood, F. G., Dept. of Educ., Washington College, Chestertown, Md.
Livingston, Thomas B., Box 4060, Texas Tech. College, Lubbock, Tex.
Lloyd - Jones, Esther, 525 West 120th St., New York, N. Y.
Lobaugh, Dean, Asst. Superintendent of Schools, Eugene, Ore.
Lodeski, Frank J., Principal, Mulligan Elem. School, Chicago, Ill.
Lodge, Helen M., Memorial University of Newfoundland, St. John's, Newfoundland
Loeffler, Roland, Modesto High School, Modesto, Calif.
Loess, Henry B., Chm., Dept. of Psych., Lake Forest College, Lake Forest, Ill.
Loew, C. C., Superintendent of Schools, Urbana, Ill.
Lofton, Mrs. Margaret Lawrence, 923 Maple Ave., Norfolk, Va.
Logan, Jack M., Superintendent of Schools, Waterloo, Iowa
Logsdon, J. D., Principal, Shorewood High School, Shorewood, Wis.
Lohmann, Victor Louis, Dir., Psycho-Educ. Clinic, State Tchrs. Col., St. Cloud, Minn.
Lola, Justita, Labay Normal School, Legaspi, Albay, Philippines
Lomax, Paul S., Ch., Dept. of Bus. Educ., New York Univ., New York, N.Y.
London, Jack, Sch. of Educ., University of California, Berkeley, Calif.
Long, Charles M., Pennsylvania State University, University Park, Pa.
Long, Isabelle, 4343 Harriet Ave. South, Minneapolis, Minn.
Longbotham, G. Thomas, 120 South Mill St., Merrill, Wis.
Longstreet, R. J., Dept. of Educ., Stetson Univ., De Land, Fla.
Lonsdale, Mrs. Maxine deLappe, 1405 Campbell Lane, Sacramento, Calif.
Lonsdale, Richard C., Sch. of Educ., Syracuse University, Syracuse, N.Y.
Loomis, Arthur K., Educ. Adv., Hq. FEC, APO 500, San Francisco, Calif.
Looney, William F., Pres., Boston Teachers College, Boston, Mass.
Loop, Alfred B., 2619 Franklin St., Bellingham, Wash.
Loree, M. Ray, Louisiana State University, Baton Rouge, La.
Lorenz, Donald, Concordia College, Portland, Ore.
Lorge, Irving, Teachers College, Columbia University, New York, N.Y.
Lorusso, Rocco E., 2386 Knapp Dr., Rahway, N.J.
Loso, Dorine, Col. of Med., Pub. Health Nurs., State Univ. of N. Y., Syracuse, N. Y.
Loughrea, Mildred, Asst. Dir., Elem. Educ., City Schools, St. Paul, Minn.
Louttit, C. M., Chm., Dept. of Psych., Wayne University, Detroit, Mich.
Lovelass, Harry D., Illinois State Normal University, Normal, Ill.
Low, Camilla M., Dept. of Educ., University of Wisconsin, Madison, Wis.
Lowe, Alberta, College of Educ., University of Tennessee, Knoxville, Tenn.
Lowe, Mrs. Herman, Western Kentucky State College, Bowling Green, Ky.
Lowe, R. N., Sch. of Educ., University of Oregon, Eugene, Ore.

Lowes, Ruth, Prof. of Educ., West Texas State Col., Canyon, Tex.
Lowry, V. A., President, General Beadle State Tchrs. College, Madison, S.D.
Lowther, William L., Prin., Livingston High School, Livingston, N. J.
Lubell, Richard M., Principal, Public School 92, Brooklyn, N.Y.
Lucas, Rev. Ernest A. J., St. Joseph's College, Collegeville, Ind.
Lucas, John J., 300 East 159th Street, New York, N.Y.
Lucash, Benjamin, 1367 Magee Avenue, Philadelphia, Penn.
Lucio, William H., Sch. of Educ., Univ. of California, Los Angeles, Calif.
Luckey, Bertha M., Psychologist, Board of Education, Cleveland, Ohio
Ludeman, LeRoy, Principal, Central High School, Aberdeen, S.D.
Ludes, Fr. Titus H., O.F.M., Quincy College, Quincy, Ill.
Ludington, John R., U.S. Office of Education, Washington, D.C.
Luecke, Mrs. Carl L., 411 Sergeant Ave., Joplin, Mo.
Luke, Brother, Institute Pedagogique St. Georges, Laval-Rapids, Que.
Luker, Arno H., Colorado State College of Education, Greeley, Colo.
Lund, S. E. Torsten, Haviland Hall, Univ. of Calif., Berkeley, Calif.
Lunt, Robert, Supt., School Union Ten, Scarborough, Me.
Lurton, Sallie E., Headmistress, Holton-Arms Schools, Washington, D.C.
Luvaas, Clarence B., Principal, Hayes Elementary School, Cedar Rapids, Iowa
Lyman, Howard B., Dept. of Psych., Univ. of Cincinnati, Cincinnati, Ohio
Lynch, James M., Superintendent of Schools, New Brunswick, N.J.
Lynch, Katharine D., Bur. for Child. with Ret. Ment. Develop., New York, N.Y.
Lynch, Mary Elizabeth, State Tchrs. Col. of Boston, Boston, Mass.
Lyons, John H., Dir., Guid. and Audio-Vis. Aids, Pub. Schls., Thompsonville,
   Conn.

Macbeth, Ruby, 69 Cannon St., Charleston, S.C.
MacDonald, Nellie V., 2770 Yonge St., Toronto, Ontario, Canada
MacFee, Mrs. Winifred C., Western Mich. College, Kalamazoo, Mich.
Mack, Esther, State College of Washington, Pullman, Wash.
MacKay, James L., 2205 West Mistletoe St., San Antonio, Tex.
MacKay, William R., 4067 Wesley Way, El Sobrante, Calif.
Mackenzie, Donald M., Dean, Blackburn College, Carlinville, Ill.
MacKenzie, Elbridge G., Anderson College, Anderson, Ind.
Mackenzie, Gordon N., Teachers College, Columbia Univ., New York, N.Y.
Mackintosh, Helen K., U.S. Office of Education, Washington, D.C.
Macklin, A. G., Dir., Div. of Basic Educ., Virginia State Col., Petersburg, Va.
MacLatchy, Josephine H., Bur. of Educ. Res., Ohio State Univ., Columbus, Ohio
MacLean, Malcolm S., Sch. of Educ., Univ. of Calif., Los Angeles, Calif.
Maddox, Clifford R., 15816 Marshfield Ave., Harvey, Ill.
Madison, Thurber H., Sch. of Music, Indiana University, Bloomington, Ind.
Madore, Normand William, West Texas State College, Canyon, Tex.
Magalona, Concepcion, 3811 O'Hara St., Pittsburgh, Pa.
Magdalen Marie, Sister, Dept. of Educ., Siena Heights College, Adrian, Mich.
Magoon, Thomas M., 2337 Doswell Ave., St. Paul, Minn.
Mahaffey, Clarence H., 4953 Edgerton Ave., Encino, Calif.
Mahler, Clarence A., Dept. of Psych., Oregon State College, Corvallis, Ore.
Mahoney, Eva, Supv., Read. Clinic, Georgetown University, Washington, D.C.
Mahoney, John J., Dir., Civic Educ. Center, Tufts College, Medford, Mass.
Mailey, James H., Sch. of Educ., Southern Methodist University, Dallas, Tex.
Major, C. L., Denison University, Granville, Ohio
Malan, Russell, Superintendent of Schools, Harrisburg, Ill.
Malaney, Jon Francis, 412½ Third St. South, Virginia, Minn.
Maline, Julian L., West Baden College, West Baden Springs, Ind.
Mallory, Berenice, U.S. Office of Education, Washington, D.C.
Maloney, Marguerite L., Asst. Dir. of Elem. Educ., City Schls., St. Paul, Minn.
Maloof, Mitchell, P.O. Box 22, Roslindale, Mass.
Malter, Morton S., Portland State Ext. Center, Portland, Ore.
Maney, Mrs. Ethel S., 121 Montgomery Ave., Bala-Cynwyd, Pa.
Mang, Brother William, Via Aurelia Antica 19, Rome, Italy
Mann, J. P., Supt. of Schools, Appleton, Wis.

Mann, V. S., Box 266, State College, Miss.
Manolakes, George, Sch. of Educ., New York University, New York, N. Y.
Mansour, Roshdy Fam, Fayoum, Egypt
Mantell, Herman P., 154 Nassau Street, New York, N.Y.
Manuel, Herschel T., University of Texas, Austin, Tex.
Manwiller, Lloyd V., South Dakota State College, Brookings, S. D.
Marc-Aurele, Paul, 162 Marois Blvd., Laval-des-Rapides, Montreal, Quebec, Canada
Margolis, Herman R., Principal, Goodrich Elem. School, Chicago, Ill.
Maria Catherine, Sister, Mount St. Vincent College, Halifax, Nova Scotia
Marinaccio, Anthony, Superintendent of Schools, Kankakee, Ill.
Markarian, Robert E., Springfield College, Springfield, Mass.
Markey, Ruth, 6038 Canal Blvd., New Orleans, La.
Markle, David H., Dir., Evening Div., Ohio Northern University, Ada, Ohio
Marks, Sallie B., 3133 Connecticut Ave., Washington, D.C.
Marksberry, Mary Lee, Blairstown, Mo.
Marquis, Norwood, School of Educ., Miami University, Oxford, Ohio
Marrinan, Edward L., Jr., 2067 Ferncliff Ave., Dayton, Ohio
Marsden, W. Ware, 2217 West 5th St., Stillwater, Okla.
Marsh, Kathleen H., Asst. Prin., Chaney School, Detroit, Mich.
Marshall, Daniel W., Dept. of Educ., Tufts University, Medford, Mass.
Marshall, Natica M., Read. Clinic, Lab. Sch., Temple Univ., Philadelphia, Pa.
Marshall, Thomas O., 2 Davis Court, Durham, N.H.
Martens, Mrs. Freda R. H., "Woodlands," Ruby, N.Y.
Martin, Clyde V., Div. of Educ., Long Beach State College, Long Beach, Calif.
Martin, Edwin D., Dir. of Research, Public Schools, Houston, Tex.
Martin, F. David, Dept. of Philos., Bucknell University, Lewisburg, Pa.
Martin, George B., Willamette University, Salem, Ore.
Martin, Howell C., Principal, Valdosta High School, Valdosta, Ga.
Martin, Ignatius A., Supt. of Diocesan Schls., Lafayette, La.
Martin, John Z., President, Upland College, Upland, Calif.
Martin, Millicent V., Inst. of Home Econ., Univ. of Illinois, Urbana, Ill.
Martin, W. Burton, Presby. Bd. of For. Missions, 156 Fifth Ave., New York, N.Y.
Martin, W. Howard, University of Connecticut, Storrs, Conn.
Martina, Sister Anne, 314 Houston Ave., Crookston, Minn.
Martini, Angiolina A., 2629 Dwight Way, Berkeley, Calif.
Martinson, Ruth A., Long Beach State College, Long Beach, Calif.
Martorana, S. V., Div. of High. Educ., U.S. Office of Education, Washington, D.C.
Mary Adelbert, Sister, S.N.D., Diocesan Supv. of Schools, Toledo, Ohio
Mary Afra, Sister, St. Mary College, Xavier, Kan.
Mary Alma, Sister, Dean, St. Mary's College, Notre Dame, Ind.
Mary Anastasia, Sister, Dean, St. Mary's College, Holy Cross, Ind.
Mary Angela Betke, Sister, Felician Psychological Clinic, Buffalo, N.Y.
Mary Aquinas, Sister, C.P.P.S., Immaculata College, Dayton, Ohio
Mary Basil, Sister, Good Counsel College, White Plains, New York
Mary Benedetta, Mother, Prin., Villa Cabrini Academy, Burbank, Calif.
Mary Benedict, Mother, Chm., Educ. Dept., Marymount College, Tarrytown, N. Y.
Mary Benedict, Sister, B.V.M., Chm., Dept. of Educ., Mundelein Col., Chicago, Ill.
Mary Berenice O'Neill, Sister, C.S.J., Pres., Col. of St. Teresa, Kansas City, Mo.
Mary Bernice, Sister, Dept. of Educ., St. John College, Cleveland, Ohio
Mary Caroline, Sister, Educ. Dept., Notre Dame College, Staten Island, N.Y.
Mary Christine Beck, Sister, Dir., Sacred Heart Jr. Col., Belmont, N.C.
Mary Clotile, Sister, Chm., Dept. of Educ., Dunbarton Col., Washington, D. C.
Mary Consuela, Sister, Immaculata College, Immaculata, Pa.
Mary Coralita, Sister, O.P., St. Mary of the Springs, Columbus, Ohio
Mary Dolores, Sister, College of St. Francis, Joliet, Ill.
Mary Dorothy, Sister, Education Dept., Barry College, Miami, Fla.
Mary Felicitas, Sister, Immaculata College, Dayton, Ohio
Mary Fidelma, Mother, Educ. Dept., Marymount College, New York, N. Y.
Mary Florita, Sister, Community Supv., Nazareth Motherhouse, Rochester, N.Y.

Mary Francesca, Sister, Georgian Court College, Lakewood, N.J.
Mary Gabrielle, Sister, Nazareth College, Nazareth, Mich.
Mary Gerold, Sister, Dean, 1209 Park Ave., Racine, Wis.
Mary Hyacinth, Sister, Our Lady of Sorrows Convent, Ladysmith, Wis.
Mary Imeldine, Sister, Marylhurst College, Marylhurst, Ore.
Mary Imeldis, Sister, Cardinal Stritch College, Milwaukee, Wis.
Mary Inez, Mother, Holy Family College, Manitowoc, Wis.
Mary Irmina, Sister, Villa Madonna College, Covington, Ky.
Mary James, Sister, Mt. St. Vincent Col., Rockingham, Nova Scotia, Canada
Mary Joseph, Sister, 35-50 158th St., Flushing, N.Y.
Mary Josephine, Sister, Mount Mary College, Milwaukee, Wis.
Mary Josephine, Sister, Rosary College, River Forest, Ill.
Mary Justinia, Sister, Notre Dame Convent, Milwaukee, Wis.
Mary Kathleen, Sister, Mt. St. Agnes College, Baltimore, Md.
Mary Kevin, Sister, *Deceased.*
Mary, Laurina, Sister, Vice-Pres., Mount Mary College, Yankton, S.D.
Mary Lawrence, Sister, Mary Manse College, Toledo, Ohio
Mary Lucille, Sister, President, Mercy College, Detroit, Mich.
Mary Marguerite, Sister, B.V.M., Principal, Gesu Convent, Milwaukee, Wis.
Mary Michael, Sister, Immaculate Heart College, Los Angeles, Calif.
Mary Muriel Hogan, Sister, Ottumwa Heights College, Ottumwa, Iowa
Mary Muriel, Sister, Marian College, Fond du Lac, Wis.
Mary Norita, Sister, St. Xavier College, Chicago, Ill.
Mary Olivia, Sister, Dean, Marian College, Indianapolis, Ind.
Mary Priscilla, Sister, Head, Dept. of Educ., Notre Dame Col., Cleveland, Ohio
Mary Regina, Sister, Elem. Sch. Supv., Sisters of Mercy Provin. House, Chicago, Ill.
Mary Regis, Sister, Principal, St. Peter's High School, Pittsburgh, Pa.
Mary Rose Agnes, Sister, Our Lady of Cincinnati College, Cincinnati, Ohio
Mary Rose Eileen, Sister, Dunbarton College of Holy Cross, Washington, D.C.
Mary of St. Michael, Sister, College of the Holy Name, Oakland, Calif.
Mary Teresa Francis McDade, Sister, Mount Carmel, Dubuque, Iowa
Mary Theodine, Sister, Dean, Viterbo College, La Crosse, Wis.
Mary Vera, Sister, C.S.A., Principal, Jefferson School, Hays, Kan.
Mary Vernice, Sister, Catholic University of America, Washington, D.C.
Mary Vincent Therese, Sister, St. Joseph's College for Women, Brooklyn, N.Y.
Marzolf, Stanley S., Illinois State Normal University, Normal, Ill.
Masling, Joseph, Dept. of Psych., Syracuse Univ., Syracuse, N.Y.
Massanari, Karl, Goshen College, Goshen, Ind.
Massey, William J., Louisiana Polytechnic Institute, Ruston, La.
Masters, Harry V., President, Albright College, Reading, Pa.
Mathews, C. O., Dept. of Educ., Ohio Wesleyan University, Delaware, Ohio
Mathias, C. Wilber, State Teachers College, Kutztown, Pa.
Mathiasen, O. F., Dept. of Educ., Antioch College, Yellow Springs, Ohio
Matricaria, D. Anthony, 73 Howard Ave., Ansonia, Conn.
Matthew, Eunice Sophia, State Dept. of Education, Nashville, Tenn.
Matthews, R. D., Dept. of Educ., Univ. of Pennsylvania, Philadelphia, **Pa.**
Matthews, Stephen J., 34 Holmes Court, Albany, N.Y.
Mattila, Ruth Hughes, 3625 North Sheffield Ave., Chicago, Ill.
Maucker, James William, President, Iowa State Tchrs. College, Cedar Falls, Iowa
Mauth, Leslie J., Ball State Teachers College, Muncie, Ind.
Mayfield, L. B., Superintendent, Sch. Dist. 49, Medford, Ore.
Mayhew, Lewis B., Box 391, East Lansing, Mich.
Mayo, Jane A., 2606 Wolfe Street, Little Rock, Ark.
Mayor, John R., Sch. of Educ., University of Wisconsin, Madison, Wis.
Max, Herbert J., Chm., Dept. of Educ., Wartburg College, Waverly, Iowa
Maziarz, Rev. Edward A., Dean, St. Joseph's College, Collegeville, Ind.
Mazyck, Harold E., Jr., Prairie View A. & M. College, Prairie View, Tex.
McAllister, David, Arkansas Polytechnic College, Russellville, Ark.
McAtee, Veva, Dir. of Guidance, 1921 David Ave., Whiting, Ind.
McBirney, Ruth, Boise Junior College, Boise, Idaho

McBrair, Marian, Assoc. Dean of Stud., Iowa State Tchrs. Col., Cedar Falls, Iowa
McBride, James H., Superintendent of Schools, Norwalk, Ohio
McCallister, J. M., 8100 South Blackstone Ave., Chicago, Ill.
McCandless, Frederick D., Albany Medical College, Albany, N.Y.
McCann, Lloyd E., Dept. of Educ., Butler University, Indianapolis, Ind.
McCann, Thomas W., 141 Sims Road, Syracuse, N.Y.
McCarthy, Raymond G., 52 Hillhouse Ave., New Haven, Conn.
McClean, Donald E., 171 Lucero Way, Menlo Park, Calif.
McClellan, James, Teachers College, Columbia University, New York, N.Y.
McClendon, LeRoy, 313 East Austin, Nacogdoches, Tex.
McClintock, James A., Drew University, Madison, N.J.
McCluer, V. C., Supt. of Schools, Ferguson, Mo.
McClure, L. Morris, Western Michigan College, Kalamazoo, Mich.
McClurkin, W. D., George Peabody College for Teachers, Nashville, Tenn.
McClusky, F. D., Sch. of Educ., University of Calif., Los Angeles, Calif.
McClusky, Howard Y., Univ. of Michigan, Ann Arbor, Mich.
McConnell, Gaither, 254 Pine Street, New Orleans, La.
McConnell, T. R., Sch. of Educ., University of California, Berkeley, Calif.
McCorkle, David B., University of Mississippi Medical Center, Jackson, Miss.
McCormick, Chester A., Col. of Educ., Wayne University, Detroit, Mich.
McCown, Roger, Sutton Hall, University of Texas, Austin, Texas
McCrary, James W., Jr., East Texas State Tchrs. College, Commerce, Tex.
McCreight, Russell W., Teachers College, University of Nebraska, Lincoln, Neb.
McCuen, Theoron L., Supt., Kern County Union High School, Bakersfield, Calif.
McCullough, Constance M., San Francisco State College, San Francisco, Calif.
McDanald, Eugene C., Jr., 1906 Little St., La Marque, Tex.
McDermott, John C., Chm., Dept. of Educ., St. John's Univ., Brooklyn, N.Y.
McDermott, Leon A., Central Mich. Col. of Educ., Mount Pleasant, Mich.
McDonald, L. R., Principal, Woodruff High School, Peoria, Ill.
McDonald, Moss, County Superintendent of Schools, Versailles, Mo.
McDonald, Mrs. V. R., Olive Branch, Miss.
McDougle, Ethel, 3776 West Thirty-third St., Cleveland, Ohio
McElhannon, Joseph C., Dept. of Educ., Baylor University, Waco, Tex.
McFadden, Mrs. LE'toile K., Asst. Dir., Nursing Educ., Emanuel Hospital, Port-
    land, Ore.
McFarland, John W., Superintendent, Public Schools, Vernon, Tex.
McGarry, Charles P., Supt., Diocese of Camden, Camden, N.J.
McGarry, Francis B., State Teachers College, East Stroudsburg, Pa.
McGaughy, Jean B., Prin., Countryside School, Barrington, Ill.
McGehee, Elise, 2343 Prytania St., New Orleans, La.
McGhehey, Marion A., Sch. of Educ., Indiana University, Bloomington, Ind.
McGill, Ida Belle, Arizona State College, Flagstaff, Ariz.
McGinnis, Frederick A., Chm., Div. of Educ., Wilberforce Uni., Wilberforce, Ohio
McGlasson, Maurice A., Central Washington College of Educ., Ellensburg, Wash.
McGuire, J. Carson, Col. of Educ., Univ. of Texas, Austin, Tex.
McHale, Kathryn, 3601 Connecticut Ave., Washington, D.C.
McIlrath, William J., State Teachers College, Florence, Ala.
McIlvaine, Franklin, State Teachers College, Lock Haven, Pa.
McIntosh, Charles W., Div. of International Educ., Dept. of Health, Educ. &
    Welfare, Washington, D.C.
McIntosh, D. C., Dean, Grad. Sch., A. & M. College, Stillwater, Okla.
McIntosh, Leslie A., Principal, Columbia High School, Richland, Wash.
McIntosh, William Ray, Superintendent of Schools, Rockford, Ill.
McIntyre, Richmond E., Principal, J. F. Gunn Elem. Sch., Burlington, N.C.
McIsaac, John S., Geneva College, Beaver Falls, Pa.
McKee, Frances M., Bemidji State Teachers College, Bemidji, Minn.
McKee, William W., Merrill Palmer School, 71 E. Ferry Ave., Detroit, Mich.
McKee, W. J., University of North Carolina, Chapel Hill, N.C.
McKelvey, Frederick H., Dir., Cen. for Educ. Serv., Ohio Univ., Athens, Ohio
McKenna, F. Raymond, Eastern Illinois State College, Charleston, Ill.
McKeough, Rev. M. J., Dean, St. Norbert College, West DePere, Wis.

McKernon, James G., 419 S. Ottawa St., Dixon, Ill.
McKillop, Anne S., Teachers College, Columbia University, New York, N.Y.
McKim, George L., Sch. of Educ., Boston College, Chestnut Hill, Mass.
McKim, Margaret G., Teachers College, Univ. of Cincinnati, Cincinnati, Ohio
*McKinney, James, Chm., Bd. of Trustees, American School, Chicago, Ill.
McKnight, Mrs. F. J., Georgia State College for Women, Milledgeville, Ga.
McLaughlin, James J., Wisconsin State College, River Falls, Wis.
McLaughlin, J. O., 606 East 6th St., Claremont, Calif.
McLaughlin, Kenneth F., Test Serv. Bur., Florida St. Univ., Tallahassee, Fla.
McLaughlin, Vincent J., School of Educ., Fordham Univ., New York, N.Y.
McLaughlin, William J., Prin., D. A. Harmon Jr. H.S., Hazelton, Pa.
McLeary, Ralph D., Superintendent of Schools, Jackson, Mich.
McLendon, Jonathon C., Dept. of Educ., Duke University, Durham, N.C.
McLure, John R., Dean, Col. of Educ., Univ. of Alabama, University, Ala.
McMahan, F. J., St. Ambrose College, Davenport, Iowa
McMahan, John Julia, New Mexico Col. of A. & M., State College, N.M.
McMahon, Mrs. G. F., Prin., Bennett Elementary School, Chicago, Ill.
McManamon, Fr. James, St. Joseph Friary, Cleveland, Ohio
McMaster, T. A., Genl. Secy., Manitoba Teachers Society, Winnipeg, Manitoba
McMillan, William A., Div. of Educ., Wiley College, Marshall, Tex.
McMillian, N. B., Kentucky Education Association, Louisville, Ky.
McMullen, Charles B., Dean, State Tchrs. College, Bridgewater, Mass.
McMullin, Ernan, University of Notre Dame, Notre Dame, Ind.
McMurray, Foster, Col. of Educ., University of Illinois, Urbana, Ill.
McMurtrey, Violet, 3365 Southwest 103rd St., Beaverton, Ore.
McNally, Crystal, 428 South Broadway, Wichita, Kan.
McNally, Harold J., Teachers College, Columbia University, New York, N.Y.
McNutt, C. R., Provost Marshall General's School, Camp Gordon, Ga.
McNutt, Franklin H., Woman's Col., Univ. of North Carolina, Greensboro, N.C.
McPhail, Harry R., Superintendent of Schools, Ames, Iowa
McPherson, Virgil L., 904 East Mayfair Ave., Orange, Calif.
McPherson, Mrs. W. M., Box 513, Brook Street, Newark Valley, N.Y.
McQueeny, Mother Mary, San Francisco Col. for Women, San Francisco, Calif.
McRae, Louie James, Principal, East Highland School, Dothan, Ala.
McSwain, E. T., Sch. of Educ., Northwestern University, Evanston, Ill.
McTigue, Mary R., Principal, Lincoln School, Chicago, Ill.
*Mead, Arthur R., 1719 Northwest 6th Ave., Gainesville, Fla.
Mease, Clyde D., Superintendent of Schools, Humboldt, Iowa
Mech, Edmund V., University of Oklahoma, Norman, Okla.
Meckel, Henry C., San Jose State Col., San Jose, Calif.
Meder, Elsa M., Houghton Mifflin Co., Boston, Mass.
Meehan, Rev. John T., Prin., Norfolk Catholic High School, Norfolk, Va.
Meeker, Alice M., State Teachers College, Paterson, N.J.
Meenes, Max, Head, Dept. of Psych., Howard University, Washington, D.C.
Meier, Frederick A., President, State Teachers College, Salem, Mass.
Melby, Ernest O., Sch. of Educ., New York Univ., New York, N.Y.
Melchert, John C., Jr., Instituto Normal Evangelico, San Pedro Sula, Honduras
Mellott, Malcolm E., Editor-in-Chief, John C. Winston. Philadelphia, Pa.
Mendenhall, C. B., Ohio State University, Columbus, Ohio
Mendoza, Romulo Y., Bureau of Public Schools, Manila, Phillippines
Menegat, Paul A., Supt. Prin., Forest Grove Union High Schl., Forest Grove, Ore.
Menge, Carleton P., University of New Hampshire, Durham, N.H.
Menge, J. W., College of Educ., Wayne Univ., Detroit, Mich.
Menger, Clara, Soc. Sci. Dept. Monticello College, Godfrey, Ill.
Mensenkamp, L. E., Prin., Freeport High School, Freeport, Ill.
Mentzer, Rosalind, Michigan State University, East Lansing, Mich.
Mercer, Lois L., 222 Prospect Ave., Findlay, Ohio
Meredith, Cameron W., Northwestern University, Evanston, Ill.
Merenda, Peter F., Res. and Eval. Branch, Naval Exam. Cen., Great Lakes, Ill.
Merritt, C. B., Col. of Educ., University of Arizona, Tucson, Ariz.
Merry, Mrs. R. V., Morris Harvey College, Charleston, W.Va.

Mersand, Joseph, Eng. Dept., Jamaica High School, Jamaica, N.Y.
Metzner, Jerome, Biology and Gen. Sci. Dept., Jamaica High School, Jamaica, N.Y.
Metzner, William, Prin., John B. Stetson Junior High School, Philadelphia, Pa.
Meyer, Charlotte, Elementary Supervisor, Public Schools, Decatur, Ill.
Meyer, George A., Col. of Educ., Drake University, Des Moines, Iowa
Meyer, Mrs. Marie, Douglass College, Rutgers University, New Brunswick, N.J.
Meyers, C. E., Sch. of Educ.. University of So. Calif., Los Angeles, Calif.
Meyers, Max B., 324 East 59th St., Brooklyn, N.Y.
Meyers, W. H., 1306 Sunset Lane, Alvin, Tex.
Michael, Lloyd S., Superintendent, Evanston Township High School, Evanston, Ill.
Michaelis, Dorothy I., 40 Evelyn Pl., Staten Island, N.Y.
Michaelis, John U., Sch. of Educ., Univ. of California, Berkeley, Calif.
Micheels, William J., Col. of Educ., Univ. of Minn., Minneapolis, Minn.
Michelson, John M., Sch. of Educ., Temple University, Philadelphia, Pa.
Mijanovich, Nada, Inst. of Child Welfare, Univ. of Minn., Minneapolis, Minn.
Mikesell, Doyle, Head, Div. of Basic Stud., Drake Univ., Des Moines, Iowa
Miles, Arnold A., 11500 Hamilton Ave., Detroit, Mich.
Miles, Matthew B., Horace Mann-Lincoln Inst., Columbia Univ., New York, N.Y.
Miles, Vaden W., Physics Dept., Wayne University, Detroit, Mich.
Milheim, Robert P., 17 East Spring St., Oxford, Ohio
Millard, C. V., Div. of Educ., Michigan State College, East Lansing, Mich.
Miller, Benjamin, Supv., Day Elementary School, Bronx, N.Y.
Miller, Carroll H., Colorado A. & M. College, Ft. Collins, Colo.
Miller, Carroll L., College of L.A., Howard Univ., Washington. D.C.
Miller, Charles, Vice-Prin., McKinley Elem. School, Newark, N.J.
Miller, Charles S., Allegheny College, Meadville, Pa.
Miller, Henry, Sch. of Educ., City College, New York, N.Y.
Miller, Ira E., Eastern Mennonite College, Harrisonburg, Va.
Miller, John L., Superintendent of Schools, Great Neck, N.Y.
Miller, Kenneth M., University of Tasmania, Hobart, Australia
Miller, Lawrence William, University of Denver, Denver, Colo.
Miller, Lebern N., Dept. of Educ., Tulsa University, Tulsa, Okla.
Miller, Louise C., 627 North Main St., Adrian, Mich.
Miller, Paul A., Superintendent of Schools, Warren, Ohio
Miller, Paul A., Superintendent of City Schools, Minot, N.D.
Miller, Paul R., Superintendent of Schools, Kane, Pa.
Miller, Ruth M., Hartwick College, Oneonta, N.Y.
Milliamson, Florence J., Bowling Green State University, Bowling Green, Ohio
Milligan, Glenn E., Psychologist, Bd. of Educ., Columbus, Ohio
Milligan, Phyllis E., 712 Fairlawn Dr., Columbus, Ohio
Milling, Euleas, 29 South Georgia Ave., Concord, N.C.
Mills, Forrest L., Racine Public Library, Racine, Wis.
Mills, Henry C., University of Rochester, Rochester, N.Y.
Mills, William H., Univ. Elem. Sch., University of Michigan, Ann Arbor, Mich.
Milner, Bessie, Principal, East Ward School, Gulfport, Miss.
Milner, Ernest J., Sch. of Educ., Syracuse University, Syracuse, N.Y.
Miniclier, G. E., Principal, Washington High School, St. Paul, Minn.
Minkler, F. W., Director of Education, Lansing, Ontario, Canada
Minnis, Roy B., Dir. of Adult Educ., State Dept. of Educ., Denver, Colo.
Minock, Daniel F., John A. Sutter Junior High School, Los Angeles, Calif.
Minogue, Mildred M., Prin., Armstrong Elem. School, Chicago, Ill.
Mintz, Norbett L., Psych. Dept., Brandeis University, Waltham, Mass.
Misner, Paul J., Superintendent of Schools, Glencoe, Ill.
Mitchell, B. F., Louisiana State Univ., Baton Rouge, La.
Mitchell, Donald P., Sch. of Educ., Rutgers University, New Brunswick, N.J.
Mitchell, Eva C., Hampton Institute, Hampton, Va.
Mitchell, Frank W., University of Otago, Dunedin, New Zealand
Mitchell, Guy Clifford, Dept. of Educ., Mississippi College, Clinton, Miss.
Mitchell, T. W., Principal, East Junior-Sen. High School, Duluth, Minn.
Mitchell, William R., Olivet College, Olivet, Mich.

Mitzel, Harold E., Div. of Tchr. Educ., 500 Park Ave., New York, N.Y.
Mock, Gordon D., 425 Hawthorne Ct., Madison, Wis.
Moe, Richard D., Dir., Tchr. Educ., Waldorf College, Forest City, Iowa
Moffatt, Maurice P., Montclair State Tchrs. College, Montclair, N.J.
Moffitt, J. C., Superintendent of Schools, Provo, Utah
Moldstad, John Alton, Audio-Visual Center, Indiana Univ., Bloomington, Ind.
Moler, Donald L., Dept. of Educ., Eastern Ill. State College, Charleston, Ill.
Moll, Boniface E., St. Benedicts College, Atchison, Kan.
Monell, Ira H., Principal, Lafayette School, Chicago, Ill.
Monell, Ralph P., Superintendent, Public Schools, Canon City, Colo.
*Monroe, Walter S., 420 Van Buren Ave., Los Altos, Calif.
Montgomery, George, Prin., West Philadelphia High School, Philadelphia, Pa.
Montgomery, Thomas S., Sam Houston State Tchrs. College, Huntsville, Tex.
Moody, Edith, Elementary Supervisor, Richmond, Calif.
Moon, James V., Superintendent of Schools, Western Springs, Ill.
Moore, Cecil L., Principal, L. L. Campbell School, Austin, Tex.
Moore, Clyde B., Stone Hall, Cornell University, Ithaca, N.Y.
Moore, Edward C., Dept. of Philos., University of Idaho, Moscow, Idaho
Moore, H. K., Arkansas A. & M. College, College Heights, Ark.
Moore, Harold E., Sch. of Educ., University of Denver, Denver, Colo.
Moore, James H., 215 East Washington Ave., Riverton, Wyo.
Moore, John W., Superintendent of Schools, Winston-Salem, N.C.
Moore, Parlett L., Principal, Carver High School, Rockville, Md.
Moorhead, Sylvester A., Sch. of Educ., Univ. of Mississippi, University, Miss.
Moran, Alfred A., Dept. of Educ., University of Detroit, Detroit, Mich.
Moreau, Rev. Jules L., Seabury-Western Theological Seminary, Evanston, Ill.
Morgan, Barton, Dept. of Educ., Iowa State College, Ames, Iowa
Morgan, Roland R., Supt. of Schools, Mooresville, N.C.
Morgart, John H., Principal, Herron Hill Junior High School, Pittsburgh, Pa.
Moriarty, Joseph F., 255 Van Houten Ave., Passaic, N.J.
Moriarty, Mary J., State Teachers College, Bridgewater, Mass.
Mork, Gordon M. A., Col. of Educ., Univ. of Minnesota, Minneapolis, Minn.
Morris, Frank E., Lmeritus Prof. of Philos., Connecticut Col., New London, Conn.
Morris, John B., Burton Hall, University of Minnesota, Minneapolis, Minn.
Morris, J. V. L., Northwestern State College, Alva, Okla.
Morris, Van Cleve, Col. of Educ., University of Georgia, Athens, Ga.
Morrison, Fanny, 169 Mt. Vernon Street, Dover, N.H.
Morrison, Gaylord D., Colorado State College of Educ., Greeley, Colo.
*Morrison, J. Cayce, 530 East 23rd St., New York, N.Y.
Morrison, Leger Roland, 16 Brown St., Warren, R.I.
Morse, Horace T., Dean, Gen. Col., Univ. of Minnesota, Minneapolis, Minn.
Mort, Paul, Teachers College, Columbia University, New York, N.Y.
Morton, R. L., Ohio University, Athens, Ohio
Mosbo, Alvin O., Administrative Asst., Public Schools, Davenport, Iowa.
Moseley, S. Meredith, Principal, Dillard High School, Fort Lauderdale, Fla.
Mosher, Frank K., Dist. Prin., Liverpool Central Schls., Liverpool, N.Y.
Mosier, Earl E., Dean, Michigan State Normal Col., Ypsilanti, Mich.
Moskowitz, Sue, Bur. of Educ. Res., Bd. of Ed., 110 Livingston St., Brooklyn, N.Y.
Moss, Roy B., Dir., Audio-Visual Center, Grambling, La.
Moss, Theodore C., 30 Collidge Dr., Snyder, N.Y.
Mourier, Regis Paul, 1921 Lee Rd., Cleveland Heights, Ohio
Moyer, James Herbert, Dept. of Educ., Penn. State Univ., University Park, Pa.
Mudge, Evelyn L., Head, Dept. of Educ., Hood College, Frederick, Md.
Mudge, John, Asst. Dist. Supt., Public Schools, Santa Maria, Calif.
Mueller, Karl J., 1007 White Oaks Rd., Campbell, Calif.
Muirhead, Joseph V., Prin., Pittsburg Evening High School, Pittsburg, Calif.
Muldoon, Hugh C., Dean, Sch. of Pharmacy, Duquesne Univ., Pittsburgh, Pa.
Mulhern, Joseph C., S.M., Chm., Educ. Dept., Spring Hill College, Mobile, Ala.
Muller, Philippe, l'Univ. et l'Ecole Normale cantonale, Neuchatel, Switzerland
Mulliner, John H., 612 North Bismark Ave., Webster Groves, Mo.
Mulrooney, Thomas W., Dir., Child Devel. & Guid., Pub. Schls., Wilmington, Del.

Mulry, Verna, Dir. of Reading, Waukesha H.S., Waukesha, Wis.
Munch, T. W., Sutton Hall, University of Texas, Austin, Tex.
Munro, C. Donald, Prin., King George School, Peterborough, Ont.
Munro, Paul M., Superintendent of Schools, Lynchburg, Va.
Muntyan, Bozidar, Col. of Educ., University of Florida, Gainesville, Fla.
Muntyan, Milosh, Sch. of Educ., Michigan State University, East Lansing, Mich.
Murnane, Patrick J., Principal, Newburyport High School, Newburyport, Mass.
Murphy, A. C., Asst. Dir., Ext. Bureau, University of Texas, Austin, Tex.
Murphy, Edna I., Box 354, Grand Rapids, Mich.
Murphy, Forrest W., Dean, Sch. of Educ., Univ. of Mississippi, University, Miss.
Murphy, George E., Dir., Read. Clinic, Penn. State Univ., University Park, Pa.
Murphy, Helen A., Sch. of Educ., Boston University, Boston, Mass.
Murphy, Mrs. Jeannie Dean, 1960 West Seventy-ninth St., Los Angeles, Calif.
Murphy, John A., 21-10 33rd Road, Long Island City, N.Y.
Murray, Lessie L., Head, Elem. Educ. Dept., Atlanta Christian Col., Wilson, N.C.
Murray, Robert E., 1916 South Sig Hill Drive, Kirkwood, Mo.
Murray, Thomas, Dept. of Educ., Sam Houston State Tchrs. Col., Huntsville, Tex.
Myers, Mrs. Emma G., Orangeville, Columbia County, Pa.
Myklebust, Per, Volda, Norway

Nafziger, Mary K., Dept. of Educ., Goshen College, Goshen, Ind.
Nagle, Orris O., 21177 Parkcrest, Harper Woods, Mich.
Nagy, O. Richard, Principal, Carteret School, Bloomfield, N.J.
Nahm, Helen, 2 Park Avenue, New York, N.Y.
Nahshon, Samuel, 1730 Penn Ave., North, Minneapolis, Minn.
Nakosteen, Mehdi, Indian Hills, Colo.
Nance, Mrs. Afton Dill, State Dept. of Education, Sacramento, Calif.
Nash, Curtis E., Central Michigan College, Mt. Pleasant, Mich.
Naslund, Robert A., Sch. of Educ., Univ. of Southern Calif., Los Angeles, Calif.
Nason, Doris E., Dept. of Educ., Univ. of Connecticut, Storrs, Conn.
Nassau, Dorothy P., Pedagogical Library, Bd. of Educ., Philadelphia, Pa.
Naumann, M. J., Concordia Seminary, Springfield, Ill.
Neal, Nellie N., 2524 Benvenue Ave., Berkeley, Calif.
Neale, Gladys E., Macmillan Company of Canada, Toronto, Ont.
Neff, Frederick Clifton, Sch. of Educ., Rutgers University, New Brunswick, N.J.
Neiderhiser, F. J., Superintendent of Schools, McClure, Ohio
Nelson, Arthur T., Asst. Superintendent of Schools, Westport, Conn.
Nelson, Carl B., 2300 Colfax Ave. South, Minneapolis, Minn.
Nelson, Constance B., University of Kansas City, Kansas City, Mo.
Nelson, Earl E., Lake County High School, Two Harbors, Minn.
Nelson, Kenneth G., New York State Dept. of Education, Albany, N.Y.
Nelson, Milton G., 166—19th Ave., Lake Worth, Fla.
Nelson, M. J., Iowa State Teachers College, Cedar Falls, Iowa
Nelson, N. P., State Teachers College, Oshkosh, Wis.
Nelson, Willard H., Alabama Polytechnic Institute, Auburn, Ala.
Nemzek, Claude L., Chm., Educ. Dept., Univ. of Detroit, Detroit, Mich.
Nesbit, Daun Wilbur, Franklin and Marshall College, Lancaster, Pa.
Nesi, Carmella, Principal, Junior High School 7, Bronx, N.Y.
Neuber, Margaut A., Pennsylvania State University, University Park, Pa.
Neuner, Elsie Flint, Dir. of Instruction, Dept. of Educ., New Rochelle, N.Y.
Newbury, Dorothy I., Dept. of Educ., Cornell College, Mount Vernon, Iowa
Newenham, R. L., Superintendent of Schools, Zion, Ill.
Newland, Kenneth E., Stephens College, Columbia, Mo.
Newman, Herbert M., Education Dept., Brooklyn College, Brooklyn, N.Y.
Newman, Louis, Principal, Akiba Hebrew Academy, Philadelphia, Pa.
Nicholas, William T., 7 Parkview Court, Pocatello, Idaho
Nichols, Augusta M., Asst. Supt. of Schools, Manchester, N.H.
Nichols, James Herbert, Elementary Principal, Georgetown, Del.
Nichols, Joe, Dean, State Normal and Ind. College, Ellendale, N.D.
Nicholson, Alice, 891 10th Ave. North, Pensacola, Fla.
Nickerson, James, Dean, Div. of Educ., Montana State Col., Bozeman, Mont.

Nielsen, William A., Bakersfield High School, Bakersfield, Calif.
Nietz, John A., Sch. of Educ., University of Pittsburgh, Pittsburgh, Pa.
Nikoloff, Nicholas, 605 Williams St., Springfield, Mo.
Nishimoto, Mitoji, International Christian Univ., Mitaka-Shi, Tokoyo, Japan
Nixon, John E., Sch. of Educ., Stanford University, Stanford, Calif.
Nixon, Lucille M., P.O Box 450, Palo Alto, Calif.
Noah, Dennis P., Dept. of Educ., Louisiana State Univ., Baton Rouge, La.
Noar, Gertrude, 225 Adams St., Brooklyn, N.Y.
Noll, Victor H., Sch. of Educ., Michigan State Univ., East Lansing, Mich.
Norberg, Kenneth D., Sacramento State College, Sacramento, Calif.
Nordberg, H. Orville, Dept. of Educ., Sacramento State Col., Sacramento, Calif.
Norem, Grant M., State Teachers College, Minot, N.D.
Norman, Ralph Paul, Col. of Engineering, Univ. of Minnesota, Minneapolis, Minn.
Norman, Wade C., 5619 Maxwell Ave., Affton, Mo.
Norris, Forbes H., Superintendent of Schools, Rockville, Md.
Norris, K. E., Prin., Sir George Williams College of Y.M.C.A., Montreal, Que.
Norris, Paul B., Exec. Secy., Iowa Div. Izaak Walton League, Indianola, Iowa
Norris, Robert B., Central Bucks Joint Schools, Doylestown, Pa.
Norrix, Loy, Superintendent of Schools, Kalamazoo, Mich.
Norton, Rev. Edward, S.V.D., 4940 South Greenwood Ave., Chicago, Ill.
Norton, John K., Teachers College, Columbia University, New York, N.Y.
Nosal, Walter S., Dir., Dept. of Educ., John Carroll Univ., Cleveland, Ohio
Novotny, Marcella, Queens Vocational High School, Long Island City, N.Y.
Nunnally, Nancy, 4028 Egbert Ave., Cincinnati, Ohio
Nutter, H. E., Head, Materials of Instruc., Univ. of Florida, Gainesville, Fla.
Nystrom, J. W., Jr., Pembroke Rd., Danbury, Conn.

Oates, Wayne E., Southern Baptist Theological Seminary, Louisville, Ky.
Oberholtzer, Kenneth E., Supt. of Schools, Denver, Colo.
O'Brien, Cyril C., Marquette University, Milwaukee, Wis.
O'Brien, Francis J., Superintendent of Schools, North Andover, Mass.
O'Brien, John W., 24 Dartmouth Circle, Swarthmore, Pa.
O'Brien, Mal, New York Univ. College for Teachers, Buffalo, N.Y.
O'Connell, Sister Margaret Mary, Pres., Col. of Notre Dame, Baltimore, Md.
O'Connor, Clarence D., Lexington Sch. for the Deaf, New York, N.Y.
O'Connor, John D., Teaching Principal, Hampshire, Ill.
O'Connor, Mrs. Marguerite O., Northern Illinois State Tchrs. Col., DeKalb, Ill.
Odell, C. W., Col. of Educ., University of Illinois, Urbana, Ill.
O'Donnell, Beatrice, Michigan State University, East Lansing, Mich.
Ogden, J. Gordon, Jr., Dept. of Educ., Florida Southern College, Lakeland, Fla.
Ogilvie, William K., Northern Illinois State College, DeKalb, Ill.
Ogle, Rachel, Franklin College, Franklin, Ind.
O'Hara, Rev. Charles M., Marquette University, Milwaukee, Wis.
O'Hearn, Mary, 1060 High Street, Dedham, Mass.
Ohlsen, Merle M., Col. of Educ., Univ. of Illinois, Urbana, Ill.
Ojemann, R. H., Child Welfare Res. Sta., State Univ. of Iowa, Iowa City, Iowa
O'Keefe, Timothy, College of St. Thomas, St. Paul, Minn.
Olander, Herbert T., University of Pittsburgh, Pittsburgh, Pa.
Oldfather, R. B., Superintendent of Schools, Painesville, Ohio
*Oldham, Mrs. Birdie V., Principal, Rochelle Elem. School, Lakeland, Fla.
Olea, Mrs. Maria, Prin., Dita School, Dita, Cuenca, Butangas, Philippines
O'Leary, Timothy F., Asst. Supt. of Catholic Schools, Boston, Mass.
Oliver, Albert Irving, Jr., Sch. of Educ., Univ. of Pennsylvania, Philadelphia, Pa.
Oliver, George J., Dept. of Educ., Col. of William and Mary, Williamsburg, Va.
Oliver, James Willard, Dept. of Philos., Univ. of Florida, Gainesville, Fla.
Oliver, Stanley C., Southwest Missouri State College, Springfield, Mo.
Olmsted, M. D., State Teachers College, Slippery Rock, Pa.
Olphert, Warwick Bruce, University of Melbourne, Melbourne, Victoria, Australia
Olsen, Hans C., Eastern Illinois State College, Charleston, Ill.
Olsen, Marion G., Principal, Public School 84, Buffalo, N.Y.

Olson, Gilma, Pennsylvania State University, University Park, Pa.
Olson, Irene, Vocational Guidance Service, Minneapolis, Minn.
Olson, R. A., Ball State Teachers College, Muncie, Ind.
Olson, Willard C., Dean, Sch. of Educ., Univ. of Mich., Ann Arbor, Mich.
O'Malley, Sarah, 1039 South Austin Blvd., Chicago, Ill.
O'Mara, J. Francis, Coord. in Cur. Develop., Pub. Schls., West Springfield, Mass.
Omwake, Eveline B., Child Study Center, Yale University, New Haven, Conn.
O'Neill, John J., State Teachers College, Boston, Mass.
Ooley, Everett B., Principal, H. A. Gray School, Edmonton, Alberta
Oppleman, Dan L., Central Washington College of Education, Ellensburg, Wash.
Oppenheimer, J. J., University of Louisville, Louisville, Ky.
Orear, Margaret Louise, Asst. Supt., City Schools, Bellflower, Calif.
Orleans, Jacob S., 12309 Monica St., Detroit, Mich.
Ormsby, Lelia T., Dept. of Educ., Sacramento State Col., Sacramento, Calif.
O'Rourke, J. Mel, Principal, Kenwood School, Chicago, Ill.
Orr, Louise, 925 Crockett St., Amarillo, Tex.
Orton, Don A., Col. of Educ., University of Utah, Salt Lake City, Utah
Osborn, John K., Central State College of Education, Mt. Pleasant, Mich.
Osborn, Wayland W., Board of Education Examiners, Des Moines, Iowa
Osburn, W. J., University of Washington, Seattle, Wash.
Ostrander, Raymond H., Supt. of Schools, Mineola, N.Y.
Ostwalt, Jay H., Dept. of Educ., Davidson College, Davidson, N.C.
O'Sullivan, Nona R., 340 West St., Randolph, Mass.
Osuna, Pedro, Dist. Supt., Yuba College, Marysville, Calif.
Oswalt, Edna R., Head, Dept. of Spec. Educ., Kent State Univ., Kent, Ohio
Oswalt, William W., Jr., Read. Supv., Lehigh County Schools, Allentown, Pa.
Otis, Jack, Dept. of Mental Health, Univ. of Illinois, Urbana, Ill.
Otterman, Lois M., Dir., Read. Clinic, Univ. of Vermont, Burlington, Vt.
Otto, Henry J., University of Texas, Austin, Tex.
Otts, John, Principal, Central High School, Charlotte, N.C.
Overstreet, George T., Retired Prin., Burnett High School, Terrell, Tex.
Ovsiew, Leon, Sch. of Educ., Temple University, Philadelphia, Pa.
Owen, Mary E., Editor, *The Instructor*, Dansville, N.Y.
Owens, Henry G., 13 Clarendon Ave., Sans Souci, Greenville, S.C.
Owings, Ralph S., Mississippi Southern College, Hattiesburg, Miss.

Pace, C. Robert, Chm., Dept. of Psych., Syracuse University, Syracuse, N.Y.
Paine, H. W., Inst. of Inter-Amer. Aff., Amer. Emb., Balboa, Canal Zone
Painter, Fred B., Superintendent, Brighton School Dist. 1, Rochester, N.Y.
Palliser, G. C., Post Office Box 1525, Wellington, New Zealand
Palmer, Albert, Dept. of Educ., Macalester College, St. Paul, Minn.
Palmer, Anne M. H., Los Angeles State College, Los Angeles, Calif.
Palmer, Frank J., 208 Church Street, North Syracuse, N.Y.
Palmer, James B., Ginn and Company, Boston, Mass.
Palmer, John C., Dir. of Guidance, Public Schools, Concord, Mass.
Palmer, Josephine S., State Teachers College, New Paltz, N.Y.
Palmer, Lulu, State Department of Education, Montgomery, Ala.
Palmquist, Marjorie Jane, 2610 Etna St., Berkeley, Calif.
Pando, Jose C., St. John's University, Brooklyn, N.Y.
Pankove, Mrs. Ethel, 41 Harriet Dr., Princeton, N.J.
Panlasigui, Isidoro, Dean, Col. of Educ., Univ. of Philippines, Quezon City,
    Philippines
Papsidero, Joseph, 139 Thompson St., North, Tonawanda, N.Y.
Park, Lawrence, Sch. of Educ., Penn. State University, University Park, Pa.
Parke, Margaret B., 430 West 118th St., New York, N.Y.
Parker, Clyde, Superintendent of Schools, Cedar Rapids, Iowa
Parker, Edna, Florida State University, Tallahassee, Fla.
Parker, Jessie M., Superintendent of Public Instruction, Des Moines, Iowa
Parker, Marjorie H., Dept. of Educ., Miner Teachers College, Washington, D.C.
Parker, Milton M., 9 Buttles Ave., Columbus, Ohio
Parkes, Mrs. Josephine, 803 W. Abram, Arlington, Tex.

Parks, Ethel, Route 2, Calhoun, Mo.
Parkyn, George W., Dir., N. Z. Council for Educ. Research, Willington, New Zealand
Parrish, William, 215 W. Downing, Tahlequah, Okla.
Parsons, Arthur Lovell, Junior High School, Winchester, Mass.
Parsons, Seth H., Dept. of Educ., New Mexico Highlands Univ., Las Vegas, N.M.
Parton, Daisy, Dept. of Educ., Univ. of Alabama, University, Ala.
Pasricha, Bal Rama, National Defence Academy, Clement Town, Dehra Dun, U.P. India
Passow, A. Harry, Teachers Col., Columbia Univ., New York, N.Y.
Paster, G. Nicholas, Dir., Stud. Activ., Roosevelt Univ., Chicago, Ill.
Pate, Mildred, Forsyth County Board of Educ., Winston-Salem, N.C.
Patrick, Robert B., Pennsylvania State University, University Park, Pa.
Pattee, Howard Hunt, P.O. Box 1211, Los Altos, Calif.
Patten, Ruth H., General Supv., Public Schools, Richmond, Calif.
Patterson, Allen D., State Teachers College, Lock Haven, Pa.
Patterson, Gordon E., Res. Dir., Santa Fe City Schools, Santa Fe, N.M.
* Patterson, Herbert, Oklahoma A. & M. College, Stillwater, Okla.
Pattison, Mattie, Dept. of Home Econ., Iowa State College, Ames, Iowa
Paul, Marvin S., 1354 Estes Ave., Chicago, Ill.
Paulien, Gunther B., University of Nebraska, Lincoln, Neb.
Paulsen, F. Robert, University of Utah, Salt Lake City, Utah
Paulson, Alice T., Principal, High School, Blue Earth, Minn.
Pauly, Frank R., Dir. of Res., Board of Educ., Tulsa, Okla.
Pavel, Harriet, Greeley Vocational School, Chicago, Ill.
Pax, Rev. Walter, Chm., Dept. of Educ., DePaul University, Chicago, Ill.
Payne, Joseph Arthur, Jr., Dean, Barber Scotia College, Concord, N.C.
Payne, Walter L., Lyons Township Junior College, La Grange, Ill.
Paynovich, Nicholas, Amphitheater High School, Tucson, Ariz.
Peacock, A. E., Supt. of Schools, Moose Jaw, Sask.
Pearson, Millie V., Oklahoma A. & M. College, Stillwater, Okla.
Peebles, Clarence M., Asst. Dean, Dental Sch., Northwestern Univ., Chicago, Ill.
Peel, J. C., Dean, Florida Southern College, Lakeland, Fla.
Peirce, Lottie M., Educ. and Vocational Counselor, Boulder, Colo.
Peisner, Earl, Sch. of Educ., Oregon State College, Corvallis, Ore.
Pella, Milton O., Univ. High School, Univ. of Wisconsin, Madison, Wis.
Pelton, Frank M., Univ. of Rhode Island, Kingston, R.I.
Pelton, Warren J., Bowling Green University, Bowling Green, Ohio
Penn, Floy L., Mt. Lebanon Public Schools, Pittsburgh, Pa.
Perdew, Philip W., University of Denver, Denver, Colo.
Peregrine, Donald, Superintendent, Starke County Schools, Knox, Ind.
Perkins, Mrs. Pearl P., Tougaloo Southern Christian Col., Tougaloo, Miss.
Perlmutter, Oscar W., St. Xavier College, Chicago, Ill.
Perrin, Porter G., Dept. of English, Univ. of Wash., Seattle, Wash.
Perry, Elizabeth W., 1588 Beacon Street, Brookline, Mass.
Perry, James Olden, Dept. of Educ., Texas Southern University, Houston, Tex.
Perry, W. D., University of North Carolina, Chapel Hill, N.C.
Perry, Winona M., Univ. of Nebraska, Lincoln, Neb.
Peters, Frank C., Tabor College, Hillsboro, Kansas
Peters, Frank R., Dept. of Educ., University of Chicago, Chicago, Ill.
Peterson, A. I., Supv. of Indian Education, Bemidji, Minn.
Peterson, Aaron D., R.R. 1, Godfrey, Ill.
Peterson, Arthur E., Supt. of Schools, Sandy City, Utah
Peterson, Elmer T., Col. of Educ., State Univ. of Iowa, Iowa City, Iowa
Peterson, Evelyn F., Dir. of Elem. Educ., Waterloo, Iowa
Peterson, Laurine, Luther College, Wahoo, Neb.
Peterson, LeRoy, Sch. of Educ., University of Wisconsin, Madison, Wis.
Peterson, M. A., Orleans, Minn.
Peterson, Wiley K., Dist. Supt., Public Schools, Hermosa Beach, Calif.
Pettiss, J. O., Dept. of Educ., Louisiana State Univ., Baton Rouge, La.
Petty, Walter T., Sacramento State College, Sacramento, Calif.

Pezzullo, Thomas J., Asst. Supt., Johnston School Dept., Johnston, R.I.
Pfau, Ed, Sch. of Educ., Michigan State University, East Lansing, Mich.
Phay, John E., Bur. of Educ. Res., Univ. of Mississippi, University, Miss.
Phearman, Leo T., Long Beach State College, Long Beach, Calif.
Phenix, Philip H., Teachers College, Columbia University, New York, N.Y.
Phillips, A. J., Exec. Secy., Mich. Educ. Assn., Lansing, Mich.
Phillips, Claude Anderson, Switzer Hall, Univ. of Missouri, Columbia, Mo.
Phillips, Donald K., Superintendent of Schools, New Rochelle, N.Y.
Phillips, Gene David, Bethany College, Bethany, W. Va.
Phillips, Murray G., University of Oklahoma, Norman, Oklahoma
Phillips, Ned, Supt. of Schools, Naches, Wash.
Phillips, Thomas A., 203 East Park St., Marquette, Mich.
Philp, William A., P.O. Box 965, Mt. Union Station, Alliance, Ohio
Phipps, George C., Principal, J. N. Thorp Elem. School, Chicago, Ill.
Piazza, Frank, Asst. Superintendent, Board of Education, Bridgeport, Conn.
Picchiotti, Natalie, Prin., Schley School, Chicago, Ill.
Pickering, Iva Viola, Friends University, Wichita, Kan.
Piekarz, Josephine A., Read. Clinic, Univ. of South Carolina, Columbia, S.C.
Pierson, Leroy R., Portland State Extension Center, Milwaukie, Ore.
Pietz, Emil T., 4444 Irving St., Denver, Colo.
Pike, Carroll Milton, Jr., Northern Ill. State Tchrs. Col., DeKalb. Ill.
Pikunas, Justin, Psych. Dept., University of Detroit, Detroit, Mich.
Piltz, Albert, Col. of Educ., University of Florida, Gainesville, Fla.
Pinckney, Paul W., Principal, Oakland High School, Oakland, Calif.
Pitcher, Leonard S., Ch., Dept. of Educ., Shelton College, Ringwood, N.J.
Pitkin, Royce S., President, Goddard College, Plainfield, Vt.
Pitt, Rt. Rev. Msgr., Sec., Catholic School Board, Louisville, Ky.
Pittman, DeWitt Kennieth, Prin., E. Mecklenburg Sr. High Schl., Matthews, N.C.
Pitts, Clara L., 1705 Kenyon St., N.W., Washington, D.C.
Plana, Juan F., Province Inspector of Prim. Inst., Camaguey, Cuba
Platz, Marvin H., San Diego State College, San Diego, Calif.
Pledger, Maud Myrtice, East Texas State Tchrs. Col., Commerce, Tex.
Plemmons, William H., Appalachian State Teachers College, Boone, N.C.
Pliska, Stanley Robert, Norfolk Div., Col. of William and Mary, Norfolk, Va.
Plog, Lawrence T., Kingston High School, Kingston, N.Y.
Plumb, Valworth R., Div. of Educ., Duluth Br., Univ. of Minn., Duluth, Minn.
Podlich, William F., Jr., 192 Vista del Cerro Dr., Tempe, Ariz.
Poffenberger, Thomas, Home Econ. Bldg., University of California, Davis, Calif.
Pogue, Graham, Dir. of Stud. Tchng., Ball State Tchrs. Col., Muncie. Ind.
Polglase, Robert J., Vice-Prin., Bloomfield Junior High Sch., Bloomfield, N.J.
Polley, Mrs. Victoria Z., Principal, Evershed School, Niagara Falls, N.Y.
Poole, Albert E., 316 Graceland Ave., Des Plaines, Ill.
Poole, Mrs. G. Cowen, Sch. of Educ., Muskegee Institute, Muskegee, Ala.
Porter, F. W., Supt. of Schools, Greenfield, Mass.
Porter, R. H., Steck Company, Austin, Tex.
Porter, Willis P., Dir., Elem. Educ., State Teachers College, Oneonta, N.Y.
Potter, Muriel, Michigan State Normal College, Ypsilanti, Mich.
Potter, Willis N., College of the Pacific, Stockton, Calif.
Potthoff, Edward F., Col. of Educ., Univ. of Illinois, Urbana, Ill.
Poulos, Thomas H., Michigan School for the Deaf, Flint, Mich.
Poulter, Maxwell W., University of Queensland, St. Lucia Brisbane, Australia
Pound, Clarence A., Purdue University, Lafayette, Ind.
Pounds, Ralph L., Teachers Col., University of Cincinnati, Cincinnati, Ohio
Powell, Mrs. Virginia L., Prin., Garfield-Buchanan Schls., Steubenville, Ohio
Power, Edward J., 20235 Prevost, Detroit, Mich.
Powers, Fred R., Superintendent, Amherst Schools, Amherst, Ohio
Powers, S. Ralph, 90 Adams Ave., Haworth, N.J.
Pratt, L. Edward, Sch. of Educ., Southern Methodist University, Dallas, Tex.
Prentis, Roy C., 224 Burton Hall, Univ. of Minnesota, Minneapolis, Minn.
Preston, Eleonora Marie, Los Angeles State College, Los Angeles, Calif.
Preston, Ralph C., Sch. of Educ., Univ. of Penn., Philadelphia, Pa.

Prestwood, Elwood L., 426 Righters Mill Rd., Gladwyne, Pa.
Prewett, Clinton R., East Carolina College, Greenville, N. C.
Price, R. Holleman, University of Mississippi, University, Miss.
Price, Robert Diddams, Teachers College, Univ. of Cincinnati, Cincinnati, Ohio
Price, Robert R., Dept. of Agric. Educ., Okla. A. & M. Col., Stillwater, Okla.
Price, Ruth Evert, Language Arts Collaborator, Public Schools, Philadelphia, Pa.
Price, Uberto, State University Teachers College, Plattsburgh, N. Y.
Prichard. Clarence, Superintendent, Township High School. Waukegan, Ill.
Probst, Joseph S., Chm., Educ. Dept., Canisius College, Buffalo, N.Y.
Proctor, Bernard S., Chrm., Dept. of Indust. Arts Educ., Hampton Inst., Va.
Prosch, M. Jean, 105 New England Ave., Summit, N.J.
Prudham, W. M., Prin., Collegiate and Vocational Inst., Owen Sound, Ont.
Prutzman, Stuart E., Superintendent of County Schools, Jim Thorpe, Pa.
Pugh, Sterling B., Prin., Washington School, New Rochelle, N.Y.
Pulsifer. Walter T., Sup. Massachusetts School Union 62, West Boylston, Mass.
Punke, Harold H., Alabama Polytechnic Institute, Auburn, Ala.
Purdy, Gordon, Asst. to President, Lincoln College, Lincoln, Ill.
Purdy, Norman E., Principal, Blue Ash School, Blue Ash, Ohio
Purdy, Ralph D., Dept. of Educ., Marshall College, Huntington, W.Va.
Puryear, R. W., Pres., Florida Normal and Indust. Mem. Col., St. Augustine, Fla.
Putnam, Rex, Superintendent of Public Instruction, Salem, Ore.

Quanbeck, Martin. Dean, Augsburg College. Minneapolis, Minn.
Quanbeck, Thor H., Dept. of Educ., Waldorf College, Forest City, Iowa
Quick, Otho J., Eastern Illinois State College, Charleston, Ill.
Quish, Bernard A., Prin., Phoebe Apperson Hearst School, Chicago, Ill.

Rabban, Meyer, Dir., The Windword School, White Plains, N.Y.
Rackley, J. R., Dean, Col. of Educ., Univ. of Okla., Norman, Okla.
Radhakrishna, K. S., Hindustani Talimi Sangh., Sevagram, Wardha, M.P., India
Radley, Arthur A., District Superintendent of Schools, Waterville, N.Y.
Ragan. William B., Dept. of Educ.. University of Oklahoma, Norman, Okla.
Rahn. Lloyd N.. Siepert Hall. Bradley University. Peoria. Ill.
Ram, M. Jaya, Page Hall, Ohio State University, Columbus, Ohio
Ramirez, Emiliano C., 278 Querino Ave., Parangue, Rizal, Philippines
Ramsden, John W., 2006 Seventh St., Columbus, Ga.
Ramsey, Curtis P., 1230 18th Ave. South, Nashville, Tenn.
Ramsey, Grover C., 517 North Parkside. Chicago. Ill.
Ramsey. J. W.. Principal. Superior-Maitland School. Northfork. W.Va.
Ramseyer, Lloyd L., President, Blufften College, Blufften, Ohio
Rand. E. W.. Southern University. Baton Rouge. La.
Randall, Edwin H., Western State College, Gunnison, Colo.
Randolph, Victor, Southern Illinois University, Carbondale, Ill.
Rankin, George R., South Division High School. Milwaukee, Wis.
Rankin, Paul T., Asst. Supt. of Schools. Detroit. Mich.
Ranney. Harriet. Upper Iowa University. Fayette. Iowa
Rappaport. Mary B.. State Education Department. Albany. N.Y.
Rarsons, R. W., Eastern Nazarene College, Wollaston, Mass.
Rasche, William F.. Dir.. Milwaukee Vocational School, Milwaukee, Wis.
Rasmussen. Elmer M.. Dean. Dana College. Blair. Neb.
Rasmussen, Glen R., Univ. of Michigan Ext. Service, Flint, Mich.
Ratliff, John A., Prin., Marshall Jr. High School, Houston, Tex.
Rattigan, Bernard T.. Catholic University of America, Washington. D.C.
Raubinger. F. M.. Commissioner of Educ., State Dept. of Educ., Trenton, N.J.
Rawson. K. O., Superintendent of Schools, Clintonville, Wis.
Ray, Ethel. Dept. of Educ., Western Illinois State College, Macomb, Ill.
Ray. Rolland. Col. of Educ., State Univ. of Iowa. Iowa City. Iowa
Reals. Willis H.. Dean, Univ. Col.. Washington University. St. Louis, Mo.
Reas. Herbert D.. Act. Dean, Sch. of Education, Seattle Univ., Seattle, Wash.
* Reavis, W. C., *Deceased.*
Red, S. B., University of Houston, Houston, Tex.

Reed, Calvin H., Tchrs. Col., University of Nebraska, Lincoln, Neb.
Reed, Charles H., Prin., Vista and MacGregor Schls., Albany, Calif.
Reed, Helen M., Col. of Educ., University of Kentucky, Lexington, Ky.
Reed, Lula B., County Supt. of Schools, Red Oak, Iowa
Reed, Richard Y., University of Miami, Coral Gables, Fla.
Rees, R. P., Headmaster, Roosevelt High School, Johannesburg, South Africa
Reeve, Jay W., 3419 Rainbow Dr., Palo Alto, Calif.
Reeves, Floyd W., Sch. of Educ., Michigan State College, East Lansing, Mich.
Reeves, Wilfred, Prin., Roosevelt School, Olympia, Wash.
Regan, Willard Philip, Jr., P. O. Box 904, Hemet, Calif.
Rehage, Kenneth J., Dept. of Educ., University of Chicago, Chicago, Ill.
Reichert, Stephen B., Jr., John Muir College, Pasadena, Calif.
Reifsnyder, Rev. John A., 9 East 12th St., Covington, Ky.
Reilley, Albert G., Asst. Supt. of Schools, Framingham, Mass.
Reilly, James J., Chm., Dept. of Educ., St. Anselm's College, Manchester, N.H.
Reinertsen, S. G., Superintendent of Schools, Moorhead, Minn.
Reinhardt, Emma, Eastern Illinois State College, Charleston, Ill.
Reisin, Seymour, 332 West 83rd St., New York, N.Y.
Reiter, M. R., Superintendent of Schools, Morrisville, Pa.
Reitze, Arnold W., 3 Lienau Place, Jersey City, N.J.
Reller, Theodore L., Sch. of Educ., University of California, Berkeley, Calif.
Remmers, Herman, Purdue University, Lafayette, Ind.
Remon, Marion E., Dir. Elem. Educ., Public Schools, Melrose, Mass.
Renard, John N., Oxnard Union High School, Oxnard, Calif.
Renouf, Edna M., Prin., Scenic Hills School, Springfield, Pa.
Resek, E. Frederick, Principal, Bridge Elem. School, Chicago, Ill.
Reuter, George S., Jr., Head, Dept. of Educ., Arkansas A. & M. Col., College
    Heights, Ark.
Reynard, Harold E., Arps Hall, Ohio State University, Columbus, Ohio
Reynolds, James W., Col. of Educ., University of Texas, Austin, Tex.
Reynolds, Maynard C., University of Minnesota, Minneapolis, Minn.
Rhode, Jerome E., Prin., High School, Milaca, Minn.
Rhodes, L. H., Principal, Central Elem. School, Alamogordo, N. M.
Rhodes, William E., Chaplain, University of Denver, Denver, Colo.
Rice, Arthur H., Mang. Editor, *Nation's Schools*, Chicago, Ill.
Rice, Charles, Springfield College, Springfield, Mass.
Rice, Ralph Samuel, Supv. Prin., North Hills Joint Schls., Pittsburgh, Pa.
Rice, Roy C., Dept. of Educ., Arizona State College, Tempe, Ariz.
Rice, Theodore D., Sch. of Educ., New York University, New York, N. Y.
Richardson, John S., Ohio State University, Columbus, Ohio
Richardson, L. S., Sup., A. & M. Consolidated Schls., College Station, Tex.
Richardson, Orvin T., Prof. of Educ., Washington Univ., St. Louis, Mo.
Richey, Herman G., Dept. of Educ., University of Chicago, Chicago, Ill.
Richey, Robert W., Sch. of Educ., Indiana University, Bloomington, Ind.
Richman, Seymour, 14 East Cheshire Pl., Staten Island, N. Y.
Rider, Chester G., Superintendent of Schools, Concord, Ark.
Ridgway, Helen A., State Dept. of Educ., Hartford, Conn.
Riedel, Mark T., Superintendent, School Dist. 41, Glen Ellyn, Ill.
Riepe, Dale, Chm., Dept. of Philos., Univ. of North Dakota, Grand Forks, N. D.
Riethmiller, Gorton, 12541 Second Ave., Highland Park, Mich.
Riggs, Edwon L., 2802 E. McDowell St., Phoenix, Ariz.
Rikkola, V. John, Dept. of Educ., State Teachers College, Salem, Mass.
Riley, T. M., Principal, Palms Junior High School, Los Angeles, Calif.
Rinsland, Henry D., Dept. of Educ., University of Oklahoma, Norman, Okla.
Riordan, Sister Dorothy Marie, College of St. Elizabeth, Convent Station, N.J.
Risinger, Robert G., Alabama Polytechnic Institute, Auburn, Ala.
Risk, Thomas M., Dept. of Educ., Univ. of South Dakota, Vermillion, S.D.
Ritchie, Harold L., Prin., Memorial School, North Haledon, N.J.
Ritchie, Harold S., Asst. Superintendent of Schools, Paterson, N.J.
Ritter, John M., Editor-in-Chief, L. W. Singer Co., Inc., Syracuse, N.Y.
Rivlin, Harry N., Chm., Dept. of Educ., Queens College, Flushing, N.Y.

Roach, Stephen F., Man. Editor, *Eastern School Law Review*, Jersey City, N.J.
Robbins, Edward T., Supt., Alamo Heights School Dist., San Antonio, Tex.
Robbins, Irving, Queens College, Flushing, N.Y.
Roberson, James A., Prin., Lamar and Valley View Schools, Abilene, Tex.
Roberts, J. B., Head, Dept. of Educ., West Texas State College, Canyon, Tex.
Roberts, L. A., Superintendent, Dallas County Schools, Dallas, Tex.
Robertson, Minns S., Col. of Educ., Louisiana State Univ., Baton Rouge, La.
Robertson, Walter J., Superintendent of City Schools, Las Vegas, N.M.
Robertson, Wanda, University of Utah, Salt Lake City, Utah
Robinette, Walter R., LaGrange College, LaGrange, Ga.
Robinson, Alice, Board of Education, Rockville, Md.
Robinson, Cliff, 561 Rose St., Salem, Ore.
Robinson, Darrol E., Plymouth Tchrs. College, Plymouth, N.H.
Robinson, H. E., Dir., Spec. Educ., Texas Education Agency, Austin, Tex.
Robinson, Mrs. Helen M., Dept. of Educ., Univ. of Chicago, Chicago, Ill.
Robinson, Joseph R., *Deceased.*
Robinson, Roy E., Superintendent of Schools, Ferndale, Mich.
Robinson, Thomas L., Alabama State College, Montgomery, Ala.
Robinson, William McK., Western State College, Kalamazoo, Mich.
Roblee, Dana B., Fed. Civil Defense Adm., Washington, D.C.
Rocchio, Patrick D., Long Beach City College, Long Beach, Calif.
Rodgers, John O., Head, Dept. of Educ., Southwestern Univ., Georgetown, Tex.
Rodriguez-Diaz, M., Alfred University, Alfred, N.Y.
Roeder, Jesse N., Supt. of Schools, Palmerton, Pa.
Roenigk, Elise Mae, R.D. No. 1, Box 43, Cabot, Pa.
Roesch, Winston L., 143 Bostwick Ave. N.E., Grand Rapids, Mich.
Roffe, Pauline E., Dir., Elem. Educ., Upper Darby Schools, Upper Darby, Pa.
Rogers, Blanche Joy, 2437 Morris Ave., Bronx, N.Y.
Rogers, John D., Prin., Mt. Lebanon Elem. Schools, Pittsburgh, Pa.
Rogers, Mother V., Dean, Duchesene College, Omaha, Neb.
Rogers, Virgil M., Dean, Sch. of Educ., Syracuse University, Syracuse, N.Y.
Rohan, William, Asst. Prin., Columbus School, Chicago, Ill.
Rohrbach, Q. A. W., Pres., State Teachers College, Kutztown, Pa.
Rolfe, Howard C., 9195 Barnett Valley Rd., Sebastopol, Calif.
Rollins, William B., Jr., 7772 Otto Street, Downey, Calif.
Rollins, Willis R., 15 Rose Brook Rd., West Hartford, Conn.
Romano, Louis, 1701 East Capitol Dr., Shorewood, Wis.
Romney, Miles C., University of Oregon, Eugene, Ore.
Rooney, Edward B., Exec. Dir., Jesuit Educ. Assn., New York, N.Y.
Rose Miriam, Sister, Holy Name College, Spokane, Wash.
Rosebrock, Allan F., Dept. of Educ., New York State Col., Albany, N.Y.
Rosemarie Julie, Sister, Educ. Dept., Col. of Notre Dame, Belmont, Calif.
Rosenthal, Alan G., 26 Leslie Pl., New Rochelle, N.Y.
Roth, Bernard, 180 East 163rd St., Bronx, N.Y.
Roth, Bernice, Dir., Test Serv., No. Ill. State Tchrs. Col., DeKalb, Ill.
Roth, G. T., Superintendent Community Unit No. 100, Jerseyville, Ill.
Rothney, John W. M., Dept. of Educ., Univ. of Wisconsin, Madison, Wis.
Rothstein, Jerome H., San Francisco State College, San Francisco, Calif.
Rothwell, Angus B., Superintendent of Schools, Manitowoc, Wis.
Rousseve, Charles B., Principal, Johnson Locett School, New Orleans, La.
Rowland, Loyd W., Dir., Louisiana Assoc. for Mental Health, New Orleans, La.
Rowland, Sydney V., Temple University, Philadelphia, Pa.
Rowley, Judge K., Dept. of Educ., Morris Brown College, Atlanta, Ga.
Rowntree, Urwin, Dir. of Educ., Brown and Sharpe Mfg. Co., Providence, R.I.
Roye, Leon Stansbury, Prin., Havre de Grace Consolidated Sch., Havre de
    Grace, Md.
Ruark, Henry C., Jr., Audio-Visual Center, Indiana University, Bloomington, Ind.
Rubinstein, Samuel R., 6 Stuyvesant Oval, Stuyvesant Town, New York, N.Y.
Rucker, Thomas J., Prin., Sigel School, St. Louis, Mo.
Ruckman, Stanley V., Oregon College of Education, Monmouth, Ore.
Ruddell, Arden K., Col. of Educ., Univ. of Minnesota, Minneapolis, Minn.

Rudisill, Mabel, Dept. of Educ., Duke University, Durham, N. C.
Rudman, Herbert C., Sch. of Educ., University of South Carolina, Columbia, S.C.
Rudolf, Kathleen Brady, Monroe High School, Rochester, N.Y.
Ruffner, Ralph W., 7213 Delfield St., Chevy Chase, Md.
Rugen, Mabel E., University of Michigan, Ann Arbor, Mich.
Rugg, Earl U., Head, Div. of Educ., Colorado State Col. of Educ., Greeley, Colo.
Rugg, Harold, Woodstock, N. Y.
Rugh, Dwight, USOM-Israel, c/o American Embassy, Tel Aviv, Israel
Rulon, Phillip J., Peabody House, 13 Kirkland St., Cambridge, Mass.
Ruman, Edward L., Dept. of Tchg., Iowa State Tchrs. College, Cedar Falls, Iowa
Rumsey, Mary H., Hannibal-LaGrange College, College Heights, Hannibal, Mo.
Rung, Wilbur K., Senior High School, Altoona, Pa.
Runyan, Charles S., Marshall College, Huntington, W. Va.
Ruppert, Ethel C., Essex Elementary School, Baltimore, Md.
Rusch, Reuben R., 805 South Chestnut St., East Lansing, Mich.
Russel, John H., University of Denver, Denver, Colo.
Russell, David H., Sch. of Educ., University of California, Berkeley, Calif.
Russell, Earle S., Superintendent of Schools, Windsor, Conn.
Russell, Edward J., Superintendent of Schools, Pittsfield, Mass.
Russell, James L., Dean, Grad. Div., West Texas State College, Canyon, Tex.
Russell, John Dale, Chancellor and Exec. Sec., Bd. of Educ. Fin., Santa Fe, N.M.
Russell, Robert D., Punahou School, Honolulu, Hawaii
Rutledge, James A., University of Nebraska, Lincoln, Neb.
Rux, David Alan, 4223 Frury Lane, Topeka, Kan.
Ruzicka, William J., 17215 Pennington St., Detroit, Mich.
Ryan, Carl J., Dean, Tchrs. Col., Athenaeum of Ohio, Cincinnati, Ohio
Ryan, Eunice G., 442 Cherokee Blvd., St. Paul, Minn.
Ryan, Francis A., Sch. of Educ., Fordham University, New York, N.Y.
Ryan, W. Carson, Dept. of Educ., Univ. of North Carolina, Chapel Hill, N.C.
Ryan, Rev. William D., Assoc. Dean, St. Stanislaus Sem., Florissant, Mo.
Ryans, David G., Sch. of Educ., Univ. of California, Los Angeles. Calif.
Ryden, Einar, Biology Annex, Purdue University, Lafayette, Ind.
Ryder, Raymond R., Div. of Educ., Purdue University, Lafayette, Ind.

Sachs, Moses B., Rabbi, Am Echod Synagogue. Waukegan, Ill.
Sabik, Adolph J., Principal, Franklin School, East Chicago, Ind.
Sahai, Prem Nath, Headmaster, S.D. Tchrs. Trng. Inst., Baijnath, Punjab, India
Sailer, T. H. P., 219 Walnut St., Engelwood, N.J.
St. Lawrence, Francis, 7102 Vanport Ave., Whittier, Calif.
St. Lawrence, Mother, Rosemont College, Rosemont, Pa.
Salerno, Salvatore W., 222 Rutledge Ave., East Orange, N.J.
Salinger, Herbert E., 2933 Sunrise Dr., Napa, Calif.
Salisbury, A. W., Superintendent of Schools, Galesburg, Ill.
Salmons, George B., Plymouth Teachers College, Plymouth, N.H.
Salsbury, Jerome C., Dir. of Curric., Board of Educ., Bloomfield, N.J.
Salser, Alden, Prin., Horace Mann Jr. High School, Wichita, Kan.
Salten, David G., Supt. of Schools, Long Beach. N.Y.
Samonte, Pablo Q., 1025-B Maria Cristina, Manila, Philippines
Samonte, Soledad E., Philippine Normal College, Manila, Philippines
Sampson, William, Principal, Henry B. Whitehorne High School, Verona, N.J.
Samson, Gordon E., Educational Policies Commission, Washington, D.C.
Samson, Ruth D., 432 S. Curson Ave., Los Angeles, Calif.
Sand, Ole, Dept. of Educ., Wayne University, Detroit, Mich.
Sanders, Richard H., 10639 Drew St., Chicago, Ill.
Sanders, William J., Supt. of Schools, Springfield, Mass.
Sanderson, Arnold T., Principal. High School. Worthington, Minn.
Sanford, Charles W., Col. of Educ., University of Illinois, Urbana, Ill.
Sanford, Helen M., Principal, Haven School. Evanston. Ill.
Sanford, R. N., Dept. of Psych., Univ. of California, Berkeley, Calif.
Sartain, Harry W., Dir. of Curric. & Research, Roseville Schls., St. Paul, Minn.
Satlow, I. David, Thomas Jefferson High School, Brooklyn, N.Y.

Sauer, Dorothy V., Dept. of Educ., Chicago Tchrs. Col., Chicago, Ill.
Saunders, Raymond J., Ramcoca Valley Reg. High School, Mount Holly, N.J.
Sausjord, Gunnar, Div. of Educ., San Francisco State Col., San Francisco, Calif.
Sauvain, Walter H., Dept. of Educ., Bucknell University, Lewisburg, Pa.
Savage, Tom K., Austin Peay State College, Clarksville, Tenn.
Sawin, Enoch I., 3711 Cambridge Rd., Montgomery, Ala.
Sawin, Philip Q., University of Wisconsin, Madison, Wis.
Saylor, Charles F., Superintendent of Schools, Jeanette, Pa.
Saylor, Galen, Dept. of Educ., University of Nebraska, Lincoln, Neb.
Scales, Eldridge E., Delaware State College, Dover, Del.
Scanlan, William J., Principal, Central High School, St. Paul, Minn.
Scarborough, Clarence C., Sch. of Educ., North Carolina State Col., Raleigh, N.C.
Scarf, Robert C., Ball State Teachers College, Muncie, Ind.
Scates, Douglas E., Col. of Educ., University of Florida, Gainesville, Fla.
Schaefer, Frances M., 7937 Paxton Ave., Chicago, Ill.
Scharf, Louis, 570 Lefferts Ave., Brooklyn, N.Y.
Schenke, Lahron H., Dept. of Educ., Drury College, Springfield, Mo.
Scherich, Millard, Dept. of Philos., Oklahoma A. & M. Col., Stillwater, Okla.
Schettler, John D., Isaac School, Phoenix, Ariz.
Schlegel, Miriam A., Dept. of Educ., Juaniata College, Huntington, Pa.
Schlichting, Harry F., University of Tulsa, Tulsa, Okla.
Schmadel, Elnora, 9842 E. Maple Ave., Bellflower, Calif.
Schmidt, Austin G., Chm., Dept. of Educ., Loyola Univ., Chicago, Ill.
Schmidt, Carl J., 205 South Wyoming St., Hazleton, Pa.
Schmidt, L. G. H., Headmaster, Tech. Sch., Roseberg, New South Wales
Schmidt, Milton W., Concordia Teachers College, River Forest, Ill.
Schmidt, Ralph L. W., Box 7703, University Station, Baton Rouge, La.
Schmidt, William S., County Superintendent of Schools, Upper Marlboro, Md.
Schmitt, Irvin H., 4808 South Thirtieth St., Arlington, Va.
Schneider, Bernhard W., Supt. of Rural Educ., Winsted, Conn.
Schneider, Renata, Gethsemane Lutheran School, St. Paul, Minn.
Schnepple, Stanley O., Supt. of Schools, Palo Alto, Calif.
Schneyer, J. Wesley, Read. Clinic, Univ. of Pennsylvania, Philadelphia, Pa.
Schnitzen, Joseph P., 1334 Monroe St., N.E., Minneapolis, Minn.
Schoeller, Arthur W., Wisconsin State College, Milwaukee, Wis.
Schoen, Lloyd R., Bob Jones University, Greenville, S.C.
Schoolcraft, Arthur A., West Virginia Wesleyan College, Buckhannon, W.Va.
Schooler, Virgil E., Indiana University, Bloomington, Ind.
Schooling, Herbert W., Dept. of Educ., Univ. of Chicago, Chicago, Ill.
Schott, M. S., Central Missouri State College, Warrensburg, Mo.
Schreiber, Herman, 80 Clarkson Ave., Brooklyn, N.Y.
Schroeder, Elroy H., Superintendent of Schools, Grand Forks, N.D.
Schrupp, M. H., San Diego State College, San Diego, Calif.
Schueler, Herbert, Dept. of Educ., Queens College, Flushing, N.Y.
Schultz, Frederick, Box 931, G.P.O., New York, N.Y.
Schunert, Jim R., San Diego State College, San Diego, Calif.
Schunk, Russell J., Lib. Div., State Dept. of Educ., St. Paul, Minn.
Schutz, Richard E., 512 West 122nd St., New York, N.Y.
Schutz, Seymour, 246 West End Ave., New York, N.Y.
Schuyler, Helen K., Kansas State Tchrs. College, Pittsburg, Kan.
Schwada, Paul L., Dean, Olivet Nazarene College, Kankakee, Ill.
Schwanholt, Dana B., Valparaiso University, Valparaiso, Ind.
Schwartz, Alfred, Dept. of Educ., Drake University, Des Moines, Iowa
Schwartz, John C., Dept. of Educ., Los Angeles State Col., Los Angeles, Calif.
Schwartz, William P., Principal, Caton School, Brooklyn, N.Y.
Schwarzenberger, Alfred J., Jefferson School, Medford, Wis.
Scobey, Mary-Margaret, Sch. of Educ., Syracuse University, Syracuse, N.Y.
Scott, Cecil Winfield, New Haven State Teachers College, New Haven, Conn.
Scott, Frances Aliene, State Dept. of Education, Charleston, W. Va.
Scott, Guy, 919 Oxford Dr., Emporia, Kan.
Scott, Helen Elizabeth, Rhode Island College of Education, Providence, R.I.

Scott, Jeanne E., Central Missouri State College, Warrensburg, Mo.
Scott, Owen, College of Educ., University of Georgia, Athens, Ga.
Scott, Walter W., Supt. of Schools, Holland, Mich.
Seagoe, May V., Sch. of Educ., University of California, Los Angeles, Calif.
Searles, Warren B., Orange County Community College, Middletown, N. Y.
Sears, J. B., Professor Emeritus of Educ., Stanford University, Stanford, Calif.
Seaton, Donald F., Supt. of Schools, Boone, Iowa
Seay, C. W., Principal, Dunbar High School, Lynchburg, Va.
Seay, Maurice F., Kellogg Foundation, Battle Creek, Mich.
Sechler, Hazel, 800 West Eighth St., Silver City, N.M.
Seeman, Myron, 521 Division St., Madison, Wis.
Segel, David, U.S. Office of Education, Washington, D.C.
Segner, Esther F., Women's Col., Univ. of North Carolina, Greensboro, N.C.
Seidel, Vaughn D., Supt., Alameda County Schools, Oakland, Calif.
Seidlin, Joseph, Dean, Grad. School, Alfred University, Alfred, N.Y.
Selby, June, Supv. of Grades, Board of Education, Watertown, N.Y.
Selke, Erich, Dept. of Educ., Univ. of North Dakota, Grand Forks, N.D.
Selleck, E. R., Supt. of Schools, Dist. 98, Berwyn, Ill.
Sellman, William N., Asst. Supt. of Schools, St. Louis, Mo.
Senour, Alfred C., 4133 Ivy Street, East Chicago, Ind.
Sensibar, Judith Jay, 4900 Woodlawn Ave., Chicago, Ill.
Serge, Henrietta E., New Haven State Teachers College, New Haven, Conn.
Serviss, Trevor K., Editor-in-Chief, D. C. Heath and Co., Boston, Mass.
Setzepfandt, A. O. H., Asst. Supt. in chg. of Elem. Educ., Tulsa, Okla.
Seubert, Eugene E., Dept. of Educ., Washington Univ., St. Louis, Mo.
Seville, George C., 134 Newcomb Road, Tenafly, N.J.
Sewell, Nelson B., Principal, Salinas Union High School, Salinas, Calif.
Sexton, Wray E., 23 Hoffman St., Maplewood, N.J.
Seyfert, Warren C., Milwaukee Country Day School, Milwaukee, Wis.
Shack, Jacob H., Asst. Supt., Curr. Div., Board of Educ., Brooklyn, N.Y.
Shaffer, R. D., Superintendent of Schools, Muncie, Ind.
Shales, J. M., Ball State Teachers College, Muncie, Ind.
Shane, Harold G., Sch. of Educ., Northwestern University, Evanston, Ill.
Shannon, Ernest B., Dean of Students, Bethany-Peniel College, Bethany, Okla.
Shannon, Gail, Col. of Educ., University of Oklahoma, Norman, Okla.
Shaplin, Judson T., 112 Avon Hill Street, Cambridge, Mass.
Shappelle, Rev. James, 5440 Moeller Ave., Norwood, Ohio
Sharlip, Lou N., Principal, Ludlow School, Philadelphia, Pa.
Shattuck, George E., Prin., Norwich Free Academy, Norwich, Conn.
Shaw, Archibald B., Supt. of Schools, Scarsdale, N.Y.
Shay, Carleton B., 12567 Everglade St., Los Angeles, Calif.
Shea, James T., Dir. of Research, School Dist., San Antonio, Tex.
Shea, Joseph J., 67 East Main St., Fredonia, N.Y.
Sheehan, Rosemary, Prin., Woodrow Wilson Jr. High School, Tulsa, Okla.
Sheldon, Muriel, Supv. of Counseling, Div. of Sec. Educ., Los Angeles, Calif.
Shelly, Colsin R., Principal, Lafavette School, Lancaster, Pa.
Shelton, Nollie W., Supt., Camden County Schools, Camden, N. C.
Shepard, Loraine V., Col. of Educ., Michigan State Univ., East Lansing, Mich.
Shepard, Robert H., Spicer Memorial College, Kirkee, Poona, India
Shepard, Samuel, Jr., Dir., Elem. Educ., Board of Education, St. Louis, Mo.
Shepherd, Gerald Q., Dept. of Educ., Los Angeles State Col., Los Angeles, Calif.
Shepherd, Lou A., Iowa State Teachers College, Cedar Falls, Iowa
Sherer, Lorraine, University of California, Los Angeles, Calif.
Sheridan, Marion C., Head, Eng. Dept., High School, New Haven, Conn.
Shigley, E. Harold, Marion College, Marion, Ind.
Shine, Joseph B., 9238 South Bishop St., Chicago, Ill.
Shipp, Frederic T., San Francisco State College, San Francisco, Calif.
Shoemaker, Francis, Teachers College, Columbia University, New York, N. Y.
Shoemaker, F. L., 15 Woodside Dr., Athens, Ohio
Shores, J. Harlan, Col. of Educ., University of Illinois, Urbana, Ill.
Short, James E., Dept. of Educ., Montana State Univ., Missoula, Mont.

Shrewsbury, Thomas B., San Francisco State College, San Francisco, Calif.
* Sias, A. B., Professor Emeritus, Ohio University, Athens, Ohio
Sickles, F. J., 296 Livingston Ave., New Brunswick, N.J.
Siebert, Edna M., Principal, Grant Elementary School, Chicago, Ill.
Siebrecht, Elmer B., 623 Fifth St., Ames, Iowa
Sieg, Martha D., Madison College, Harrisonburg, Va.
Siewers, Grace L., Librarian, Salem College, Winston-Salem, N.C.
Silas, Gordon, Director, Teacher Educ., Roanoke College, Salem, Va.
Silber, John R., Box 2109, Yale Station, New Haven, Conn.
Silvern, Leonard C., 13 Cleveland Pl., Yonkers, N.Y.
Simmons, I. F., Supt., Jefferson County Bd. of Educ., Birmingham, Ala.
Simmons, Patricia C., Whittier College, Whittier, Calif.
Simms, Naomi, Dept. of Educ., Kent University, Kent, Ohio
Simon, Arthur M., 123 Lott Ave., Brooklyn, N.Y.
Simon, Donald L., Principal, High School, Bloomington, Ind.
Simpson, Alfred D., *Deceased.*
Simpson, Ray H., Col. of Educ., University of Illinois, Urbana, Ill.
Simpson, William H., 2409 Huntleigh Court, Oklahoma City, Okla.
Sims, Harold W., 305 West 94th Pl., Chicago, Ill.
Sims, Verner M., Col. of Educ., University of Alabama, University, Ala.
Sinclair, J. H., Occidental College, Los Angeles, Calif.
Singer, Arthur, Jr., Northern Illinois State College, DeKalb, Ill.
Singletary, James D., Dept. of Educ., Prairie View Col., Prairie View, Tex.
Singleton, Carlton M., Col. of Educ., State Univ. of Iowa, Iowa City, Iowa
Singleton, Gordon G., 2104 Gorman Ave., Waco, Tex.
Singleton, Stanton J., Col. of Educ., University of Georgia, Athens, Ga.
Sininger, Harlan, New Mexico Highlands Univ., Las Vagas, N.M.
Sires, Ely, Loyola University, Chicago, Ill.
Sitz, Herbert A., Martin Luther College, New Ulm, Minn.
Skaggs, Darcy A., P.O. Box 395, Baldwin Park, Calif.
Skard, Aase Gruda, Fjellyn 2, Lysaker, Norway
Skatzes, D. H., Old Washington High School, Old Washington, Ohio
Skelton, Claude N., Asst. Prin., Soldan-Blewett High School, St. Louis, Mo.
Skinner, Mary Lou, U.S. Public Health Service, 42 Broadway, New York, N.Y.
Skogsberg, Alfred H., Principal, Bloomfield Junior High School, Bloomfield, N.J.
Slay, Ronald J., Michigan State Normal College, Ypsilanti, Mich.
Slebodnick, Edward B., 17 C. S. Fairway, Pullman, Wash.
Sletten, R. Signe, Supv., Lab. Sch., State Tchers. Col., Mankato, Minn.
Sligo, Joseph Richard, 1791 West 4th St., Reno, Nev.
Sloan, Paul W., State Univ. College for Teachers, Buffalo, N.Y.
Slobetz, Frank, State Teachers College, St. Cloud, Minn.
Slutz, Frank D., 16 Lexington Ave., Dayton, Ohio
Small, Florence Lovell, Div. of Educ., Bethune-Cookman Col., Daytona Beach, Fla.
Small, Mrs. Turie E. Thornton, 554 South Campbell St., Daytona Beach, Fla.
Small, William Jack, Educ. Dept., Roosevelt College, Chicago, Ill.
Smallenburg, Harry W., Dir. of Research & Guid., County Schls., Los Angeles, Calif.
Smiley, Marjorie B., Hunter College, New York, N.Y.
Smith, Agnes Marie, Sister, Brescia College, Owensboro, Ky.
Smith, Ara K., Prin., Elston Jr. High School, Michigan City, Ind.
Smith, B. Othanel, Dept. of Educ., Univ. of Ill., Urbana, Ill.
Smith, C. A., 7220 Lindell Ave., St. Louis, Mo.
Smith, Calvin S., 5705 South 1700 West, Murray, Utah
Smith, Dasil A., Dept. of Educ., Univ. of Utah, Salt Lake City, Utah
Smith, David R., *Deceased.*
Smith, Denis C., Provincial Inspector of Schools, Nelson, B.C., Canada
Smith, Dora V., 201 Burton Hall, University of Minnesota, Minneapolis, Minn.
Smith, Emmitt D., West Texas State Col., Canyon, Tex.
Smith, Mrs. Gertrude S., 17786 Beaverland, Detroit, Mich.
Smith, Henry P., Fraser Hall, University of Kansas, Lawrence, Kan.

Smith, Ida T., Sch. of Educ., Oklahoma A. & M. College, Stillwater, Okla.
Smith, J. Edward, Regional Supt., Central Bucks Joint Schls., Doylestown, Pa.
Smith, Mrs. Josephine C., Dir. of Elem. Educ., Pub. Schls., Washington, D.C.
Smith, Kathleen, Sch. of Medicine, Washington University, St. Louis, Mo.
Smith, Kathryn H., Dir., Tchr. Placement, Oregon State Col., Corvallis, Ore.
Smith, Linda C., Dept. of Educ., Cortland State Tchrs. Col., Cortland, N.Y.
Smith, Lloyd N., Dept. of Educ., Indiana State Teachers Col., Terre Haute, Ind.
Smith, Martha W., State Department of Education, Montgomery, Ala.
Smith, Mrs. Mary G., Vice-Prin., Madison Junior High School, Newark, N.J.
Smith, Menrie M., 1018 West 17th St., Anniston, Ala.
Smith, Nila B., Sch. of Educ., N.Y. Univ., Washington Square, New York, N.Y.
Smith, Paul E., Asst. Supt. of Schools, Rochester, N.Y.
Smith, Philip G., Dept. of Educ., Western Reserve University, Cleveland, Ohio
* Smith, Raymond A., Sch. of Educ., Texas Christian Univ., Fort Worth, Tex.
Smith, Russell B., Dept. of Educ., Marshall College, Huntington, W.Va.
Smith, Russell W., Principal, Campbell School, East Moline, Ill.
Smith, Ruth L., Dir., Student Tchg., State Teachers College, Towson, Md.
Smith, Sara E., Dept. of Educ., Western Maryland College, Westminster, Md.
*Smith, Stephen E., East Texas Baptist College, Marshall, Tex.
Smith, T. O., Superintendent, City Schools, Ogden, Utah
Smith, Vernon G., Winchester Rd., New London, Conn.
Smith, Walter D., Dept. of Psych., Florida State Univ., Tallahassee, Fla.
Smith, W. Holmes, El Camino College, Calif.
Smith, William N., South Carolina State College, Orangeburg, S.C.
Smith, Woodward C., 318 S. Washington Ave., Mt. Pleasant, Mich.
Smither, Ethel L., Binford Junior High School, Richmond, Va.
Smotherman, T. Edwin, Col. of Educ., W. Virginia Univ., Morgantown, W. Va.
Snader, Daniel W., Col. of Educ., Univ. of Illinois, Urbana, Ill.
Snarr, Otto W., Jr., Supv., Extension Classes, Univ. of Wyoming, Laramie, Wyo.
Snarr, Mrs. Ruth G., County Supt. of Schls., Montgomery City, Mo.
Snider, Glenn R., Col. of Educ., University of Oklahoma, Norman, Okla.
Snider, Hervon L., Sch. of Educ., University of Idaho, Moscow, Idaho
Snively, Donald L., Assoc. Supt., Darby Twp. Sch. Dist., Glenholden, Pa.
Snyder, Harvey B., Dept. of Educ., Pasadena College, Pasadena, Calif.
Snyder, Jerome R., 1700 Wethersfield Rd., Austin, Tex.
Snyder, Ruth C., 1217 Walnut St., Utica, N.Y.
Snyder, Walter E., Superintendent of Schools, Salem, Ore.
Snyder, Wayne T., 4247 Bellefontaine Ave., Kansas City, Mo.
Socher, E. Elona, 1415 Clearview St., Philadelphia, Pa.
Soderquist, H. A., 25340 Orchard Lake Rd., Farmington, Mich.
Solberg, Kristen, 407 113th St., Tacoma, Wash.
Solomon, Ruth H., Albany Medical College, Albany, N.Y.
Soloway, Jack, 2436 North Albany Ave., Chicago, Ill.
Sommers, Mildred, Dept. of Instr., Bd. of Educ., Jackson, Mich.
Sonstegard, Manford, Iowa State Teachers College, Cedar Falls, Iowa
Sorenson, Garth, 17741 Lull St., Reseda, Calif.
Sorenson, Helmer E., Oklahoma A. & M. College, Stillwater, Okla.
Sorenson, R. H., Guidance Dir., Public Schools, St. Cloud, Minn.
Southall, Maycie, George Peabody College for Teachers, Nashville, Tenn.
Southerlin, W. B., State Educational Finance Comm., Columbia, S.C.
Sowards, G. Wesley, Teachers College, Columbia University, New York, N.Y.
Spain, Clarence H., Principal, Binford Jr. High School, Richmond, Va.
Spalding, Willard B., Genl. Ext. Div., Oregon Syst. of Higher Educ., Portland, Ore.
Spalke, E. Pauline, Lawrence Road, Salem Depot, N.H.
Sparling, Edward J., President, Roosevelt University, Chicago, Ill.
Spaulding, Seth, The Ford Foundation, P.O. Box 1397, Rangoon, Burma
Spaulding, William E., Vice-Pres., Houghton-Mifflin Co., Boston, Mass.
Spence, Ralph B., Teachers College, Columbia Univ., New York, N.Y.
Spencer, E. M., Dept. of Educ., Fresno State College, Fresno, Calif.
Spencer, Peter L., Harper Hall, Claremont Colleges, Claremont, Calif.
Spitz, Thomas A., Sch. of Educ., City College, New York, N.Y.

Spitzer, Herbert, Univ. Elem. Sch., State Univ. of Iowa, Iowa City. Iowa
Springer, Robert L., 139 Bromleigh Rd., Stewart Manor, Garden City, N. Y.
Springman, John H., Superintendent of Schools. Glenview. Ill.
Sproud, Dorothy G., Chief Psych., State Mental Hyg. Clinic, Berkeley, Calif.
Sprowles, Lee, University of Georgia, Athens, Ga.
Stack, Mrs. Thelma D., Milwaukee State Tchrs. Col., Milwaukee, Wis.
Stahlecker, Lotar, Kent State University, Kent, Ohio
Staiger, Ralph C., Dir., Read. Clinic. Mississippi Southern Col.. Hattiesburg, Miss.
Staiger, Roger P., Alumni Association, Ursinus Col., Collegeville, Pa.
Stair, Jean, Asst. Dir., Visiting Nurse Assn., New Haven, Conn.
Stalnaker, John M., 1075 Elm St., Winnetka, Ill.
Stanford, Madge. Dept. of Educ.. Southern Methodist Univ., Dallas, Tex.
Stanton, Jeannette E., Ohio Wesleyan University, Delaware, Ohio
Stapay, Peter P., Dean, Panzer College of Phys. Educ. and Hyg., East Orange, N.J.
Staple, Flora M., University of Minnesota, Duluth Branch, Duluth, Minn.
Stapleton, Edward G., Superintendent of County Schools, Towson, Md.
Starner, Norman Dean, Wyalusing, Pa.
Stathers, A. J., Prin., Jane Lew High School, Jane Lew, W.Va.
Stauffer, Russell G.. Dir.. Read. Clinic. Univ. of Delaware. Newark, Del.
Stearns, Harry L., Superintendent of Schools, Englewood, N.J.
Stecklein, John Ellsworth, 211 Burton Hall, Univ. of Minn., Minneapolis, Minn.
Steel, Harry J., State Univ. College for Teachers, Buffalo, N.Y.
Steel, Wade A., Superintendent, Leyden High School, Franklin Park, Ill.
Steele, H. L.. Head. Dept. of Educ.. Idaho State College. Pocatello. Idaho
Steeves, Frank L., Col. of Educ., University of North Dakota, Grand Forks, N.D.
Steffek, Ralph L., Superintendent of Schools, East Detroit, Mich.
Stegall, Alma L., Dept. of Educ., Virginia State College, Petersburg, Va.
Stegeman, William H., Dir. of Res., Educ. Center. City Schls., San Diego, Calif.
Stein, Michael W., Lee H. Kellogg School, Falls Village, Conn.
Steinberg, Warren L., 4418 Corinth Ave., Culver City, Calif.
Steinemann, Kathryn P., Minster Public Schools, Minster, Ohio
Steinhauer, Milton H., Sch. of Educ., Rutgers Univ., New Brunswick, N.J.
Steininger, Earl W., 515 6th Ave., N.E., Independence, Iowa
Stellhorn. A. C.. Lutheran Schools. St. Louis. Mo.
Steltenpohl, Elizabeth H., Manhattanville Col. of Sacred Heart, Purchase, N.Y.
Steph, Harlan J., Dean of Men, Midwestern University, Wichita Falls, Tex.
Stephan, Paul M., 100 Lincoln Ave., Riverside, Ill.
Stephens, J. M., Dept. of Educ., Johns Hopkins Univ., Baltimore, Md.
Stern, Mrs. Rose R., 451 Bergen Ave., Jersey City, N.J.
Sternberg, William N., Prin., Public School 611, Bronx, New York, N.Y.
Sternlieb, Ida B., 234 East 15th St., New York, N.Y.
Stetson, G. A., Superintendent of Schools, West Chester, Pa.
Steudler, Mary M., Teachers College of Connecticut. New Britain. Conn.
Stevens, Glenn Z., Pennsylvania State University, University Park, Pa.
Stevens, Godfrey D., Cincinnati Pub. Schools. Cincinnati. Ohio
Stevens, J. H., Principal, Holloway High School, Murfreesboro, Tenn.
Stewart, A. W., 37 Winthrop Rd., Columbus, Ohio
Stewart, Charles T.. Col. of Educ., Univ. of Maryland. College Park, Md.
Stewart, Frederick H., Prin.. I. A. Sheppard School, Philadelphia, Pa.
Stewart, Glen C., Dept. of Music, Alma College, Alma, Mich.
Stickler, W. Hugh, Dir., Educ. Res., Florida Sta. Univ., Tallahassee, Fla.
Stielstra, William, History Dept., Alma College, Alma, Mich.
Stienstra. Clifford C.. Principal. High School. Fertile. Minn.
Stier, Lealand D., Dept. of Educ., Santa Barbara Coll., Goleta, Calif.
Stillman, Calvin W., Cobb Hall, University of Chicago, Chicago, Ill.
Stoddard, George D., 1041 Kingston Rd., Princeton, N.J.
Stoke, Stuart M., Head, Educ. Dept., Mount Holyoke Col., South Hadley, Mass.
Stokes, Maurice S., Savannah State College, Savannah, Ga.
Stollberg, Robert, San Francisco State College, San Francisco, Calif.
Stolt, Edna B., State Superintendent of Public Instruction, Cheyenne, Wyo.
Stone, Gladys, Supt., Monterey County Schools, Salinas, Calif.

Stone, L. Gordon, Wisconsin State College, River Falls, Wis.
Stone, L. Joseph, Vassar College, Poughkeepsie, N. Y.
Stonebraker, W. Chester, Principal, Green School, Dist. 5, Roseburg, Ore.
Stonehocker, D. Doyle, Dean, Junior College, Burlington, Iowa
Stordahl, Kalmer E., 717 Four-Mile Rd., Alexandria, Va.
Stottler, Richard Husted, University of Maryland, College Park, Md.
Stoughton, Robert W., Consultant, State Dept. of Educ., Hartford, Conn.
Strain, Mrs. Sibyl M., 25 Alfred Lane, Bloomfield, N. J.
Strand, William H., Col. of Educ., Univ. of Minnesota, Minneapolis, Minn.
*Strang, Ruth, Teachers College, Columbia University, New York, N.Y.
Stratemeyer. Florence, Teachers College. Columbia University, New York. N.Y.
Strattner, Mary Jane, Skinner Hall, Univ. of Massachusetts, Amherst, Mass.
Stratton, L. T., Dept. of Educ., Findlay College, Findlay, Ohio
Strawe, Walter V., Principal, Lowell School, Chicago, Ill.
* Strayer, George D., Teachers College, Columbia University, New York, N.Y.
Strayer, George D., Jr., Col. of Educ., Univ. of Washington. Seattle, Wash.
Strebel, Jane D., Board of Educ. Library, Minneapolis, Minn.
Strem, Bruce E., 222 West Gardner Street, Long Beach, Calif.
Streng, Alice, Wisconsin State College, Milwaukee, Wis.
Strickland, C. G., Sch. of Educ., Baylor University, Waco, Tex.
Strickler. Robert E., 3538 Halliday, St. Louis, Mo.
Stroker, Kenneth, Superintendent, Com. Cons. Dist. Schls., Joliet, Ill.
Stroud, J. B., State University of Iowa. Iowa City, Iowa
Stuart, Alden T., Superintendent of Schools, Wellsville, N.Y.
Stubbs, G. T., Oklahoma A. & M. College. Stillwater. Okla.
Stumpf, W. A.. Box 6126 College Station. Durham. N.C.
Stunkard, Clayton L., University of Minnesota, Minneapolis, Minn.
Sturgill, Mrs. Evelyn Ethington, 1013 N. Center St., Casa Grande, Ariz.
Sugden, W. E.. Supt. of Schools, River Forest, Ill.
Sullivan, Bernice W., Read. Dir., Cabell County Schls., Huntington, W.Va.
Sullivan, Helen Blair. Sch. of Educ., Boston University. Boston, Mass.
Sullivan, James B., State Teachers College, Salem, Mass.
Sullivan, Joseph V., 29 Salem Way, Yonkers, N.Y.
Sun, Huai Chin. Chm., Grad. Div. of Educ.. Bishop College, Marshall, Tex.
Sundaram, M. S., Educ. Secy., Embassy of India, Washington, D.C.
Supernau, C. J., College of L. A.. Marquette Univ.. Milwaukee. Wis.
Sutherland, Margaret, Col. of Educ., Univ. of California, Davis, Calif.
Suttell, Lloyd, Col. of Educ., Univ. of Puerto Rico, Rio Piedros, Puerto Rico
Sutton, Elizabeth, Granville, Tenn.
Swann, Reginald L., Teachers Col. of Conn., New Britain, Conn.
Swanson, Herbert L.. Principal. City Schools, Manhattan Beach, Calif.
Swanson, Lloyd W., San Jose State College, San Jose, Calif.
Swartout. S. G.. State Teachers College, Brockport. N.Y.
Swartz, David J., Asst. Supt. of Schls., Div. of Hous., Brooklyn, N.Y.
Swearingen, Mildred. Florida State Univ., Tallahassee. Fla.
Swenson, Esther J., Col. of Educ.. Univ. of Alabama. University, Ala.
Swenson, Lloyd G., Adams State College, Alamosa, Colo.
Swertfeger, Floyd F., Longwood College, Farmville, Va.
Swift, G. C., Supt. of Schools. Watertown. Conn.
Swift, Leonard F., Col. of Educ., University of Illinois, Urbana, Ill.
Swinehart, George B.. Supv. Prin., Boyertown Pub. Schls., Boyertown, Pa.
Sylla, Ben A., Supt. of Schools, Chicago Heights, Ill.

Taba, Hilda. San Francisco State College. San Francisco. Calif.
Tackett, William Marshall, Valparaiso University, Valparaiso, Ind.
Tadelman, Joseph J., Kelly High School, Chicago, Ill.
Tadena, Tomas, Rogers Center, Indiana University, Bloomington, Ind.
Taillon, Brother Leopold, Dean of Educ., St. Joseph Univ., New Brunswick, Can.
Tait, Arthur T.. 5523 Rumsey Dr., Riverside, Calif.
Tajima, Yuri, Roosevelt University, Chicago, Ill.
Tallman. R. W., 2024 Avalon Road, Des Moines, Iowa

Tan, Hasan, Gazi Eğitim Enstitüsü, Ankara, Turkey
Tannenbaum, Abraham, Teachers College, Columbia University, New York, N.Y.
Tanner, B. William, 5241 Melvin Dr., Toledo, Ohio
Tanruther, E. M., Indiana State Teachers College, Terre Haute, Ind.
Tapper, Inga B., 348 Forest Dr., Cedar Rapids, Iowa
Tarbell, R. W., 5117 West Washington Blvd., Milwaukee, Wis.
Tatum, Beulah Benton, Goucher College, Towson, Md.
Taylor, Bob E., State Dept. of Vocational Education, Phoenix, Ariz.
Taylor, Charles H., Superintendent of Schools, Midland Park, N.J.
Taylor, George Allen, 905 West Margate Tr., Chicago, Ill.
Taylor, L. O., Dept. of Educ., University of Omaha, Omaha, Neb.
Taylor, Marvin, Div. of Educ., Queens College, Flushing, N.Y.
Taylor, Marvin J., 527 Somerville Dr., Pittsburgh, Pa.
Taylor, Paul L., P. O. Box 330, Pine Bluff, Ark.
Taylor, Ralph, Audio-Visual Co-ord., San Diego County Schools, San Diego, Calif.
Taylor, William H., Superintendent of Schools, Vicksburg, Mich.
Tead, Ordway, 49 East Thirty-third St., New York, N.Y.
Tempero, Howard E., Tchrs. Col., University of Nebraska, Lincoln, Neb.
Temple, F. L., Dept. of Educ., University of Alabama, University, Ala.
Templeton, Robert G., Summer St., Manchester, Mass.
Templin, Mildred C., Inst. of Child Welfare, Univ. of Minn., Minneapolis, Minn.
Tengquist, Howard W., Research Chemist, Western Condensing Co., Appleton, Wis.
Tenney, Charles D., Vice-President, Southern Illinois University, Carbondale, Ill.
Ter Keurst, Arthur J., Central Mo. State Tchrs. Col., Warrensburg, Mo.
Terrill, Mrs. Pearl L., Dunbar High School, Arcadia, Okla.
Terry, Paul W., Sch. of Educ., Univ. of Alabama, University, Ala.
Tetz, Henry E., Superintendent of Schools, Dist. 13C, Independence, Ore.
Thayer, H. C., 2259 Fox Ave., Madison, Wis.
Theisen, W. W., Asst. Superintendent of Schools, Milwaukee, Wis.
Thelen, Herbert A., Dept. of Educ., University of Chicago, Chicago, Ill.
Theodore, Georgia, Chicago Teachers College, Chicago, Ill.
Thevaos, Deno G., Pennsylvania State University, University Park, Pa.
Thissen, Mollie, R. 2, Ellendale, Minn.
Thomann, Don F., Principal, Athens High School, Athens, Ohio
Thomas, Dorothy B., 2111 Salisbury St., Pittsburgh, Pa.
Thomas, George Isaiah, Principal, Campus School, New Paltz, N.Y.
Thomas, Hobart F., San Francisco State College, San Francisco, Calif.
Thomas, J. A., Prin., Stanley Humphries High School, Castlegar, B.C., Canada
Thomas, L. M., Dean of Instr., Nebraska State Tchrs. Col., Kearney, Neb.
Thomas, R. Murray, Dept. of Educ., State Teachers College, Brockport, N.Y.
Thomas, Ruth H., N. Y. State Col. of Home Econ., Cornell Univ., Ithaca, N.Y.
Thomas, Ruth M., Dir., Div. of Educ., Central State College, Wilberforce, Ohio
Thompson, Anton, 715 Locust Ave., Long Beach, Calif.
Thompson, Charles H., Dean, Graduate School, Howard Univ., Washington, D.C.
Thompson, D. H., Central Washington College of Educ., Ellensburg, Wash.
Thompson, Emmett C., Sacramento State College, Sacramento, Calif.
Thompson, Fred R., Col. of Educ., University of Maryland, College Park, Md.
Thompson, G. E., Superintendent of Schools, St. Charles, Ill.
Thompson, Orrin G., Supt., Public Schools, Elgin, Ill.
Thompson, Ralph H., Western Washington College of Educ., Bellingham, Wash.
Thompson, Ray, Counselor-Trainer, North Carolina College, Durham, N.C.
Thomson, Proctor, Pitzer Hall, Claremont Men's College, Claremont, Calif.
Thorndike, Robert L., Teachers College, Columbia University, New York, N.Y.
Thorne, Edmund H., Supt. of Schools, West Hartford, Conn.
Thorngate, J. H., Vice-Principal, Senior High School, Eau Claire, Wis.
Thornton, James W., Jr., Vice-Pres., Orange Coast Coll., Costa Mesa, Calif.
Thorp, Marion A., Prin., Adaire-Chandler Schools, Philadelphia, Pa.
Thorp, Mary T., Dir., Henry Barnard School, Providence, R.I.
Threlkeld, Archie L., Jamaica, Vt.
Threlkeld, Curtis H., 219 South Orange Ave., South Orange, N.J.

Thuma, Mary, 126 South College Dr., Bowling Green, Ohio
Thurston, Edmund W., Superintendent of Schools, Westwood, Mass.
Tidwell, Robert E., Stillman College, Tuscaloosa, Ala.
Tiedeman, Herman R., Illinois State Normal University, Normal, Ill.
Tiedman, Stuart C., Dept. of Educ., Drake University, Des Moines, Iowa
Tierney, Marie, Chicago Teachers College, Chicago, Ill.
Tiffany, Burton C., Asst. Supt., Chula Vista City Schls., Chula Vista, Calif.
Tillinghast, Charles C., Ridgefield Road, Wilton, Conn.
Tilton, J. W., Dept. of Educ., Yale University, New Haven, Conn.
Timberlake, Mary E., Newberry College Library, Newberry, S. C.
Tingle, Mary J., Col. of Educ., Univ. of Georgia, Athens, Ga.
Tinker, Miles A., University of Minnesota, Minneapolis, Minn.
Tinsley, Lacy B., Principal, West End High School, Fayetteville, Tenn.
Tinson, John T., 637 West 6th St., Ontario, Calif.
Tireman, L. S., Educ. Dept., Univ. of New Mexico, Albuquerque, N.M.
Toles, Caesar F., Dir., Bishop Junior College, Dallas, Tex.
Tomaszewski, Edward J., 107 10th St., Windber, Pa.
Tong, Howard F., Junction City High School, Junction City, Ore.
Tongaw, Margaret, 2720 Manhattan Ave., Manhattan Beach, Calif.
Tonne, Herbert A., Sch. of Educ., New York University, New York, N.Y.
Toops, Herbert A., Dept. of Psych., Ohio State University, Columbus, Ohio
Topp, Robert F., Dean, Grad. Sch., National College of Education, Evanston, Ill.
Torrey, Robert D., Sec. Curr. Co-ord., Plumas Univ. Sch. Dist., Quincy, Calif.
Totten, W. Fred, Pres., Flint Jr. College, Flint, Mich.
Townsend, Edward Arthur, 525 East Eighty-ninth St., New York, N.Y.
Townsend, Loran G., Dean, Col. of Educ., Univ. of Missouri, Columbia, Mo.
Townsend, Virgil L., Kathleen High School, Kathleen, Fla.
Trabue, M. R., Dean, Sch. of Educ., Penn. State Univ., University Park, Pa.
Tracy, Elaine M., Dept. of Educ., St. Olaf College, Northfield, Minn.
Tracy, L. L., Jr., Kansas State Teachers College, Pittsburg, Kan.
Trainkaus, William K., New Haven State Teachers College, New Haven, Conn.
Traister, Harold W., Dept. of Educ., State Tchrs. College, California, Pa.
Trapanese, Menna G., 18 Westervelt Place, Jersey City, N.J.
Travelstead, Chester C., Sch. of Educ., Univ. of South Carolina, Columbia, S.C.
Travis, Vaud A., Chm., Dept. of Educ., Northwestern State Col., Tahlequa, Okla.
Traxler, Arthur E., Educational Records Bureau, New York, N.Y.
Treacy, John P., 2111 North Fifty-ninth St., Milwaukee, Wis.
Tremaine, Donahue L., 56 Violet Ave., Buffalo, N.Y.
Tremblay, Francis W., Apt. 10, Bldg. 313, Stanford Village, Stanford, Calif.
Trescott, B. M., Kirk Lane, Media, Pa.
Trible, Dierdre, Supv., Special Educ., Public Schools, Evansville, Ind.
Triggs, Frances O., 419 West 119th St., New York, N.Y.
Trillingham, C. C., County Supt. of Schls., Los Angeles, Calif.
Trione, Verdun, 838 Franquette Ave., Santa Rosa, Calif.
Triptow, Richard F., St. Patrick High School, Chicago, Ill.
Tronsberg, Josephine, University of Pittsburgh, Pittsburgh, Pa.
Troth, Harold R., Prin., Jane Addams School, Dayton, Ohio
Troutwein, Marvin E., Augsburg College, Minneapolis, Minn.
Trow, William Clark, School of Educ., Univ. of Mich., Ann Arbor, Mich.
Troxel, O. L., Colorado State College of Education, Greeley, Colo.
Troyer, Lewis, National College of Education, Evanston, Ill.
Trump, J. Lloyd, Col. of Educ., Univ. of Illinois, Urbana, Ill.
Trusal, Maurice E., Dir. of Curriculum, Public Schools, Williamsport, Pa.
Tsuge, Mrs. Haruko, International House, Univ. of Chicago, Chicago, Ill.
Tudyman, Al, Dir. Spec. Educ., Oakland Public Schools, Oakland, Calif.
Tumlinson, J. E., Box 249, Lampasas, Tex.
Turner, Howard, Southern Louisiana Institute, Lafayette, La.
Turner, Rex Allwin, Pres., Alabama Christian Col., Montgomery, Ala.
Turner, Robert B., Coral Gables High School, Coral Gables, Fla.
Twente, J. W., Dept. of Educ., University of Kansas, Lawrence, Kan.
Twichell, William S., County Superintendent of Schools, Newark, N.J.

Twombly, John J., Northern Illinois State College, DeKalb, Ill.
Tydings, R. N., Hobbs Municipal Schools, Hobbs, N.M.
Tyler, Fred T., Sch. of Educ., Univ. of California, Berkeley, Calif.
Tyler, I. Keith. Ohio State University, Columbus. Ohio
Tyler, Ralph W., 202 Junipero Serra Blvd., Stanford, Calif.
Tyson, George R., Ursinus College, Collegeville, Pa.

Udstuen, Sadie B., Illinois State Normal University, Normal, Ill.
Ullrich, George, 42 Rowley St., Rochester, N.Y.
Ulmer, T. H., Superintendent, Hartsville Area Schls., Hartsville, S. C.
Umberger, Willis H., State Dept. of Education, Norwich, Conn.
Umstattd, J. G., University of Texas, Austin, Tex.
Underwood, Mrs. Anna, Fairview High School, Fairview. Okla.
Underwood, Helen B., Dir., Sch. of Voc. Nursing, Vallejo Col., Vallejo, Calif.
Unger, Mrs. Lloyd G., 128 Barry Point Rd., Riverside, Ill.
Unruh, Adolph, Dept. of Educ., Washington University, St. Louis, Mo.
Unzicker, Samuel P., Dept. of Educ., State Teachers Col., Paterson, N.J.

Vakil, K. S., 119 Marzleanabad, Andheri, Bombay. India
Valenti, J. J., Dept. of Educ., Loyola University, Chicago, Ill.
Valentine, E. A., Jr., Capt., Officers Open Mess, APO 937 c/o PM, Seattle, Wash.
Van Bruggen, John A., Dept. of Educ., Calvin College, Grand Rapids, Mich.
Van Buskrib, Edgar F., 1502 Bass Ave., Columbia, Mo.
Van Campen, Marion, Head, Elem. Educ. Dept., Kent State Univ., Kent, Ohio
Vander Beke. George E.. Registrar, Marquette University, Milwaukee. Wis.
Vander Horck, Karl J., Col. of Educ., Univ. of Minnesota, Minneapolis, Minn.
Vanderlinden, J. S., Superintendent, Dawson Consolidated Schls., Dawson, Iowa
VanderMeer, A. W., Pennsylvania State University, University Park, Pa.
Vander Werf, Lester S., Dean, Col. of Educ., Northeastern University, Boston,
     Mass.
Van Dyke, L. A., State University of Iowa, Iowa City, Iowa
Van Loan, W. L., Supt. of Schools. Corvallis. Ore.
Van Nastrand, M. Eugene, State Teachers College, St. Cloud, Minn.
Van Ness, Carl C., Vice-Pres., Appleton-Century-Crofts Co., New York, N.Y.
Van Ness, Paul H., Prin., Central Ave. and Warren St. Schls.. Newark. N.J.
Van Ormer, Edward B., Pennsylvania State University, University Park, Pa.
Van Patter, Vernon E., Chm., Dept. of Educ., Wisconsin State Coll., Superior, Wis.
Van Putten. M. W., Superintendent of Schools, Eveleth. Minn.
Van Roekel, B. H., Michigan State University, East Lansing, Mich.
Van Wegenen, M. J., University of Minnesota, Minneapolis, Minn.
Van Zwoll, James A., University of Maryland. College Park, Md.
Varn, Guy L.. Supt., City Schools, Columbia, S.C.
Vasey, Hamilton G.. Superintendent of Schools, Fargo, N.D.
Vaughan, Warren T., Jr., 506 Boston Post Rd., Weston, Mass.
Verseput. Robert F.. Dover High School. Dover. N.J.
Vett, John George, State University Teachers College, New Paltz, N.Y.
Vickers, Robert C., Ohio State Univ., Columbus, Ohio
Vickery, Verna L.. 714 East Thomas, Hammond, La.
Vikner, Carl F., 215 Burton Hall, University of Minnesota, Minneapolis, Minn.
Villano, George R., 1620 Detroit St., Denver, Colo.
Vincent, Harold S., Superintendent of Schools, Milwaukee, Wis.
Vineyard, Jerry J., Superintendent of Schools, Arkansas City, Kan.
Voelker. Paul H.. Asst. Dir.. Special Educ., Public Schls.. Detroit, Mich.
Voigt, Virginia E., Seton Hall University, South Orange, N. J.
Voirol, Eula C., 4927 Bell Ave.. Kansas City. Mo.
Volberding. Eleanor. Dept. of Educ., No. Ill. State Tchrs. Col.. DeKalb, Ill.
Volle, Arthur H., Dean of Students, Wheaton College, Wheaton, Ill.
Volz, H. H., Camp Peary, Williamsburg, Va.
Vonk, Paul Kenneth, University of Miami Branch, Coral Gables, Fla.
Von Schlichten, Erwin, Dept. of Psych., Union College, Schenectady, N.Y.
Votaw, Daniel C., 3535 Sterne St., San Diego, Calif.

Vredevoe, Lawrence E., Sch. of Educ., Univ. of California, Los Angeles, Calif.

* Waddell, C. W.. 1365 Midvale Ave., Los Angeles, Calif.
Wade, D. E., R.D. 1, New Paltz, N. Y.
Waggoner, Sherman G., Teachers College of Conn., New Britain, Conn.
Wagner, Carl E.. 7421 Zephyr Place. Maplewood. Mo.
Wagner, Elmer E., Sch. of Educ., Univ. of So. California, Los Angeles, Calif.
Wagner, Robert W., Dept. of Photography, Ohio State Univ., Columbus, Ohio
Waine, Sidney I., 842 44th St., Brooklyn, N. Y.
Wakefield, Troy M., Route 4, Box 414, Gainesville, Fla.
Wakeman, Seth, Dept. of Educ., Smith College, Northampton, Mass.
Walcott, Fred G., Univ. High School, Univ. of Michigan, Ann Arbor, Mich.
Waldron, Margaret L., St. Mary-of-the-Woods, Ind.
* Walker, E. T., Bigfork, Mont.
Walker, K. P., Supt. of Schools, Jackson, Miss.
Walker, Knox, Asst. Supt., Fulton County Schools, Atlanta, Ga.
Walker, Mrs. Virginia L., 2644 West Market St., Akron, Ohio
Wall, G. S., Dept. of Educ., Stout State College, Menomonie, Wis.
Wall, William Michael, Supervising Principal, Winnipeg, Manitoba, Canada
Wallace, Mrs. Frances P., Supv., Harrison County Schools, Marshall, Tex.
Wallace, Morris S., Dept. of Educ., Texas Tech. College, Lubbock, Tex.
Wallar, Gene A., San Jose State College, San Jose, Calif.
Walsh, J. Hartt, Dean, Col. of Educ., Butler University, Indianapolis, Ind.
Walsh, Michael F., Commissioner of Educ., 205 Benefit St., Providence, R.I.
Walter, Raymond L., Box 201, Millbrook, Ala.
Walter, Robert B.. Chief Deputy Supt.. County Schools, Los Angeles, Calif.
Walters, Everett L., Wisconsin State College, La Crosse, Wis.
Walther, Herbert K., USOM to Ethiopia, c/o State Dept. Mail Rm., Washington, D.C.
Walvoord, Anthony C., Box 2845, T.S.C.W. Station, Denton, Tex.
Wampler, W. Norman, Supt. of Schools, Bellflower, Calif.
Wanamaker, Pearl A., State Supt. of Public Instruction, Olympia, Wash.
Wandt, Edwin, Los Angeles State College, Los Angeles, Calif.
Wang, Charles K. A., Los Angeles State College, Los Angeles, Calif.
Ward, John Henry, Texas College, Tyler, Tex.
Ward, W. H.. Dir., Ext. Div., Univ. of South Carolina, Columbia, S.C.
Wardeberg, Helen, 108 Stone Hall, Cornell University, Ithaca, N.Y.
Warren, John S., Dir., Teacher Educ., Hendrix College, Conway, Ark.
Warriner, Clell C., Principal, Okmulgee High School, Okmulgee, Okla.
Warriner, David A.. Louisiana College, Pineville, La.
Warwick, Raymond, Principal, Public School, Riverton, N.J.
Washburne, Carleton W., Brooklyn College, Brooklyn, N.Y.
Washington, Booker T., Principal, Williston Ind. School, Wilmington, N.C.
Wasson, Margaret. 3705 University Blvd., Dallas. Tex.
Wasson, Roy J., Superintendent of Schools, Colorado Springs, Colo.
Waterman, Floyd T., Baker Elementary School, Great Neck, N.Y.
Waters, E. Worthington, Maryland State College, Princess Anne, Md.
Watkins, Ralph K., University of Missouri, Columbia, Mo.
Watson, C. Hoyt, President. Seattle Pacific College, Seattle, Wash.
Watson, E. H.. East Texas Teachers College, Commerce, Tex.
Watson, Jack M., Indiana University, Bloomington, Ind.
Watson, N. E., Supt., Northfield Twp. High School, Northbrook, Ill.
Watson, Norman E., Dean of Stud. Pers., Orange Coast Col., Costa Mesa, Calif.
Watson, Warren N., Dean, Sch. of Educ.. Seattle Pacific Col., Seattle, Wash.
Watson, William C., 29 Woodstock Rd., Mt. Waverley, Victoria, Australia
Watt, John Stewart, Knox College. Galesburg. Ill.
Wattenberg, William W.. Wayne University, Detroit, Mich.
Watters, Rev. Loras J., Loras College, Dubuque, Iowa
Watts, B. C., School of Educ., Southern Methodist Univ., Dallas, Tex.
Watts, Morrison L.. Dept. of Educ., Prov. of Alberta, Edmonton, Alba.
Weaver, David A., President, Shurtleff College, Alton, Ill.
Weaver, David O., 3033 John Marshal Dr., Arlington, Va.

Weaver, Edward K., Sch. of Educ. Atlanta University, Atlanta, Ga.
Weaver, J. Fred, Sch. of Educ., Boston Univ., Boston, Mass.
Weaver, John E., Washington Missionary Col., Takoma Park, Washington, D.C.
Weaver, P. C., Pennsylvania State University, University Park, Pa.
Webb, Tom, 2137 Neil Ave., Columbus, Ohio
Weber, Clarence A., Sch. of Educ., Univ. of Conn., Storrs, Conn.
Weddington, Rachel T., Howard University, Washington, D.C.
Weeks, James S., 2 Crestmont Ter., Oneonta, N.Y.
Wegener, Frank Corliss, University of Texas, Austin, Tex.
Weida, Mrs. Ethelyn Y., Supv., Special Classes, Union H.S. Dist., Compton, Calif.
Weidner, Mrs. Bruce V., 308 N. University Ave., Oxford, Ohio
Weifenbach, William, Dean, Eve. Div., Kansas City Univ., Kansas City, Mo.
Weinrich, Ernest F., Asst. Supt., Public Schools, Schenectady, N.Y.
Weir, Thomas A., 4729 Oakridge, St. Louis, Mo.
Weisiger, Louise P., Dir. of Research, Public Schools, Richmond, Va.
Weiss, George D., Supv., Stud. Tchg., State Teachers College, Kutztown, Pa.
Welch, Mrs. Arthuryne J., Tennessee A. & I. State Univ., Nashville, Tenn.
Welch, Carolyn M., 830 Chauncey Rd., Penn Valley, Narberth, Pa.
Welch, Cornelius A., Dean, Sch. of Educ., Bonaventure Col., Bonaventure, N.Y.
Welch, Earl E., Editor-in-Chief, Silver Burdett Co., Morristown, N.J.
Welch, Eleanor W., Illinois State Normal University, Normal, Ill.
Weldon, J. Elmer, Georgetown College, Georgetown, Ky.
Wellck, Arthur Albert, University of New Mexico, Albuquerque, N.M.
Welling, Helen F., 333 East McWilliams St., Fon du Lac, Wis.
Welsh, Walter C., Sch. of Ind. Art, New York, N.Y.
Wendt, Paul R., Audio-visual Aids, Southern Illinois Univ., Carbondale, Ill.
Wenger, Roy E., International Christian University, Tokyo, Japan
Wenk, J. H., Sussex School, Shaker Heights, Ohio
Wente, Walter H., Academic Dean. St. John's Col., Winfield, Kan.
Wentz, Howard A., Supv. Prin., Nether Providence Sch. Dist., Wallingford, Pa.
Wernick, Leo J., 2040 West Adams St., Chicago, Ill.
Wesley, Charles H., Pres., Central State College, Wilberforce, Ohio
Wesley, Edgar B., Box 1201, Los Altos, Calif.
Wesley, Willena, Principal, Fairport Elem. School, Dayton, Ohio
West, Allan M., Exec. Secy., Utah Education Assn., Salt Lake City, Utah
West, Guy A., Pres., Sacramento State College, Sacramento, Calif.
West, Roscoe L., President, State Teachers College, Trenton, N.J.
West, William A., General College, Univ. of Minnesota, Minneapolis, Minn.
West, William H., Superintendent of Schools, Belvidere, N.Y.
Westbrook, Charles H., 17 Towana Rd., Richmond, Va.
Westfall, Byron L., Indiana State Teachers College, Terre Haute, Ind.
Westlund, Hildur L., 2015 Baxter Ave., Superior, Wis.
Westover, Frederick L., Box 1553, University, Ala.
Weyer, F. E., Dean, Hastings College, Hastings, Neb.
Whaley, Lloyd, Pennsylvania State University, University Park, Pa.
Wheat, H. G., Col. of Educ., West Virginia University, Morgantown, W.Va.
Wheat, Leonard B., Duluth Branch, Univ. of Minnesota, Duluth, Minn.
Wheeler, Bruce E., Asst. Supt. of Schools, Springfield, Ill.
Wheeler, Eldon G., Hinsdale Twp. High School, Hinsdale, Ill.
Wheeler, Joseph A., Principal, Benjamin Franklin School, Miami, Fla.
Wheeler, Lester R., Dir., Read. Clinic, University of Miami, Coral Gables, Fla.
Wheeler, Mrs. Olive Boone, Box 818, Austin 64, Tex.
Whelan, James F., Chm., Dept. of Educ., Loyola University, New Orleans, La.
Whipple, Carl E., Superintendent, Sch. Dist. of Warren Borough, Warren, Pa.
Whipple, Earl G., Principal, Elmhurst Jr. High School, Elmhurst, Ill.
Whipple, Gertrude, Wayne University, Detroit, Mich.
Whisler, H. M., 292 East Broadway, Danville, Ind.
Whitcomb, Charles L., Superintendent of Schools, Haverhill, Mass.
White, George L., Dir., Educ. Serv., Silver Burdette Co., New York, N.Y.
White, Mrs. Helen B., P.O. Box 144, Tujunga, Calif.
White, J. B., Dean, Col. of Educ., University of Florida, Gainesville, Fla.

White, John C., Principal, Mesa High School, Mesa, Ariz.
White, Kenneth B., Dean of Instr., State Teachers Col., Paterson, N.J.
White, Kenneth H., Fort Hays Kansas State College, Hays, Kan.
White, Vern A., 4142 Elm Avenue, Long Beach, Calif.
White, Verna, Sch. of Educ., Syracuse University, Syracuse, N. Y.
Whitehead, Willis A., 13124 Shaker Square, Cleveland, Ohio
Whitelaw, John B., Glen Hills, Rockville, Md.
Whitesel, John A., Miami University, Oxford, Ohio
Whitley, Paul N., Prin., John Oliver Secondary Sch., Vancouver, B. C., Canada
Whitney, Algard P., Col. of Educ., Univ. of Illinois, Urbana, Ill.
Whitson, Willie, State Teachers College, Kirksville, Mo.
Whitten, James M., Gorham State Teachers College, Gorham, Me.
Whittier, C. Taylor, Dir. of Instr., Pinellas County Schools, Clearwater, Fla.
Wickes, Mrs. Una S., Counselor, Pasadena High School, Pasadena, Calif.
Wigell, Wayne W., Joliet Junior College, Joliet, Ill.
Wiggin, Gladys A., Col. of Educ., University of Maryland, College Park, Md.
Wiggin, Richard G., Asst. State Supv. of Art Educ., Richmond, Va.
Wiggins, Forrest Oran, Allen University, Columbia, S. C.
Wiggins, Sam P., George Peabody College for Teachers, Nashville, Tenn.
Wilburn, D. Banks, Dean, Tchrs. Col., Marshall College, Huntington, W.Va.
Wilkerson, H. Clifton, 542 Market St., Platteville, Wis.
Wilkinson, John A., Dept. of Educ., Univ. of Chicago, Chicago, Ill.
Wilks, William T., State Teachers College, Troy, Ala.
Willard, Robert L., Utica College, Utica, N.Y.
Willey, Ivan R., Col. of Educ., University of Wyoming, Laramie, Wyo.
Willey, Lawrence V., Jr., 26 Garden Apts., Geneva, N. Y.
Williams, Arleigh T., College of Marin, Kentfield, Calif.
Williams, Beatrice, State Teachers College, St. Cloud, Minn.
Williams, Byron B., University of Rochester, Rochester, N. Y.
Williams, Charles Albert, John Marshall Junior High School, Houston, Tex.
Williams, Charles C., North Texas State College, Denton, Tex.
Williams, Chester Spring, Col. of Educ., Univ. of Oklahoma, Norman, Okla.
* Williams, Claude L., P. O. Box 201, Steger, Ill.
Williams, Cyrus P., Wharton County Jr. College, Wharton, Tex.
Williams, Edward V., 855 Fair St., S. W., Atlanta, Ga.
Williams, E. I. F., Heidelberg College, Tiffin, Ohio
Williams, Fannie C., Principal, Valena C. Jones School, New Orleans, La.
Williams, Fountie N., Principal, Broadway School, Clarksburg, W.Va.
Williams, Frederick Allen, Dean, Grad. Sch., A. & T. College, Greensboro, N.C.
Williams, Harold A.,1260 Fairlawns Ave., Morgantown, W.Va.
Williams, Howard Y., Jr., Dir., St. Paul Read. Clinic, St. Paul, Minn.
Williams, Jacob T., Principal, Carver High School, Gadsden, Ala.
Williams, James Harry, Asst. Prin., Armstrong High School, Richmond, Va.
Williams, John D., Long Beach State College, Long Beach, Calif.
Williams, Maurice C., 520 Gayley Ave., Los Angeles, Calif.
Williams, Nat. Supt. of Schools, Lubbock, Tex.
Williams, Ralph R., 7458 Kingston Ave., Chicago, Ill.
Williams, Wilbert W., Dean of Students, Wilberforce Univ., Wilberforce, Ohio
Williams, Wilbur A., Michigan State Normal College, Ypsilanti, Mich.
Williams, W. Morris, San Francisco Unified Sch. Dist., San Francisco, Calif.
Williamson, E. C., Northeast High School, Philadelphia, Pa.
Williamson, Stanley E., Dept. of Sci. Educ., Oregon State Col., Corvallis, Ore.
Williamson, Walter W., 1820 Cromwood Rd., Baltimore, Md.
Willis, Jeanne LaRay, South Carolina State College, Orangeburg, S. C.
Wills, Benjamin G., 1550 Bellamy St., Santa Clara, Calif.
Willson, Gordon L., Supt. of Schools, Baraboo, Wis.
Wilson, David H., Lodi, N.Y.
Wilson, Frank T., Hunter College, New York, N.Y.
Wilson, George D., Kentucky State College, Frankfort, Ky.
Wilson, J. A. R., Santa Barbara College, Goleta, Calif.
Wilson, Mary C., Supv., Lincoln Parish Schools, Ruston, La.

Wilson, Merle A., Principal, Howe Elementary School, Des Moines, Iowa
Wilson, Russell E., Sch. Equip. Div., Brunswick-Balke-Collender Co., Chicago, Ill.
Wilson, Walter E., Superintendent of Schools, Metuchen, N. J.
Wilson, William G., Supt., Elem. Dist. 14, Public Schls., Chicago, Ill.
Wiltse, Earl W., Supt. of Schools, Grand Island, Neb.
Winchell, Karl F., Exec. Secy., Wyoming Educ. Assn., Cheyenne, Wyo.
Windom, John Henry, Harris Teachers College, St. Louis, Mo.
Wingo, G. Max, Sch. of Educ., University of Michigan, Ann Arbor, Mich.
Winn, Columbia, Madison College, Harrisonburg, Va.
Winslow, Marion B., Superintendent Sch. Dist. 9C, Coos Bay, Ore.
Winston, Ethna B., Elizabeth City State Tchrs. Col., Elizabeth City, N. C.
Wirth, Arthur G., Dept. of Educ., Brooklyn College, Brooklyn, N. Y.
Wise, Joseph M., 108-14 65th Rd., Forest Hills, N.Y.
Withall, John, National Educ. Assn., 1201 Sixteenth St. NW, Washington, D. C.
Witherington, Henry C., Registrar, Belmont College, Nashville, Tenn.
Witherspoon, Wade H., Jr., Prin., Elizabeth Heights School, Great Falls, S. C.
Witt, Paul W. F., Teachers College, Columbia University, New York, N.Y.
Witte, Cyril M., Dept. of Educ., Loyola College, Baltimore, Md.
Witter, Sanford C., Superintendent of Schools, Igloo, S. D.
Witty, Paul A., School of Educ., Northwestern University, Evanston, Ill.
Wixon, John L., Contra Costa Junior College, El Cerrito, Calif.
Wixted, William G., Hunter College, New York, N.Y.
Wochner, Raymond E., Arizona State College, Tempe. Ariz.
Woelfel, Norman, Dir., Tchg. Aids Lab., Ohio State University, Columbus, Ohio
Woellner, Robert C., Dir., Voc. Guid. & Plac., Univ. of Chicago, Chicago, Ill.
Wolbrecht, Walter F., 316 Parkwood, Kirkwood, Mo.
Wolf, Lloyd L., 3515 Madison Rd., Cincinnati, Ohio
Wolf, Ruth, Dir., Spec. Services, County Schools, Los Angeles, Calif.
Wolfe, Josephine B., Parkwood Manor, State Rd., Upper Darby, Pa.
Wolfe, W. D., Superintendent of Schools, Lawrence, Kan.
Wolfram, Donald J., Dean, Alma White College, Zarephath, N.J.
Wolk, Mrs. Samuel J. B., 420 East 23rd St., New York, N.Y.
Woo, K. K., 547 2nd Ave., San Francisco, Calif.
Wood, C. B., Dept. of Educ., Univ. of British Columbia, Vancouver. B.C.
Wood, Crispin M., 483rd T.C.Gru., APO 75, c/o PM, San Francisco, Calif.
Wood, Darrell E., 1419 Washington St., Emporia, Kan.
Wood, Ernest R., Sch. of Educ., New York University, New York, N.Y.
Wood, Joseph E., Prin., Glenfield Junior High School, Montclair, N.J.
Wood, Roi S., Superintendent of Schools, Joplin, Mo.
Wood, W. Clement, Head, Dept. of Educ., Ft. Hays Kan. State Col., Hays, Kan.
Woodhull, James E., Voc. Educ. Dept., Colorado A. & M. Coll., Fort Collins, Colo.
Woodring, Wiley F., Elem. Prin., Southwest Missouri St. Col., Springfield, Mo.
Woodruff, Olive, Kent State University, Kent, Ohio
Woods, Robert K., Wisconsin State College, Platteville, Wis.
Woodside, J. Barnes, Supt. of Schools, Willoughby, Ohio
Woodson, C. C., Principal, Carver High School, Spartanburg, S.C.
Woodward, Myrle A., 124 High Rock Lane, Westwood, Mass.
Woodworth, Denny, Col. of Educ., Drake University, Des Moines, Iowa
Woodworth, I. R., Dept. of Educ., Sacramento State College, Sacramento, Calif.
Woody, Thomas, Sch. of Educ., University of Pennsylvania, Philadelphia, Pa.
Woofter, J. A., 412 South Union St., Ada, Ohio
Wool, Max L., 101 Bay State Rd., Boston, Mass.
Woolf, Kenneth A., Supt. of Schls., Wayne Twp., Mountain View, N.J.
Woollatt, Lorne H., Dir. of Research, Public Schools, Baltimore, Md.
Wooton, Flaud C., Dept. of Educ., Univ. of California, Los Angeles, Calif.
Wotnoski, Helen C., 222½ E. St. Paul Street, Spring Valley, Ill.
Wotring, Clayton W., Cedar Crest College, Allentown, Pa.
Wozencraft, Marian, Fenn College, Cleveland, Ohio
Wray, Shirl D., Kokomo High School, Kokomo, Ind.
Wrenn, C. Gilbert, Buton Hall, Univ. of Minnesota, Minneapolis, Minn.
Wright, C. O., Exec. Secy., Kansas State Tchrs. Assn., Topeka, Kan.

Wright, Mrs. Roberta Peddy, Dept. of Educ., A. & I. State Col., Nashville, Tenn.
Wrightstone, J. Wayne, Dir., Bureau of Educ. Res., Bd. of Educ., Brooklyn, N.Y.
Wronski, Stanley P., Sch. of Educ., Boston University Boston, Mass.
Wubben, Horace J., President, Mesa County Junior Col., Grand Junction, Colo.
Wyeth, E. R., 3 Iris St., Burwood, Melbourne, Australia
Wynne, John P., Head, Dept. of Educ., State Tchrs. College, Farmville, Va.

Yancey, Mrs. B. W., Headmistress, Louise L. McGehee Sch., New Orleans, La.
Yaple, Graydon W., Dean of Faculty, Wilmington College, Wilmington, Ohio
Yauch, Wilbur A., Head, Dept. of Educ., No. Ill. St. Tchrs. Col., DeKalb, Ill.
Yeokum, Charles F., 1618 Tennessee St., Lawrence, Kan.
Yeuell, Gladstone H., University of Alabama, University, Ala.
Yoakam, Gerald A., Cathedral of Learning, Univ. of Pittsburgh, Pittsburgh, Pa.
Young, Albert T., Jr., School Psychologist, Falls Church, Va.
Young, Charles W., Bowling Green State University, Bowling Green, Ohio
Young, Francis Allan, State College of Washington, Pullman, Wash.
Young, F. Roman, Loyola University, Chicago, Ill.
Young, Horace A., Jr., Texas Southern University, Houston, Tex.
Young, J. E. M., Brandon College, Brandon, Manitoba, Canada
Young, John J., Superintendent of Schools, Mishawaka, Ind.
Young, Kenneth E., California State Polytechnic College, San Dimas, Calif.
Young, Lloyd P., President, Keene Teachers College, Keene, N.H.
Young, Paul A., Supt., York Com. High School, Elmhurst, Ill.
Young, William E., Dir., Div. of Elem. Educ., State Educ. Dept., Albany, N.Y.
Youngs, Joseph P., Gallaudet College, Washington, D.C.
Yu, Yung Juin, 734 Auburn Ave., Buffalo, N.Y.
Yuhas, Theodore F., Prin., Campus Sch., State Tchrs. Col., Mankato, Minn.
Yunghans, Ernest E., R.R. 7, Wayne Ter., Fort Wayne, Ind.

Zaeske, Arnold, 2323 Sixth St., Peru, Ill.
Zahorsky, Mrs. Metta, 361 East Guava, Oxnard, Calif.
Zawadski, Bohdan, Dept. of Psych., City College of New York, New York, N.Y.
Zellner, Aubrey, Dept. of Educ., St. John's Univ., Collegeville, Minn.
Zim, Herbert S., Dept. of Educ., Univ. of Illinois, Urbana, Ill.
Zimmerman, Mrs. Alice B., Woman's Col., Univ. of North Carolina, Greensboro, N.C.
Zintz, Miles V., 2216 Main Street, Cedar Falls, Iowa
Zipper, Joseph H., 2306 Parade St., Erie, Pa.
Zulauf, Romeo M., Northern Illinois State Teachers College, DeKalb, Ill.
Zwetschke, Earl T., Long Beach State College, Long Beach, Calif.
Zwikstra, Mary, 177 Linden Ave., Oak Park, Ill.

INFORMATION CONCERNING THE NATIONAL SOCIETY FOR THE STUDY OF EDUCATION

1. PURPOSE. The purpose of the National Society is to promote the investigation and discussion of educational questions. To this end it holds an annual meeting and publishes a series of yearbooks.

2. ELIGIBILITY TO MEMBERSHIP. Any person who is interested in receiving its publications may become a member by sending to the Secretary-Treasurer information concerning name, title, and address, and a check for $5.00 (see Item 5).

Membership is not transferable; it is limited to individuals, and may not be held by libraries, schools, or other institutions, either directly or indirectly.

3. PERIOD OF MEMBERSHIP. Applicants for membership may not date their entrance back of the current calendar year, and all memberships terminate automatically on December 31, unless the dues for the ensuing year are paid as indicated in Item 6.

4. DUTIES AND PRIVILEGES OF MEMBERS. Members pay dues of $4.00 annually, receive a cloth-bound copy of each publication, are entitled to vote, to participate in discussion, and (under certain conditions) to hold office. The names of members are printed in the yearbooks.

Persons who are sixty years of age or above may become life members on payment of fee based on average life-expectancy of their age group. For information, apply to Secretary-Treasurer.

5. ENTRANCE FEE. New members are required the first year to pay, in addition to the dues, an entrance fee of one dollar.

6. PAYMENT OF DUES. Statements of dues are rendered in October for the following calendar year. Any member so notified whose dues remain unpaid on January 1, thereby loses his membership and can be reinstated only by paying a reinstatement fee of fifty cents.

School warrants and vouchers from institutions must be accompanied by definite information concerning the name and address of the person for whom membership fee is being paid. Statements of dues are rendered on our own form only. The Secretary's office cannot undertake to fill out special invoice forms of any sort or to affix notary's affidavit to statements or receipts.

Cancelled checks serve as receipts. Members desiring an additional receipt must enclose a stamped and addressed envelope therefor.

7. DISTRIBUTION OF YEARBOOKS TO MEMBERS. The yearbooks, ready prior to each February meeting, will be mailed from the office of the distributors, only to members whose dues for that year have been paid. Members who desire yearbooks prior to the current year must purchase them directly from the distributors (see Item 8.)

8. COMMERCIAL SALES. The distribution of all yearbooks prior to the current year, and also of those of the current year not regularly mailed to members in exchange for their dues, is in the hands of the distributor, not of the Secretary. For such commercial sales, communicate directly with the University of Chicago Press, Chicago 37, Illinois, which will gladly send a price list covering all the publications of this Society. This list is also printed in the yearbook.

9. YEARBOOKS. The yearbooks are issued about one month before the February meeting. They comprise from 600 to 800 pages annually. Unusual effort has been made to make them, on the one hand, of immediate practical value, and, on the other hand, representative of sound scholarship and scientific investigation.

10. MEETINGS. The annual meeting, at which the yearbooks are discussed, is held in February at the same time and place as the meeting of the American Association of School Administrators.

Applications for membership will be handled promptly at any time on receipt of name and address, together with check for $5.00 (or $4.50 for reinstatement). Applications entitle the new members to the yearbook slated for discussion during the calendar year the application is made.

5835 Kimbark Ave.
Chicago 37, Illinois

NELSON B. HENRY, *Secretary-Treasurer*

PUBLICATIONS OF THE NATIONAL SOCIETY FOR THE STUDY OF EDUCATION

NOTICE: Many of the early Yearbooks of this series are now out of print. In the following list, those titles to which an asterisk is prefixed are not available for purchase.

Distributed by
THE UNIVERSITY OF CHICAGO PRESS, CHICAGO 37, ILLINOIS
1956